Beginning Math and Physics for Game Programmers

Contents at a Glance

Beginning Math and Physics for Game Programmers

Wendy Stahler

800 East 96th Street, 3rd Floor, Indianapolis, Indiana 46240
An Imprint of Pearson Education
Boston • Indianapolis • London • Munich • New York • San Francisco

Beginning Math and Physics for Game Programmers

International Standard Book Number: 0-7357-1390-1

Library of Congress Catalog Card Number: 2003106775

Printed in the United States of America

First printing: March 2004

09 08 07 06 05 04   7 6 5 4 3 2 1

Interpretation of the printing code: The rightmost double-digit number is the year of the book's printing; the rightmost single-digit number is the number of the book's printing. For example, the printing code 04-1 shows that the first printing of the book occurred in 2004.

Trademarks

Warning and Disclaimer

Publisher
Stephanie Wall

Production Manager
Gina Kanouse

Executive Development Editor
Lisa Thibault

Senior Project Editor
Kristy Hart

Copy Editor
Gayle Johnson

Senior Indexer
Cheryl Lenser

Proofreader
Sheri Cain

Composition
Amy Hassos

Manufacturing Coordinator
Dan Uhrig

Interior Designer
Kim Scott

Cover Designer
Aren Howell

Media Developer
Jay Payne

Marketing
Scott Cowlin
Tammy Detrich

Publicity Manager
Susan Nixon

This book is dedicated to Doug.

Thank you for always believing in me.

Table of Contents

About the Author

**Wendy Stahler** was the first course director of the Game Design and Development Program at Full Sail Real World Education in Winter Park, Florida. During her six years at Full Sail, she concentrated much of her time toward developing the math and physics curriculum. Wendy is also an adjunct professor at Rollins College in the IT department, and just recently took on her next challenge of IT training in the corporate world. Wendy graduated from Rollins College earning an Honors BA in mathematics with a concentration in computer science, and an MA in corporate communication and technology, graduating with honors.

About the Technical Reviewers

These reviewers contributed their considerable hands-on expertise to the entire development process for *Beginning Math and Physics for Game Programmers*. As the book was being written, these dedicated professionals reviewed all the material for technical content, organization, and flow. Their feedback was critical to ensuring that *Beginning Math and Physics for Game Programmers* fits our readers' need for the highest-quality technical information.

Roberto Colnaghi, Jr. has a bachelor's degree in computer science and is a Microsoft Certified Professional. Acting in complex web systems and online services, lately using the Microsoft .NET Framework, he's founding a game company with a focus on online games. He teaches courses on Microsoft technologies for web development at Microsoft Certified Training Centers. Roberto has a big personal library, with books on multiplayer games to genetic programming topics, and he participates in game development communities and mailing lists. He's starting his master's degree in artificial intelligence. He has written articles, games, and material on game programming for Windows in the university and online communities.

Kevin Mack is a game designer, currently working on *Medal of Honor: Pacific Assault* for Electronic Arts. Before joining EA, he designed games for Disney Interactive, Cadillac, and Kronos Digital Entertainment, he worked as a programmer on a real-time 3D action-adventure game for Creative Capers Entertainment, and he served as an information architect with Razorfish LA. His discovery of game development allowed him to channel an earlier body of work in documentary film and database development for New York's capital markets into a single medium. He studied undergraduate film at New York University, and he earned his MFA in film directing from the American Film Institute. He now lives in Pasadena, California.

Acknowledgments

Mom and Dad—thank you for your encouragement.

Hap Aziz—thank you for introducing me to the crazy world of gaming.

Dr. Douglas Child and Dr. Donald Griffin—thank you for advising me on the original curriculum development.

Gene Woolcock and Tony Judice—thank you for jump-starting my math and computer science career back in junior high school.

Stephanie Wall and Lisa Thibault—thank you for your patience and support.

Marc Mencher—thank you for pushing me to write this book.

Thanks to Cody Kahrizi and Dustin Clingman for their programming expertise and contributions to the book. Thanks also to my programmers Dustin Henry, Mike Wiggand, and Mike Fawcett.

And a special thank-you to all my students for your inspiration.

Tell Us What You Think

As the reader of this book, you are the most important critic and commentator. We value your opinion and want to know what we're doing right, what we could do better, what areas you'd like to see us publish in, and any other words of wisdom you're willing to pass our way.

As the Associate Publisher for New Riders Publishing/Peachpit Press, I welcome your comments. You can fax, email, or write me directly to let me know what you did or didn't like about this book—as well as what we can do to make our books stronger. When you write, please be sure to include this book's title, ISBN, and author, as well as your name and phone or fax number. I will carefully review your comments and share them with the author and editors who worked on the book.

Please note that I cannot help you with technical problems related to the topic of this book, and that due to the high volume of email I receive, I might not be able to reply to every message.

Fax: 317-428-3280

Email: stephanie.wall@peachpit.com

Mail: Stephanie Wall
            Associate Publisher
            New Riders Publishing/Peachpit Press
            800 East 96th Street, 3rd Floor
            Indianapolis, IN 46240 USA

Introduction

When I was asked to develop a math and physics for game programming curriculum six years ago, there were absolutely no reference books strictly on that topic were available. At the time, there were many articles in industry magazines and bits and pieces scattered throughout many books on game development in general, but no books focused on game programming applications of math and physics. I tackled this scavenger hunt with great enthusiasm. As I compiled information from traditional math and physics textbooks and articles and excerpts from game programming books, the core of this book emerged.

As I researched and refined my course materials for the game design and development program at Full Sail, more and more publications surfaced. Eventually several books in this specific area appeared on the shelves, but most of them were so intense that they made my head spin! That is when I decided to take a step back in the process and provide a foundation for eager programmers to be able to tackle the difficult books currently available. This book is not the last one you will ever read on the topic of math and physics for game programming. I hope it serves as a stepping-stone at the beginning of an ongoing learning process.

Who Is This Book For?

This book is for anybody interested in the programming side of game development. Code samples and references to the open-source demos on the companion CD have been provided in every chapter, so if you are already familiar with C++ you will definitely walk away with a deeper understanding of these foundational topics in math & physics for programming games. However, programming experience is not necessary if you focus on the math and physics topics conceptually and then try the self-assessment questions. You can always come back and revisit the code samples after you've started an introductory course in C++. This is not a book about 3D programming per se. Rather, it's a foundational tool for the math and physics involved in 3D programming. In addition, this book is not a replacement for more-advanced volumes on 3D math—it's a stepping-stone to those volumes. It provides the foundation you will need to tackle advanced topics in realistic 3D simulation. A strong background in algebra is required for optimal success with this book. Geometry and trigonometry are both strongly recommended.

How Is This Book Organized?

The first half of this book provides a mathematical foundation for the physics topics discussed in the second half.

Chapter 1 starts with the point and line. Both items are defined in 2D and 3D, and then applications in collision detection are discussed.

Chapter 2 provides a brief overview of geometry topics specific to game programming. The Pythagorean theorem, the distance formula, and the midpoint formula are reviewed. The equations of several geometric shapes, such as circle, parabola, and sphere, are defined. Then these topics are used for more approaches to collision detection.

Chapter 3 provides a brief overview of trigonometry topics that are used frequently in coding games. The six trigonometric functions are defined, along with their identities. In addition, the use of C++ math functions and measuring angles in radians are discussed.

Chapter 4 introduces the concept of using vectors to describe physical quantities. Various vector formats are introduced, and all the necessary mathematical operations for vectors, such as addition/subtraction, scalar multiplication, dot product, cross product, and normalizing, are defined.

Chapter 5 defines a matrix as well as all the mathematical operations used for matrices, including addition/subtraction, scalar multiplication, matrix multiplication, and transpose.

Chapter 6 describes the most common use of matrices—transformations. Matrices can control all the movement of objects in a game, including translation, scaling, and rotation. Great attention is given to optimization techniques for game programming.

Chapter 7 prepares you to deal with the units of physical quantities. Converting all measurements to the same units is critical when coding.

Chapter 8 introduces physics. Velocity, acceleration, and their relationship to time and displacement are defined in terms of one dimension.

Chapter 9 introduces the concept of derivative in terms of velocity and acceleration. It serves as a very brief introduction to derivative calculus.

Chapter 10 expands the topics of the previous two chapters into two and three dimensions. In particular, this chapter pays close attention to projectile motion.

Chapter 11 examines the forces that cause objects to move. Sir Isaac Newton coined three laws that govern almost all motion near the surface of the earth. This chapter links those laws to the earlier chapters that describe how objects move.

Chapter 12 defines two different types of energy. It provides an alternative approach, an energy approach, to modeling the motion of objects in games.

Chapter 13 examines the fun part of games—collisions. Without collisions there would be no interactivity. This chapter discusses how objects should move as a result of hitting each other.

Chapter 14 wraps up with a discussion of rotational motion. Many of the earlier physics topics are then redefined in terms of angular motion as opposed to linear.

Appendix A lists important formulas that are featured throughout the book.

Appendix B is a reference of great resources you can turn to for more information.

Each chapter contains several examples and then provides practice questions with the answers so that you can check your answers. Many of the chapters also contain a "Visualization Experience." These sections each relate to one of the demos provided on the companion CD. Some demos simply illustrate an important concept from the chapter, and others are completely interactive. The C++ code for each demo is also provided so that you can see how they were done.

What Will I Take Away from This Book?

If you complete all the activities for every chapter, you should come away with a strong enough understanding of the underlying mathematical principles to be able to structure and implement common 3D physics problems and recognize their implementations in existing systems. From here, you'll be positioned at a decent jumping-off point to dive into, understand, and begin to apply the rationale behind 3D operations in game engines, and you'll have enough information to begin tackling the more advanced texts on the subject.

Remember, this is only the beginning. Take the foundation provided in this text and use it to investigate deeper topics in the field. Appendix B contains several titles that take these concepts to a whole new level. Let this book empower you to start that long and crazy path toward realistic 3D physics simulation. You can do it!

Chapter 1

Points and Lines

Have you ever thought about programming a game and wondered where to start? How does the computer know where to place objects? And how does it make them move? This chapter addresses those questions and lays the groundwork for the rest of the book. This chapter first defines the point so that you can position objects on the flat 2D screen or in a complex 3D world. This chapter establishes standards for the coordinate systems; they are consistent throughout this book. From there, you can examine the idea of a line in both 2D and 3D. The point gives a position, but a line can determine a motion path or even the edge of an object. After discussing all the characteristics of a line (including slope), this chapter concludes with a discussion of line-line collision detection in a game setting.

The Point Defined

In the world of game programming, you will deal with many different types of functions. In general, a **function** is a rule that takes in information (input) and returns new information (output). In programming, you can write functions that take in various types of input, such as variables, text, or numbers, and return a different type of information or even perform an action as output. In a well-written program, you should compartmentalize repeatable tasks in functions so that the code is kept simple and clean. Let's take a look at an example of a well-commented and useful function:

```
// purpose: determine whether a number is a power of 2
// input: the number being checked
// output: true if it's a power of 2, else false
bool powOfTwo(int num)
{
    return !(num & (num - 1));
}
```

This function is passed in any integer and returns a `true` or `false` answer on whether the number is a power of 2—for example, 16, 32, 64, ...

However, in mathematics a function is limited to just numbers: It takes in a number, applies a rule to it, and then returns a new number. There are two ways to define a function in mathematics. First, you could list a set of ordered pairs consisting of an input followed by its corresponding output. For example, the following ordered pairs define a function: (0,0), (1,2), (2,4), (3,6), and (4,8). You also might have seen this written in tabular form, as shown in Table 1.1.

Table 1.1   Ordered Pairs in Tabular Form

x	y
0	0
1	2
2	4
3	6
4	8

Although setting up a lookup table like this is simple and fast, this approach has some problems. If you feed a number into the tabular function and no entry is listed for it, you get an error message. Looking at Table 1.1, what would happen if you had an input of 5? There's no entry for an input of 5, so the computer wouldn't know what to do with it. Related to that is another issue with using a lookup table: An entry must exist for every possible input, and that could lead to a *very* large table that takes up a lot of storage. This leads to a better method.

The second way to define a function is by using a **formula**, or an equation that relates two numbers. The function just discussed can also be written as $y = 2x$, where x is the input and y is the output. Try plugging each of the ordered pairs into the equation.

Does it work? Then clearly both definitions describe the same function. The benefit of using this second approach, though, is that it accommodates any numeric input, not just the five numbers listed in the table. With a function that can take any real number as input, this approach uses a great deal less storage space than a table.

Now let's look at an area in which functions are commonly used: putting things on the screen. When you write game programs, often you ask the computer to place objects on the screen, but how does the computer know where to put them? Traditionally, game programmers use the Cartesian coordinate system to pinpoint any particular location on the screen. The **Cartesian coordinate system** consists of a horizontal x-axis and a vertical y-axis. Each individual point can be defined by an ordered pair with an x-coordinate followed by a y-coordinate, written as (x,y). The origin is the point where the two axes intersect; its coordinates are $(0,0)$. From the origin, positive x values are to the right, and negative x values are to the left. Likewise, positive y values go up, and negative y values go down.

Example 1.1: Graphing 2D Locations

You want to place six objects (A through F) on the screen. Graph their locations on a Cartesian coordinate system: A(0,0), B(1,2), C(4,3), D(–1,2), E(–2,–1), and F(3,–2).

Solution

The points are graphed in Figure 1.1.

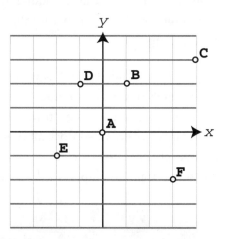

Figure 1.1   Points A through F graphed on the Cartesian coordinate system.

Now you can use functions to move objects around on the screen based on their *x* and *y* coordinates.

> **NOTE**
>
> Be careful not to confuse the Cartesian coordinate system with screen coordinates. Notice that the positive y-axis points up on the Cartesian system. Unfortunately, monitors have been set up to read top to bottom, so screen coordinates use down for the positive *y* direction. See Figure 1.2.

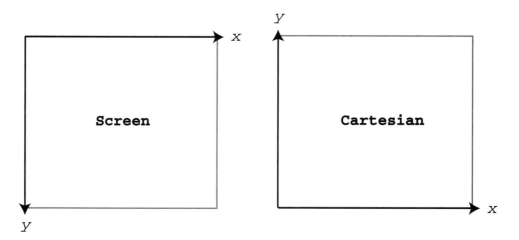

Figure 1.2   The screen coordinate system.

In the overall rendering pipeline, the last step is to convert from Cartesian coordinates to screen coordinates. Chapter 6, "Transformations," addresses how to do that. For now, keep in mind that everything you do will be within the Cartesian coordinate system, meaning that positive *y* is up.

This same coordinate system can be extended to 3D as well. All you have to do is add a third axis: the z-axis. Unfortunately, there are no industry standards at this point. Some packages use a *y*-up world, and some use a *z*-up world. Some engines use a right-handed system, and others use a left. What does all this mean? In the end it's quite arbitrary what you name each axis. Just be clear on what labels you are using for each individual project. This book uses the *y*-up, right-handed coordinate system, as shown in Figure 1.3.

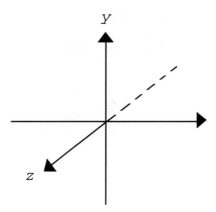

Figure 1.3   The y-up, right-handed coordinate system.

Notice in this system that the positive x-axis is to the right, the positive y-axis is up, and the positive z-axis comes out of the screen toward the viewer. The y-up name is quite obvious, but the right-handed label might not make much sense. Using your right hand, fold your pinky and ring fingers down. Point your thumb to the right (positive x direction) and your pointer finger up (positive y direction). You'll see that your middle finger comes forward (positive z direction). Try doing the same thing with your left hand. If your left thumb points to the right (positive x direction) and your pointer finger is up (positive y direction), your middle finger is forced to point backward (positive z direction for the left-handed system). I've chosen to use the y-up, right-handed system for several reasons:

➤ It's the system used in traditional mathematics.

➤ It's the system used by a majority of programmers (but not all).

➤ It's the system used by OpenGL.

Using this system, you can pinpoint any location in 3D space by giving its coordinates as an ordered triple (x,y,z).

Example 1.2: Graphing a 3D Location

Give the coordinates of point P pictured in Figure 1.4.

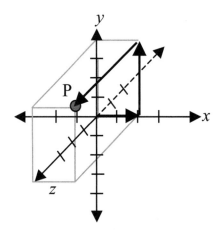

Figure 1.4   A 3D point P.

Solution

To get to point P, you must travel two units to the right, four units up, and five units forward, so the point can be described by the ordered triple (2,4,5).

Traditional mathematicians use the parentheses notation. However, you might see some programmers use notations such as <2,4,5> or [2 4 5] to represent the same point. We'll discuss these notations more in Chapters 4, "Vector Operations," and 5, "Matrix Operations." In code, there is also more than one way to store coordinates. Many programmers will prefer to use simple data types, while others will choose the lengthy (though powerful) object-oriented method and wrap the points in a class or structure.

```
// Some various data types which can be used to store points
// 1. an array of floats.  The advantage lies in speed, ease,
//     and low memory cost
float 3dPoint[3];

// 2. a structure holding 3 floats. The advantage lies in the
//     ability to overload operators and define functions
struct 3dPoint
{
    float x, y, z;
```

```
    // The overloaded addition operator
    3dPoint operator+(const 3dPoint &P2) const
    {
        3dPoint temp = {     this->x + P2.x,
                        this->y + P2.y,
                        this->z + P2.z
                   };

        return temp;
    }
};
```

Using this structure, adding two points is as simple as follows:

```
3Dpoint A, B, C;
C = A + B;
```

Also, it is a good idea to get into the habit of thinking of coordinate systems as they appear in games. In almost all 2D games, the world's coordinate system is defined by the origin, (0, 0), appearing at the top-left corner of the screen with the x and y values increasing to the right and the bottom. Generally, screen coordinates are in pixels, so if your game is running in 800×600 resolution, your screen coordinates would extend 800 right along the X axis and 600 down along the Y axis. In 3D games, it is important to remember that most games are written facing down the negative Z-axis, and the size of the units is generally pre-determined by whatever API you happen to be using.

> 2D points are represented by an ordered pair (x,y).
>
> 3D points are represented by an ordered triple (x,y,z).

Self-Assessment

1. Give the coordinates of the 2D points A through E shown in Figure 1.5.

2. Plot the following points on the grid provided in Figure 1.6: A(3,1), B(−3,1), C(0,2), D(−2,0), E(−1,−2).

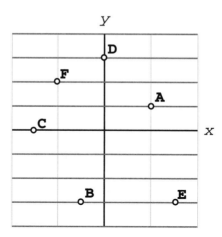

Figure 1.5   2D points A through E.

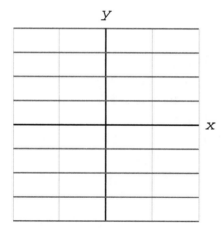

Figure 1.6   A blank grid.

3. Give the coordinates of 3D point P shown in Figure 1.7.

4. Give the coordinates of 3D point Q shown in Figure 1.8.

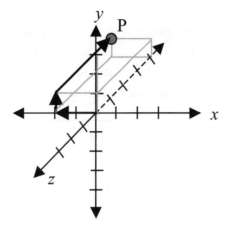

Figure 1.7   3D point P.

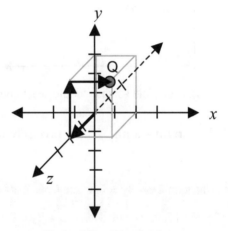

Figure 1.8   3D point Q.

The Line Defined

A **linear equation** is a special kind of function. Remember in the preceding section, when we defined a function by a set of ordered pairs or points? Each of those points is an **individual solution** for the equation $y = 2x$. The **complete solution** is *all* the points that satisfy the equation. If you began plotting individual solutions to a linear equation, an interesting pattern would emerge.

Look at the table for the linear equation $y = 2x$ again. The table offers five individual solutions to the equation. Before you look at Figure 1.9, plot these five points and see if you can figure out the pattern. If you're not sure, try some additional solutions. As you plot more and more solutions, a line starts to emerge, as shown in Figure 1.9. This line is the complete solution for the linear equation $y = 2x$.

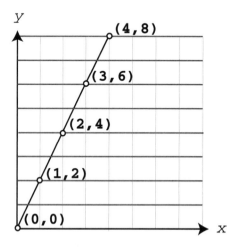

Figure 1.9   The complete solution for the linear equation $y = 2x$.

So what is the pattern? That's right—a line. That's precisely why it's called a linear equation.

The graph of an equation of the form **Ax + By = C**, where A and B are not both 0, is a straight line.

Conversely, every straight line is an equation of the form **Ax + By = C**, where A and B are not both 0.

In general, the easiest way to graph a linear equation is to transform the equation so that the y is alone on one side. Then choose a value for x, substitute it in the equation, and find a value for y. Although two ordered pairs are enough to determine the graph of a line, it's better to use a third point as a check.

TIP
Be smart when choosing values of x; keep them small and manageable. It's usually helpful to use 0 as one of your x values.

Example 1.3: Graphing a Line

Graph the equation $3x - 2y = 8$.

Solution

1. Transform the equation to get y alone on one side:

   $3x - 2y = 8$

   $-2y = -3x + 8$

   $y = (3/2)x - 4$

2. It's much easier to graph points with integer coordinates, so choose x values such as 0, 2, and 4. When you plug these three values into the equation, you get the following three ordered pairs as individual solutions:

   $(0,-4)$, $(2,-1)$, $(4,2)$

3. Graph these three points, and draw the line connecting them. (Technically, you need only two points to determine the line, but the third point serves as a double check.)

   The graph of the line $3x - 2y = 8$ is shown in Figure 1.10.

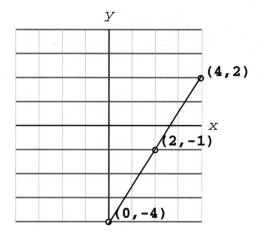

Figure 1.10   The complete solution for the linear equation $3x - 2y = 8$.

Example 1.4: Graphing a Horizontal Line

Graph the equation $y = 3$.

Solution

This one is a little tricky; at first glance it doesn't look like the equation of a line. However, if you think of it as

$$0x + 1y = 3$$

it matches the Ax + By = C form.

1. Try to find three individual solutions that satisfy the equation.

2. Pick three x values, such as 0, 1, and –1. When you plug them into the equation, you get the three ordered pairs (0,3), (4,3), and (–4,3). Actually, no matter which x values you choose, the corresponding y value is always 3.

3. Plot the three points, and draw the line connecting them.

   The graph of the line $y = 3$ is shown in Figure 1.11.

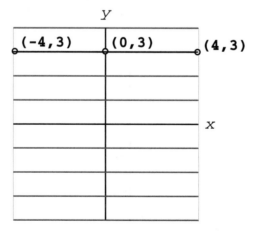

Figure 1.11   The complete solution for the linear equation $y = 3$.

> **NOTE**
> At this point, we have defined the equation of a line in 2D: Ax + By = C. The next section investigates this linear equation in even more detail and extends it to 3D.

Self-Assessment

State whether the following equations are linear (that is, if the complete solution is a line):

1. $2x - y = 5$

2. $-x + 5y = 0$

3. $x = -1$

4. $y + x^2 = 5$

Graph the following linear equations:

5. $x - 2y = 0$

6. $-3x + y = 4$

7. $x = 1$

Properties of Lines

Now that we've defined the equation of a line, let's look at its properties a little more closely. One of the most important elements of a line is its **slope**, or steepness. Figure 1.12 shows a hill (a straight line) that rises steadily at a rate of 50m of vertical "rise" for each 100m of horizontal "run."

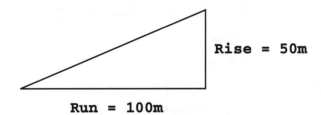

Figure 1.12   A hill represented by a straight line.

The steepness of this incline is measured by the ratio of its rise to its run, which in this case is 50/100, or 50%. This same hill can be mathematically represented by the linear equation $1/2x - y = c$, as shown in Figure 1.13.

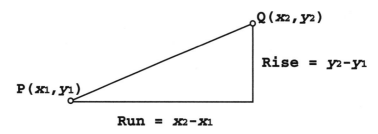

Figure 1.13   Line $1/2x - y = c$ with slope $1/2$.

Look at the coordinates of points P and Q. As you can see, the line rises at a rate of one vertical unit for every two horizontal units. This means that the line's steepness, or **slope**, is rise/run = $1/2$. In general, subscript notation is used to name any two points $P(x_1, y_1)$ and $Q(x_2, y_2)$ on a nonvertical line to define slope, which we will denote as m.

$$slope = m = \frac{\Delta y}{\Delta x} = \frac{y_2 - y_1}{x_2 - x_1}$$

It doesn't matter which two points you choose; the slope ratio is always the same for any two points on the same line. Look at the graph of $1/2x - y = 0$, shown in Figure 1.14.

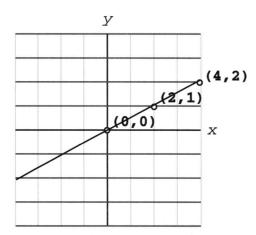

Figure 1.14   Line $1/2x - y = 0$ with slope $1/2$.

Points P and Q and the origin all lie on the same line. If you use points P and Q to calculate the slope, you get $m = (2–1)/(4–2) = 1/2$. If you use point P and the origin, you get $m = (1–0)/(2–0) = 1/2$. Either way, the slope is still $1/2$.

Example 1.5: The Slope Between Two Points

Find the slope between points (1,5) and (–2,0).

Solution

Slope = $m = (y_2-y_1)/(x_2-x_1) = (0–5)/(–2–1) = (–5)/(–3) = 5/3$.

Let's take a look at how we would solve this same problem in code, using a function specifically designed to calculate the slope between 2D points:

```
// purpose: calculate the slope of a line given 2 points
// input:   P1 - an array of 2 floats representing point 1
//               P2 - an array of 2 floats representing point 2
// output: the slope between our 2 points
float slopeBetweenPoints(float *P1, float *P2)
{
    return (P2[1] - P1[1]) / (P2[0] - P1[0]) ;
}
```

Example 1.6: The Slope of a Line

Now let's combine this idea of slope with the graph of a line, which was discussed in the preceding section.

Determine the slope of the following two lines, and graph both lines on the same Cartesian coordinate system:

a. $y = 1/2x + 1$

b. $–3x + 6y = –12$

Solution

Find two pairs of coordinates for each line, and then use the slope formula.

a. (0,1) and (4,3) both satisfy $y = 1/2x + 1$.

Using the slope formula, you get $m = (3–1)/(4–0) = 2/4 = 1/2$.

b. (0,–2) and (3,–1/2) both satisfy $–3x + 6y = –12$.

Using the slope formula, you get $m = ([-1/2] - -2)/(3-0) = (3/2)/3 = 1/2$.

Now that you have two points on each line, you can plot the two points and connect them with a line, as shown in Figure 1.15.

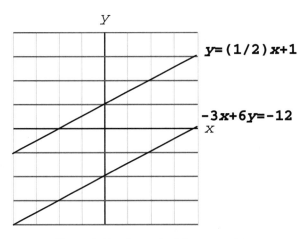

Figure 1.15 A graph of lines a and b.

Look at the graphs of these two equations. They both have slope $1/2$, and they're parallel to each other. That makes sense, doesn't it? If they both rise at the same rate, they must be **parallel**. In fact, looking at the slope can tell you an awful lot about the graph of a line. If the slope is a negative number, the graph falls as it goes from left to right. If the slope is a positive number (as in Example 1.6), the graph rises as it goes from left to right. If the slope of a line is 0, the graph is a horizontal line. Last, if the denominator of the slope formula is 0, the slope is undefined. When the slope is undefined, the graph is a vertical line. These few rules will help you visualize the graph of a line based on its slope.

Notice that in Example 1.6 the two lines are parallel because their slopes are equal. Another interesting relationship between the two slopes occurs if the lines are **perpendicular**, or if they intersect at right angles. (Another fancy word for perpendicular is **orthogonal**, so you might come across that term in programming as well.) The interesting rule is that any time you multiply the slopes of two perpendicular lines, you always get −1. This means that the two slopes must be negative reciprocals of each other.

If two lines are perpendicular, $m_1 m_2 = -1$, or $m_1 = -\dfrac{1}{m_2}$ or $m_2 = -\dfrac{1}{m_1}$.

A function in code which would encompass this formula would look like this:

```
// purpose: to determine the slope of the line perpendicular to
// ourselves
// input:  slope - the slope of our line
// output: the slope of a line perpendicular to us
float perpSlope(float slope)
{
    return -1 / slope;
}
```

Let's take a look at a useful application of this concept. Say for instance that you are making a game in which it is important to know whether or not a collision occurs at a right angle. Knowing that the slope of a line that is perpendicular to another line is −1 over that slope, then if two lines are perpendicular, the product of their slopes will be −1.

```
// purpose: to determine whether two lines are perpendicular
// input:  slope1 - the slope of the first line
//         slope2 - the slope of our second line
// output: true if the lines are perpendicular, else false
bool arePerp(float slope1, float slope2)
{
    if(slope1 * slope2 == -1)
        return true;

    return false;
}
```

Look back at Example 1.6 for a moment. You calculated the slope by finding two points on the line and then using the slope formula. If the equation is in standard form ($Ax + By = C$), there's a shortcut for finding the slope.

For any line in standard form, $Ax + By = C$, the slope $m = -A/B$.

The second equation from Example 1.6 is in standard form: $-3x + 6y = -12$. Because it's in standard form, you can use this new shortcut. The slope $= -A/B = -(-3)/6 = 1/2$. That's the same slope you found using two points on the line. Just be careful with the plus and minus signs; it's very easy to lose track of them.

Example 1.7: Finding the Slope of a Line

Find the slope of the line $2x + y = 5$.

Solution

Don't panic because there's no number in front of the y; it just means that B=1. (If there is no y, B must be 0.)

$$\text{slope} = m = -A/B = -2/1 = -2$$

This shortcut works with linear equations in standard form, but there are two other forms for the equation of a line that you might find more useful.

Slope-intercept form:

$y = mx + b$

Point-slope form:

$(y-y_1) = m(x-x_1)$, where (x_1, y_1) is a point on the line.

Let's look at each one more closely.

The slope-intercept form is probably the most often recalled form of the three. It's used quite frequently in code because the y, or the output, is equal to the rest of the equation, which is the common format for equations in code. You already know that the m represents slope, but you might not have realized that the b represents the **y-intercept**, or the point where the line crosses the y-axis. This form is convenient for trying to visualize the graph, because you immediately know where it crosses the y-axis, and you also know how steep its incline is from the slope.

> **NOTE**
> The y-intercept is the point on the line where $x = 0$. Similarly, the x-intercept is the point on the line where $y = 0$.

Interestingly enough, the point-slope form of a linear equation has many benefits over the other two forms. What if you needed to generate an equation based on two points? For example, you might know your current location and the point you want to move to, but you need the equation of a line to take you there. The point-slope form provides an easier way to get that equation, because all you need is a point on the line and the slope. After you compute the slope, you have both pieces of information for the line.

Example 1.8: Finding the Equation of a Line

Your game character is currently at point (50,200) on the screen. The player clicks the point (150,400), indicating that he wants to go there. Find the equation to take him in a straight-line path to the desired location.

Solution

To generate an equation in point-slope form, all you need is the slope and one of the two points on the line:

$$\text{Slope} = m = (400–200)/(150–50) = 200/100 = 2$$

You could use either of the two points, because they're both on the line. Use the starting point, (50,200). Now you just have to plug those two items into the point-slope equation:

$$(y–y_1) = m(x–x_1)$$
$$(y–200) = 2(x–50)$$

What's interesting is that if you want your answer in slope-intercept form instead, all it takes is two quick algebraic steps:

$$(y–200) = 2(x–50)$$

$$y–200 = 2x–100$$

$$y = 2x+100$$

When it's time for your character to animate along that line, you'll want to use the slope-intercept form to find out where to place it on the y-axis for each x. Notice in this example that the point-slope form gives you an easy way to derive the line, and the slope-intercept form provides an easy way to use it.

Now let's combine this process with the idea of perpendicular lines that was discussed earlier.

Example 1.9: Finding the Equation of a Perpendicular Line

An object in your game is currently moving along the line $y = 2/3x + 20$. When it gets to the point (30,40), the player presses the directional button, forcing the object to turn 90° to the left and continue along that line. Find the equation for the line of the new path.

Solution

Just like the last example, if you find a point on the line and the slope, you can quickly generate an equation in point-slope form. You already know a point on the line, because the object was at (30,40) when it turned, so all you really need to find is the perpendicular slope.

If the slope of the original line is 2/3, the negative reciprocal is –3/2. Therefore, the slope of the new line must be –3/2.

Now you just have to plug those two items into the point-slope equation:

$$(y-y_1) = m(x-x_1)$$
$$(y-40) = -3/2(x-30)$$

If you like, you can even put that answer back in slope-intercept form:

$$(y-40) = -3/2(x-30)$$
$$(y-40) = (-3/2)x + 45$$
$$y = (-3/2)x + 85$$

Example 1.9 is illustrated in Figure 1.16.

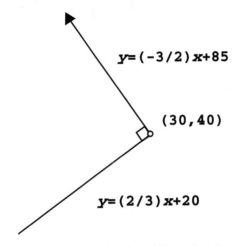

Figure 1.16   Illustration of Example 1.9.

> **NOTE**
> In Chapter 4, you'll find out how to perform this process using vector operations, which makes it easier to move to 3D.

In addition to quickly generating an equation, another benefit of the point-slope equation is that it can easily be extended to 3D. In 2D, a point and a slope can define a line. Looking back at Example 1.9, the starting point of the new line (30,40) and the slope −3/2 define the line. Another way to represent the line is with a slightly different notation that will make more sense when you get to the vector chapter (Chapter 4). The vector notation represents the point in the form <x,y> or <30,40> and the slope as <Δx, Δy> or <2,−3>. This allows you to define a 3D line as a 3D point <x,y,z> and a 3D "slope" as <$\Delta x,\Delta y,\Delta z$>.

Example 1.10: Defining a Line in 3D

Your game character is currently at point (50,200,75) in your 3D world. You want him to move to the point (100,50,225). Find the line that will take him in a straight-line path to the desired location.

Solution

You already know a point on the line, <50,200,75>, so all you need to find is Δx, Δy, and Δz:

$$\Delta x = 100-50 = 50$$

$$\Delta y = 50-200 = -150$$

$$\Delta z = 225-75 = 150$$

Therefore, the line can be defined by the point <50,200,75> and the change in position <50,–150,150>.

Self-Assessment

Compute the slope between the following pairs of points:

1. (0,10) and (5,0)

2. (3,5) and (1,9)

3. (2,–1) and (6,1)

4. (–2,–5) and (1,4)

5. (–3,5) and (–4,$^7/_2$)

6. (9,8) and (9,–7)

7. (4,2) and (–2,1)

8. (3,7) and (–8,7)

9. How are the lines from questions 1 and 2 related?

10. Describe what the line in question 6 looks like.

11. Describe what the line in question 8 looks like.

Find the slope of the following lines:

12. $2x + 3y = 10$

13. $x - 5y = 0$

14. $2y = 8$

15. $x + y = -7$

Find the equation of a line connecting the following pairs of points:

16. $(0,10)$ and $(5,0)$

17. $(3,5)$ and $(1,9)$

18. $(2,-1)$ and $(6,1)$

19. $(-2,-5)$ and $(1,4)$

20. $(2,0,-1)$ and $(3,4,5)$

21. $(-3,1,5)$ and $(0,8,-2)$

Applications in Collision Detection

There will be times in game programming when you'll want to know if and where two lines intersect. The lines might represent the side of a building or the ground or the path of an object. You might need to program a conditional based on the intersection of two such lines. Now that you know how to find the equations of these lines, you can put the two equations together to form a **system of linear equations**. Then you can solve the system mathematically. This section first discusses the three types of solutions you might find, and then it describes methods of finding the numeric solution.

When solving a system of two linear equations, you're really searching for the intersection of two lines. The **solution set** is the set of all the points that satisfy both equations. Figures 1.17, 1.18, and 1.19 illustrate the three possible outcomes for a system of two linear equations. In Figure 1.17, the two lines

$$2x + 3y = 3$$

$$-x + 3y = -6$$

intersect at exactly one point. This point is labeled P, and on the graph it looks as if P has the coordinates (3,–1). This is easy to verify; just plug these coordinates into each equation to check. The graph doesn't always show the point of intersection so clearly. The next section looks at how to calculate the point of intersection numerically.

$$2(3) + 3(-1) = 3$$

$$6 - 3 = 3 \checkmark$$

$$-(3) + 3(-1) = -6$$

$$-3 - 3 = -6 \checkmark$$

Notice that the graphs of these two lines have different slopes.

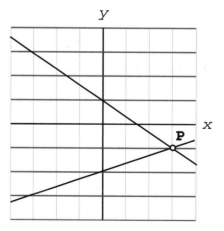

Figure 1.17   Two lines intersecting at one point.

In Figure 1.18, the lines

$$-3x + 6y = 6$$

$$-x + 2y = 2$$

coincide, or overlap. This time the solution set is not just one point; it's the infinite set of all the points on either line. Notice that the graphs of these two equations have the same slope and the same y-intercept.

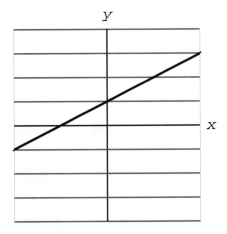

Figure 1.18   Two lines that coincide.

Finally, in Figure 1.19, the two lines

$$-x + 2y = 2$$

$$-x + 2y = -2$$

are parallel. The solution set is the empty set, because the two equations have no points in common. They will never intersect. Notice that the graphs of these two equations have the same slope but different y-intercepts.

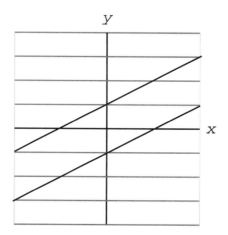

Figure 1.19   Two lines that never intersect.

As you can see, the number of solutions for a system of linear equations is related to the slope and the y-intercept of the equations. Let's summarize the three possibilities.

Theorem

A system of two linear equations in the same plane has

- Exactly one solution if the two graphs have different slopes.
- An infinite set of solutions if both graphs have the same slope and y-intercept.
- *No* solution if the graphs have the same slope but different y-intercepts.

This is a very systematic procedure that can quickly and easily be implemented in code. Here is the algorithm, or step-by-step process, in pseudocode:

Find the slope of both lines, m_1 and m_2.

1. If $m_1 \neq m_2$, output one solution.

2. If $m_1 = m_2$, find the y-intercept of both lines, b_1 and b_2.

   If $b_1 \neq b_2$, output zero solutions.

   If $b_1 = b_2$, output infinite solutions.

Example 1.11: A System of Linear Equations

Graph the following system of linear equations (two lines), and state the size of the solution set (specify how many points of intersection exist).

$$x + y = 2$$

$$-x + 2y = -2$$

Solution

Both lines are graphed in Figure 1.20. It looks as though they intersect at one point close to the point (2,0). The graph isn't always so clear, so verify it numerically using the algorithm:

1. Find both slopes, m_1 and m_2. Both lines are in standard form, so you can use the $-A/B$ shortcut.

   $$m_1 = -1/1 = -1$$

   $$m_2 = -(-1)/2 = 1/2$$

2. The slopes are not the same ($m_1 \neq m_2$), so there must be one point of intersection.

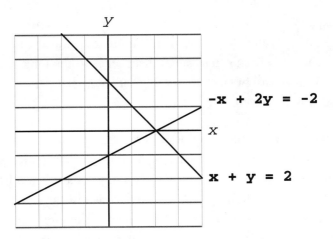

Figure 1.20 A graph of two lines in Example 1.11.

Example 1.12: Line-Line Collision Detection

A ball on the screen is moving along the straight path described by the line $-x + 2y = -2$. A wall has been placed along the line $3x - 6y = -6$. Will the ball ever hit the wall?

Solution

You could graph these two lines like you did in Example 1.11, but the graphs can sometimes be misleading, so go straight to the algorithm.

1. You might find that it's easier to pick off the slope and the y-intercept by putting both lines in slope-intercept form:

   $-x + 2y = -2 \rightarrow y = \frac{1}{2}x - 1$

   $3x - 6y = -6 \rightarrow y = \frac{1}{2}x + 1$

2. Find both slopes: $m_1 = \frac{1}{2}$ and $m_2 = \frac{1}{2}$.

3. If $m_1 = m_2$, find both y-intercepts: $b_1 = -1$ and $b_2 = 1$.

4. If $b_1 \neq b_2$, output zero solutions, because they are parallel and will never intersect. This means that the ball will never hit the wall.

This algorithm is very important to use when you're expecting two lines to intersect. What would happen if, in the preceding example, you were expecting the ball to hit the wall? That's right—you'd get stuck in an infinite loop waiting for something that will never happen. This check can save you headaches in the long run, so verify in the code that the two lines will in fact intersect if that's a crucial part of the gameplay. It's a quick check, so why not use it?

After you've checked to see that two lines intersect at one point, you might want to know what that point of intersection is. You can find its coordinates using one of two methods: linear combination or substitution. You might have heard the expression "two equations with two unknowns." This refers to two linear equations with two variables you need to find—in this case, x and y. Either of these two methods will work anytime you have two equations and two variables for which to solve.

Let's discuss **linear combination** first. Basically, you use the properties of equality to transform the system of equations into an equivalent system that is easier to work with. You do this by multiplying both sides of an equation by the same nonzero number. You want to multiply each equation by some number so that both equations have either the same x coefficient or the same y coefficient. (Remember that the coefficient is the number in front of the x or the y.) Suppose you have the following system of two linear equations:

$3x + 2y = 10$

$4x + 3y = 6$

Try to transform the system so that both equations have the same y coefficient. To do that, you must first multiply both sides of the top equation by 3. That gives you $9x + 6y = 30$, which is still equal to $3x + 2y = 10$. Then you multiply both sides of the bottom equation by 2 to get $8x + 6y = 12$. This gives you an equivalent system (the same two lines), only this time the y coefficients are equal:

$9x + 6y = 30$

$8x + 6y = 12$

The next step is to combine the two equations into one. You do this by subtracting one from the other. Subtract the bottom one from the top one:

$9x + 6y = 30$

$-(8x + 6y = 12)$

$x + 0y = 18$

$x = 18$

The equation $x = 18$ is called the linear combination of the two original equations. Now you know that the x-coordinate of the solution is 18. All you have to do now is plug 18 back into one of the original equations to find the y-coordinate. If you plug 18 in for x in the top equation, you get

$3(18) + 2y = 10$

so $y = -22$

Therefore, the solution to this system of equations is (18,–22). What does this mean? Remember that the solution is the point where the two lines intersect. The following summarizes the steps of the linear combination method:

1. Choose which variable you'd like to eliminate (*x* or *y*).

2. Multiply both sides of each equation by some nonzero number so that the coefficients of the variable you are trying to eliminate match. (Keep in mind that it's much easier to work with small numbers.)

3. Subtract one equation from the other to find the system's linear combination.

4. Solve for the solution's first variable.

5. Substitute that back into one of the original equations to solve for the other variable.

It might help to step through an example using this new method.

Example 1.13: Finding the Point of Intersection Using the Linear Combination Method

A car in your game is traveling along a straight-line path defined by $3x + 5y = 8$, and a wall is placed along another line defined by $x + 3y = 4$. If the car continues on the same path, will it hit the wall? If so, at what point will it hit?

Solution

1. Check to see if the car will hit the wall. The slope of the first line is –3/5, and the slope of the second line is –1/3, so they will intersect.

2. Now you can use linear combination to find the exact point of intersection for these two lines:

    $3x + 5y = 8$

    $x + 3y = 4$

3. Choose the variable you'd like to eliminate. Try to get rid of the *x* variable.

4. You must multiply by nonzero numbers so that the x coefficients are equal. In this case all we have to do is multiply the bottom equation by 3 on both sides. That will give us an equivalent system of:

$3x + 5y = 8$

$3x + 9y = 12$

5. If you subtract the bottom equation from the top one, you get $0x - 4y = -4$.

(You could have just as easily subtracted the top from the bottom; that would have worked too.)

6. The equation found in step 5 can be solved for y: $-4y = -4$ can be reduced to $y = 1$.

7. Substitute 1 for y in one of the original equations to solve for x. It might be easier to use the bottom original equation.

8. Substituting for y, you get $x + 3(1) = 4$, or $x = 1$. So the solution must be the point $(1, 1)$.

Now let's turn our attention to the second method of solving a system of two linear equations, which is **substitution**. This method requires a lot of simple algebra. You still have to find the solution one coordinate at a time. First you must choose one of the original equations and solve it in terms of one variable, which means that one variable is on one side of the equals sign while everything else is on the other side. Suppose one of the equations in your system is

$x + 2y = 5$

To solve this equation in terms of x, you must subtract $2y$ from both sides, which gives you

$x = -2y + 5$

Then you substitute that equation for x in the system's second equation. So if the second equation is

$3x - 2y = -1$

substituting gives you

$$3(-2y + 5) - 2y = -1$$

This is where all the algebra comes into play. At this point, you want to solve for y. If you perform the algebra properly, you will find that

$$3(-2y + 5) - 2y = -1$$

$$-6y + 15 - 2y = -1$$

$$-8y + 15 = -1$$

$$-8y = -16$$

$$y = 2$$

The final step is the same as it would be with the linear combination method. You must plug 2 in for y in one of the original equations so that you can solve for x. If you plug it into the first equation, you get

$$x + 2(2) = 5$$

so $x = 1$

This means that the solution is the point $(1, 2)$.

Just as we did for linear combination, let's review the steps for the substitution method:

1. Choose one of the original equations, and solve it in terms of one variable. (Get one variable on the left of the equals sign and everything else on the right.)

2. Substitute this equation into the other original equation. (At this point one of the variables should be eliminated.)

3. Solve for the remaining variable.

4. Substitute the value found in step 3 into one of the original equations to solve for the other variable.

Now let's step through another example.

Example 1.14: Finding the Point of Intersection Using the Substitution Method

Solve the following system using the substitution method:

$$-3x + y = 8$$
$$5x - 2y = 9$$

Solution

1. Examine the two original equations. It will be easier to solve for y in the first equation, because it has a coefficient of 1. You can do this quickly by adding $3x$ to each side. That gives you

$$y = 3x + 8$$

2. Substitute the equation from step 1 for y in the bottom original equation. The result is

$$5x - 2(3x + 8) = 9$$

(As you can see, the y has been eliminated.)

3. Solve the equation found in step 2 for x:

$$5x - 2(3x + 8) = 9$$

$$5x - 6x - 16 = 9$$

$$-x = 25$$

$$x = -25$$

4. Substitute -25 for x in one of the original equations so that you can solve for y. If you plug it into the top equation, you get

$$-3(-25) + y = 8$$

so $y = -67$

This means that the solution is the point $(-25, -67)$.

Both of the methods discussed in this section can be used to solve any system of two linear equations that has exactly one solution. However, it might be easier to use substitution when one of the variables has a coefficient of 1. Otherwise, it might be easier to use the linear combination method. Knowing which method to use in a particular situation can save you a lot of time. That is why it's a good idea to be comfortable with both methods.

So we are now confronted with the question of how to define lines and check for collision between them in code. Consider if we define a line by its slope and any point along that line. In that instance, the equation for a line would look as follows:

$$y - y1 = m(x - x1)$$

where m is the slope of the line and (x1,y1) is any point along the line. Rewriting this in terms of y, and looking at two different lines, we get:

$$y = m1(x - x1) + y1$$
$$y = m2(x - x2) + y2$$

By setting the equations equal to each other and solving for x, we get:

$$x = (m1x1 - m2x2 + y2 - y1) / (m1 - m2)$$

So, let's write a function which, when given two lines, will return their point of intersection. This function assumes that we have already established that these lines are not parallel:

```
// purpose: find the point of intersection between two lines
// input: L1Point- a 2D point along our first line
//        L1Slope- the slope of our first line
//        L2Point- a 2D point along our second line
//        L2Slope- the slope of our second line
// output: our array of float holding our point
float *lineIntersect(float *L1Point, float L1Slope,
                float *L2Point, float L2Slope)
{
    // A temp array for holding our answer
```

```
    float temp[2] = {0, 0};
    // Solve for our x value of the solution
    temp[0] = (L1Slope * L1Point[0] - L2Slope * L2Point[0] +
              L2Point[1] - L1Point[1]) / (L1Slope - L2Slope);
    // Use our new-found value to solve for our y value
    temp[1] = L1Slope(temp[0] - L1Point[0]) + L1Point[1];

    return temp;
}
```

Self-Assessment

Give the slope and y-intercept for each equation and the number of solutions for the system:

1. $x + y = 7$

2. $x - 3y = -6$

3. $x + 4y = 8$
   $x - 3y = -2$
   $-x + 3y = -6$
   $x/4 + y = 2$

4. $x - y = 5$

5. $x + 3y = -1$

6. $3x - 5y = -8$
   $5x + y = 0$
   $2x + 6y = -5$
   $3x + 5y = 8$

Solve the following systems of linear equations using the linear combination method:

7. $6x - 5y = 7$

8. $1/2x + 2y = 3$
   $x - 7y = -1$
   $4x - 5y = 24$

Solve the following systems of linear equations using the substitution method:

9. $3x - 2y = -6$

10. $4x + 3y = 8$
    $x + 5y = 15$
    $2x + y = 6$

Self-Assessment Solutions

The Point Defined

1. A(2,1), B(–1,–3), C(–3,0), D(0,3), E(3,–3)

2. The answer is shown in Figure 1.21.

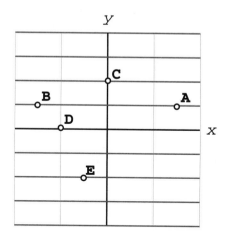

Figure 1.21   Graph of points A through E.

3. (–2,1,–4)

4. (2,3,2)

The Line Defined

1. Yes

2. Yes

3. Yes

4. No

5. The answer is shown in Figure 1.22.

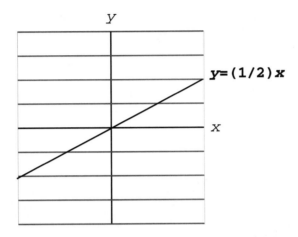

Figure 1.22   Graph of x – 2y = 0.

6. The answer is shown in Figure 1.23.

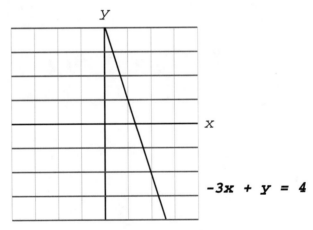

Figure 1.23   Graph of –3x + y = 4.

7. The answer is shown in Figure 1.24.

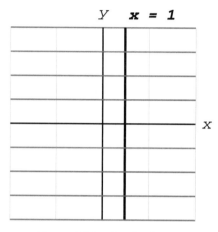

Figure 1.24   Graph of x = 1.

Properties of Lines

1. $m = -2$

2. $m = -2$

3. $m = 1/2$

4. $m = 3$

5. $m = 3/2$

6. $m = $ undefined

7. $m = 1/2$

8. $m = 0$

9. They are parallel.

10. Vertical

11. Horizontal

12. $m = -2/3$

13. $m = 1/5$

14. $m = 0$

15. $m = -1$

16. $(y-10) = -2(x)$ or $y = -2x + 10$

17. $(y-5) = -2(x-3)$ or $y = -2x + 11$

18. $(y+1) = \frac{1}{2}(x-2)$ or $y = \frac{1}{2}x - 2$

19. $(y-4) = 3(x-1)$ or $y = 3x + 1$

20. point $<2,0,-1>$ and vector $<1,4,6>$

21. point $<-3,1,5>$ and vector $<3,7,-7>$

Applications in Collision Detection

1. $m_1 = -1, b_1 = 7, m_2 = \frac{1}{3}, b_2 = \frac{2}{3}$; one solution

2. $m_1 = \frac{1}{3}, b_1 = 2, m_2 = \frac{1}{3}, b_2 = -2$; zero solutions

3. $m_1 = -\frac{1}{4}, b_1 = 2, m_2 = -\frac{1}{4}, b_2 = 2$; infinite solutions

4. $m_1 = 1, b_1 = -5, m_2 = -5, b_2 = 0$; one solution

5. $m_1 = -\frac{1}{3}, b_1 = -\frac{1}{3}, m_2 = -\frac{1}{3}, b_2 = -\frac{5}{6}$; zero solutions

6. $m_1 = \frac{3}{5}, b_1 = \frac{8}{5}, m_2 = -\frac{3}{5}, b_2 = \frac{8}{5}$; one solution

7. $(2,1)$

8. $(6,0)$

9. $(0,3)$

10. $(5,-4)$

Chapter 2

Geometry Snippets

This chapter addresses all the geometry topics that appear throughout the book. In fact, this collection of geometric methods can be used in nearly every game programming challenge you are likely to encounter. The Pythagorean theorem surfaces whenever you use vectors to control movement or when you use right triangles to model various scenarios. The distance formula is used in both collision detection and the physics of motion. Parabolas are used to represent projectile paths in 2D and 3D motion. Finally, circles and spheres are used to model round objects and motion paths, but most importantly, they can be used as bounding geometry for collision detection. This chapter concludes with a demo from the companion CD-ROM that shows bounding circles being used for collision detection.

Distance Between Points

Often in programming, you want to know the distance between two points on the screen. It could be two objects about to collide or two characters about to interact. Or maybe the artificial intelligence is waiting for the player to come within a certain distance of the enemy before it attacks. Whatever the situation, it's important to be able to quickly calculate that distance between two points on those objects. The easiest way to do that is to use the **Pythagorean theorem**.

The Pythagorean Theorem

$a^2 + b^2 = c^2$

where *a* and *b* are the legs of a right triangle and *c* is the hypotenuse.

The Pythagorean theorem is illustrated in Figure 2.1.

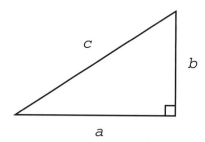

Figure 2.1 $a^2 + b^2 = c^2$.

NOTE

The Pythagorean theorem works only for right triangles, not just any triangle. The small box inside the triangle indicates that sides *a* and *b* intersect at a 90° angle, which means that the triangle is a right triangle.

The converse of this theorem is also true.

The Converse of the Pythagorean Theorem

If *a*, *b*, and *c* are the lengths of the three sides of a triangle, and $a^2 + b^2 = c^2$, the triangle is a right triangle with a hypotenuse of length *c*.

You'll see that the Pythagorean theorem is used extensively in Chapter 4, "Vector Operations," but for now you can use it to investigate the distance between two points on the screen. Suppose you have two points, $P_1(x_1, y_1)$ and $P_2(x_2, y_2)$, as shown in Figure 2.2.

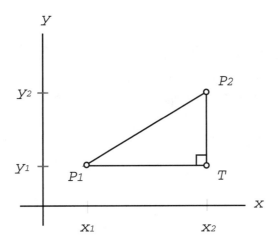

Figure 2.2   The distance between points p$_1$ and p$_2$.

You can draw a right triangle with line segment P$_1$P$_2$ as its hypotenuse. The third vertex of this triangle has the coordinates T(x_2, y_1). As you can see, side P$_1$T has length ($x_2 - x_1$), and side P$_2$T has length ($y_2 - y_1$). Now you can use the Pythagorean theorem:

$$(P_1P_2)^2 = (P_1T)^2 + (P_2T)^2$$

$$= (x_2 - x_1)^2 + (y_2 - y_1)^2$$

This can be summarized in a simple formula, the *distance formula*.

The Distance Formula in 2D

$$P_1P_2 = \sqrt{(x_2 - x_1)^2 + (y_2 - y_1)^2}$$

where $P_1(x_1, y_1)$ and $P_2(x_2, y_2)$ are points on the line.

The following function takes in two arrays of floats, each size 2, which represent points in 2D space and returns the distance between them. Notice the use of the `sqrt()` function that exists in the `<cmath>` header file and returns the square root of whatever number is passed into it. Also note the use of the `pow()` function which takes in two parameters. It returns the first parameter raised to the power of the second. While the pow function is quite useful, it is a bit slower than simply multiplying the numbers manually in the code. For instance, `pow(x, 2)` is not as fast as `x * x`. However, if using a Microsoft compiler, using the `#pragma intrinsic` command in the preprocessor section of your code will greatly increase the speed of most math function calls:

```
#pragma intrinsic(sqrt, pow)
```

continues

continued

This allows most math function calls to be sent directly to the math co-processor rather than being sent to the function stack. (For more information on the `intrinsic` command, do a search for `intrinsic` in your MSDN library.) Also notice that we are type-casting our answer to a float before it is returned. This is to avoid a truncation compiler warning due to possible loss of information when changing from a double to a float. This can also be avoided by using the less common `sqrtf()` and `powf()` which take input and return output as floats rather than doubles.

```
// purpose: to calculate the distance between two points
// input: P1- an array of 2 floats representing point 1
//         P2- an array of 2 floats representing point 2
// output: the distance between the two points
float distance2D(float *P1, float *P2)
{
    // Calculate our distance and return it
    return (float)sqrt(pow(P2[0] - P1[0], 2) + pow(P2[1] -
    ➥ P1[1], 2);
}
```

Example 2.1: The Distance Between Two Screen Points

If one object is centered at (25,80), and another is centered at (55,40), what is the distance between their two centers?

Solution

$$P_1P_2 = \sqrt{(x_2 - x_1)^2 + (y_2 - y_1)^2}$$

$$= \sqrt{(55 - 25)^2 + (40 - 80)^2}$$

$$= \sqrt{(30)^2 + (-40)^2}$$

$$= \sqrt{900 + 1600}$$

$$= \sqrt{2500}$$

$$= 50$$

Let's combine the distance formula with the Pythagorean theorem in another example.

Example 2.2: Checking for a Right Triangle

A triangle is defined by the following three vertices: A(20,50), B(100,90), and C(70,150). Check to see if it's a right triangle.

Solution

The three points are graphed in Figure 2.3, but you can't tell for sure just by looking at the figure; you need numerical proof.

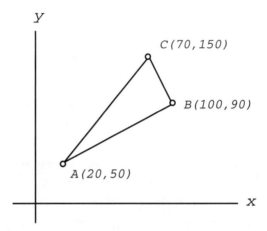

Figure 2.3 Triangle ABC.

According to the converse of the Pythagorean theorem, if the lengths of the three sides fit $a^2 + b^2 = c^2$, it's a right triangle. First, find the lengths by using the distance formula three times, once for each side.

For side AB:

$$AB = \sqrt{(100-20)^2 + (90-50)^2}$$

$$= \sqrt{80^2 + 40^2}$$

$$= \sqrt{6400+1600}$$

$$= \sqrt{8000}$$

For side BC:

$$BC = \sqrt{(70-100)^2 + (150-90)^2}$$

$$= \sqrt{(-30)^2 + (60)^2}$$

$$= \sqrt{900 + 3600}$$

$$= \sqrt{4500}$$

For side CA:

$$CA = \sqrt{(70-20)^2 + (150-50)^2}$$

$$= \sqrt{50^2 + 100^2}$$

$$= \sqrt{2500 + 10000}$$

$$= \sqrt{12500}$$

Now, plug these three lengths into the Pythagorean theorem to see if it fits:

$$a^2 + b^2 = c^2$$

$$(\sqrt{8000})^2 + (\sqrt{4500})^2 = (\sqrt{12500})^2$$

$$8000 + 4500 = 12,500$$

$$12500 = 12500 \checkmark$$

Therefore, it is a right triangle.

The distance formula can also be extended to three dimensions. All you have to do is take the z-coordinates into account as well.

The Distance Formula in 3D

$$P_1P_2 = \sqrt{(x_2 - x_1)^2 + (y_2 - y_1)^2 + (z_2 - z_1)^2}$$

where $P_1(x_1,y_1,z_1)$ and $P_2(x_2,y_2,z_2)$ are points on the line.

Example 2.3: The Distance Between Two 3D Points

If one object is centered at (25,80,30) and another is centered at (55,40,100), what is the distance between their two centers?

Solution

$$P_1P_2 = \sqrt{(x_2 - x_1)^2 + (y_2 - y_1)^2 + (z_2 - z_1)^2}$$

$$= \sqrt{(55 - 25)^2 + (40 - 80)^2 + (100 - 30)^2}$$

$$= \sqrt{(30)^2 + (-40)^2 + (70)^2}$$

$$= \sqrt{900 + 1600 + 4900}$$

$$= \sqrt{7400}$$

$$\approx 86$$

Another very helpful formula related to the distance formula is the midpoint formula. There might be times when you'll need the point exactly halfway between two objects on the screen. When that happens, just look up the following formula.

The Midpoint Formula in 2D

$$M\left(\frac{x_1 + x_2}{2}, \frac{y_1 + y_2}{2}\right)$$

is the midpoint between $P_1(x_1,y_1)$ and $P_2(x_2,y_2)$.

The following function takes two points, P1 and P2, as input and returns the midpoint. Notice in this function that we are using the `new` keyword to allocate memory to our `temp` variable. Make sure to clean up this memory when it is no longer needed by using the `delete` keyword. Also remember to use brackets when freeing the memory because we are using brackets to create the memory:

```
delete [] temp;
```

continues

continued

```
// purpose: calculate the midpoint of a line segment
// input: P1- an array of 2 floats representing point 1
//        P2- an array of 2 floats representing point 2
// output: the midpoint between the two points
float *find2DMidPoint(float *P1, float *P2)
{
    // Allocate enough memory to our pointer
float *temp = new float[2];
    // Calculate our midpoint
    temp[0] = (P1[0] + P2[0]) / 2.0f;
    temp[1] = (P1[1] + P2[1]) / 2.0f;
    // Return our answer
    return temp;
}
```

Example 2.4: The Midpoint Between Two Screen Points

If one object is centered at (25,80) and another is centered at (55,40), what is the midpoint between them?

Solution

The midpoint is really just the average of the two *x*s and the two *y*s:

$$M\left(\frac{x_1 + x_2}{2}, \frac{y_1 + y_2}{2}\right)$$

$$M\left(\frac{25 + 55}{2}, \frac{80 + 40}{2}\right)$$

$$M\left(\frac{80}{2}, \frac{120}{2}\right)$$

$$M\left(40,60\right)$$

> **NOTE**
>
> Be careful with the plus and minus signs. Notice that the distance formula subtracts the *x*s and the *y*s, but the midpoint formula adds them.

Just like with the distance formula, the midpoint formula can be extended to 3D by simply adding a z component.

The Midpoint Formula in 3D

$$M\left(\frac{x_1 + x_2}{2}, \frac{y_1 + y_2}{2}, \frac{z_1 + z_2}{2}\right)$$

is the midpoint between $P_1(x_1, y_1, z_1)$ and $P_2(x_2, y_2, z_2)$.

Our 3D midpoint function in code is not much different from our 2D function, differing only in the addition of a third point. Once again, be sure to use `delete` to clean up the memory that is allocated before the program ends:

```
// purpose: calculate the midpoint of a line segment in 3D
// input: P1- an array of 3 floats representing point 1
//           P2- an array of 3 floats representing point 2
// output: the midpoint between the two points
float *find3DMidPoint(float *P1, float *P2)
{
    // Allocate enough memory to our pointer
float *temp = new float[3];
    // Calculate our midpoint
    temp[0] = (P1[0] + P2[0]) / 2.0f;
    temp[1] = (P1[1] + P2[1]) / 2.0f;
    temp[2] = (P1[2] + P2[2]) / 2.0f;
    // Return our answer
    return temp;
}
```

Example 2.5: The Midpoint Between Two 3D Points

If one object is centered at (25,80,30) and another is centered at (55,40,100), what is the midpoint between them?

Solution

Use the 3D extension of the midpoint formula:

$$M\left(\frac{x_1 + x_2}{2}, \frac{y_1 + y_2}{2}, \frac{z_1 + z_2}{2}\right)$$

$$M\left(\frac{25 + 55}{2}, \frac{80 + 40}{2}, \frac{30 + 100}{2}\right)$$

$$M\left(\frac{80}{2}, \frac{120}{2}, \frac{130}{2}\right)$$

$$M\left(40, 60, 65\right)$$

At this point, you should be able to

➤ Find the length of one side of a right triangle if given the other two

➤ Test for a right triangle using the converse of the Pythagorean theorem

➤ Find the distance between two points in 2D and 3D

➤ Compute the midpoint between two points in 2D or 3D

These topics are revisited in future chapters, so stay tuned!

Self-Assessment

1. Find the length of side b, as shown in Figure 2.4.

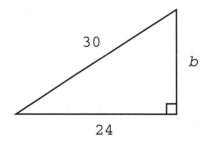

Figure 2.4 Find side b.

2. A triangle is defined by the following vertices: (30,75), (25,0), and (–50,45). Is it a right triangle?

3. Find the distance between points (30,80) and (150,130).

4. Find the distance between points (20,50,10) and (100,120,40).

5. Find the midpoint between points (30,80) and (150,130).

6. Find the midpoint between points (20,50,10) and (100,120,40).

Parabolas

Think about the last time you threw a baseball or kicked a soccer ball. Did it follow a straight-line path through the air? No, it probably had more of a curved or arclike path. In fact, any projectile follows what is called a parabolic path. A **parabola** is really just a fancy name for a symmetric bump, or arc. The bump can be upside-down or sideways, as shown in Figure 2.5, but one side is always a mirror image of the other.

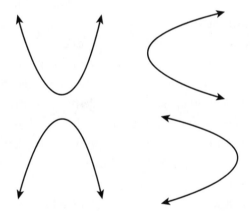

Figure 2.5 Four different types of parabolas.

You will use two components of the parabola to determine its equation. The first is the **vertex**, which is the very tip of the bump. The second is the **axis of symmetry**, which goes through the vertex and splits the parabola right down the middle so that each side is a reflection of the other. There are actually two forms for the equation of a parabola—one for the up-and-down version with a vertical axis of symmetry, and one for the sideways version with a horizontal axis of symmetry.

A Parabola with a Vertical Axis

$y=a(x-h)^2+k$, with vertex (h,k) and axis of symmetry $x=h$.

A Parabola with a Horizontal Axis

$x=a(y-k)^2+h$, with vertex (h,k) and axis of symmetry $y=k$.

> **NOTE**
>
> The term vertex is also used in the context of polygonal modeling. Don't confuse that type of vertex with this one, which is more like the apex of a curve.
>
> Also, both forms use (h,k) for the vertex, but notice that the positions of h and k in the actual equations switch.
>
> Finally, note that the axis of symmetry is either a horizontal or vertical line that always goes through the vertex.

When making a rough sketch of a parabola, you must consider two additional features. First, if the equation is in the form $y=a(x-h)^2+k$, the parabola opens either up or down. If it looks like $x=a(y-k)^2+h$, it opens sideways. Notice in the up-and-down version that you can plug in different values for x and then solve for y. In the sideways version, you interpolate along the y-axis and solve for x. Second, the constant a determines in which direction the parabola opens and how wide or skinny the opening is. If a is a positive number, the parabola opens up if it looks like $y=a(x-h)^2+k$ or opens to the right if it's $x=a(y-k)^2+h$. If a is negative, the parabola opens downward or to the left. Also, the closer a gets to 0, the wider the opening. Likewise, the farther a gets from 0 (positive or negative), the skinnier the opening. These are just some tips to help you estimate where a parabola will fall and how to make adjustments to model whatever you like.

Example 2.6: Sketching a Parabola

Roughly sketch the parabola $y = (-\frac{1}{3})(x-2)^2 + 3$.

Solution

1. Determine whether this is an up/down version or a sideways version. Because the x is squared and the y is not, this one must be vertical.

2. Now that you know which form it is, you know where to look for h and k. In this case, the vertex is $(2,3)$.

3. The last thing to look for is the a, which describes the opening. For this parabola, $a=-\frac{1}{3}$, so it must open down, and the opening is relatively wide.

4. The parabola is sketched in Figure 2.6. The axis of symmetry $(x=2)$ is drawn for you to see, but it is not part of the parabola's graph.

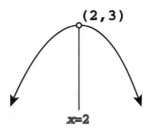

Figure 2.6   The graph of $y = (-\frac{1}{3})(x-2)^2 + 3$.

Example 2.7: Sketching Another Parabola

Roughly sketch the parabola $x = y^2 + 5$.

Solution

1. Determine whether this is an up/down version or a sideways version. Because the y is squared and the x is not, this one must be horizontal.

2. Now that you know which form it is, you know where to look for h and k. In this case, the vertex is $(5,0)$. Notice that the y is by itself, which is the same as $(y-0)$, so k must be 0.

3. The last thing to look for is the *a*, but nothing's there. If nothing is in the *a* position, *a* must equal 1. For this parabola, *a*=1, so it must open to the right. The opening is relatively wide, but not as wide as the last one.

4. The parabola is sketched in Figure 2.7. Notice that the axis of symmetry is just the x-axis (*y*=0).

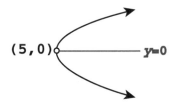

Figure 2.7   The graph of $x = y^2 + 5$.

Now that you are familiar with the parabolic equation, you can use it to model a projectile's motion path. Graphing it precisely is not nearly as important as knowing how to adjust the equation to fit your needs. Plenty of shareware programs available online will graph the parabolic equation for you if you want to see the precise graph. What is more important for you is knowing how to modify the equation to fit your needs. Think about what values you might plug into the equation to model a line drive versus a pop fly in a baseball game. Chapter 10, "Motion in Two and Three Dimensions," looks more closely at how to model a projectile's motion with a parabolic equation. Perhaps you know an object's starting point and initial velocity, and you want to track its height as it travels horizontally. The parabolic equation will track it for you!

Self-Assessment

Give the vertex of the following parabolas:

1. $y = 10(x-4)^2 + 7$

2. $x = -2(y-5)^2 + 1$

3. $y = (x+3)^2 + 2$

4. $x = -3y^2 - 12$

5. $y = (x+1)^2$

Sketch the graph of the following parabolas:

6. $y = 10(x-1)^2 + 3$

7. $x = y^2 - 2$

Circles and Spheres

It's very important to be familiar with the equation of a circle. You might want to draw a circle on the screen, which means graphing the equation. You might want to trace the motion of an object on a circular path. You might even want to use a bounding circle on your object for collision detection. In any of these cases, you need to manipulate the equation of a circle. Remember that in a flat plane (such as the screen), a *circle* is the set of all points at a given distance, called the **radius**, from a given fixed point, the **center**. Therefore, just those two elements, the center and the radius, can determine an equation for the circle. Which equation gives you the distance between the center and a point on the circle? That's right—the Pythagorean theorem. Notice the similarity between the Pythagorean theorem and the equation of a circle.

In code, we can define circles or spheres in the same way as math: by storing the center and the radius. The following two structures are an example of a circle and sphere as defined in code:

```
struct circle
{
    float center[2];
    float radius;
};

struct sphere
{
    float center[3];
    float radius;
};
```

The Equation of a Circle

$(x-h)^2 + (y-k)^2 = r^2$

where the center is (h,k) and the radius is r.

Look at the circle shown in Figure 2.8.

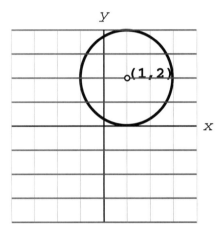

Figure 2.8 The graph of $(x-1)^2 + (y-2)^2 = 4$.

It's centered at point $(1, 2)$ and has a radius of 2. Now look up the distance formula from the beginning of this chapter. For each point (x, y) on the circle, you have

$(x-1)^2 + (y-2)^2 = 2^2$

or

$(x-1)^2 + (y-2)^2 = 4$

You might recognize the Pythagorean theorem more easily when the circle is centered at the origin. If you plug in $(0,0)$ for (h,k), look at what happens to the circle equation.

Equation of a Circle Centered at the Origin

$x^2 + y^2 = r^2$

where the center is $(0,0)$ and the radius is r.

Example 2.8: Sketching a Circle

Roughly sketch the circle $x^2 + (y+1)^2 = 9$.

Solution

You need to know only two things to sketch a circle: the center and the radius.

1. To find the center pattern, match back to the general form, which is $(x-h)^2 + (y-k)^2 = r^2$. The center has coordinates (h,k). Looking at the equation, $x^2 + (y+1)^2 = 9$, $h=0$ and $k=-1$. Therefore, the center of this circle is $(0,-1)$.

2. The other thing you need is the radius. This one is easy; just look at the number by itself on the right side. That number is r^2, so just take the square root, and you have the radius. In this case, $r^2=9$, so r=3.

3. Now that you have the center $(0,-1)$ and the radius of 3, you can sketch the circle. This is done for you in Figure 2.9.

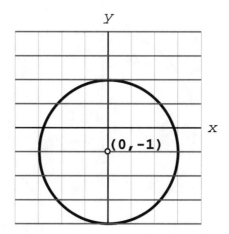

Figure 2.9   The graph of $x^2 + (y+1)^2 = 9$.

> **NOTE**
> Be careful with the plus and minus signs when looking for the center. Notice in the general form that minus signs are inside the parentheses. This means that if there's a plus sign, it's really minus a negative, so your h or k is actually a negative number, like the k in Example 2.8.

Example 2.9: Sketching Another Circle

Roughly sketch the circle $x^2 + y^2 = 16$.

Solution

You need to know only two things to sketch a circle: the center and the radius.

1. To find the center pattern, match back to the general form, which is $(x-h)^2 + (y-k)^2 = r^2$. The center has coordinates (h,k). Looking at the equation, $x^2 + y^2 = 16$, you can see that there are no parentheses and no h and k. This just means that h and k are 0, so the center of this circle is the origin $(0,0)$.

2. The other thing you need is the radius. Don't forget that the 16 is r^2, so just take the square root, and you have the radius, which in this case is 4.

3. Now that you have the center $(0,0)$ and the radius of 4, you can sketch the circle. This is done for you in Figure 2.10.

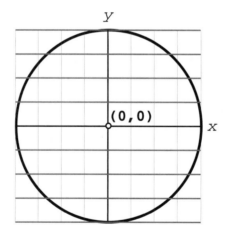

Figure 2.10   The graph of $x^2 + y^2 = 16$.

Now that you can visualize a circle based on its equation, let's go the other way. Suppose you want to generate an equation for a circle based on a situation in your game.

Example 2.10: Finding a Circle Equation

In your game, you have decided to use a bounding circle for the collision detection on your car as it drives up an incline. The car's center point is (20,50), and the farthest vertex has coordinates (60,80), as shown in Figure 2.11. Find an equation to represent the bounding circle.

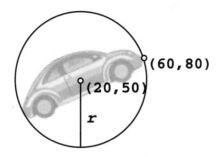

Figure 2.11   A bounding circle on a car.

Solution

To determine an equation, you need the circle's center and radius.

1. The center of your object has been given: (20,50). This means that h=20 and k=50. You can substitute those values into the general equation for a circle, which gives you

$$(x–20)^2 + (y–50)^2 = r^2$$

2. Now you just need to find the radius. Remember that the radius is defined as the distance from the center to any point on the circle, so all you have to do is use the distance formula for the center point (20,50) and the point on the circle (60,80):

$$r = \sqrt{(x_2 - x_1)^2 + (y_2 - y_1)^2}$$

$$r = \sqrt{(60 - 20)^2 + (80 - 50)^2}$$

$$r = \sqrt{(40)^2 + (30)^2}$$

$$r = \sqrt{1600 + 900}$$

$$r = \sqrt{2500}$$

$$r = 50$$

3. Now that you have the radius of 50, you can plug it into the equation, which gives you

$(x{-}20)^2 + (y{-}50)^2 = 2500$

Although it makes sense to discuss circles in 2D, you need to address spheres for three dimensions. A **sphere** is what you get when a circle revolves about its center point. Picture a basketball or a tennis ball; they are examples of spheres. Spheres can be used to define objects such as balls, or they can be used as bounding geometry for complex-shaped objects such as cars or spaceships. Quite often, game developers use bounding spheres to simplify collision detection between two objects that don't require precise collision. Just like a circle, the sphere is defined by a center and a radius. The only difference is that the center point has three coordinates rather than two.

Equation of a Sphere

$(x{-}h)^2 + (y{-}k)^2 + (z{-}l)^2 = r^2$

where the center is (h,k,l) and the radius is r.

Notice what happens again when the center is the origin, (0,0,0).

Equation of a Sphere Centered at the Origin

$x^2 + y^2 + z^2 = r^2$

where the center is (0,0,0) and the radius is r.

Example 2.11: The Center and Radius of a Sphere

In your game, you have decided to use a bounding sphere for the collision detection. The center point of your object is (20,50,−30), and the farthest vertex has coordinates (60,80,−20). Find an equation to represent the bounding sphere.

Solution

To determine an equation, you need the sphere's center and radius.

1. The center of your object has been given: (20,50,–30). This means that h=20, k=50, and l=–30. You can substitute these values into the general equation for a sphere, which gives you

$$(x–20)^2 + (y–50)^2 + (z+30)^2 = r^2$$

2. Now you just need to find the radius. Remember that the radius is defined as the distance from the center to any point on the sphere, so all you have to do is use the distance formula with the center point (20,50,–30) and the point on the sphere (60,80,–20):

$$r = \sqrt{(x_2 - x_1)^2 + (y_2 - y_1)^2 + (z_2 - z_1)^2}$$

$$r = \sqrt{(60 - 20)^2 + (80 - 50)^2 + (-20 + 30)^2}$$

$$r = \sqrt{(40)^2 + (30)^2 + (10)^2}$$

$$r = \sqrt{1600 + 900 + 100}$$

$$r = \sqrt{2600}$$

3. Now that you have the radius of $\sqrt{2600}$, you can plug that into the equation, which gives you

$$(x–20)^2 + (y–50)^2 + (z+30)^2 = 2600$$

> **NOTE**
> Just like with the circle, be careful with the plus and minus signs when plugging in the center's coordinates.

Now that we've discussed the equation of a circle and the equation of a sphere, you can use them to define round objects in your game, such as a ball. You can use them to define a circular path for an object. You can also use them as bounding geometry for collision detection, which is addressed in the next section.

Self-Assessment

Give the center and radius of the following circles:

1. $(x-30)^2 + (y-10)^2 = 400$

2. $(x+20)^2 + (y-90)^2 = 100$

3. $(x+50)^2 + y^2 = 625$

Find the equation of a circle that meets the following criteria:

4. center = (40,–25), radius = 30

5. center = (0,0), radius = 15

6. center = (–10,40), circle goes through the point (20,50)

Give the center and radius of the following spheres:

7. $(x-10)^2 + (y-30)^2 + (z-50)^2 = 1600$

8. $x^2 + y^2 + z^2 = 100$

9. $(x-50)^2 + y^2 + (z+40)^2 = 1$

Find the equation of a sphere that meets the following criteria:

10. center = (40,–25,30), radius = 10

11. center = (0,0,0), radius = 22

12. center = (10,0,–60), circle goes through the point (10,50,–30)

Applications in Collision Detection

The preceding section alluded to using circles and spheres for bounding geometry in your game. Certainly you can use other shapes, but the circle and sphere are simple shapes to work with numerically, and the test for collisions between circles and spheres is much faster than any other test. This test might lack precision, but because it's so fast, this test is perfect as the first line of defense. Let's look more closely at how to use these equations to mathematically determine whether two objects have collided.

Let's start with the two-dimensional circle, and then we'll expand the same process to 3D. Quite often, when you have an odd-shaped object such as a car, it's difficult to perform precise collision detection on the shape. One very common solution is to place it inside a bounding circle and just perform the collision detection on the circle instead. As you saw in a previous example, the car can be placed in a bounding circle defined by $(x–h)^2 + (y–k)^2 = r^2$, as shown in Figure 2.12.

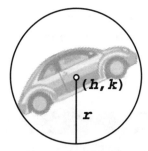

Figure 2.12   A general bounding circle on a car.

Now you can investigate the collision detection of two cars placed in bounding circles. Both circles are defined by a center and a radius, as shown in Figure 2.13.

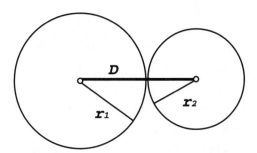

Figure 2.13   Two bounding circles barely touching.

Notice that in Figure 2.13 the two circles are just barely touching. When this is the case, you can see that the distance (D) between the two centers must equal the sum of the two radii (r_1+r_2). This means that if the two circles are overlapping (that is, colliding), the distance between the centers must be *less than* the sum of the two radii (r_1+r_2), as shown in Figure 2.14.

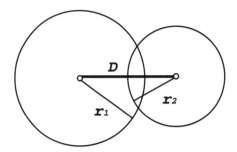

Figure 2.14   Two bounding circles overlapping.

This observation results in a simple less-than-or-equal-to check. Earlier in this chapter we reviewed the distance formula, so that can be used to calculate the distance between the two centers. Then you just have to compare that distance to the sum of the two radii (r_1+r_2).

Circle-Circle Collision Detection

Given two circles $(x-h_1)^2 + (y-k_1)^2 = r_1^2$ and $(x-h_2)^2 + (y-k_2)^2 = r_2^2$, if $\sqrt{(h_2-h_1)^2+(k_2-k_1)^2} \le (r_1+r_2)$ a collision occurs.

NOTE
The circles do not have to be the same size for this method to work. They can have different-length radii based on the size of the objects inside.

Keep in mind that in video games objects move frame by frame, so this function must be set up inside a loop so that it's rechecked each frame. Also remember that as you move objects frame by frame, the motion is not smooth. The objects kind of jump a short distance each frame. This means that two objects might not touch at all in one frame and then overlap in the next frame; they might skip over the instant where they were just barely touching. That is why it's necessary to do a less-than-or-equal-to check rather than just an equal check.

Example 2.12: Circle-Circle Collision

Suppose you are coding the collision detection for a 2D racing game, and you decide to use bounding circles. In the current frame, one car's bounding circle is defined by the equation $(x-50)^2 + (y-20)^2 = 900$, and the other car's bounding circle is defined by the equation $(x+10)^2 + (y-10)^2 = 400$. Have they collided yet?

Solution

1. To perform this collision detection, you first must determine the center and the radius for each bounding circle. The first circle has center (50,20) and a radius of 30, and the second circle has center (−10,10) and a radius of 20.

2. Calculate the distance (D) between the two centers:

$$D=\sqrt{(h_2 - h_1)^2 + (k_2 - k_1)^2}$$

$$D=\sqrt{(-10-50)^2 + (10-20)^2}$$

$$D=\sqrt{(-60)^2 + (-10)^2}$$

$$D=\sqrt{3600+100}$$

$$D=\sqrt{3700}$$

$$D \approx 60.83$$

3. Finally, you need to check to see if $D \leq (r_1+r_2)$. In this case, $(r_1+r_2) = 30+20 = 50$, so D is not $\leq (r_1+r_2)$, which means that there is *no* collision.

As soon as you start coding this, you'll find that the square-root function is very expensive, meaning that it takes a lot of processing power. There is a quick and easy way to eliminate the square root and speed up this collision check. If you square both sides of the inequality, the same less-than-or-equal-to relationship is true. You can see in Example 2.12 that if 60.83 is not less than 50, $(60.83)^2$ is still not less than $(50)^2$. This faster method (Optimized Circle-Circle Collision Detection) is as follows.

Optimized Circle-Circle Collision Detection

Given two circles $(x-h_1)^2 + (y-k_1)^2 = r_1^2$ and $(x-h_2)^2 + (y-k_2)^2 = r_2^2$, if $(h_2-h_1)^2 + (k_2-k_1)^2 \leq (r_1+r_2)^2$, there is a collision.

By now you can probably guess just how to extend this process to 3D. Rather than using bounding circles, you can use bounding spheres in 3D. Again, an equation for the bounding sphere can be determined by the model's center and the radius to its farthest vertex. After that, it's just a frame-by-frame check to see if the spheres have overlapped. We'll stick with the faster version from here on out.

Optimized Sphere-Sphere Collision Detection

Given two spheres $(x-h_1)^2 + (y-k_1)^2 + (z-l_1)^2 = r_1^2$ and $(x-h_2)^2 + (y-k_2)^2 + (z-l_2)^2 = r_2^2$, if $(h_2-h_1)^2 + (k_2-k_1)^2 + (l_2-l_1)^2 \leq (r_1+r_2)^2$, there is a collision.

The following simple function can be used to detect whether or not two spheres have collided. In this example, we will be using the sphere struct which we defined earlier, and which has been repeated here for ease. Notice that in calculating the distance between the centers of the spheres, we are not using square root but rather comparing the value against the sum of the radii squared. This is a slight but effective optimization that can dramatically improve your frame rate if there are a large number of sphere-to-sphere collision checks that are required every frame.

```
struct sphere
{
    float center[3];
    float radius;
};
// purpose: to detect a collision between 2 spheres
// input:   S1- our first sphere, passed by reference
//          S2- our second sphere, passed by reference
// output: true if there is a collision, else false
bool ColBetweenSpheres(sphere &S1, sphere &S2)
{
    return (pow(S2.center[0] - S1.center[0], 2) +
            pow(S2.center[1] - S1.center[1], 2) +
            pow(S2.center[2] - S1.center[2], 2)) <
            pow(S1.radius + S2.radius, 2));
}
```

Take note of the fact there is no complicated if-else statement in the function. Should the comparison of the two values resolve to true, then there has been a collision and that very answer can be returned. Should the comparison resolve to false, there has been no collision, and that answer can also be returned.

Example 2.13: Sphere-Sphere Collision

Suppose you are coding the collision detection for a 3D racing game, and you decide to use bounding spheres. In the current frame, one car's bounding sphere is defined by the equation $(x-30)^2 + (y-20)^2 + (z+10)^2 = 1600$, and the other car's bounding sphere is defined by the equation $x^2 + (y-40)^2 + (z+50)^2 = 2500$. Have they collided yet?

Solution

1. To perform this collision detection, you first must determine the center and the radius for each bounding sphere. The first sphere has center $(30,20,-10)$ and a radius of 40, and the second sphere has center $(0,40,-50)$ and a radius of 50.

2. Calculate the distance (D) between the two centers:

$$D = \sqrt{(h_2 - h_1)^2 + (k_2 - k_1)^2 + (l_2 - l_1)^2}$$

$$D = \sqrt{(0-30)^2 + (40-20)^2 + (-50+10)^2}$$

$$D = \sqrt{(-30)^2 + (20)^2 + (-40)^2}$$

$$D = \sqrt{900 + 400 + 1600}$$

$$D = \sqrt{2900}$$

$$D \approx 53.85$$

3. Finally, you need to check to see if $D \le (r_1 + r_2)$. In this case, $(r_1 + r_2) = 40 + 50 = 90$, so $D \le (r_1 + r_2)$, which means that *yes*, there is a collision.

Bounding circles and spheres are a simple approach to collision detection. They're a relatively fast method, but they're not always the most accurate. Look back at Figure 2.11, where we first used a bounding circle on the car. Notice all the empty space within the circle? That space is dangerous, because it could cause false collisions. This phenomenon is illustrated in Figure 2.15.

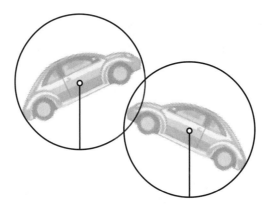

Figure 2.15 False collisions.

One way to avoid false collisions is to use a different shape that fits your model more closely. Just make sure that you can define the shape with an equation of some sort so that you can perform a numeric check. Another way is to set up a hierarchy of circles. Start by checking for a collision between the two original bounding circles. If the check you performed earlier returns no collision, there's no problem. However, if it returns a collision, it might be a false alarm, so at that point you could perform a closer check. In other words, set up a conditional that states that if no collision occurs, keep going. If there is a collision, do a closer check. In this closer check, you can use several smaller bounding circles that fit the object more closely. This gives you better accuracy, but it takes extra processing time if there's a possibility of a collision. If the two larger circles aren't overlapping, there's no sense in taking the time to check all the smaller circles. Figure 2.16 shows how you might use smaller circles to get a tighter fit on the car.

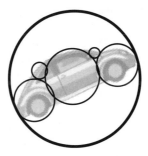

Figure 2.16 A circle hierarchy on a car.

> **NOTE**
> Whether you follow up the initial check with smaller circles or any other more precise check, the one large bounding circle or sphere is always a fast approach for the first test.

The preceding chapter looked at intersecting lines, and this chapter examined intersecting circles and spheres. Collision detection is a significant part of any game engine, because it manages the interaction of all the individual objects in your game world. There will always be new ways of approaching collision detection that are faster or more accurate, but this discussion gives you a foundation for investigating alternative methods.

Self-Assessment

1. Suppose you are coding the collision detection for a 2D baseball game, and you decide to use bounding circles. In the current frame, one player's bounding circle is defined by the equation $(x-70)^2 + (y-20)^2 = 1600$, and the baseball's bounding circle is defined by the equation $(x-50)^2 + (y-60)^2 = 256$. Have they collided yet?

2. Suppose you are coding the collision detection for a 3D football game, and you decide to use bounding spheres. In the current frame, one player's bounding sphere is defined by the equation $(x-50)^2 + y^2 + (z+20)^2 = 1600$, and the football's bounding sphere is defined by the equation $(x-60)^2 + (y-70)^2 + (z+50)^2 = 400$. Have they collided yet?

3. What might be an extra step you could take to avoid false collisions when working with bounding spheres?

Visualization Experience: Collision Detection

On the CD-ROM, you will find a demo named Circles. Here's a brief description from the programmer:

This example is used to demonstrate the movement and collision of two circles with the bounds of the screen and each other. The circles are placed in random positions on the screen and are given random directions to travel in. To maintain simplicity, true vector reflection is not used for the collision of the balls. Instead, a basic reflection algorithm is used to maintain the appearance of true reflection.

—Dustin Henry

Go ahead and run the demo by double clicking circles.exe. You'll see the two balls bounce around and occasionally collide with each other. Behind the scenes, the computer is checking frame by frame to see if they have hit each other using the circle-circle collision method described in the preceding section.

You can view the source code by double-clicking circles_code.txt. If you scroll down far enough, you'll see the section responsible for the circle-circle collision detection, which is shown in Listing 2.1.

Listing 2.1   Circle-Circle Collision

```
////////////////////////////////////////////////////////////////
// checkBallCollision : Check for a collision with another ball
//
// In : ball2 - the ball to check collision with
//
// Return : True if there was a collision with another ball
////////////////////////////////////////////////////////////////
bool Ball::checkBallCollision(Ball &ball2)
{
    // The radius of the balls
    int radius1 = diameter / 2;
    int radius2 = ball2.diameter / 2;

    // The center point of the first ball
    POINT center1;
    center1.x = radius1 + bounds.left;
    center1.y = radius1 + bounds.top;

    // The center point of the second ball
    POINT center2;
    center2.x = radius2 + ball2.bounds.left;
    center2.y = radius2 + ball2.bounds.top;

    // The distance between the two balls' centers
    double distance = sqrt(SQUARE(center2.x - center1.x) +
    ➥ SQUARE(center2.y - center1.y));

    // See if they have collided
    if (distance <= radius1 + radius2)
```

You might notice that as a bonus the programmer has also included collision detection between the balls and the edge of the screen. This uses a bounding-box approach to collision detection, because the screen is made up of four straight lines.

You might want to revisit this demo after reading Chapter 14, "Rotational Motion," which discusses collision response.

Self-Assessment Solutions

Distance Between Points

1. $b = 18$

2. No

3. 130

4. $\sqrt{12200} \approx 110.45$

5. (90,105)

6. (60,85,25)

Parabolas

1. (4,7)

2. (1,5)

3. (−3,2)

4. (−12,0)

5. (−1,0)

6. The answer is shown in Figure 2.17.

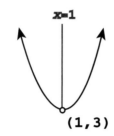

Figure 2.17 $y = 10(x{-}1)^2 + 3$.

7. The answer is shown in Figure 2.18.

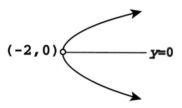

Figure 2.18 $x = y^2{-}2$.

Circles and Spheres

1. center = (30,10), radius = 20

2. center = (−20,90), radius = 10

3. center = (−50,0), radius = 25

4. $(x{-}40)^2 + (y{+}25)^2 = 900$

5. $x^2 + y^2 = 225$

6. $(x{+}10)^2 + (y{-}40)^2 = 1000$

7. center = (10,30,50), radius = 40

8. center = (0,0,0), radius = 10

9. center = (50,0,−40), radius = 1

10. $(x{-}40)^2 + (y{+}25)^2 + (z{-}30)^2 = 100$

11. $x^2 + y^2 + z^2 = 484$

12. $(x-10)^2 + y^2 + (z+60)^2 = 3400$

Applications in Collision Detection

1. Yes

2. No

3. Set up a hierarchy of spheres, and check the smaller ones only if the larger spheres have collided.

Chapter 3

Trigonometry Snippets

KEY TOPICS

- Degrees Versus Radians
- Trigonometric Functions
- Trigonometric Identities
- Using Math Libraries in C++

This chapter sets up standards for dealing with angles. Not only are they used for rotation, but they're also used to establish direction for vectors. This chapter also defines the trigonometric functions, which are used whenever you want to model wavelike oscillating motion or model a scenario with a right triangle. They are also used extensively in Chapter 4, "Vector Operations," when we discuss vectors. The last two sections focus on identities for manipulating trig functions within equations and using the trig functions in C++. This chapter lays the groundwork for all the chapters that follow.

Degrees Versus Radians

Before we can delve into the world of trigonometry, it's imperative that we discuss angles and set standards for working with them. Obviously, angles are used for rotation, which we'll discuss in Chapters 6, "Transformations," and 14, "Rotational Motion,". They can also be used to establish a direction, which you'll see done in Chapter 4 and throughout the physics chapters. Let's identify the standards that will be used in those future chapters.

Every angle consists of two rays that intersect at a point called the **vertex**. We'll call one ray the initial side and the other ray the terminal side. To place an angle in standard position, we'll use the Cartesian coordinate system. The vertex should be at the origin (0,0), and the initial side *always* falls on the positive x-axis, as shown in Figure 3.1.

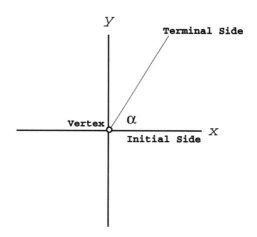

Figure 3.1   An angle in standard position.

From the positive x-axis, measure out positive angles counterclockwise and negative angles clockwise. This determines the position of the terminal side. Remember that a full revolution is 360°. If the angle happens to be 90°, or a right angle, the terminal side falls on the positive y-axis, and if the angle is 180°, the terminal side falls on the negative x-axis. Notice the α symbol in Figure 3.1. Another standard that's widely accepted is to use Greek letters (such as alpha [α], beta [β], and theta [θ]) to represent angles, so don't be thrown when you come across these characters in our discussion of angles.

Example 3.1: A Positive Angle in Standard Position

Draw a 60° angle in standard position.

Solution

Start with the vertex at the origin and the initial side on the positive x-axis. From there, measure out 60° counterclockwise, and draw the terminal side, as shown in Figure 3.2.

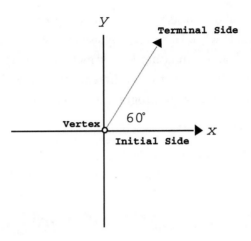

Figure 3.2 A 60° angle in standard position.

Example 3.2: A Negative Angle in Standard Position

Draw a –100° angle in standard position.

Solution

Start with the vertex at the origin and the initial side on the positive x-axis. From there, measure out 100° clockwise, and draw the terminal side, as shown in Figure 3.3.

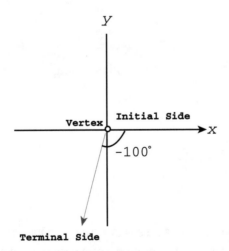

Figure 3.3 A –100° angle in standard position.

So far, we've only talked about measuring angles in degrees because that's what you're probably most comfortable with. However, angles can also be measured in radians. Just like you can measure a distance in either feet or meters, you can measure angles in either degrees or radians. They're just two different units. Most likely, you'll estimate an angle in degrees but you'll have to program it in radians, so you need a conversion between the two.

Earlier, I said that a full revolution is 360°; it's also $2\pi^R$. This means that half a revolution is 180°, or π^R. That's the basis of the conversion.

Degrees to Radians

Angle in degrees * $= \left(\dfrac{\pi^R}{180°}\right)$ Angle in radians

---

> **NOTE**
> Don't be thrown by the "R" superscript (^{R}); it's just a label for radians, like the degree symbol (°). Try to get into the habit of always labeling your angles with one of these two symbols (° or ^{R}). Otherwise, it won't always be clear to your teammates which unit you're working in.

Example 3.3: Converting Degrees to Radians

Convert 120° to radians.

Solution

To convert from degrees to radians, multiply your angle by the fraction $\left(\dfrac{\pi^R}{180°}\right)$:

$$120° * \left(\frac{\pi^R}{180°}\right) = \left(\frac{120°\pi^R}{180°}\right) = \left(\frac{2\pi^R}{3}\right)$$

> **NOTE**
> The standard for writing an angle in radians is to leave it as a fraction times π^R, as shown in Example 3.3. However, if you want to express it as a decimal number, just plug in $\pi \approx 3.141592654$.

> It is important to note that all the C++ trig functions—such as sin(), cos(), and tan()—take input in radians, and all inverse trig functions—such as asin(), acos(), and atan()—return angles in radians as well. It is a good idea when using angles to create a `#define` at the top of your math library which can be used to easily convert from degrees to radians and vice versa.
>
> ```
> #define RadToDeg 57.29577951f
> #define DegToRad 0.017453293f
> ```
>
> Multiplying an angle in radians by `RadToDeg` will convert that number into degrees, while multiplying a number in degrees by `DegToRad` will convert it into radians.

To go the opposite direction, from radians to degrees, just multiply the angle in radians by the reciprocal of the conversion factor you just used.

Radians to Degrees

Angle in radians $* = \left(\dfrac{180°}{\pi^R}\right)$ Angle in degrees.

Example 3.4: Converting Radians to Degrees

Convert $\left(\dfrac{6\pi^R}{5}\right)$ to degrees.

Solution

To convert from radians to degrees, multiply your angle by the fraction $\left(\dfrac{180°}{\pi^R}\right)$:

$$\left(\frac{6\pi^R}{5}\right)\left(\frac{180°}{\pi^R}\right) = \left(\frac{6\pi^R(180°)}{5\pi^R}\right) = \left(\frac{6(180°)}{5}\right) = 216°$$

> **NOTE**
>
> Notice in Example 3.4 that the π^R on the top of the fraction cancels out the π^R on the bottom of the fraction. It's very easy to get the two conversion factors mixed up, so use the units as a guide. Make sure that the fraction is flipped in such a way that the original units cancel out the way you want them to.

At this point, we have established standards for discussing angles. Typically, Greek letters are used to represent angles. Also, a direction can be established by expressing an angle in standard position. In addition, you can now convert angles between degrees and radians.

Self-Assessment

Draw the following angles in standard position:

1. 120°

2. 270°

3. −45°

Convert the following angles from degrees to radians:

4. 60°

5. 270°

6. 45°

Convert the following angles from radians to degrees:

7. $\left(\dfrac{3\pi^R}{4}\right)$

8. $\left(\dfrac{\pi^R}{3}\right)$

9. $\left(\dfrac{2\pi^R}{5}\right)$

Trigonometric Functions

The trigonometric functions often surface in game programming. Any time you model a scenario with a right triangle (which happens often on a gridlike screen), the trig functions come in handy. We'll also use them in the vector chapter (Chapter 4) and again in all the 2D and 3D physics chapters. In addition, we'll look at the graphs of sine and cosine, because they can be used for any kind of oscillating (wavelike) motion. But before we get too carried away, let's define these functions from scratch.

The trigonometric functions are all defined in terms of a right triangle; they're really just relationships between two of the three sides. Look at the triangle shown in Figure 3.4. It's a right triangle, so you can use it to define sine, cosine, and tangent.

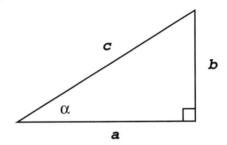

Figure 3.4   A right triangle.

Notice that angle α is labeled. It is important to always indicate which angle the function is taking as input. The trig functions are useless without an angle as input. In this case, use α to set up the definitions of sine (sin), cosine (cos), and tangent (tan).

Trigonometric Functions

$$\sin \alpha = \frac{opp}{hyp} = \frac{b}{c}$$

$$\cos \alpha = \frac{adj}{hyp} = \frac{a}{c}$$

$$\tan \alpha = \frac{opp}{adj} = \frac{b}{a}$$

where *opp* = the side opposite α, *adj* = the side adjacent to α, and *hyp* = the hypotenuse.

> **NOTE**
>
> These trig functions apply *only* to a right triangle. They will not work for any other type of triangle.

As you can see, sine, cosine, and tangent are simply fractions, or ratios, relating two out of the three sides of the right triangle. The reference angle determines which sides to use. Notice that if you use the other nonright angle, that switches which side is opposite and which side is adjacent, so always include the reference angle.

Example 3.5: Defining Sine, Cosine, and Tangent

If α is an angle in standard position, and (12,5) is a point on its terminal side, find $\sin \alpha$, $\cos \alpha$, and $\tan \alpha$.

Solution

1. To talk about the trig functions, we need to establish a right triangle. Figure 3.5 shows a right triangle created using the point (12,5) on the terminal side.

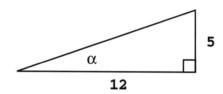

Figure 3.5   A right triangle for Example 3.5.

2. The coordinates of the point (12,5) give you the length of two sides. You can use the Pythagorean theorem to calculate the length of the third side:

$$c = \sqrt{12^2 + 5^2} = \sqrt{144 + 25} = \sqrt{169} = 13$$

3. Now all you have to do is apply the definitions of sine, cosine, and tangent:

$$\sin \alpha = \frac{opp}{hyp} = \frac{b}{c} = \frac{5}{13}$$

$$\cos \alpha = \frac{adj}{hyp} = \frac{a}{c} = \frac{12}{13}$$

$$\tan \alpha = \frac{opp}{adj} = \frac{b}{a} = \frac{5}{12}$$

There are actually six trigonometric functions total. We've already defined the first three in terms of the triangle shown in Figure 3.4. The other three functions, cosecant (csc), secant (sec), and cotangent (cot), are simply reciprocals of the first three.

Other Trigonometric Functions

$$\csc \alpha = \frac{1}{\sin \alpha} = \frac{hyp}{opp}$$

$$\sec \alpha = \frac{1}{\cos \alpha} = \frac{hyp}{adj}$$

$$\cot \alpha = \frac{1}{\tan \alpha} = \frac{adj}{opp}$$

where *opp* = the side opposite α, *adj* = the side adjacent to α, and *hyp* = the hypotenuse.

Because these last three functions are simply reciprocals, most of the time all you need are the first three: sine, cosine, and tangent. However, there might be times when you simplify a formula and you end up with a fraction involving sine, cosine, or tangent. In those special cases, it might further optimize your code to use one of these last three functions instead.

Even though these trigonometric functions sound intimidating, they're really just functions that have been preprogrammed into your calculator. You can access them using buttons, just like the multiply function or the square root function. If you have a scientific calculator, take a minute to familiarize yourself with its trig functions. If you have Windows installed on your computer, it comes with a calculator on the Accessories menu. If you switch the View to scientific, you'll see that the trig functions appear on the left side. Type in **30**, and then click the sine button. You should get 0.5. Notice that you can also switch to radian mode at the top and enter the angle in radian mode if you want. Most scientific calculators give you that option. You might want to practice using your calculator with some of the frequently used angles shown in Table 3.1.

Table 3.1   Trigonometric Functions for Frequently Used Angles

α (Degrees)	α (Radians)	sin α	cos α	tan α
0	0	0	1	0
30	π/6	0.5	0.8660	0.5774
45	π/4	0.7071	0.7071	1
60	π/3	0.8660	0.5	1.7321
90	π/2	1	0	—
120	2π/3	0.8660	−0.5	−1.7321
180	π	0	−1	0
270	3π/2	−1	0	—
360	0	0	1	0

Many programmers prefer to create a look-up table for trigonometric functions before the actual game loop begins to run. This can greatly increase the speed at which trig values can be calculated in code. An example of creating a look-up table follows:

```
// This will hold our values
float sin_table[360];
// Fill in our table
for(int i = 0; i < 360; ++i)
{
    // Remember our DegToRad #define from before, PI / 180
    sin_table[i] = sin(i * DegToRad);
}
```

Having created this sin table, the program no longer needs to call upon the sin() function to calculate the value, but would rather look it up in this way:

```
// Calculate the sine of any angle
float value = sin_table[abs((int)angle) % 360];
```

By typecasting the angle to an int, then getting its absolute value and using the modulus operator, we ensure that regardless of the size of our angle, we won't be blowing out of our array bounds. It is also important to note, however, that if the #pragma intrinsic command is used to make the trig functions intrinsic in a Microsoft compiler, the amount of optimization created by using a look-up table becomes virtually negligible.

```
#pragma intrinsic(sin, cos, tan)
```

> **NOTE**
> Check your MSDN library for a list of compiler switches which need to be turned on in order to make the trig functions intrinsic. Also be warned that the intrinsic commands *cannot* be used on these functions while in debug mode, so only use this option when you are ready to create your final release build.

Let's look at a couple examples to see how these trigonometric functions are actually used.

Example 3.6: Using Cosine

Suppose your game character shoots an arrow at a target in the air. He's aiming at a 60° angle, and the arrow follows a straight-line path for 50 pixels. If the sun is directly overhead, how far must the shadow travel across the ground?

Solution

1. This scenario can be modeled with a right triangle. Place the angle in standard position, and label the hypotenuse with a length of 50 pixels, as shown in Figure 3.6.

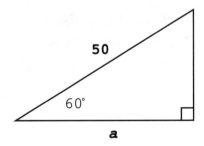

Figure 3.6   A right triangle for shooting an arrow.

2. You can see that you're actually looking for the length of the bottom side of the right triangle. Call it *a*.

3. The cosine function sets up a relationship between the adjacent side *a* and the hypotenuse, so use that:

$$\cos 60° = \frac{adj}{hyp} = \frac{a}{50}$$

50 (cos 60°) = *a*

4. Using the Windows calculator, type in the angle: **60**. Then click the cos button. This should give you 0.5. Last, multiply that by the 50 pixels, which gives you 25.

This means that the shadow must travel 25 pixels across the ground.

Notice that when you know the angle, you use the regular cosine function in the calculator. The calculator actually returns the value of the ratio (adjacent/hypotenuse) for that angle. What if you were working backwards? That is, what if you know the fraction and you want the angle measure? This requires using the inverse of one of the trigonometric functions. The inverse is written with a –1 superscript, and the letters "arc" are placed in front of the name. For example, the inverse cosine function is written $\cos^{-1}$ and is pronounced "arccosine." Many calculators use the 2nd function or the Shift key for the inverses. Check your calculator to find them. The Windows calculator has a check box for the inverse function.

Let's revisit the shooting-arrow example for practice with the inverse function.

Example 3.7: Using the Inverse Tangent

Suppose your game character shoots an arrow at a target in the air. He's standing 100 pixels away from the target, which is 400 pixels off the ground. What angle should he aim at if the arrow will follow a straight-line path?

Solution

1. This scenario can be modeled with a right triangle. This time, you know the lengths of the two sides, as shown in Figure 3.7.

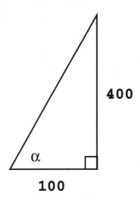

Figure 3.7   Another right triangle for shooting an arrow.

2. This time you're looking for the angle in standard position. Call it α.

3. The tangent function sets up a relationship between the opposite side and the adjacent side, so use that:

$$\tan \alpha \ = \ \frac{opp}{adj} = \frac{400}{100} = 4$$

$$\tan \alpha \ = \ 4$$

$$\alpha = \tan^{-1}(4)$$

4. Using the Windows calculator, type in the ratio of the opposite side divided by the adjacent side: 4. Click the Inv (inverse) check box. Then click the tan button. This should give you approximately 76°.

This means that the player must aim at a 76° angle in standard position to hit the target.

Let's find out how to solve a similar problem in code by using a function which will return the angle between two objects in standard position, given their locations:

```
// purpose: to calculate the angle between 2 objects in 2D space
// input:    P1 - the location of the first object
//           P2 - the location of the second object
// output: the angle between the objects in degrees
float calcAngle2D(float *P1, float *P2)
{
    // Calculate our angle
    float ang = (float)atan((P2[1] - P1[1]) / (P2[0] - P1[0])) *
    ➥ RadToDeg;
    // In the event that the angle is in the first quadrant
    if(P2[1] < P1[1] && P2[0] > P1[0])
        return ang;
    // In the event of second or third quadrant
    else if((P2[1] < P1[1] && P2[0] < P1[0]) ||
    (P2[1] > P1[1] && P2[0] < P1[0]))
        return ang + 180;
    // If none of the above, it must be in the fourth
    else
        return ang + 360;
}
```

Of importance in this function is the means through which we figure out the actual angle based on the returned value of atan(). Remember that the sine of angles is positive in the first and second quadrants, the cosine of angles is positive in the first and fourth quadrants, while the tangent of angles is positive in the first and third quadrants. All the inverse trig functions will always return the angle in the first quadrants if passed in a positive value. If passed in a negative value, however, asin() and atan() will return the angle in the fourth quadrant, while acos() will return the angle in the second quadrant. Therefore in this example, we must check the object's positions in relation to themselves to see which quadrant our angle is truly in, and then add either 180 or 360 to get that angle in standard position.

> **NOTE**
> When you know the angle measure, use the regular sine, cosine, or tangent function. If you want to return the angle, use one of the inverse functions.

The last thing this section needs to address is the graph of sine and cosine. You might have seen a sound wave before; that's exactly what the graphs of sine and cosine look like.

First, you'll examine the graph of $y=\sin(x)$, and then you'll compare it to the graph of $y=\cos(x)$. You can use Table 3.1 to plot a couple reference angles to get started. If you use the angle in degrees column for the x values, the sin α column would represent the corresponding y values. If you used your calculator for the sine of some of the angles in between, you'd find that they all fall on the curve graphed in Figure 3.8.

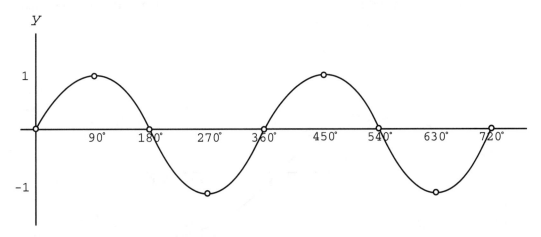

Figure 3.8   Graph of y=sin(x).

Notice that the graph has a pattern that repeats every 360° (or $2\pi^R$); this is called the *fundamental period*. There are ways to alter the period if you need to stretch or squish the graph horizontally to fit your needs. To change the period, simply place a number in front of the x. Fractions stretch the graph, and larger numbers compact it.

Example 3.8: Stretching the Sine Wave Horizontally

Graph the equation $y=\sin(1/2x)$.

Solution

1. The easiest way to start is to plug in several x values and calculate the corresponding y. Table 3.2 shows a few key points.

Table 3.2   Points on y=sin(1/2x)

x	y
0°	0
180°	1
360°	0
540°	−1
720°	0

2. After you've plotted these key points, try plugging in a few more. You'll find that they all fall in the curve shown in Figure 3.9.

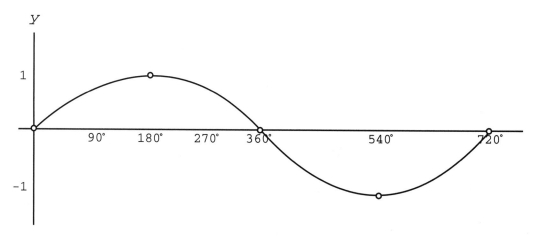

Figure 3.9   Graph of y=sin(1/2x).

Example 3.9: Squishing the Sine Wave Horizontally

Graph the equation $y=\sin(2x)$.

Solution

1. The easiest way to start is to plug in several x values and calculate the corresponding y. Table 3.3 shows a few key points.

Table 3.3   Points on y=sin(2x)

x	y
0°	0
45°	1
90°	0
135°	−1
180°	0

2. After you've plotted these key points, try plugging in a few more. You'll find that they all fall in the curve shown in Figure 3.10.

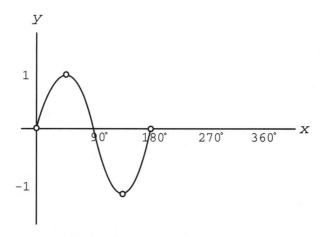

Figure 3.10   Graph of y=sin(2x).

Look back at the last two examples. Notice that when you place ½ in front of the x, the sine wave repeats every 720° instead of every 360°. Then, when you place a 2 in front of the x, the pattern repeats every 180°. This leads to the first characteristic of the sine wave.

Period of the Sine Wave

For y=sin(Bx), the period = $\dfrac{360°}{|B|}$.

> **NOTE**
>
> The period measures how often the sine wave repeats. We put the absolute value symbol around *B* because a negative sign would not affect the period.
>
> Also note that if there is no number in the *B* position, *B*=1, which brings us back to the fundamental period of 360°.

You can also stretch or squish the sine graph vertically by placing a number in front of the sine function, which changes the *amplitude*. This time a fraction squishes the graph, and a large number stretches it. Be careful, because this is the opposite of the period.

Example 3.10: Stretching the Sine Wave Vertically

Graph the equation $y=2\sin x$.

Solution

1. The easiest way to start is to plug in several x values and calculate the corresponding y. Table 3.4 shows a few key points.

Table 3.4 Points on $y=2\sin x$

x	y
0°	0
90°	2
180°	0
270°	−2
360°	0

2. After you've plotted these key points, try plugging in a few more. You'll find that they all fall in the curve shown in Figure 3.11.

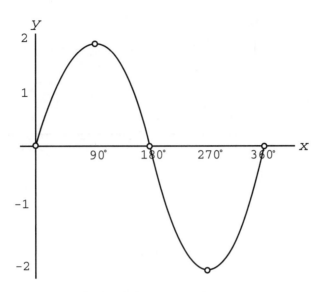

Figure 3.11   Graph of y=2sin(x).

Example 3.11: Squishing the Sine Wave Vertically

Graph the equation $y = \frac{1}{2}\sin x$.

Solution

1. The easiest way to start is to plug in several x values and calculate the corresponding y. Table 3.5 shows a few key points.

Table 3.5   Points on $y = \frac{1}{2}\sin x$

x	y
0°	0
90°	1/2
180°	0
270°	−1/2
360°	0

2. After you've plotted these key points, try plugging in a few more. You find that they all fall in the curve shown in Figure 3.12.

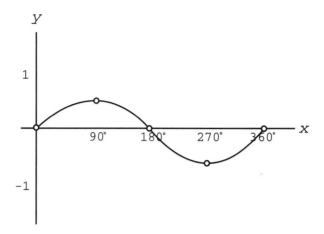

Figure 3.12   Graph of y=^{1}/$_2$sin(x).

Notice that the sine wave normally fluctuates between 1 and –1. When you place a 2 in front of the sine, the graph goes as high as 2 and as low as –2. Then, when you place ^{1}/$_2$ in front of the sine, the graph cycles between ^{1}/$_2$ and –^{1}/$_2$. This leads to the second characteristic of the sine wave.

Amplitude of the Sine Wave

For y=Asin(x), the amplitude = |A|.

> **NOTE**
>
> The amplitude measures how high and low the sine wave fluctuates. We put the absolute value symbol around A because a negative sign would not affect the amplitude.
>
> You might want to use a small amplitude for something like the motion of a ship on the water.

These same two characteristics apply to the cosine function in exactly the same way. The only difference is that the cosine function is offset to the left by 90°. Figure 3.13 shows the graph of y=cosx. Notice that the highest point crosses at the y-axis rather than at 90°. Everything else is identical, just shifted 90° to the left.

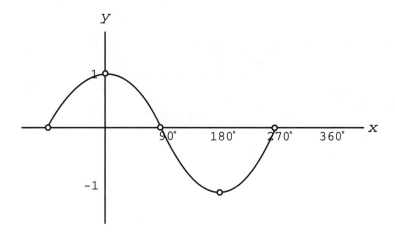

Figure 3.13   Graph of y=cos(x).

This section has defined all six trigonometric functions. These functions can now be used in our study of vectors in the next chapter. They can also be used whenever you model a situation with a right triangle or whenever you want an object to follow a wavelike motion path.

Self-Assessment

Using your calculator, find the value of the following trigonometric functions:

1. $\sin 45°$

2. $\cos 125°$

3. $\tan -35°$

4. Find $\sin\alpha$, $\cos\alpha$, and $\tan\alpha$ for the angle shown in Figure 3.14.

5. Find the degree measure of angle α in Figure 3.14.

6. Find $\cot -35°$.

7. Find $\csc 20°$.

8. Find $\sec 45°$.

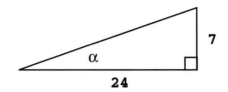

Figure 3.14   A right triangle for question 4.

State the period and amplitude of the following equations:

9. $y=5\sin3x$

10. $y=3\cos x$

11. $y=\cos4x$

12. $y=5\sin x$

13. $y=-2\cos(^1\!/_2x)$

14. $y= ^1\!/_2\sin(-2x)$

Trigonometric Identities

Now that we've defined the six trigonometric functions, several trig identities (or rules) allow you to algebraically manipulate equations that have the trig functions embedded in them. You never know when these identities might prove useful. Remember that when you're programming, every operation takes additional processing time, so always try to reduce formulas to their simplest terms. Of course, this might involve one or more of these identities.

The first identity is the *unit circle,* which is the circle centered at the origin with a radius of 1. The equation for the unit circle is $x^2+y^2=1$. For any point on the unit circle, you can create a right triangle with one angle in standard position, as shown in Figure 3.15.

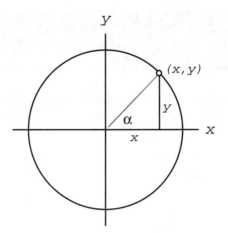

Figure 3.15   The unit circle.

Notice that the hypotenuse is the radius, which has a length of 1 unit. Now you can apply the definitions of sine and cosine:

$\sin\alpha = y/1 = y$ and $\cos\alpha = x/1 = x$

so $y = \sin\alpha$

and $x = \cos\alpha$

This is true for any point on the unit circle.

> **NOTE**
> This is a great trick for remembering the sine and cosine of multiples of 90°. At 90°, 180°, 270°, and 360°, the unit circle intersects the axes, so it's very easy to pick off the x and y coordinates, which give you sine and cosine. For example, at 90°, the unit circle has coordinates (0,1). Therefore, $\sin 90°=1$ and $\cos 90°=0$.

Now that you know $y = \sin\alpha$ and $x = \cos\alpha$, you can substitute sine and cosine into the equation of the unit circle for x and y. This gives you your first trig identity.

Unit Circle Identity

$\cos^2\alpha + \sin^2\alpha = 1$

There's also a very interesting relationship among tangent, sine, and cosine. If you look back at the definitions of the first three trigonometric functions, you'll see that

$\sin\alpha = \text{opp/hyp}$ and $\cos\alpha = \text{adj/hyp}$

This means that , $\dfrac{\sin\alpha}{\cos\alpha} = \dfrac{opp/hyp}{adj/hyp} = \dfrac{opp}{adj}$ which is the definition of $\tan\alpha$.

This leads to the next two identities.

Tangent and Cotangent

$\tan\alpha = \dfrac{\sin\alpha}{\cos\alpha}$

$\cot\alpha = \dfrac{\cos\alpha}{\sin\alpha}$

There are also a couple interesting negative angle identities. Try plugging a couple angles into your calculator to verify that they're true.

Negative Angles

$\sin(-\alpha) = -\sin\alpha$

$\cos(-\alpha) = \cos\alpha$

$\tan(-\alpha) = -\tan\alpha$

Example 3.12: Verifying One of the Negative Angle Identities

Using $\alpha = 30°$, verify that $\sin(-\alpha) = -\sin\alpha$.

Solution

1. Find $\sin(-30°)$ using a calculator. You should find that $\sin(-30°) = -0.5$.

2. Find $-\sin(30°)$ using a calculator. You should find that $\sin(30°) = 0.5$, so $-\sin(30°) = -0.5$.

   In this case, the identity holds true.

Next let's look at the sum and difference identities for sine.

Sum and Difference Identities for Sine
$\sin(\alpha_1 + \alpha_2) = \sin\alpha_1\cos\alpha_2 + \cos\alpha_1\sin\alpha_2$
$\sin(\alpha_1 - \alpha_2) = \sin\alpha_1\cos\alpha_2 - \cos\alpha_1\sin\alpha_2$

Example 3.13: $\sin(90°+\alpha)$

Simplify $\sin(90°+\alpha)$.

Solution

1. Apply the new sum identity for sine:

   $\sin(\alpha_1 + \alpha_2) = \sin\alpha_1\cos\alpha_2 + \cos\alpha_1\sin\alpha_2$

   $\sin(90° + \alpha) = \sin90°\cos\alpha + \cos90°\sin\alpha$

2. Reduce it by taking the sine and cosine of 90°:

   $\sin(90° + \alpha) = (1)\cos\alpha + (0)\sin\alpha$

   $\sin(90° + \alpha) = \cos\alpha$

Example 3.14: sin(180°−α)

Simplify $\sin(180°-\alpha)$.

Solution

1. Apply the new difference identity for sine:

$$\sin(\alpha_1 - \alpha_2) = \sin\alpha_1\cos\alpha_2 - \cos\alpha_1\sin\alpha_2$$

$$\sin(180° - \alpha) = \sin180°\cos\alpha - \cos180°\sin\alpha$$

2. Reduce it by taking the sine and cosine of 180°:

$$\sin(180° - \alpha) = (0)\cos\alpha - (-1)\sin\alpha$$

$$\sin(180° - \alpha) = \sin\alpha$$

The cosine has very similar sum and difference identities.

Sum and Difference Identities for Cosine

$$\cos(\alpha_1 + \alpha_2) = \cos\alpha_1\cos\alpha_2 - \sin\alpha_1\sin\alpha_2$$

$$\cos(\alpha_1 - \alpha_2) = \cos\alpha_1\cos\alpha_2 + \sin\alpha_1\sin\alpha_2$$

Example 3.15: cos(180°+α)

Simplify $\cos(180°+\alpha)$.

Solution

1. Apply the new sum identity for cosine:

$$\cos(\alpha_1 + \alpha_2) = \cos\alpha_1\cos\alpha_2 - \sin\alpha_1\sin\alpha_2$$

$$\cos(180° + \alpha) = \cos180°\cos\alpha - \sin180°\sin\alpha$$

2. Reduce it by taking the sine and cosine of 180°:

$$\cos(180°+\alpha) = (-1)\cos\alpha - (0)\sin\alpha$$

$$\cos(180°+\alpha) = -\cos\alpha$$

Example 3.16: cos(90°−α)

Simplify cos(90°−α).

Solution

1. Apply the new difference identity for cosine:

$$\cos(\alpha_1 - \alpha_2) = \cos\alpha_1\cos\alpha_2 + \sin\alpha_1\sin\alpha_2$$

$$\cos(90° - \alpha) = \cos90°\cos\alpha + \sin90°\sin\alpha$$

2. Reduce it by taking the sine and cosine of 90°:

$$\cos(90° - \alpha) = (0)\cos\alpha + (1)\sin\alpha$$

$$\cos(180° + \alpha) = \sin\alpha$$

This section contains quite a few trig identities, from the unit circle identity all the way through the sum and difference identities. As a programmer, you should know that the trigonometric functions are fairly expensive (they take more processing power than a simple multiply or add function), so your goal should always be to minimize the number of trig functions called in your code. The next section looks at the syntax for actually using these functions in C++.

Self-Assessment

1. Using the unit circle, find sin(180°) and cos(180°).

2. Using the values you found in question 1, verify that the unit circle identity is true for 180°.

3. Find tan(30°) *without* using the tangent function on your calculator.

4. Find sin(2α) using the sum identity.

5. Find cos(2α).

6. If you had to use a lookup table for sine values and you could store only values up through sin(90°), how might you find sin(120°)?

Using Math Libraries in C++

As you start programming, you'll find that it's not necessary to reinvent the wheel. Many functions have already been written a thousand times, so why rewrite them? The trigonometric functions have already been mastered, and they're out there to be used. If you're coding in C++, you can include the math.h library, which already contains function calls for sine, cosine, tangent, and their inverses.

> **NOTE**
> Whenever you want to use these function calls, make sure you include math.h at the beginning of your code by using the following line:
>
> ```
> #include <math.h>
> ```

The sine, cosine, and tangent functions take in a double and output a double. The input, or parameter, is an angle expressed in radians, and the output is a decimal number between –1 and 1. Remember that the angle must be in radians, so you might need to perform a last-minute conversion from degrees to radians (see the first section of this chapter). Quite often, programmers first define a constant for π:

$$\pi = 3.14159265$$

and then use it later to convert from degrees to radians. A typical sine function call looks like this:

```
result = sin (angle*pi/180);
```

Once again, perhaps the best way to create a constant for repeated use is the #define the value in the top of a frequently used header file.

```
#define PI 3.14159265f
#define RadToDeg 57.29577951f
#define DegToRad 0.017453293f
```

The cosine and tangent functions use the exact same format.

math.h Trig Functions

sine: double sin (double *x*)

cosine: double cos (double *x*)

tangent: double tan (double *x*)

return a number between −1 and 1 when an angle in radians is input.

The inverse trig functions are also defined in math.h. Remember that the inverses are used to return the angle (see the second section of this chapter). These three functions also take in a double and return the angle in radians as a double. Again, you can always convert back to degrees if you want. The functions are actually labeled asin, acos, and atan.

math.h Inverse Trig Functions

arcsine: double asin (double *x*)

arccosine: double acos (double *x*)

arctangent: double atan (double *x*)

return an angle in radians when a double value (*x*) is input.

A typical line of code looks like this:

```
angle = asin (input)*180/pi;
```

NOTE

Don't forget to include the math.h library just like before:

```
#include <math.h>
```

You can also include the more frequently used <cmath> library, because it's a bit more compatible.

Also note that there are restrictions on the input for asin and acos; they are defined only for values between −1 and 1.

> **TIP**
>
> Division is a more expensive operation than multiplication, so you might want to consider defining another constant equal to $1/\pi$ (0.31830989) and then multiply instead of divide.

> **NOTE**
>
> Now we have truly set the stage to deal with vectors in future chapters. In this section you tackled the function calls in C++ for the trigonometric functions and their inverses. This is where all the previous sections start to come together in terms of programming. Now you can move forward with their applications in game programming.

Self-Assessment Solutions

Degrees Versus Radians

1. The answer is shown in Figure 3.16.

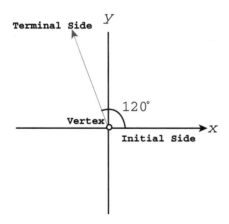

Figure 3.16   The solution to question 1.

2. The answer is shown in Figure 3.17.

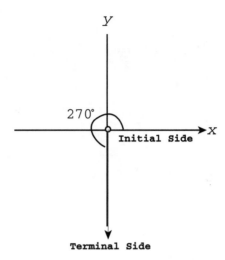

Figure 3.17   The solution to question 2.

3. The answer is shown in Figure 3.18.

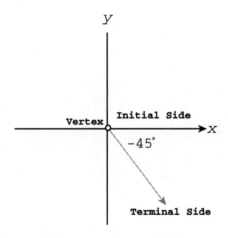

Figure 3.18   The solution to question 3.

4. $\left(\dfrac{\pi^R}{3}\right)$

5. $\left(\dfrac{3\pi^R}{2}\right)$

6. $\left(\dfrac{\pi^R}{4}\right)$

7. 135°

8. 60°

9. 72°

Trigonometric Functions

1. 0.7071

2. −0.5736

3. −0.7002

4. $\sin\alpha = \frac{7}{25} = 0.28$, $\cos\alpha = \frac{24}{25} = 0.96$, $\tan\alpha = \frac{7}{24} = 0.29$

5. $\alpha = 16.26°$

6. −1.4281

7. 2.9238

8. 1.4142

9. per = 120°, amp = 5

10. per = 360°, amp = 3

11. per = 90°, amp = 1

12. per = 360°, amp = 5

13. per = 720°, amp = 2

14. per = 180°, amp = $\frac{1}{2}$

Trigonometric Identities

1. $\sin(180°) = 0$ and $\cos(180°) = -1$

2. $\sin^2(180°) + \cos^2(180°) = 0^2 + (-1)^2 = 1$, so it is true for 180°.

3. $\tan(30°) = \sin(30°)/\cos(30°) = 0.5/0.8660 = 0.5774$

4. $\sin(2\alpha) = \sin(\alpha+\alpha) = \sin\alpha\cos\alpha + \cos\alpha\sin\alpha$

5. $\cos(2\alpha) = \cos\alpha\cos\alpha - \sin\alpha\sin\alpha = \cos^2(\alpha) - \sin^2(\alpha)$

6. Use the sum identity for sine:
   $\sin(90°+30°) = \sin90°\cos 30° + \cos90°\sin 30° = \cos 30° + 0 = 0.8660$

Chapter 4

Vector Operations

This chapter is dedicated to defining and working with vectors. Vectors are a comparatively new invention. They entered mathematical parlance in the 19th century, as mathematicians and physicists wrestled with the need to describe motion rather than static placement. The regular numbers that you're used to dealing with are called scalar values, and they can be used to describe an amount or static placement. Unfortunately, though, these scalar values can't be used to describe an object's motion, because they have no way of indicating direction. Over the years, you've probably performed operations such as addition and multiplication on scalar numbers more often than you can count. This chapter revisits operations like that but for vectors, which include direction and govern all the motion in most games. This chapter sets up the rules for mathematically working with vectors so that you can use them in future chapters.

Vector Versus Scalar

Whenever you introduce a quantity in your game, you must distinguish whether it's a vector quantity or a scalar quantity. The difference between the two lies in the direction.

You've been working with scalar quantities since you learned to count. A **scalar** is just a number; sometimes it's called a magnitude without any direction. A **vector** quantity has both magnitude and direction. For example, suppose your friend is having car trouble, and he calls and asks you to come pick him up because he's only 2 miles away. You say no problem and hop in your car. But how will you find him? If he had said 2 miles due east on your street, you might have had a better chance of locating him. That's the difference between vectors and scalars. The scalar version of 2 miles doesn't give you enough information. The vector version of 2 miles due east gives you the direction you need to find your buddy. The direction makes all the difference in the world. So a scalar quantity is just a number, or a magnitude. A vector quantity is a magnitude with direction included. This might seem like a minor distinction, but it makes a world of difference when you start simulating motion.

Vector Versus Scalar

Scalar = magnitude only

Vector = magnitude + direction.

In code, scalars can be stored in any number of variable types designed to hold numbers, depending on the range of values which need to be stored. Anything from a char, which can hold values from −128 and 127, to an unsigned long, which can hold values between 0 and 18,446,744,073,709,551,616 (or 2 to the power of 64), to a double, which can hold values between +/-1.7E +/-308 (up to 15 digits). There are, however, no built-in data types designed specifically for storing vectors, although 3D API's like OpenGL and Direct3D each have a standard which they adhere to. Therefore, vectors can be stored in code as either an array of floats or as a user-defined data type:

```
// An array of 3 floats is one way to store a vector, i j and k
float 3Dvector[3] = { 0, 0, 0 };
// A user-defined data type is another
struct 3Dvector
{
float x, y, z;
};
```

By using a data type, it is possible to create an extremely powerful structure or class which can encompass almost every operation which could be needed. This will be covered in more detail in further chapters.

When you're programming, always be sure to include the direction whenever you're dealing with an object in motion. Some quantities, such as time and points, can't have a direction, so a scalar number is fine. However, quantities such as displacement, velocity, and force describe an object in motion, so always include the direction.

You might not be familiar with the terms **displacement** and **velocity**. Displacement is the vector version of distance, and velocity is the vector version of speed. For example, 55mph is just a scalar, so we call it speed. However, 55mph due east is a vector, so we call it velocity. These two quantities are discussed in greater detail in Chapter 8, "Motion in One Dimension."

The trickiest part of working with vectors is dealing with the direction. In one dimension there are only two possible directions, so positive or negative can be used to indicate which one. For example, if all an object can do is move left or right on the screen, positive numbers indicate to the right, and negative numbers indicate to the left. Similarly, we often use positive numbers for up and negative numbers for down when dealing with vertical motion.

> **NOTE**
>
> Chapter 1, "Points and Lines," discussed the different coordinate systems for 3D. In this book, up, right, and out from the screen are the positive directions, and down, left, and back behind the screen are the negative directions. Be sure to pay close attention to the coordinate system defined by the engine you are working with.

Example 4.1: *Pong*: Positive Displacement

Suppose you're programming the motion of the paddle in a *Pong* game. The paddle can only move up and down. If the center of the paddle starts at (20,50) and moves to (20,400), what is its displacement?

Solution

Looking at the y-coordinates, you can see that the paddle moves from the 50-pixel mark to the 400-pixel mark. Therefore, its displacement must be 350 pixels.

Example 4.2: *Pong*: Negative Displacement

Again, you're programming the motion of the paddle in a *Pong* game. The paddle can only move up and down. If the center of the paddle starts at (20,400) and moves to (20,50), what is its displacement?

Solution

Looking at the y-coordinates, you can see that this time the paddle moves from the 400-pixel mark to the 50-pixel mark. Therefore, its displacement must be –350 pixels.

> **NOTE**
>
> Notice that, in one dimension, positive or negative is all you need to indicate the direction. Example 4.1 had a positive displacement, but when you flipped the positions in Example 4.2, the displacement became negative.

When dealing with displacement, direction is very important. There's a very big difference between distance (the scalar) and displacement (the vector). When calculating displacement, all you care about is where the object starts and where it ends. Whatever happens in between doesn't matter. Football is a great example of displacement versus distance. Suppose your receiver catches the football on the 20-yard line and starts running. There's a blocker in the way, so the receiver circles around the blocker, avoids the other defender running toward him, and eventually gets tackled on the 50-yard line.

If you look at his path mapped out in Figure 4.1, you can see that he runs much farther than 30 yards. However, as far as you're concerned for the game, he gained 30 yards for the team. The positive 30 yards is his displacement even though the actual distance traveled is much more. If you ignored direction completely, you'd be concerned with the scalar version, distance. That is the critical difference between distance and displacement.

Displacement

Displacement = final position – initial position

$\Delta x = x_f - x_i.$

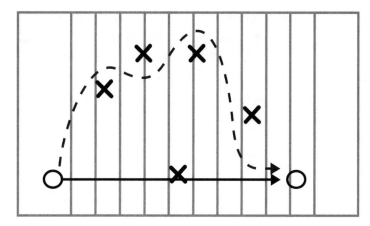

Figure 4.1   A football player's displacement.

> **NOTE**
> Remember that, when calculating displacement, where direction matters, all you need to know is the starting point and the ending point. Only for the scalar version of distance do you care what happens in between.

Example 4.3: Distance Versus Displacement

This time, you're playing a simple version of *Mario Brothers* where all he can do is move left and right (he can't jump yet). Suppose Mario starts out with a horizontal position of 200 pixels. He starts to move to the right, but at the 250-pixel mark he realizes he missed a mushroom, so he backs up to the 100-pixel mark to get the mushroom. Then he runs forward to meet the princess at the 450-pixel mark. What's his overall displacement, and what's his actual distance traveled?

Solution

1. Calculate displacement first. Mario starts out at the 200-pixel mark and ends up at the 450-pixel mark. Overall, his displacement is final position – initial position = 400 pixels – 200 pixels = 250 pixels.

2. You can ignore direction when calculating distance, so add up the length of each segment of Mario's run. From 200 pixels to 250 pixels is 50 pixels. From there he goes another 150 pixels to the mushroom, so that's 200 pixels so far. Then he runs 350 pixels toward the princess, so that's 550 pixels total distance traveled.

Notice that distance and displacement are quite often very different values, as they were with Mario. Also, notice that you lose all the information about what happens in the middle when all you look at is displacement. You might want to consider breaking the motion into smaller time intervals so that you don't miss anything. Looking back at Mario, you might want to consider separating that scenario into three segments. Remember that, when coding, you need to use displacement to maintain the direction, so you might want to work with three segments: +50 pixels, –150 pixels to the mushroom, and +350 pixels to the princess.

> **NOTE**
> If you choose to program a game in real time, your time intervals will hopefully be close to 1/30 of a second, so you won't risk losing much information between frames.

Scalars are no big deal, because you've been working with them all your life. However, this vector idea might be new, and the trick lies in dealing with the direction. Motion in one dimension is easy, because positive or negative can indicate the direction of vector quantities. The rest of this chapter is dedicated to dealing with vectors in 2D and 3D, which are a little more complicated to work with.

Self-Assessment

1. What's the difference between a vector and a scalar quantity?

2. Is "–65 feet" an example of a vector or a scalar?

3. Is "35 seconds" an example of a vector or a scalar?

4. If a runner on a straight track starts at the 5-ft. marker and stops at the 65-ft. marker, what's his displacement?

5. If a confused runner on a straight track starts at the 65-ft. marker and stops at the 5-ft. marker, what's his displacement?

6. Suppose you're playing *Pong*, and the paddle starts with a y-coordinate of 250 pixels. You move it down to the 100-pixel mark to hit the ball. Then you move up 300 pixels in anticipation of the next hit. As the ball approaches, you realize you're a little off, so you move down 20 pixels. What's the paddle's overall displacement?

7. What is the actual distance that the paddle in question 6 travels?

8. In a baseball game, a player gets caught in a rundown when trying to steal second. After running back and forth, he ends up safely back on first base. What's his overall displacement for that play?

Polar Coordinates Versus Cartesian Coordinates

In the preceding section, you found that positive or negative is sufficient for the direction of a vector in one dimension. However, in 2D and 3D, positive or negative just isn't enough. There are two different forms for describing a vector in 2D: polar coordinates and Cartesian coordinates. **Polar coordinates** are a little more intuitive, so let's look at them first.

> **Polar Coordinates**
>
> Vector A $= \|A\|$ @ θ
>
> where $\|A\|$ is the magnitude of A and θ is the direction.

Figure 4.2 illustrates polar coordinates.

$\|A\|$

θ

Figure 4.2   Vector A expressed in polar coordinates.

> **NOTE**
> Notice that vector A is a capital letter. This text uses capital letter notation for vectors. Some sources use the arrow notation, which is written Ā. They both mean the same thing. Also note that the @ symbol is pronounced "at." For example, 20m @ 30° is read as "20 meters at 30 degrees in standard position."

Polar coordinates are the easiest way to visualize what a vector looks like. This is why we spent time establishing a standard position for angles in Chapter 3, "Trigonometry Snippets." Now when we express a vector as a magnitude with a direction, the direction is simply an angle in standard position. This takes care of all the possible directions in 2D.

Cartesian coordinates are less intuitive, but that is the form used for coding vectors. Rather than describe a vector by its length and direction, you can also describe it by its horizontal and vertical displacement, much like with the Cartesian coordinate system. These two pieces are called the horizontal and vertical components, and they're written in what I call "i and j form."

Cartesian Coordinates (Components)

Vector $B = b_1\hat{i} + b_2\hat{j}$

where $\hat{i}$ is one unit in the x direction and $\hat{j}$ is one unit in the y direction.

Figure 4.3 illustrates Cartesian coordinates.

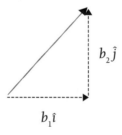

Figure 4.3   Vector B expressed in Cartesian coordinates.

> **NOTE**
> The i and j form might look strange because of the "caps" over the i and j. Just read $\hat{i}$ as "in the x direction" and $\hat{j}$ as "in the y direction." For example, $3\hat{i} + 4\hat{j}$ is read as "3 in the x direction and 4 in the y direction." The $\hat{i}$ and $\hat{j}$ are actually vectors themselves. They both have a magnitude of 1 and point in the directions of the positive x and y axes.
>
> Also note that the components might be negative, which just indicates left or down rather than right or up.

The computer screen is set up in a gridlike fashion, which is why coding is done in Cartesian coordinates. Quite often you plan with vector quantities in polar form but then need to code them in Cartesian form. Therefore, let's look at the process of converting from polar coordinates to Cartesian. If you look at vector A shown in Figure 4.4, you'll see that you can create a right triangle and use the trig functions to convert from polar to Cartesian coordinates.

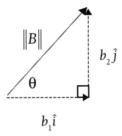

Figure 4.4   Converting from polar to Cartesian coordinates.

> **Converting from Polar to Cartesian Coordinates**
>
> For vector $A = \|A\| @ \theta$,
>
> $A = a_1\hat{i} + a_2\hat{j}$
>
> where $\|A\|\cos\theta$ and $\|A\|\sin\theta$.

Example 4.4: Converting from Polar to Cartesian Coordinates

Vector A is a displacement vector. Convert A = 20m @ 30° to Cartesian coordinates.

Solution

You can use sine and cosine to break A into components:

$a_1 = \|A\|\cos\theta = 20\cos30° \approx 20(0.8660) \approx 17.32$

$a_2 = \|A\|\sin\theta = 20\sin30° = 20(0.5) = 10$

Therefore, A = 17.32$\hat{i}$ + 10$\hat{j}$ in component form.

Converting from Cartesian to Polar Coordinates

For vector B = $b_1\hat{i}$ + $b_2\hat{j}$,

$\|B\| = \sqrt{(b_1)^2 + (b_2)^2}$ and $\theta = \tan^{-1}\left(\dfrac{b_2}{b_1}\right)$.

Figure 4.5 illustrates this process.

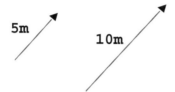

5m   10m

Figure 4.5   Converting from Cartesian to polar coordinates.

Example 4.5: Converting from Cartesian to Polar Coordinates

Convert vector B = 3$\hat{i}$ + 4$\hat{j}$ to polar coordinates.

Solution

1. Calculate the magnitude of B:

   $$\|B\| = \sqrt{(b_1)^2 + (b_2)^2} = \sqrt{3^2 + 4^2} = \sqrt{9+16} = \sqrt{25} = 5$$

2. Calculate the direction:

   $$\theta = \tan^{-1}\left(\frac{b_2}{b_1}\right) = \tan^{-1}\left(\frac{4}{3}\right) \approx 53.1°$$

Therefore, B = 5 units @ 53.1° in polar coordinates.

Let's take a look at some functions which could solve the preceding problems for us. First, we need to define our data types that we're going to be using:

```
// A structure for holding a vector in component form
struct 2Dvector_comp
{
```

```
float x, y;
};
// A structure for holding a vector in magnitude/direction form
struct 2Dvector_polar
{
float mag, dir;
};
```

Now let's write two functions which convert from component to magnitude/direction form and vice versa:

```
// purpose:  to convert a vector from magnitude/direction to
➡ component form
// input:    vec- a vector in magnitude/direction form
// output:   our converted vector
2Dvector_comp_PolarToCompConversion(2Dvector_polar vec)
{
// A temporary variable which will hold our answer
2Dvector_comp temp;
// Fill in our values
temp.x = mag * cos(dir * PI / 180);
temp.y = mag * sin(dir * PI / 180);
// Return our answer
return temp;
}

// purpose:  to convert a vector from component to
➡ magnitude/direction form
// input:    vec- a vector in component form
// output:   our converted vector
2Dvector_polar_CompToPolarConversion(2Dvector_comp vec)
{
// A temporary variable which will hold our answer
2Dvector_polar temp = { 0, 0 };
// Calculate our magnitude using the Pythagorean theorom
temp.mag = sqrtf(vec.x * vec.x + vec.y * vec.y);
// Error check to prevent a divide-by-zero issue in our next
➡ section
```

```
if(temp.mag == 0)
return temp;
// Caculate our angle. We are using asin() which will return an
➥ angle
// in either the 1st or the 4th quadrant
temp.dir = (180 / PI) * asin(vec.y / temp.mag);
// Adjust our angle in the event that it lies in the 2nd or 3rd
➥ quadrant
if(vec.x < 0)
temp.dir += 180;
// Adjust our angle in the event that it lies in the 4th quadrant
else if(vec.x > 0 && vec.y < 0)
temp.dir += 360;
// Return our new vector
return temp;
}
```

Another benefit of Cartesian form (besides the fact that the computer requires it) is that it can very easily be extended to 3D.

Cartesian Coordinates (Components) in 3D

Vector $B = b_1\hat{i} + b_2\hat{j} + b_3\hat{k}$

where $\hat{i}$ is one unit in the x direction, $\hat{j}$ is one unit in the y direction, and $\hat{k}$ is one unit in the z direction.

If you haven't already noticed, as mathematical concepts get implemented in the world of programming, often the notations change. A vector in Cartesian form is often written as a single-row or single-column matrix rather than in the traditional i and j form.

For example, the 2D matrix $A = 5\hat{i} + 6\hat{j}$ might also be written as $[5\ 6]$ or $\begin{bmatrix} 5 \\ 6 \end{bmatrix}$.

Similarly, a 3D vector $B = 7\hat{i} + 8\hat{j} + 9\hat{k}$ may be written as $[7\ 8\ 9]$ or $\begin{bmatrix} 7 \\ 8 \\ 9 \end{bmatrix}$.

The discussion of normalizing vectors in the "Scalar Multiplication" section later in this chapter, uses a single-row matrix to represent a vector in Cartesian coordinates, so don't be intimidated.

Self-Assessment

1. Vector A is a velocity vector. Convert A = 25m/s @ 45° to Cartesian coordinates.

2. Convert vector B = $12\hat{i} + 5\hat{j}$ to polar coordinates.

3. Vector C is a force vector. Convert C = 200N @ 60° to Cartesian coordinates.

4. Convert vector D = $8\hat{i} - 6\hat{j}$ to polar coordinates.

Vector Addition and Subtraction

Whether your vectors represent displacements or velocities or forces, there might be times when you need to add or subtract them. We'll revisit this process in Chapters 10, 11, 12, and 14. We'll look at this process graphically first, and then we'll throw in the numbers.

When trying to organize vector quantities graphically, it is common to use an arrow for each vector. The arrow's length corresponds to the vector's magnitude, and the way it's pointing represents the direction. Because these arrows are drawn to scale, it's important to always work within the same scale (that is, all meters or all feet, but not both). That way, a vector with a magnitude of 5m appears to be half as long as a vector with a magnitude of 10m, as shown in Figure 4.6.

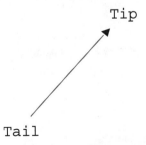

Figure 4.6   Two vectors represented by arrows.

We'll call the pointy end of the vector the tip and the other end the tail, as shown in Figure 4.7.

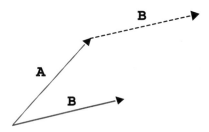

Figure 4.7 Vector tip and tail.

Now you can use the tip-to-tail method of adding vectors. One great thing about vectors is that they're not anchored to any one location. As long as the arrow stays the same length and keeps pointing in the same direction, it can be moved anywhere. To add two vectors graphically, just slide one so that it's tip-to-tail with the other, as shown in Figure 4.8.

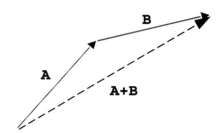

Figure 4.8 Vector A tip-to-tail with vector B.

As soon as they're tip-to-tail, draw a new vector from the tail of the first one to the tip of the second one.

Think of the vectors shown in Figure 4.9 as displacement vectors on a road map. If you travel along vector A and then turn and follow vector B, you really go from the beginning of A to the end of B.

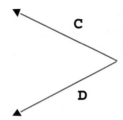

Figure 4.9   Vector A plus vector B.

Example 4.6: Adding Vectors Graphically

Find C + D for the vectors pictured in Figure 4.10.

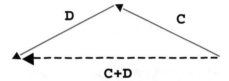

Figure 4.10   Vectors C and D.

Solution

1. Slide vector D so that it's tip-to-tail with C. Be sure to keep D the same length and pointing in the same direction.

2. Draw a new vector C + D from the tail of C to the tip of D.

3. The final vector is shown in Figure 4.11.

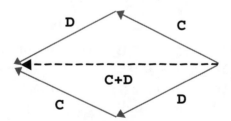

Figure 4.11   Vector C + D.

Look at the drawing of C + D. Notice that you could have also slid C tip-to-tail with D and gotten the same final vector (see Figure 4.12).

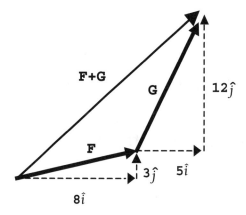

Figure 4.12 C + D = D + C.

Now try attaching some numbers to these vectors. You might have noticed in the preceding example that the length of vector C + D is much shorter than the length of C plus the length of D. That's because, with vectors, direction is taken into account. In other words:

$$\|A + B\| \neq \|A\| + \|B\|$$

For this reason, you cannot add vectors in polar coordinates unless they're in the same direction. Always convert vectors to Cartesian coordinates before attempting to add them. As soon as the two vectors are in Cartesian coordinates, just add "like" components. In other words, add the two $\hat{i}$ s and the two $\hat{j}$ s.

Adding Vectors Numerically

$A + B = (a_1 + b_1)\hat{i} + (a_2 + b_2)\hat{j}$

for vectors $A = a_1\hat{i} + a_2\hat{j}$ and $B = b_1\hat{i} + b_2\hat{j}$.

Example 4.7: Adding Vectors Numerically

Calculate C + D for vectors $C = 8\hat{i} + 3\hat{j}$ and $D = 5\hat{i} + 12\hat{j}$.

Solution

1. Set this up graphically. Slide vector D so that it's tip-to-tail with C. Be sure to keep D the same length and pointing in the same direction.

2. Now draw a new vector C + D from the tail of C to the tip of D, as shown in Figure 4.13.

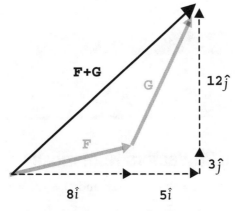

Figure 4.13   Vector C + D again.

3. The only way to calculate C + D numerically is to calculate the total amount in the x direction and the total amount in the y direction. In other words, add the two $\hat{i}$ components and add the two $\hat{j}$ components. In this case:

$$C + D = (8+5)\hat{i} + (3+12)\hat{j} = 13\hat{i} + 15\hat{j}$$

This is illustrated in Figure 4.14.

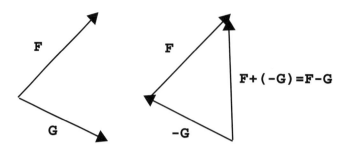

Figure 4.14 Adding corresponding components.

> **NOTE**
> Notice that Example 4.7 starts with both vectors in Cartesian coordinates. If you had been planning in polar coordinates, you would first have to convert them and then add. You might need to refer to the preceding section for the conversion process.

The same method for adding vectors also applies to 3D. Again, the coordinates *must* be in Cartesian form for you to add them numerically.

Adding 3D Vectors Numerically

$$A + B = (a_1 + b_1)\hat{i} + (a_2 + b_2)\hat{j} + (a_3 + b_3)\hat{k}$$

for vectors $A = a_1\hat{i} + a_2\hat{j} + a_3\hat{k}$ and $B = b_1\hat{i} + b_2\hat{j} + b_3\hat{k}$.

Example 4.8: Adding 3D Vectors Numerically

Calculate $C + D$ for 3D vectors $C = 9\hat{i} + 5\hat{j} - 2\hat{k}$ and $D = -2\hat{i} + \hat{j} + 4\hat{k}$.

Solution

$$C + D = (a_1 + b_1)\hat{i} + (a_2 + b_2)\hat{j} + (a_3 + b_3)\hat{k}$$

$$= (9 - 2)\hat{i} + (5 + 1)\hat{j} + (-2 + 4)\hat{k}$$

$$= 7\hat{i} + 6\hat{j} + 2\hat{k}$$

As you can see, adding vectors is quite simple when they're in Cartesian coordinates. Subtracting is equally simple—just subtract "like" components.

Subtracting Vectors Numerically

$A - B = (a_1 - b_1)\hat{i} + (a_2 - b_2)\hat{j}$

for vectors $A = a_1\hat{i} + a_2\hat{j}$ and $B = b_1\hat{i} + b_2\hat{j}$.

The same process applies to 3D subtraction.

Subtracting 3D Vectors Numerically

$A - B = (a_1 - b_1)\hat{i} + (a_2 - b_2)\hat{j} + (a_3 - b_3)\hat{k}$

for vectors $A = a_1\hat{i} + a_2\hat{j} + a_3\hat{k}$ and $B = b_1\hat{i} + b_2\hat{j} + b_3\hat{k}$.

Notice that subtracting vectors is the same as adding the negative of the second vector. In other words, you flip the signs of each component in the second vector and then add. If you're trying to visualize this graphically, it's the same as flipping the direction of the second vector and then adding them tip-to-tail. This is illustrated in Figure 4.15.

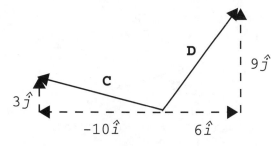

Figure 4.15   Subtracting equals adding the negative.

Example 4.9: Subtracting 3D Vectors Numerically

Calculate C − D for 3D vectors $C = 9\hat{i} + 5\hat{j} - 2\hat{k}$ and $D = -2\hat{i} + \hat{j} + 4\hat{k}$.

Solution

$C - D = (a_1 - b_1)\hat{i} + (a_2 - b_2)\hat{j} + (a_3 - b_3)\hat{k}$

$= (9 + 2)\hat{i} + (5 - 1)\hat{j} + (-2 - 4)\hat{k}$

$= 11\hat{i} + 4\hat{j} - 6\hat{k}$

So far, we have discussed two different forms of representing a vector: Cartesian coordinates (components) and polar coordinates (magnitude and direction). We've used the laws of right triangles (Pythagorean theorem and trigonometric functions) to convert between the two forms. Then we looked at adding and subtracting vectors in both 2D and 3D, which is fairly simple when the vectors are already in Cartesian coordinates. The next few sections look at how multiplication works with vectors.

Self-Assessment

1. Convert vector A = 20ft @ 80° to Cartesian coordinates.

2. Convert vector $B = 6\hat{i} + 8\hat{j}$ to polar coordinates.

3. Using vectors A and B in the previous two questions, find the vector A + B.

4. Using vectors A and B in the previous three questions, find the vector A − B.

5. Using vectors C and D shown in Figure 4.16, find vector C + D.

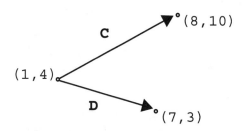

Figure 4.16 Adding vectors C and D.

6. Calculate F + G for 3D vectors $F = 2\hat{i} - 4\hat{j} - \hat{k}$ and $G = -5\hat{i} + 3\hat{j} + 6\hat{k}$.

7. Calculate F − G for 3D vectors $F = 2\hat{i} - 4\hat{j} - \hat{k}$ and $G = -5\hat{i} + 3\hat{j} + 6\hat{k}$.

Scalar Multiplication

I'm sure for many years you have been multiplying scalars by other scalars. Remember, a scalar quantity is just an ordinary number. Let's turn our attention to a scalar times a vector. If you think about a vector expressed in polar coordinates, all you have is a magnitude and a direction. When you multiply a scalar by that vector, all you're really doing is changing the magnitude by scaling it up or down. If the scalar value is a whole number, the magnitude gets larger. Likewise, if the scalar is a fraction less than 1, the magnitude gets smaller.

Scalar Multiplication in Polar Coordinates

$c\mathbf{A} = c\|A\| @ \theta$

for any scalar c and vector $\mathbf{A} = \|A\| @ \theta$.

Example 4.10: Scalar * Vector in Polar Coordinates

Calculate 5A if vector A = 3ft @ 22°.

Solution
5A = 5(3ft @ 22°) = 15ft @ 22°

If you're trying to visualize the effect scalar multiplication has on a vector, take a look at Figure 4.17.

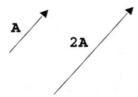

Figure 4.17   2 * vector A.

Remember that vectors are often represented by arrows with a length that corresponds to the magnitude, and the way the vector is pointing indicates the direction. As you can see, vector 2A is twice as long as A, but it still points in the exact same direction.

If you're already set up to program a vector and it's in Cartesian coordinates, you can still perform scalar multiplication without converting back to polar coordinates. Simply multiply each component by the scalar value, and that will have the same effect.

Scalar Multiplication in Cartesian Coordinates

$$cA = ca_1\hat{i} + ca_2\hat{j}$$

for any scalar c and vector $A = a_1\hat{i} + a_2\hat{j}$.

Example 4.11: Scalar * Vector in Cartesian Coordinates

Calculate $1/2A$ if vector $A = 12\hat{i} + 4\hat{j}$.

Solution

$$\tfrac{1}{2}A = \tfrac{1}{2}(12\hat{i}) + \tfrac{1}{2}(4\hat{j}) = 6\hat{i} + 2\hat{j}$$

Quite often in programming, you'll hear the term **normalization** used. It's really just a fancy word for scaling the magnitude of a vector down to 1. Quite often, a vector is used to simply establish a direction. In fact, $\hat{i}$ and $\hat{j}$ are perfect examples of that. The $\hat{i}$ is really just a vector that's one unit long in the positive x direction. Likewise, the $\hat{j}$ is a vector with a magnitude of 1 in the positive y direction. In future sections, you'll see applications where a vector with length 1 is used to establish a direction.

Normalizing a vector in polar coordinates is very simple. Just change the magnitude to 1 and leave the direction the same. However, in the context of programming, the vector will most likely be in Cartesian coordinates before you need to normalize it. In this case you must first calculate the magnitude of the vector and then divide each component by the magnitude. Essentially, you are performing a scalar multiplication by 1 over the magnitude.

Normalizing a 2D Vector

$$\hat{A} = \frac{1}{\|A\|}A = \begin{bmatrix} \dfrac{a_1}{\|A\|} & \dfrac{a_2}{\|A\|} \end{bmatrix}$$

for any vector $A = [a_1\ a_2]$.

This process happens even more frequently in 3D.

Normalizing a 3D Vector

$$\hat{A} = \frac{1}{\|A\|} A = \left[\frac{a_1}{\|A\|} \quad \frac{a_2}{\|A\|} \quad \frac{a_3}{\|A\|} \right]$$

for any vector A = [a_1 a_2 a_3].

NOTE
The symbol for a normalized vector is the cap. For example, when A has a magnitude of 1, it can be written as Â.

Example 4.12: Normalizing a Vector

Normalize vector A = [5 0 −12].

Solution

1. The first thing you need to find is the magnitude of A. (You might need to refer to the "Polar Coordinates Versus Cartesian Coordinates" section earlier in this chapter.)

$$\|A\| = \sqrt{5^2 + 0^2 + (-12)^2} = \sqrt{25 + 0 + 144} = \sqrt{169} = 13.$$

2. Now that you know the magnitude, all that's left to do is divide each component by it:

$$\hat{A} = \left[\frac{a_1}{\|A\|} \quad \frac{a_2}{\|A\|} \quad \frac{a_3}{\|A\|} \right] = \left[\frac{5}{13} \quad \frac{0}{13} \quad \frac{-12}{13} \right]$$

NOTE
To check yourself, you can always calculate $\|\hat{A}\|$. It should always equal 1 if you normalized correctly.

As you can see, scalar multiplication has the effect of scaling a vector's magnitude up or down. The direction always stays the same; only the magnitude changes. Also, the process of normalization is a great example of a scalar times a vector. The next natural question to ask is, "How do I multiply two vectors?" This question is not answered quite as easily, but it is addressed in the next two sections.

Self-Assessment

1. Does scalar multiplication affect a vector's magnitude or direction?

2. Calculate $(-1/3)A$ if vector A = 12m/s @ 43°.

3. Calculate $6B$ if vector $B = 3\hat{i} - \hat{j}$.

4. Normalize vector $C = [24\ 10]$.

5. Normalize vector $D = [0\ 7\ 24]$.

Dot Product

Remember when you first learned the multiplication tables? Your teacher probably told you that 2 times 3 could be written as 2×3 or as $2 \bullet 3$, and that they mean the same thing. This statement is true for scalar quantities. However, it's *not* true for more complex structures, such as vectors. We'll first look at $2 \bullet 3$, which is called the dot product. Then we'll investigate the cross product, 2×3, in the next section.

The most important thing to remember about the dot product of two vectors is that it always returns a scalar value. Let's first discuss *how* to calculate it, and then we'll talk about what that number represents.

> **NOTE**
> Some math texts call the dot product of two vectors the **scalar product** because that is what the dot product returns.

The Dot Product in 2D

$A \bullet B = a_1 b_1 + a_2 b_2$

for any 2D vectors $A = [a_1\ a_2]$ and $B = [b_1\ b_2]$.

Notice that you take the product of the two x components and add it to the product of the two y components. This process results in a single number. You might have already guessed how to extend this process to 3D.

The Dot Product in 3D

$A \bullet B = a_1b_1 + a_2b_2 + a_3b_3$

for any 3D vectors $A = [a_1 \; a_2 \; a_3]$ and $B = [b_1 \; b_2 \; b_3]$.

NOTE

The dot product can be performed on vectors of any dimension, not just 2D and 3D. You'll see an example of higher dimensions in Chapter 5, "Matrix Operations," which looks at multiplying matrices. Even though there might not be a physical representation of 4D or even 10D vectors, the only restriction on the dot product is that both vectors must be the same size.

The dot product is a very powerful vector operation; there's a lot of information embedded in that single number. The first point of note is that it gives you information about the angle between the two vectors (if they are 2D or 3D).

Perpendicular Check

If $A \bullet B = 0, A \perp B$.

NOTE

The $\perp$ symbol might be unfamiliar; it's the symbol for perpendicular. So if $A \bullet B = 0$, A is perpendicular to B.

This is a very efficient way to check for perpendicular lines. For 2D vectors, it requires only two multiplications and one addition. For 3D vectors it requires three multiplications and two additions and then a check to see if it's equal to 0. If the dot product is *not* equal to 0, its sign (positive or negative) provides helpful information.

Positive or Negative Dot Product

If $A \bullet B < 0$ (negative), $\theta > 90°$

If $A \bullet B > 0$ (positive), $\theta < 90°$

where θ is the angle between vectors A and B.

Example 4.13: Checking for an Object in View

Suppose the camera in your game is currently sitting at (1,4), and vector C = [5 3] represents the camera view. You know that an object's location is (7,2). If the camera can see only 90° in each direction, is the object in view?

Solution

1. The first thing you need to find is the vector that points from the current camera position to the object's position, as shown in Figure 4.18.

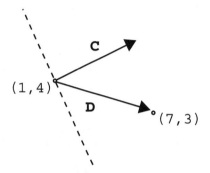

Figure 4.18   Camera view.

You can find the vector from the camera to the object by subtracting the camera's position from the object's position. Call it vector D = [(7 − 1) (2 − 4)] = [6 −2].

2. Calculate C • D:

C • D: 5(6) + 3(−2) = 30 − 6 = 24

3. Because C • D > 0, the angle between the camera's view and the vector to the object must be less than 90°, which means that the object is in view.

This quick comparison works if all you want to know is if the angle between the two vectors is greater than or less than 90°. If you need more information about the angle, the dot product can also be used to find the angle's exact degree measure.

The Angle Between Two Vectors

$$A \cdot B = \|A\|\|B\| \cos\theta$$

where θ is the angle between vectors A and B.

Example 4.14: The Angle Between Two Vectors

Suppose vector C = [5 2 –3] represents the way you are currently moving (current velocity), but you want to turn and follow vector D = [8 1 –4]. What is the angle of rotation between your current vector C and the desired vector D?

Solution

1. The first thing you need to find to use this new formula is C • D:

   C • D = 5(8) + 2(1) –3(–4) = 40 + 2 + 12 = 54

2. The next thing you need is the magnitude of each vector. (You might need to flip back earlier in this chapter for a review of how to find the magnitude when you know the components.)

   $$\|C\| = \sqrt{5^2 + 2^2 + (-3)^2} = \sqrt{25+4+9} = \sqrt{38}$$

   $$\|D\| = \sqrt{8^2 + 1^2 + (-4)^2} = \sqrt{64+1+16} = \sqrt{81}$$

3. Plug these three things into the new formula to calculate θ:

   $$C \cdot D = \|C\|\|D\| \cos\theta$$

   $$54 = \sqrt{38}(\sqrt{81}) \cos\theta$$

   $$\frac{54}{\sqrt{38}(\sqrt{81})} = \cos\theta$$

   $$0.9733 \approx \cos\theta$$

   $$\theta \approx \cos^{-1}(0.9733)$$

   $$\theta \approx 13.3°$$

   The player must turn 13.3° to follow the new vector.

One convenient property of the dot product is that it provides the length of the **projection** of one vector onto another. To visualize the projection, look at Figure 4.19. Vector A is being projected onto vector B. Imagine that a light source is directly above vector A, and it's shining down on vector B. The length projection is the length of vector A's shadow along the line defined by vector B. The only snag is that the vector being projected onto vector B must be normalized, which means that it has a length of 1. (This idea of projection will resurface in future chapters.)

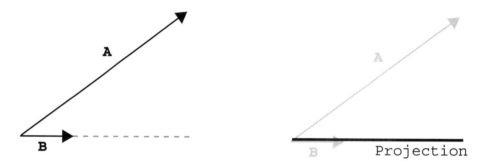

Figure 4.19   Projection of A onto B.

The dot product is a very powerful operation that will come up in many later chapters. You'll see it next in Chapter 5. In terms of programming, it's a relatively inexpensive operation, so you'll see it used in many applications. The next section discusses the other method of "multiplying" vectors—the cross product. I believe you'll find the dot product much simpler, but they have very different uses.

Self-Assessment

1. Find A • B for vectors A = [−2 8] and B = [4 1].

2. Find C • D for vectors C = [−1 4 2] and D = [3 0 5].

3. Are vectors A and B in question 1 perpendicular?

4. Find the angle between vectors C and D in question 2.

5. Suppose the camera in your game is currently sitting at (0,0) and vector F = [4 9] represents the camera view. You know that the location of an object is (3,−2). If the camera can see only 90° in each direction, is the object in view?

Cross Product

The preceding section looked at one way to "multiply" vectors—the dot product. This section examines the cross product. The biggest difference between the two is that the dot product returns a scalar value and the cross product returns another vector. Let's look at the method for calculating the cross product.

> **NOTE**
> Some math texts refer to the cross product of two vectors as the **vector product** because that is what the cross product returns.

Cross Product

$A \times B = [(a_2 b_3 - a_3 b_2)\ (a_3 b_1 - a_1 b_3)\ (a_1 b_2 - a_2 b_1)]$

for any two vectors $A = [a_1\ a_2\ a_3]$ and $B = [b_1\ b_2\ b_3]$.

Example 4.15: Cross Product

Find the cross product of vectors $A = [5\ -6\ 0]$ and $B = [1\ 2\ 3]$.

Solution

The cross product returns another vector, so you can calculate each component using the formula just described.

$A \times B = [(a_2 b_3 - a_3 b_2)\ (a_3 b_1 - a_1 b_3)\ (a_1 b_2 - a_2 b_1)]$

$= [(-6(3) - 0(2))\ (0(1) - 5(3))\ (5(2) - -6(1))]$

$= [(-18 - 0)\ (0 - 15)\ (10 + 6)]$

$= [-18\ -15\ 16]$

> **NOTE**
> After you practice calculating a few cross products, you might notice the pattern for which it was named. Just be careful with all the plus and minus signs; it's very easy to make an error.

The most notable characteristic of the cross product is that it returns another vector that is perpendicular to both the original vectors. For this reason, it only makes sense to apply the cross product to 3D vectors.

Perpendicular Vectors

A × B is perpendicular to both vectors A and B.

When you try to visualize the cross product, as shown in Figure 4.20, you might notice that it has two possible directions.

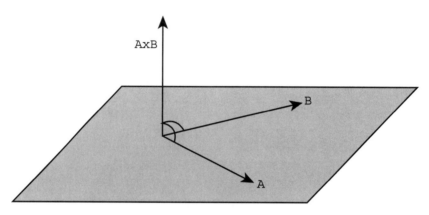

Figure 4.20 A × B.

The plane that contains vectors A and B has two perpendicular directions, "up" and "down." You can use the right-hand rule to determine which direction is given by the cross product. Place your right wrist at the point where A and B intersect, with your fingers pointing along A. As you curl your fingers toward B, your thumb points in the direction of A × B. Try reversing A and B; you should find that you get the opposite direction for B × A.

The Cross Product Is Not Commutative

A × B ≠ B × A

In fact, A × B = −(B × A) for any two 3D vectors A and B.

Because the cross product has the unique property of producing a third vector perpendicular to the original two, you can use the cross product to calculate the **surface normal**. Any two 3D vectors can define a surface. The surface normal is a vector that is perpendicular to the surface, and it has a length of 1.

Now that we've covered the important vector operations, it's time to construct a fully functional 3D vector class. Something to be careful of when naming your class is to avoid calling it simply "vector," as there is already a vector class defined in the Microsoft STL libraries. This code can be typed directly into a header (*.h) file and compiled as-is.

```cpp
#ifndef _3DVECTOR_H_
#define _3DVECTOR_H_

class 3Dvector
{
private:
    float x, y, z;
public:
        // purpose:      Our constructor
        // input:        ex- our vector's i component
        //               why- our vector's j component
        //               zee- our vector's k component
        // output:       no explicit output
        3Dvector(float ex = 0, float why = 0, float zee = 0)
{
    x = ex;    y = why; z = zee;
}

// purpose:     Our destructor
    // input:    none
    // output:   none
~3Dvector() { }

// purpose:     calculate the magnitude of our invoking vector
// input:       no explicit input
// output:      the magnitude of our invoking object
float getMagnitude()
{
```

```
        return sqrtf(x * x + y * y + z * z);
}


// purpose:   multiply our vector by a scalar value
// input:     num - the scalar value being multiplied
// output:    our newly created vector
3Dvector operator*(float num) const
{
        return 3Dvector(x * num, y * num, z * num);
}


// purpose:     multiply our vector by a scalar value
// input:       num - the scalar value being multiplied
//              vec - the vector we are multiplying to
// output:      our newly created vector
friend 3Dvector operator*(float num, const 3Dvector &vec)
{
        return 3Dvector(vec.x * num, vec.y * num, vec.z * num);
}


// purpose:     Adding two vectors
// input:       vec - the vector being added to our invoking
➥ object
// output:      our newly created sum of the two vectors
3Dvector operator+(const 3Dvector &vec) const
{
        return 3Dvector(x + vec.x, y + vec.y, z + vec.z);
}


// purpose:     Subtracting two vectors
// input:       vec - the vector being subtracted from our
➥ invoking object
// output:      our newly created difference of the two vectors
3Dvector operator-(const 3Dvector &vec) const
{
        return 3Dvector(x - vec.x, y - vec.y, z - vec.z);
}
```

```
// purpose:     Normalize our invoking vector *this changes our
➥ vector*
// input:       no explicit input
// output:      none
void normalize3Dvector(void)
{
    float mag = sqrtf(x * x + y * y + z * z);
    x /= mag;  y /= mag; z /= mag
}


// purpose:    Dot Product two vectors
// input:       vec - the vector being dotted with our invoking
➥ object
// output:       the dot product of the two vectors
float dot3Dvector(const 3Dvector &vec) const
{
    return x * vec.x + y * vec.y + z * vec.z;
}


// purpose:   Cross product two vectors
// input:     vec- the vector being crossed with our invoking
➥ object
// output:    our newly created resultant vector
3Dvector cross3Dvector(const 3Dvector &vec) const
{
    return 3Dvector( y * vec.z - z * vec.y,
             z * vec.x - x * vec.z,
             x * vec.y - y * vec.x);
}

};

#endif
```

Surface Normal

Surface normal = $(A\hat{X}B) = \dfrac{AxB}{\|AxB\|}$

for any two 3D vectors A and B.

Example 4.16: Surface Normal

A surface is defined by two vectors, A = [5 –2 0] and B = [1 2 3]. Find the surface normal so that it can be used to determine the resulting motion after a collision.

Solution

1. The cross product returns another vector that's perpendicular.

$$A \times B = [(a_2b_3 - a_3b_2)\ (a_3b_1 - a_1b_3)\ (a_1b_2 - a_2b_1)]$$

$$= [(-2(3) - 0(2))\ (0(1) - 5(3))\ (5(2) - -2(1))]$$

$$= [(-6 - 0)\ (0 - 15)\ (10 + 2)]$$

$$= [-6\ -15\ 12]$$

2. Find the magnitude of A × B:

$$\|AxB\| = \sqrt{(-6)^2 + (-15)^2 + (12)^2} = \sqrt{36 + 225 + 144} = \sqrt{405} \approx 20.125$$

3. The last step is to normalize A × B:

$$\left[\frac{-6}{20.125}\ \ \frac{-15}{20.125}\ \ \frac{12}{20.125}\right] \approx \left[-0.298\ \ 0.745\ \ 0.596\right]$$

Let's use the already-created 3Dvector class to solve this problem:

```
#include <iostream>
using namespace std;
#include "3Dvector.h"

int main()
{
    // Let's define our two vectors
    3Dvector A(5, -2, 0);
```

```
3Dvector B(1, 2, 3);
// Calculate our cross product
3Dvector C = A.cross3Dvector(B);
// Normalize our new vector
C.normalize3Dvector();
// Print our answer to the screen
cout << C.x << "i " << C.y << "j " << C.z << "k\n";

    return 0;
}
```

Last, you can also use the cross product to calculate the angle between two vectors. When you're given a choice, the dot product is faster for finding the angle. However, if you already have the cross product calculated, it might be easier to use the following method.

The Angle Between Two Vectors

$$\|AxB\| = \|A\|\|B\|\sin\theta$$

for any two 3D vectors A and B.

Example 4.17: The Angle Between Two Vectors

Find the angle between vectors A = [5 −2 0] and B = [1 2 3].

Solution

1. The first thing you need to calculate is A × B:

$$A \times B = [(a_2b_3 - a_3b_2)\ (a_3b_1 - a_1b_3)\ (a_1b_2 - a_2b_1)]$$

$$= [(-2(3) - 0(2))\ (0(1) - 5(3))\ (5(2) - -2(1))]$$

$$= [(-6 - 0)\ (0 - 15)\ (10 + 2)]$$

$$= [-6\ -15\ 12]$$

2. Find the magnitude of A × B:

$$\|AxB\| = \sqrt{(-6)^2 + (-15)^2 + (12)^2} = \sqrt{36 + 225 + 144} = \sqrt{405}$$

3. Now you need the magnitude of A and B:

$$\|A\| = \sqrt{(5)^2 + (-2)^2 + (0)^2} = \sqrt{25 + 4 + 0} = \sqrt{29}$$

$$\|B\| = \sqrt{(1)^2 + (2)^2 + (3)^2} = \sqrt{1 + 4 + 9} = \sqrt{14}$$

4. The last step is to plug these values into the formula and solve for θ:

$$\|AxB\| = \|A\|\|B\| \sin\theta$$

$$\sqrt{405} = \sqrt{29}\sqrt{14}\sin\theta$$

$$\frac{\sqrt{405}}{\sqrt{29(14)}} = \sin\theta$$

$$0.99876 \approx \sin\theta$$

$$\theta \approx \sin-1(0.99876)$$

$$\theta = 87.2°$$

Now let's add this function into our defined class for calculating the angle between two vectors:

```
float angleBetween3Dvectors(const 3Dvector &vec) const
{
    return (acos(dot3Dvector(vec) / (getMagnitude() *
    ➥ vec.getMagnitude())))
        * (180 / PI);
}
```

This section first defined the cross product. Remember that the cross product returns another 3D vector, and the dot product returns a scalar value. We also revisited the process of normalization when we calculated the surface normal. Also, the cross product can be used to calculate the angle between two vectors in almost the same way as the dot product. Now that we've discussed both types of "vector multiplication," you'll see them in action in C++ code in the next section.

Self-Assessment

1. Find A × B for vectors A = [2 –3 5] and B = [–1 0 4].

2. Find the surface normal for vectors A and B in question 1.

3. Find the angle between vectors A and B using the cross product you found in question 1.

Visualization Experience

On the CD-ROM you will find a demo named Matrix Vortex. Here's a brief description from the programmer, Kaveh Kahrizi:

> *The Matrix Vortex is designed to make you familiar with the various matrix and vector operations in a visually stimulating setting. All the math code resides in the* MatCalc *class, which is in* MatCalc.cpp *and* MatCalc.h. *The minimum system requirements for the program are a 700MHz processor, a graphics card with 8MB of memory, and 64MB of RAM. The interface is fairly intuitive and can be navigated with the left mouse button. You enter input using the keyboard; the Backspace key corrects mistakes. When you enter a matrix or vector, Tab and Shift-Tab may be used to move through the squares. Esc quits the program.*

The Matrix Vortex performs all the vector operations discussed in this chapter. Run the demo by double-clicking Mat_Calc.exe. Various vector and matrix sizes appear on the left side of the screen. Ignore the matrix selections for now. You'll use them in the next chapter.

Start with 3D vector addition. Click "3 × 1 vector." Plug in the values 12, 3, and –5, using the Tab key between entries. When you click Enter, the vector $\begin{bmatrix} 12 \\ 3 \\ -5 \end{bmatrix}$ should appear at the top of the screen. Click the operation you want to use— in this case, Addition. Click the size vector you want to add to the first vector. Notice that only the 3 × 1 choice is available. That's because you can only add vectors that are the same size. Click "3 × 1 vector" and enter the values –2, 0, and 4 for the vector, again using the Tab key between entries. When you click Enter, the second vector should appear at the top of the screen. Check to see that the values you entered are correct, and then click Solve. The vector $\begin{bmatrix} 10 \\ 3 \\ -1 \end{bmatrix}$ should appear at the bottom of the screen. When you're ready to try another vector operation, click Clear to start over.

Try going back through all the self-assessment questions and using the Matrix Vortex to check your answers. You might want to make up a few problems of your own. Do them by hand first and then use the Matrix Vortex to check yourself.

Self-Assessment Solutions

Vector Versus Scalar

1. A scalar is just a plain old number, or a magnitude only. A vector has both magnitude and direction.

2. Vector

3. Scalar

4. +60 feet

5. −60 feet

6. +130 pixels

7. 470 pixels

8. 0

Polar Coordinates Versus Components

1. $A = 17.68\hat{i} + 17.68\hat{j}$

2. $B = 13$ units @ $22.6°$

3. $C = 100\hat{i} + 173.21\hat{j}$

4. $D = 10$ units @ $36.9°$

Vector Addition and Subtraction

1. $A = 3.5\hat{i} + 19.7\hat{j}$

2. $B = 10$ units @ $53.1°$

3. $A + B = 9.5\hat{i} + 27.7\hat{j}$

4. $A - B = -2.5\hat{i} + 11.7\hat{j}$

5. $C + D = 13\hat{i} + 5\hat{j}$

6. $F + G = -3\hat{i} - \hat{j} + 5\hat{k}$

7. $F - G = 7\hat{i} - 7\hat{j} - 7\hat{k}$

Scalar Multiplication

1. Magnitude only

2. $(-1/3)A = -4$m/s @ $43°$

3. $6B = 18\hat{i} - 6\hat{j}$

4. $\hat{C} = \left[\dfrac{24}{26} \quad \dfrac{10}{26}\right] = \left[\dfrac{12}{13} \quad \dfrac{5}{13}\right]$

5. $\hat{D} = \left[\dfrac{0}{25} \quad \dfrac{7}{25} \quad \dfrac{24}{25}\right]$

Dot Product

1. 0

2. 7

3. Yes

4. $74.81°$

5. No

Cross Product

1. $[-12 \ -13 \ -3]$

2. $\left[\dfrac{-12}{17.94} \quad \dfrac{-13}{17.94} \quad \dfrac{-3}{17.94}\right] \approx [-0.67 \ -0.72 \ -0.17]$

3. $44.9°$

Chapter 5

Matrix Operations

KEY TOPICS

- Equal Matrices
- Matrix Addition and Subtraction
- Scalar Multiplication
- Matrix Multiplication
- Transpose
- Visualization Experience

The preceding chapter defined all the possible mathematical operations for vectors. This chapter defines a matrix and then revisits all those operations in terms of matrices. You'll find in Chapter 6, "Transformations," that matrices can be used to move 2D objects around on the screen and manipulate 3D objects within the world coordinate system. Before you can use matrices, we have to address how they operate. If you're comfortable with vector operations, that will serve as a helpful foundation for learning matrix operations.

Equal Matrices

Matrices can be used to organize a set of numbers in rows and columns in your game. You might be familiar with the term **array**, which is a grid-like system for organizing any type of information (numbers, variables, text, even arrays). A **matrix** is just an array that is limited to storing numbers. We discussed an example of a matrix in the preceding chapter. In some places we used a single-row matrix to represent a vector. A matrix can have as many rows or columns as you need. We used a single row for one vector. You could also use a matrix with many rows to store all the vertices of an object in your game. In that case, each row would represent an individual point. You, as the programmer, can give any meaning you like to each row and column. We'll discuss more applications in Chapter 6, but we must first look at all the mathematical operations again in terms of matrices.

On paper, it's important to always use brackets ([]) around each matrix. If you get lazy and use straight lines, that indicates something completely different, so make sure it's brackets. Within the brackets you arrange numbers in a grid of rows and columns. Each number is called an **entry**, and each entry is denoted by its row and column location. Look at matrix A in Figure 5.1.

$$A = \begin{bmatrix} 1 & 2 & 3 \\ 4 & 5 & 6 \\ 7 & 8 & 9 \end{bmatrix}$$

Figure 5.1 Matrix A.

If you needed to access the 3, you would ask the computer to get the number located in row 0, column 2. In C++, rows and columns start at 0, not 1. Figure 5.2 shows the location of each entry.

$$A = \begin{bmatrix} a_{00} & a_{01} & a_{02} \\ a_{10} & a_{11} & a_{12} \\ a_{20} & a_{21} & a_{22} \end{bmatrix}$$

Figure 5.2 Entry locations.

To create code to manipulate matrices, there are several things to consider. Does your application require fixed size or resizable matrices for calculation? If you choose to take the former perspective, there are certain ways that you can organize matrix definitions for ease of use rather than unneeded flexibility. Here is an example of a fixed sized matrix:

```
typedef struct
  {
    float x[3][3];
  } Matrix3X3;
```

If you wanted to access the 3 in matrix A using this method, it would look like this:

```
Matrix3X3 A;
A.index[0][2];
```

The row is always given first, and then the column.

The other contemplated option would involve creating a class that would allow the programmer to create matrices of any size. This is a much more elegant and reusable solution to the problem, but also can cause potential overhead when making large numbers of calculations.

If you decide to create a matrix class, you'll then need to decide how the matrix is to be represented within the class. Will it hold pointers to floats? Will you use the Standard Template Library to make a vector of vectors? A Linked List? Any one of these types will work, but each one has its own expectations regarding the implementation. A fully implemented matrix class will also have overloaded operators that will allow for easy use of the math operations which are defined for matrices as well as for ease of access to the matrix data.

Another thing to consider regarding game development is the fact that most graphics APIs like DirectX and OpenGL already contain their own matrix types that are used when programming graphics. That doesn't mean that a good programmer can get by without understanding matrix math. Because the focus in this book is on the mathematics, our discussion will stick with the more straightforward matrix presented in the first example. When evaluating a solution, always try to find shortcuts that can be used to speed up the process. The example code in this chapter emphasizes understanding over speed, so don't settle for the examples as anything more than a starting point. All matrix examples in this chapter as well as in Chapter 6 will use the fixed defined matrix types. Refer to the accompanying programs to see the complete list of matrix definitions that are used. Most of them can be distilled from the type name.

Example 5.1: Defining Matrices

What are the dimensions of matrix B, and how would you locate the entry that has a value of 5?

Solution

1. Look at matrix B in Figure 5.3. It has two rows and three columns, so its dimensions are 2×3.

$$B = \begin{bmatrix} -1 & 4 & -3 \\ 5 & 0 & -2 \end{bmatrix}$$

Figure 5.3   Matrix B.

2. Look for the 5. It's in the second row and first column, but remember that rows and columns are numbered starting with 0. This means that the 5 is in row 1, column 0.

For two matrices of the same dimensions, entries in the same row and column location are called **corresponding entries**. Two matrices are equal if and only if they have the same dimensions *and* all their corresponding entries are equal. If two matrices have different dimensions, they can never be equal. Also, if two matrices have the same dimensions, and all the corresponding entries are equal except one, they are not equal.

Equal Matrices

Two matrices are equal if

- Both matrices have equal dimensions.
- *All* corresponding entries are equal.

Example 5.2: Equal Matrices?

In Figure 5.4, are matrices C and D equal?

$$C = \begin{bmatrix} 1 & 2 & 3 \\ 4 & 5 & 6 \end{bmatrix} \qquad D = \begin{bmatrix} 1 & 2 & 3 \\ 4 & 5 & 6 \\ 7 & 8 & 9 \end{bmatrix}$$

Figure 5.4   Matrices C and D.

Solution

1. The first thing you need to check is the dimensions of each matrix. Matrix C is a 2×3 matrix, and D is a 3×3 matrix.

2. Because the dimensions are not the same, these two matrices cannot be equal. Even though some of the corresponding entries are equal, the matrices must also be the same size.

Example 5.3: Equal Matrices?

In Figure 5.5, are matrices F and G equal?

$$F = \begin{bmatrix} 1 & 2 & 3 \\ 4 & 5 & 6 \\ 0 & 8 & 9 \end{bmatrix} \qquad G = \begin{bmatrix} 1 & 2 & 3 \\ 4 & 5 & 6 \\ 7 & 8 & 9 \end{bmatrix}$$

Figure 5.5 Matrices F and G.

Solution

1. The first thing you need to check is the dimensions of each matrix. Matrix F is a 3×3 matrix, and G is a 3×3 matrix. This is a good sign.

2. Now you must check corresponding entries. Most of them are equal. However, look at the entries in row 2, column 0. Because they are not equal, matrices F and G are not equal.

How can we test equality of matrices using code? Most accesses to matrix will center on the use of for loops. The for loops will be sure to step through each index, performing the needed operations. This method is fundamental to working with all advanced matrix math, so make sure that it becomes ingrained.

Here is an example of a way to test two 3×3 matrices for equality:

```
bool areMatricesEqual(Matrix3X3 a, Matrix3X3 b)
    {
        int errorFlag = 0;
        for(int i = 0;i<3;i++)
          {
            for(int j=0;j<3;j++)
              {
                if((a.index[i][j]) != (b.index[i][j]))
                errorFlag = 1;
```

```
        }
      }
    //test for an error in equality.
    if(errorFlag == 1)
        return false;
    else
        return true;
}
```

This function will access each location in the first matrix and compare it against the second. Should an error be found, the errorFlag is set and will cause the function to return false. Check the Chapter 5 programming examples to see this equality test in action. Can you think of a way to do this faster? (Hint: If any entry is found to be wrong the matrices will be considered not equal.)

This section began with a discussion of what matrices are and how to describe them. After we established some standards for working with matrices, we discussed checking for equality. Now that you have a working vocabulary for matrices, the next section moves to adding and subtracting matrices.

Self-Assessment

1. What are the dimensions of matrix H, shown in Figure 5.6?

$$H = \begin{bmatrix} 1 \\ 2 \\ 3 \end{bmatrix}$$

Figure 5.6   Matrix H.

2. How would you describe the entry in matrix H (see Figure 5.6) that has a 2 in it?

3. What are the dimensions of matrix J, shown in Figure 5.7?

$$J = \begin{bmatrix} 3 & 5 & 15 & -2 & 0 \\ 0 & -3 & 1 & 8 & 2 \\ -1 & 2 & 12 & 4 & 7 \\ 10 & 8 & -5 & 0 & -5 \end{bmatrix}$$

Figure 5.7   Matrix J.

4. In Figure 5.7, what number is stored in row 2, column 3 of matrix J?

5. In Figure 5.8, are matrices K and L equal?

$$K = \begin{bmatrix} 1 & 2 & 0 & 2 \\ 0 & 1 & -5 & 4 \\ 9 & 0 & 3 & -6 \\ 2 & -3 & 1 & 4 \end{bmatrix} \quad L = \begin{bmatrix} 1 & 2 & 0 \\ 0 & 1 & -5 \\ 9 & 0 & 3 \end{bmatrix}$$

Figure 5.8   Matrices K and L.

6. In Figure 5.9, are matrices M and N equal?

$$M = \begin{bmatrix} 2 & -3 \\ 0 & 1 \\ -1 & 5 \end{bmatrix} \quad N = \begin{bmatrix} 2 & -3 \\ 0 & 6 \\ -1 & 5 \end{bmatrix}$$

Figure 5.9   Matrices M and N.

Matrix Addition and Subtraction

Now that we've discussed checking for equal matrices, addition and subtraction will follow quite naturally. The preceding section said that corresponding entries are positioned in the same row and column location, and if two matrices are the same size with equal corresponding entries, they must be equal. For you to add matrices, they must also have the same dimensions. You just add corresponding entries.

Adding Matrices
For two matrices of the same size, add the corresponding entries.

> **NOTE**
>
> Always remember that two matrices must have the same dimensions for you to add them (just like equal matrices).
>
> Also, some math texts refer to a matrix's dimensions as its **order**, so don't be thrown if you see that term used.

Example 5.4: Adding Matrices

Find A + B for matrices A and B in Figure 5.10.

$$A = \begin{bmatrix} 1 & 4 & 7 \\ 2 & 5 & 8 \\ 3 & 6 & 9 \end{bmatrix} \qquad B = \begin{bmatrix} -3 & 9 & 4 \\ 0 & 1 & -1 \\ 5 & -2 & 0 \end{bmatrix}$$

Figure 5.10   Adding matrices A and B.

Solution

1. Always make sure that both matrices are the same size before you attempt to add them. In this case, A and B are both 3×3, so you can add them together.

2. Add all the corresponding entries. Add the two entries in row 0, column 0, which means that $1 + (-3) = -2$, and so forth.

Figure 5.11 shows the end result of adding all the corresponding entries.

Here is a sample function that shows how to add matrices in code:

```
Matrix3X3 addMatrices(Matrix3X3 a, Matrix3X3 b)
    {
       Matrix3X3 temp;
          for(int i = 0;i<3;i++){
             for(int j=0;j<3;j++){
```

```
            temp.index[i][j] = (a.index[i][j] + b.index[i][j]);
            }
        }
    return temp;
    }
```

This function returns a Matrix3×3 that contains the result of the addition. We access each location adding the values contained and store them out into a separate matrix to return. Check the Chapter 5 programming examples to see an example of matrix addition using this function.

One quick tip! A 4×4 matrix has 16 locations to hold data. If you are adding two of them, you have to manually enter 32 individual data locations. This is not a bad thing unless you actually have work to do. It's useful to create quick random matrices based on a user-entered seed value to speed up the process to verify that your code is working. Here is a quick example:

```
//create a random matrix controlled by the seed
Matrix3X3 createRandom3X3Matrix(int seed)
    {
    Matrix3X3 temp;

        for(int i = 0;i<3;i++)
            {
            for(int j=0;j<3;j++)
                {
                    temp.index[i][j] = rand()%seed;
                }
            }
        return temp;
    }
```

Using random isn't really a great way to get truly random data, but that is a discussion for another time.

$$A + B = \begin{bmatrix} -2 & 13 & 11 \\ 2 & 6 & 7 \\ 8 & 4 & 9 \end{bmatrix}$$

Figure 5.11 Matrix A + B.

Subtracting matrices works exactly the same way; you just subtract corresponding entries.

Subtracting Matrices

For two matrices of the same size, subtract the corresponding entries.

NOTE
When subtracting matrices by hand, it's easy to lose track of plus and minus signs. You might want to consider adding the negative of the second matrix. Just flip the signs of each entry in the second matrix, and then add them.

Example 5.5: Subtracting Matrices

Find A − B for matrices A and B in Figure 5.10 (see Example 5.4).

Solution

1. Always make sure that both matrices are the same size before you attempt to subtract them. In this case, A and B are both 3×3, so you can subtract them.

2. Subtract all the corresponding entries. Subtract the two entries in row 0, column 0, which means that $1 - (-3) = 4$, and so forth.

3. Figure 5.12 shows the end result of subtracting all the corresponding entries.

$$A - B = \begin{bmatrix} 4 & -5 & 3 \\ 2 & 4 & 9 \\ -2 & 8 & 9 \end{bmatrix}$$

Figure 5.12 Matrix A – B.

Subtracting matrices in code is just like working with addition. Here is a function that adds two 4×4 matrices:

```
Matrix4X4 subtractMatrices(Matrix4X4 a, Matrix4X4 b)
{
        Matrix4X4 temp;

        for(int i = 0;i<4;i++)
            {
            for(int j=0;j<4;j++)
                {
                temp.index[i][j] = (a.index[i][j] - b.index[i][j]);
                }
            }
        return temp;
    }
```

The same principle applies here as with addition. Visit each index in the array and subtract the components from each other. The sample code for Chapter 5 contains a functional example using this code.

The most important thing to remember with adding and subtracting matrices is that they must be the same size. If you ask the computer to add or subtract matrices that are different sizes, it will most likely crash. The other place to be careful is when subtracting matrices; it's very easy to make a mistake when subtracting negative entries. Quite often, careless errors in subtracting matrices lead to the most frustrating bugs to locate, so take your time.

Self-Assessment

1. Find C + D for matrices C and D in Figure 5.13.

$$C = \begin{bmatrix} 2 & 3 \\ -1 & 0 \end{bmatrix} \quad D = \begin{bmatrix} -5 & 1 \\ 0 & 6 \end{bmatrix}$$

Figure 5.13   Matrices C and D.

2. Find C − D for matrices C and D in Figure 5.13.

3. Find F + G for matrices F and G in Figure 5.14.

$$F = \begin{bmatrix} -2 & 5 \\ 1 & 4 \\ 7 & 0 \end{bmatrix} \quad G = \begin{bmatrix} 0 & 3 \\ 8 & -1 \\ -2 & 6 \end{bmatrix}$$

Figure 5.14   Matrices F and G.

4. Find F − G for matrices F and G in Figure 5.14.

Scalar Multiplication

The preceding chapter discussed scalar multiplication with vectors. Remember, a vector is just a single row or single-column matrix, so scalar multiplication works the same way with matrices as it does with vectors. In fact, the preceding section had an example of scalar multiplication in the discussion of subtraction. At one point, there was a suggestion that rather than subtracting corresponding entries, you might want to add the negative of the second matrix. Flipping the sign of each entry is the same as multiplying the matrix by −1.

Scalar Multiplication

$$cA = \begin{bmatrix} ca_{00} & ca_{01} & \cdot & \cdot & \cdot \\ ca_{10} & \cdot & & & \\ \cdot & & \cdot & & \\ \cdot & & & \cdot & \\ \cdot & & & & ca_{nn} \end{bmatrix}$$

for any scalar value c and any size matrix A.

Just like flipping the sign of each entry, simply multiply each entry by the scalar value. This process works for any size matrix (not just square matrices) and any scalar (even fractions and negative numbers).

Example 5.6: Scalar * Matrix

Find $-5B$ for matrix $B = \begin{bmatrix} 3 & 6 & -4 \\ 0 & -1 & 2 \end{bmatrix}$.

Solution

Simply multiply each entry by -5:

$$-5B = \begin{bmatrix} -15 & -30 & 20 \\ 0 & 5 & -10 \end{bmatrix}$$

Processing scalar multiplication is the first step to doing some seriously cool work with matrices. This function shows how to multiply matrices by scalar values.

```
Matrix3X3 scalarMultiply(Matrix3X3 a, float scale)
    {
        Matrix3X3 temp;

        for(int i = 0;i<3;i++)
          {
          for(int j=0;j<3;j++)
            {
                temp.index[i][j] = (a.index[i][j] * scale);
            }
          }
        return temp;
    }
```

Again, we visit each position and multiply it through by the specified scale parameter. Hopefully, you are beginning to see a pattern with matrix usage. The sample programs for this chapter contain example programs that can perform scalar multiplication. Be sure to check them out!

Now that you can add and subtract matrices as well as multiply and divide by scalars, you can perform any combination of those operations to algebraically manipulate matrices in equations. The same rules of algebra and order of operations for scalar numbers apply to matrices as well. The only difference is that you're adding or multiplying matrices rather than single numbers.

Example 5.7: Equations with Matrices

Given matrices $A = \begin{bmatrix} 4 & 5 \\ 1 & -2 \end{bmatrix}$ and $B = \begin{bmatrix} 0 & -1 \\ -3 & 2 \end{bmatrix} = $, find matrix X if $2X = 3A - B$.

Solution

1. Look at the equation $2X = 3A - B$. If you need to solve for matrix X, you need to use the rules of algebra to get X by itself, which means multiplying both sides by $1/2$ (or dividing by 2):

   $2X = 3A - B$

   $1/2(2X) = 1/2(3A - B)$

   $X = 1/2(3A - B)$

2. The same order of operations you would use on numbers applies here as well. This means that you start inside the parentheses with the $3A - B$:

$$\overset{3A}{\begin{bmatrix} 12 & 15 \\ 3 & -6 \end{bmatrix}} + \overset{-B}{\begin{bmatrix} 0 & 1 \\ 3 & -2 \end{bmatrix}} = \overset{3A-B}{\begin{bmatrix} 12 & 16 \\ 6 & -8 \end{bmatrix}}$$

3. The last step in this case is to multiply each entry in matrix $(3A - B)$ by $1/2$ (or divide by 2):

$$\overset{\frac{1}{2}(3A-B)}{\begin{bmatrix} 6 & 8 \\ 3 & -4 \end{bmatrix}} = X$$

So far, we've discussed adding and subtracting matrices as well as multiplying and dividing matrices by scalar quantities. This lets you algebraically manipulate matrices in an equation just as you would plain old numbers and variables. The next natural question to ask is, "How do I multiply a matrix times a matrix?" That is precisely what the next section addresses.

Self-Assessment

1. If $A = \begin{bmatrix} -2 & 3 & 5 \\ 0 & 1 & -4 \\ 10 & 0 & -1 \end{bmatrix}$, find $-3A$.

2. If $B = \begin{bmatrix} 6 & -8 & -2 \\ 0 & 10 & -4 \\ 12 & 0 & -16 \end{bmatrix}$, find $1/2B$.

3. Using matrices A and B from questions 1 and 2, find matrix X if $-1/4X = 1/2B - 3A$.

Matrix Multiplication

The preceding section looked at multiplying a scalar and a matrix. The next logical step is to investigate the product of two matrices, or a matrix times another matrix. This process involves the dot product, so you might want to flip back to Chapter 4, "Vector Operations," for a quick review of the dot product before proceeding.

You can multiply matrices by taking a series of dot products. Keep in mind two important aspects of the dot product:

➤ The two vectors must have the same number of entries to take the dot product.

➤ The dot product returns a scalar quantity (a single number).

Let's start by looking at two 2×2 matrices. Matrices to be multiplied don't have to be square and don't have to be the same size, but there are restrictions, which we'll examine next. For now, I will tell you that you can multiply a 2×2 by a 2×2. Doing so gives you another 2×2.

Multiplying Two 2×2 Matrices

$$AB = \begin{bmatrix} (a_{00}b_{00} + a_{01}b_{10}) & (a_{00}b_{01} + a_{01}b_{11}) \\ (a_{10}b_{00} + a_{11}b_{10}) & (a_{10}b_{01} + a_{11}b_{11}) \end{bmatrix}$$

for any matrix $A = \begin{bmatrix} a_{00} & a_{01} \\ a_{10} & a_{11} \end{bmatrix}$ and $B = \begin{bmatrix} b_{00} & b_{01} \\ b_{10} & b_{11} \end{bmatrix}$.

This might look crazy at first glance, but take a closer look at the entry in row 0, column 0. Does it look familiar? It's the dot product of row 0 in A and column 0 in B.

Now look at the entry in row 0, column 1; it's the dot product of row 0 in A and column 1 in B. The same is true for the other two entries.

Each entry is determined by its location. The entry is a single number that you find using the dot product of the corresponding row in the first matrix and the corresponding column of the second matrix.

Example 5.8: Multiplying Two 2×2 Matrices

Given matrices $A = \begin{bmatrix} 4 & 5 \\ 1 & -2 \end{bmatrix}$ and $B = \begin{bmatrix} 0 & -1 \\ -3 & 2 \end{bmatrix}$, find matrix AB.

Solution

$$AB = \begin{bmatrix} (a_{00}b_{00} + a_{01}b_{10}) & (a_{00}b_{01} + a_{01}b_{11}) \\ (a_{10}b_{00} + a_{11}b_{10}) & (a_{10}b_{01} + a_{11}b_{11}) \end{bmatrix}$$

$$= \begin{bmatrix} 4(0) + 5(-3) & 4(-1) + 5(2) \\ 1(0) - 2(-3) & 1(-1) - 2(2) \end{bmatrix}$$

$$= \begin{bmatrix} (0 - 15) & (-4 + 10) \\ (0 + 6) & (-1 - 4) \end{bmatrix}$$

$$= \begin{bmatrix} -15 & 6 \\ 6 & -5 \end{bmatrix}$$

This example takes four separate dot products—one for each entry. Remember the first aspect of the dot product? For you to take a dot product, both vectors must have the same number of entries. This means that for a matrix multiplication to be defined, the number of columns in the first matrix must equal the number of rows in the second matrix. That's the only way to ensure that the number of entries in the rows of the first matrix matches the number of entries in the columns of the second matrix.

Is the Product Defined?

For matrix multiplication AB, the number of columns in A must equal the number of rows in B.

If you check, and the product is defined, the next step is to find the size of the answer so that you can go through and take the dot product for each entry. If the matrix multiplication is defined, you can find the size of the answer with this next rule.

The Size of the Product

If AB is defined, the size of matrix AB is the number of rows in A by the number of columns in B.

It's easy to mix up these two rules, but a visual method might help you keep them straight. If you write down the dimensions of each matrix, as shown in Figure 5.15, the two inside numbers must be equal.

$$AB = \begin{array}{c} A \\ \begin{bmatrix} 4 & 3 & -2 \\ -1 & 0 & 5 \end{bmatrix} \end{array} \begin{array}{c} B \\ \begin{bmatrix} 1 \\ 2 \\ 3 \end{bmatrix} \end{array}$$

$$2\text{x}\mathbf{3} \qquad \mathbf{3}\text{x}1$$

Figure 5.15 A visual trick for matrix multiplication.

If the two inside numbers are not equal, stop right there. The product is not defined. If they are equal, you can multiply the two matrices. The next step is to find the size of the answer. Conveniently, the two outside numbers give you the dimensions of the answer. In Figure 5.15 you can see that the two inside numbers are both 3, so the product is defined. The size of the product is 2x1, which was given by the two outside numbers. As soon as you know the size of the answer, the rest is just a series of dot products. In this case, the product has only two entries, so there are only two dot products to calculate. Figure 5.16 shows the final product.

$$AB = \begin{bmatrix} 4 & 3 & -2 \\ -1 & 0 & 5 \end{bmatrix} \begin{bmatrix} 1 \\ 2 \\ 3 \end{bmatrix} = \begin{bmatrix} 4(1)+3(2)-2(3) \\ -1(1)+0(2)+5(3) \end{bmatrix} = \begin{bmatrix} 4+6-6 \\ -1+0+15 \end{bmatrix} = \begin{bmatrix} 4 \\ 14 \end{bmatrix}$$

Figure 5.16   The product of matrices A and B.

Example 5.9: Multiplying Two Different-Sized Matrices

Using the two matrices shown in Figure 5.15, is the product BA defined?

Solution

1. Before you attempt to multiply two matrices, always check to see if the product is defined. To use the new visual trick, write down the dimensions of each matrix. This is done in Figure 5.17.

$$BA = \begin{bmatrix} 1 \\ 2 \\ 3 \end{bmatrix} \begin{bmatrix} 4 & 3 & -2 \\ -1 & 0 & 5 \end{bmatrix}$$

3x1   **2x3**

Figure 5.17   Product BA.

2. Check the two inside numbers. In this case, $2 \neq 1$, which means that the columns in B $\neq$ the rows in A, so the product is not defined. You can't calculate BA.

Remember that earlier you calculated AB; it was defined, and it returned a 2x1 matrix. However, when you flipped the order and tried to multiply B times A, it was not defined. This tells you that matrix multiplication is *not* commutative.

Matrix Multiplication Is Not Commutative

AB ≠ BA

for any size matrices A and B.

In some cases, when you flip the order, the product is still defined. However, you'll find that in most cases you get a completely different result. For example, let's look back at Example 5.8. When you multiplied A times B, you got the following product:

$$AB = \begin{bmatrix} -15 & 6 \\ 6 & -5 \end{bmatrix}$$

Notice that when you calculate BA, you get a very different result:

$$BA = \begin{bmatrix} 0 & -1 \\ -3 & 2 \end{bmatrix} \begin{bmatrix} 4 & 5 \\ 1 & -2 \end{bmatrix}$$

$$= \begin{bmatrix} 0(4) - 1(1) & 0(5) - 1(-2) \\ -3(4) + 2(1) & -3(5) + 2(-2) \end{bmatrix}$$

$$= \begin{bmatrix} 0 - 1 & 0 + 2 \\ -12 + 2 & -15 - 4 \end{bmatrix}$$

$$= \begin{bmatrix} -1 & 2 \\ -10 & -19 \end{bmatrix}$$

In this case, both AB and BA are defined, but the products are completely different.

Matrix multiplication is definitely more complicated than scalar multiplication. Just remember the three-step process:

1. Check to see if the product is defined (two inside numbers).

2. If product is defined, find its dimensions (two outside numbers).

3. Go through each entry one at a time. Based on the entry's location, take the dot product of the corresponding row in the first matrix and the column in the second matrix.

To get matrices multiplying in code, the same set of rules must apply. The product must be defined. It is the programmer's responsibility to make sure the product is defined before trying to multiply.

Here is a function that allows us to multiply two 3×3 matrices:

```
Matrix3X3 multiply3X3Matrices(Matrix3X3 a, Matrix3X3 b)
    {
        Matrix3X3 temp = createFixed3X3Matrix(0);

      for(int i = 0;i<3;i++)
          {
          for(int j=0;j<3;j++)
              {
              for(int k=0;k<3;k++)
                  {
                      temp.index[i][j] += (a.index[i][k] *
                      ➥b.index[k][j]);
                  }
              }
          }
      return temp;
    }
```

Before just accepting this function as a working example, you should make sure you can trace down the values that would be contained inside the matrices each step of the way. This triple `for` loop will allow us to make sure that each entry is process just like a dot product from the previous chapter. The accuracy of this function is critical when you are trying to limit bugs in calculations.

Multiplications are used in 3D games frequently to allow an object to rotate. Given that this happens often in 3D games, can you think of a faster way to process this multiplication?

This process is only slightly different when multiplying two different sized matrices:

```
Matrix3X1 multiplyMatrixNxM(Matrix3X3 a, Matrix3X1 b)
    {
        Matrix3X1 temp;
        temp.index[0] = 0.0f;
        temp.index[1] = 0.0f;
        temp.index[2] = 0.0f;

                for(int i=0;i<3;i++)
                {
                 for(int j=0;j<3;j++)
                 {
                  temp.index[i] += (a.index[i][j] * b.index[j]);
                 }
                }

        return temp;
    }
```

Here, we only need to visit one component of the 3×1 Matrix. Notice the step being taken to initialize the matrix. This step hasn't been listed in earlier code snips to save space, but remember to do this step. Initialize any temporary matrices that you plan to use, especially when working with multiplication. The provided sample code for this chapter contains useful examples of both sets of matrix multiplication in action.

One other really useful function that can be mentioned here is the printMatrix() function. It's a good idea to have a way to print out the information contained in the matrix. These are used throughout the sample code and are great for debugging. Here is an example of how to print out a matrix:

```
void printMatrix(Matrix4X4 a)
    {
        for(int i = 0;i<4;i++)
            {
            for(int j=0;j<4;j++)
                {
                float temp = a.index[i][j];
```

```
                    cout<<temp<<" ";
                }
            cout<<"\n";
        }
    }
```

This chapter uses generic matrices. Remember that you can attach meaning to each row and column, as you saw with the vectors. The next chapter attaches meaning to the rows and columns of the matrices so that you can use them to move objects around on the screen.

After you have written some basic matrix math programs using some of these methods, be sure to test the work that was done on paper through the new programs. Are the values the same? If not, which one is in error? Don't lose sight of the importance of working the solutions out on paper. In the inevitable situation where you are spending hours bug-hunting, you will need to go back to paper at one point or another to verify calculations. Don't rely completely on the machine for verification.

One key concept is that the computer executes algorithms to solve problems that we are already familiar with. It is important to understand the method before coding anything.

Before moving on to Chapter 6, make sure that you have reviewed the basic functions that are contained in the matrix library in the accompanying source code. That file will be used frequently in the next chapter.

Self-Assessment

For each of the following pairs of matrices, check to see if the product is defined. If it is, calculate the product.

1. $\begin{bmatrix} 3 & 7 \\ -2 & 0 \end{bmatrix}\begin{bmatrix} 0 & -5 \\ 1 & 4 \end{bmatrix}$

2. $\begin{bmatrix} 0 & -5 \\ 1 & 4 \end{bmatrix}\begin{bmatrix} 3 & 7 \\ -2 & 0 \end{bmatrix}$

3. $\begin{bmatrix} 1 \\ 2 \\ 0 \end{bmatrix} \begin{bmatrix} 4 & 0 \\ -1 & 3 \end{bmatrix}$

4. $\begin{bmatrix} 1 \\ 2 \\ 3 \end{bmatrix} \begin{bmatrix} 2 & -3 & 0 \\ 0 & 1 & -2 \\ -4 & 5 & 10 \end{bmatrix}$

5. $\begin{bmatrix} 2 & -3 & 0 \\ 0 & 1 & -2 \\ -4 & 5 & 10 \end{bmatrix} \begin{bmatrix} 1 \\ 2 \\ 3 \end{bmatrix}$

6. $\begin{bmatrix} 2 & 0 & -1 & 0 \\ 0 & 1 & 5 & 1 \\ -1 & 3 & -2 & 0 \end{bmatrix} \begin{bmatrix} 1 & 2 \\ 2 & 5 \\ 3 & -1 \\ 4 & 0 \end{bmatrix}$

Transpose

The last matrix operation you need for future chapters is the **transpose**. This operation is used in Chapter 6 when we discuss the differences between OpenGL and DirectX. The transpose is a simple yet powerful operation. So far, we've used the row and column location to designate a particular entry. The transpose operation simply swaps each entry's row and column. The transpose can be applied to any size matrix, but we'll look at a 3×3 first so that you can quickly spot the pattern.

Transpose for a 3×3 Matrix

If A = $\begin{bmatrix} a_{00} & a_{01} & a_{02} \\ a_{10} & a_{11} & a_{12} \\ a_{20} & a_{21} & a_{22} \end{bmatrix}$, $A^{T} = \begin{bmatrix} a_{00} & a_{10} & a_{20} \\ a_{01} & a_{11} & a_{21} \\ a_{02} & a_{12} & a_{22} \end{bmatrix}$.

NOTE
The ^{T} superscript is the symbol for transpose, so the transpose of matrix A is written as A^{T}.

Example 5.10: Transpose of a 3×3 Matrix

If B = $\begin{bmatrix} 1 & 4 & 7 \\ 2 & 5 & 8 \\ 3 & 6 & 9 \end{bmatrix}$, find B^T.

Solution

1. The transpose operation flips each entry's row and column, so let's go through them one at a time. The 1 is in row 0, column 0, so when you flip the row and column, it stays the same. The 2, however, is in row 1, column 0, so the transpose sends it to row 0, column 1. The 3 goes from row 2, column 0 to row 0, column 2.

2. If you go through each entry and swap (transpose) the row and column, you'll find that everything flips about the diagonal, where the row is equal to the column. You should end up with a matrix that looks like this:

$B^T = \begin{bmatrix} 1 & 2 & 3 \\ 4 & 5 & 6 \\ 7 & 8 & 9 \end{bmatrix}$

Notice that the transpose of a 3×3 matrix is another 3×3 matrix. If the original matrix is not square, the transpose changes the size, because the rows and columns are swapped. That means that a 3×1 matrix becomes a 1×3. This happens anytime you take the transpose of a vector.

Example 5.11: Transpose of a Vector

If C = $\begin{bmatrix} 4 \\ 5 \\ 6 \end{bmatrix}$, find C^T.

Solution

1. The transpose operation flips each entry's row and column, so let's go through them one at a time. The 4 is in row 0, column 0, so when you flip the row and column, it stays the same. The 5, however, is in row 1, column 0, so the transpose sends it to row 0, column 1. The 6 goes from row 2, column 0 to row 0, column 2.

2. This process leaves you with a single-row vector:

$$B^T = \begin{bmatrix} 4 & 5 & 6 \end{bmatrix}$$

Again, the transpose can be applied to any size matrix. Just remember that the dimensions swap as well as each entry's row and column location.

Transpose

For any size matrix A, each entry a_{mn} moves to a_{nm} in A^T.

Example 5.12: Transpose of a Matrix

If $D = \begin{bmatrix} 2 & -1 & 3 & 8 \\ 0 & 5 & 1 & 4 \end{bmatrix}$, find D^T.

Solution

1. The transpose operation flips each entry's row and column, so let's go through them one at a time. The 2 is in row 0, column 0, so when you flip the row and column, it stays the same. The 0, however, is in row 1, column 0, so the transpose sends it to row 0, column 1. Notice that the 0 and the −1 end up swapping positions.

2. You could continue to flip each entry one at a time. However, you might have noticed that the first row becomes the first column and the second row becomes the second column.

3. This process results in the following matrix:

$$D^T = \begin{bmatrix} 2 & 0 \\ -1 & 5 \\ 3 & 1 \\ 8 & 4 \end{bmatrix}$$

This final operation is deceptively simple. Let's see how we can accomplish this in code to transpose a 4×4 matrix:

```
Matrix4X4 transpose4X4Matrix(Matrix4X4 a)
    {
        Matrix4X4 temp;
```

```
for(int i = 0;i<4;i++)
  {
    for(int j=0;j<4;j++)
      {
        temp.index[i][j] = a.index[j][i];
      }
  }
return temp;
}
```

As soon as you have discovered an organized way to swap rows and columns, it can be calculated quickly. You might want to experiment with writing a function that calculates the transpose; all you need is a systematic method of swapping each entry's row and column. Again, we will revisit this operation in the next chapter, and you'll see just how useful it can be in programming.

Self-Assessment

For each of the following pairs of matrices, check to see if the product is defined. If it is, calculate the product.

1. $\begin{bmatrix} 7 & 13 \\ 0 & 10 \end{bmatrix}$

2. $\begin{bmatrix} 0 & -5 \\ 1 & 4 \end{bmatrix}$

3. $\begin{bmatrix} 1 \\ 2 \\ 0 \end{bmatrix}$

4. $\begin{bmatrix} 2 & -3 & 0 \\ 0 & 1 & -2 \\ -4 & 5 & 10 \end{bmatrix}$

5. $\begin{bmatrix} 2 & 0 & -1 & 0 \\ 0 & 1 & 5 & 1 \\ -1 & 3 & -2 & 0 \end{bmatrix}$

6. $\begin{bmatrix} 1 & 2 \\ 2 & 5 \\ 3 & -1 \\ 4 & 0 \end{bmatrix}$

Visualization Experience

On the CD-ROM, you will find a demo named Matrix Vortex. Here's a brief description from the programmer, Kaveh Kahrizi:

> *The Matrix Vortex is designed to make you familiar with the various matrix and vector operations in a visually stimulating setting. All the math code resides in the* `MatCalc` *class, which is in* `MatCalc.cpp` *and* `MatCalc.h`*. The minimum system requirements for the program are a 700MHz processor, a graphics card with 8MB of memory, and 64MB of RAM. The interface is fairly intuitive and can be navigated with the left mouse button. You enter input using the keyboard; the Backspace key corrects mistakes. When you enter a matrix or vector, Tab and Shift-Tab may be used to move through the squares. Esc quits the program.*

The Matrix Vortex performs all the matrix operations discussed in this chapter. Go ahead and run the demo by double-clicking Mat_Calc.exe. Various vector and matrix sizes appear on the left side of the screen.

Start with a 3×3 times a 3×1. Click "3×3 matrix." Remember that the order in which you multiply the matrices is important. In this case, you must start with the 3×3 for the multiplication to be defined. Now plug in the following values, using the Tab key between entries:

$$\begin{bmatrix} 1 & 0 & 5 \\ 0 & 1 & 6 \\ 0 & 0 & 1 \end{bmatrix}$$

When you click Enter, the matrix should appear at the top of the screen.

Click the operation you want to use—in this case, Multiplication. Click the size of matrix you want to multiply by the first matrix. This time, select "3×1 vector." Notice that not all the choices are available. You can select only the ones that are defined for this particular matrix multiplication. Enter the following values, again using the Tab key between entries:

$$\begin{bmatrix} 12 \\ 3 \\ 1 \end{bmatrix}$$

When you click Enter, the second matrix should appear at the top of the screen. Check to see that the values you entered are correct, and then click Solve. The vector

$$\begin{bmatrix} 17 \\ 9 \\ -1 \end{bmatrix}$$

should appear at the bottom of the screen. When you're ready to try another matrix operation, click Clear to start over.

Try going back through all the self-assessment questions and using the Matrix Vortex to check your answers. You might want to make up a few problems of your own. Do them by hand first, and then use the Matrix Vortex to check yourself.

Self-Assessment Solutions

Equal Matrices

1. 3×1

2. The entry in row 1, column 0

3. 4×5

4. 4

5. No

6. No

Matrix Addition and Subtraction

1. $C + D = \begin{bmatrix} -3 & 4 \\ -1 & 6 \end{bmatrix}$

2. $C - D = \begin{bmatrix} 7 & 2 \\ -1 & -6 \end{bmatrix}$

3. $F + G = \begin{bmatrix} -2 & 8 \\ 9 & 3 \\ 5 & 6 \end{bmatrix}$

4. $F - G = \begin{bmatrix} -2 & 2 \\ -7 & 5 \\ 9 & -6 \end{bmatrix}$

Scalar Multiplication

1. $-3A = \begin{bmatrix} 6 & -9 & -15 \\ 0 & -3 & 12 \\ -30 & 0 & 3 \end{bmatrix}$

2. $1/2B = \begin{bmatrix} 3 & -4 & -1 \\ 0 & 5 & -2 \\ 6 & 0 & -8 \end{bmatrix}$

3. $X = \begin{bmatrix} -36 & 52 & 64 \\ 0 & -8 & -40 \\ 96 & 0 & 20 \end{bmatrix}$

Matrix Multiplication

1. $\begin{bmatrix} 7 & 13 \\ 0 & 10 \end{bmatrix}$

2. $\begin{bmatrix} 10 & 0 \\ -5 & 7 \end{bmatrix}$

3. Undefined

4. Undefined

5. $\begin{bmatrix} -4 \\ -4 \\ 36 \end{bmatrix}$

6. $\begin{bmatrix} -1 & 5 \\ 21 & 0 \\ -1 & 15 \end{bmatrix}$

Transpose

1. $\begin{bmatrix} 7 & 0 \\ 13 & 10 \end{bmatrix}$

2. $\begin{bmatrix} 0 & 1 \\ -5 & 4 \end{bmatrix}$

3. $\begin{bmatrix} 1 & 2 & 0 \end{bmatrix}$

4. $\begin{bmatrix} 2 & 0 & -4 \\ -3 & 1 & 5 \\ 0 & -2 & 10 \end{bmatrix}$

5. $\begin{bmatrix} 2 & 0 & -1 \\ 0 & 1 & 3 \\ -1 & 5 & -2 \\ 0 & 1 & 0 \end{bmatrix}$

6. $\begin{bmatrix} 1 & 2 & 3 & 4 \\ 2 & 5 & -1 & 0 \end{bmatrix}$

Chapter 6

Transformations

KEY TOPICS

- Translation
- Scaling
- Rotation
- Concatenation
- Visualization Experience

After all the discussion of how to work with matrices, you're finally ready to look at one of the most common uses of matrices in game programming: affine transformations. **Transformations** is really just a fancy word for moving objects around in your world. It encompasses movement such as forward and backward or up and down motion, scaling objects larger or smaller, and even rotating objects. The term **affine** indicates that the essential shape of the object being moved is preserved. This chapter first looks at how to apply the transformation in two dimensions, and then it extends the process to 3D. In the end, you'll be able to set up combos that control any type of motion you can think of, all with a single matrix. If at any point you find yourself struggling with the mathematical operations, flip back to Chapter 5, "Matrix Operations," for a quick review.

Translation

Let's start with the simple motion of moving objects left, right, up, and down on a flat 2D screen. The fancy name for moving objects in these directions is **translation**. Objects can be translated using both matrix addition and matrix multiplication. If all you plan to do is translate an object, you should definitely use matrix addition, because it is by far faster and easier. However, if you plan to scale and/or rotate your object in the same frame, you have to perform the translation using matrix multiplication instead. Let's tackle the addition method first.

Most people already have an intuitive feel for translation using addition after working with the Cartesian coordinate system. Suppose you had an object at point P(1,2) and you wanted to move it three units to the right and one unit up. What would you do? Well, if you add 3 to the x-coordinate and 1 to the y-coordinate, the object would end up three units to the right and one unit up. That gives you a new location of (1+3,2+1) = (4,3). You can indicate the new position with P', so your object would end up at point P'(4,3) after translating three to the right and one up.

That approach is simple if you're translating only one point or even just a few points. However, most models in games are defined by hundreds, if not thousands, of points, so you need a more systematic way of adding 3 to every x and 1 to every y. You could set up a loop and perform the following on each point:

$x'=x+3$

$y'=y+1$

This can be rewritten with matrices:

$$\begin{bmatrix} x' \\ y' \end{bmatrix} = \begin{bmatrix} x \\ y \end{bmatrix} + \begin{bmatrix} 3 \\ 1 \end{bmatrix}$$

Remember that when adding matrices you just add corresponding entries, so the matrix format is really the same as the two equations above it. The matrices are more efficient for organizing values in code, so you can set up a loop that inputs the original location and returns the new location of each vertex.

You might not always know the numeric values of the change in x and the change in y when you set up the code. You might have to wait for user input to determine how far you want the object to move. That's fine. Just set up a generic matrix equation and then plug in the values as soon as they become available.

Earlier in this book, we used the delta symbol (Δ) for "change in," but there's no delta key on the keyboard, so most programmers use *dx* for change in x and *dy* for change in y. This leads to the general form for translation by addition.

2D Translation by Addition

$$\begin{bmatrix} x' \\ y' \end{bmatrix} = \begin{bmatrix} x \\ y \end{bmatrix} + \begin{bmatrix} dx \\ dy \end{bmatrix}$$

NOTE

The values for *dx* and *dy* are not restricted to positive numbers. If *dx* is negative, it just indicates to the left instead of to the right, and a negative *dy* indicates down rather than up.

Example 6.1: 2D Translation by Addition

Set up a general matrix equation that will move 2D objects 50 pixels to the right and 100 pixels down on the computer screen, and then use it to move a triangle with vertices at A(20,30), B(0,200), and C(300,400).

Solution

1. Set up the matrix equation. To move 50 pixels to the right and 100 pixels down, *dx* must be 50, and *dy* must be −100 (negative because it's down):

   $$\begin{bmatrix} x' \\ y' \end{bmatrix} = \begin{bmatrix} x \\ y \end{bmatrix} + \begin{bmatrix} 50 \\ -100 \end{bmatrix}$$

2. Now you have to plug in each old point and add the matrices to see where it moved. First, plug in the old location of vertex A(20,30):

   $$\begin{bmatrix} x' \\ y' \end{bmatrix} = \begin{bmatrix} 20 \\ 30 \end{bmatrix} + \begin{bmatrix} 50 \\ -100 \end{bmatrix} = \begin{bmatrix} 70 \\ -70 \end{bmatrix}$$

   So A' is the point (70,−70).

3. If you repeat step 2 with the old locations of B and C, you get the new locations B'(50,100) and C'(350,300). By moving all three vertices, you have moved the whole triangle.

4. Figure 6.1 shows the old location with dashed lines and the new location with solid lines.

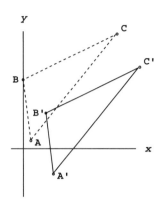

Figure 6.1   Triangle ABC before and after translation.

In Example 6.1 you translated a simple triangle with three vertices. Keep in mind, however, that most models are defined by many more vertices than that. Most polygonal models are covered by hundreds (or thousands) of triangles, but if you can translate one triangle, you can translate many.

You can also translate objects in 3D simply by adding one more entry to each matrix for the z-coordinate.

3D Translation by Addition

$$\begin{bmatrix} x' \\ y' \\ z' \end{bmatrix} = \begin{bmatrix} x \\ y \\ z \end{bmatrix} + \begin{bmatrix} dx \\ dy \\ dz \end{bmatrix}$$

Example 6.2: 3D Translation by Addition

Set up a general matrix equation that will move 3D objects 100 pixels to the left, 200 pixels up, and 50 pixels back (behind the screen), and then use it to move a triangle with vertices at A(40,0,100), B(0,350,200), and C(−100,200,−10).

Solution

1. Set up the matrix equation. To move 100 pixels to the left, 200 pixels up, and 50 pixels back, $dx = -100$, $dy = 200$, and $dz = -50$. (If you can't remember which direction is positive or negative, you can always flip back to Chapter 1, "Points and Lines.")

$$\begin{bmatrix} x' \\ y' \\ z' \end{bmatrix} = \begin{bmatrix} x \\ y \\ z \end{bmatrix} + \begin{bmatrix} -100 \\ 200 \\ -50 \end{bmatrix}$$

2. Now you have to plug in each old point and add the matrices to see where it moved. First, plug in the old location of vertex A(40,0,100):

$$\begin{bmatrix} x' \\ y' \\ z' \end{bmatrix} = \begin{bmatrix} 40 \\ 0 \\ 100 \end{bmatrix} + \begin{bmatrix} -100 \\ 200 \\ -50 \end{bmatrix} = \begin{bmatrix} -60 \\ 200 \\ 50 \end{bmatrix}$$

So A' is the point (-60,200,50).

3. If you repeat step 2 with the old locations of B and C, you get the new locations B'(-100,550,150) and C'(-200,400,-60). By moving all three vertices, you have moved the whole triangle.

Translation by addition is pretty straightforward. Here is an example of how to translate a 3D point using addition:

```
Matrix3X1 translate3DByAddition(Matrix3X1 start, Matrix3X1 trans)
    {
        Matrix3X1 temp;
        temp = addMatrices(start,trans);
        return temp;
    }
```

It is much more common to translate 3D points in games using matrices than it is 2D values. Generally speaking, a basic unit of a game that might represent the player will contain an x and y value. For example, if the player needs to have a position set 10 units to the right, one way to do this is to get away from the matrix notation:

```
Player.setX(Player.getX()+10);
```

If you are feeling comfortable with the matrix notation, feel free to keep it. It will actually be more beneficial when the emphasis comes to working with 3D points as well as rotation in 2D.

Again, if all you need to do is translate an object, use matrix addition. However, if you plan to also scale or rotate the object, you need to use matrix multiplication. You can set up a matrix equation in much the same way. Then, all you need to do is plug in each original location one at a time and multiply the matrices to find the new location.

2D Translation by Multiplication

$$\begin{vmatrix} x' \\ y' \\ 1 \end{vmatrix} = \begin{vmatrix} 1 & 0 & dx \\ 0 & 1 & dy \\ 0 & 0 & 1 \end{vmatrix} \begin{vmatrix} x \\ y \\ 1 \end{vmatrix}$$

where dx = change in x and dy = change in y.

Notice that the old point and the new point have an extra 1 on the end. It's not actually part of the point, but it needs to tag along for the matrix math to work. You might want to research "homogeneous coordinates" for further explanation.

Also, take note of the order in which the matrices are multiplied. If the order were switched (old point * translation matrix), the product would no longer be defined, and the program would crash. Remember from Chapter 5, "Matrix Operations," that the order in which you multiply matrices is critical. The number of columns in the first matrix must equal the number of rows in the second matrix. In this case, you must set it up to be a 3×3 times a 3×1, not the other way around.

Make sure that the matrix equation is always set up in that order—translation matrix * old point.

Let's repeat Example 6.1 using matrix multiplication and see if we get the same results.

Example 6.3: 2D Translation by Multiplication

Set up a general matrix equation (using matrix multiplication) that will move 2D objects 50 pixels to the right and 100 pixels down on the computer screen, and then use it to move a triangle with vertices at A(20,30), B(0,200), and C(300,400).

Solution

1. Set up the matrix equation. To move 50 pixels to the right and 100 pixels down, dx must be 50, and dy must be -100 (negative because it's down):

$$\begin{bmatrix} x' \\ y' \\ 1 \end{bmatrix} = \begin{bmatrix} 1 & 0 & 50 \\ 0 & 1 & -100 \\ 0 & 0 & 1 \end{bmatrix} \begin{bmatrix} x \\ y \\ 1 \end{bmatrix}$$

2. Now you have to plug in each old point and multiply the matrices to see where it moved. First, plug in the old location of vertex A(20,30):

$$\begin{bmatrix} x' \\ y' \\ 1 \end{bmatrix} = \begin{bmatrix} 1 & 0 & 50 \\ 0 & 1 & -100 \\ 0 & 0 & 1 \end{bmatrix} \begin{bmatrix} 20 \\ 30 \\ 1 \end{bmatrix} = \begin{bmatrix} 1(20) + 0(30) + 50(1) \\ 0(20) + 1(30) - 100(1) \\ 0(20) + 0(30) + 1(1) \end{bmatrix} = \begin{bmatrix} 70 \\ -70 \\ 1 \end{bmatrix}$$

So A' is the point (70,–70), which is exactly what you found before.

3. If you repeat step 2 with the old locations of B and C, you get the new locations B'(50,100) and C'(350,300), just like last time. By moving all three vertices, you have moved the whole triangle. Notice that it ends up moving to the same place, as it did in Example 6.1.

If you look closely at the matrix multiplication, you can see the important role that the extra 1 plays. Notice the dot product that you calculated for x'. You kept the old x (multiply by 1), ignored the old y (multiply by 0), and added dx (multiply by 1). Then, to calculate y', you ignored the old x, kept the old y, and added dy. You needed that extra 1 to add the dx and dy.

The same thing happens when you translate 3D objects using matrix multiplication.

Let's take a quick look at one way to handle this in code. Here is a function that will multiply a 2D point using matrix multiplication:

```
Matrix3X1 translate2DByMultiplication(Matrix3X1 start,float dx,
➥float dy)
    {
        Matrix3X3 temp;
        Matrix3X1 result;

        //Zero out the matrix.
        temp = createFixed3X3Matrix(0);

        //setup the 3x3 for multiplication;
        temp.index[0][0] = 1;
        temp.index[1][1] = 1;
        temp.index[2][2] = 1;

        //put in the translation amount
        temp.index[0][2] = dx;
        temp.index[1][2] = dy;

        result = multiplyMatrixNxM(temp,start);
        return result;
    }
```

There are some important things to note here. First of all, we go through and set up the positions [0][0];[1][1];[2][2] to the value of 1. The reason for this is so that the dot product will work out. Then we set the additional positions by the amount we want to move by in each direction. Once that is settled, we multiply the 3×3 matrix against our matrix that was holding our original position. The step to setting up the matrix for proper evaluation will become much more important as we move toward 3D multiplication.

3D Translation by Multiplication

$$
\begin{bmatrix} x' \\ y' \\ z' \\ 1 \end{bmatrix} = \begin{bmatrix} 1 & 0 & 0 & dx \\ 0 & 1 & 0 & dy \\ 0 & 0 & 1 & dz \\ 0 & 0 & 0 & 1 \end{bmatrix} \begin{bmatrix} x \\ y \\ z \\ 1 \end{bmatrix}
$$

where dx = change in x, dy = change in y, and dz = change in z.

The process for 3D is the same as that for 2D; the only difference is that you're now using a 4×4 translation matrix. Notice that the extra 1 is still along for the ride so that the matrix math works out.

Example 6.4: 3D Translation by Multiplication

Set up a general matrix equation (using matrix multiplication) that will move 3D objects 100 pixels to the left, 200 pixels up, and 50 pixels back (behind the screen), and then use it to move a triangle with vertices at A(40,0,100), B(0,350,200), and C(–100,200,–10).

Solution

1. Set up the matrix equation. To move 100 pixels to the left, 200 pixels up, and 50 pixels back, $dx = -100$, $dy = 200$, and $dz = -50$. (If you can't remember which direction is positive or negative, you can always flip back to Chapter 1.)

$$
\begin{bmatrix} x' \\ y' \\ z' \\ 1 \end{bmatrix} = \begin{bmatrix} 1 & 0 & 0 & -100 \\ 0 & 1 & 0 & 200 \\ 0 & 0 & 1 & -50 \\ 0 & 0 & 0 & 1 \end{bmatrix} \begin{bmatrix} x \\ y \\ z \\ 1 \end{bmatrix}
$$

2. Now you have to plug in each old point and add the matrices to see where it moved. First, plug in the old location of vertex A(40,0,100):

$$
\begin{bmatrix} x' \\ y' \\ z' \\ 1 \end{bmatrix} = \begin{bmatrix} 1 & 0 & 0 & -100 \\ 0 & 1 & 0 & 200 \\ 0 & 0 & 1 & -50 \\ 0 & 0 & 0 & 1 \end{bmatrix} \begin{bmatrix} 40 \\ 0 \\ 100 \\ 1 \end{bmatrix} = \begin{bmatrix} 1(40) + 0(0) + 0(100) - 100(1) \\ 0(40) + 1(0) + 0(100) + 200(1) \\ 0(40) + 0(0) + 1(100) - 50(1) \\ 0(40) + 0(0) + 0(100) + 1(1) \end{bmatrix} = \begin{bmatrix} -60 \\ 200 \\ 50 \\ 1 \end{bmatrix}
$$

So A' is the point (–60,200,50), just like last time.

3. If you repeat step 2 with the old locations of B and C, you get the new locations B'(–100,550,150) and C'(–200,400,–60). By moving all three vertices, you have moved the whole triangle. Notice that again you have found the same new location as you did using matrix addition.

Translation through multiplication is very similar for 3D. The major difference is that you are working with 4×4 and 4×1 matrices. The rest is fairly straightforward. Here is the function that translates 3D by multiplication:

```
Matrix4X1 translate3DByMultiply(Matrix4X1 start,float dx,
➥float dy,float dz)
    {
        Matrix4X4 temp;
        Matrix4X1 result;

        //Zero out the matrix.
        temp = createFixed4X4Matrix(0);

        //setup the 4X4 for multiplication;
        temp.index[0][0] = 1;
        temp.index[1][1] = 1;
        temp.index[2][2] = 1;
        temp.index[3][3] = 1;

        //put in the translation amount
        temp.index[0][3] = dx;
        temp.index[1][3] = dy;
        temp.index[2][3] = dz;

        result = multiplyMatrixNxM(temp,start);
        return result;
    }
```

Again, we go through and initialize the important components of the matrix, then use the starting coordinates to set the rightmost column. The result is a 4×1 matrix that holds the new position of the point.

> **NOTE**
>
> Notice that each time you calculate the new location, the last entry is always a 1. In code, you're wasting precious time if you calculate the extra 1 for every vertex. All you really need to find is x', y', and z', so don't bother calculating the last entry each time. Can you implement this as a small optimization into the translation code?

The beginning of this section said that matrix addition is by far easier and faster. After practicing both methods, I think you'll agree. Unfortunately, the only way to combine translation with scaling and rotating is to use matrix multiplication. The good news is that if you feel comfortable with translation, scaling and rotating should fall right into place for you.

Self-Assessment

Using the matrix equation provided, find the new locations of the following vertices:

$$\begin{bmatrix} x' \\ y' \end{bmatrix} = \begin{bmatrix} x \\ y \end{bmatrix} + \begin{bmatrix} 40 \\ -20 \end{bmatrix}$$

1. D(30,80)

2. E(−50,200)

3. F(100,0)

4. Set up a general matrix equation (using matrix addition) that will move 3D objects 50 pixels to the right, 300 pixels down, and 0 pixels back (behind the screen), and then use it to move a triangle with vertices at G(200,−30,−50), H(90,0,−40), and J(−400,50,−100).

5. Set up a general matrix equation (using matrix multiplication) that will move 2D objects 200 pixels to the left and 20 pixels up on the computer screen. Then use it to move a triangle with vertices at L(−100,30), M(50,−80), and N(70,0).

6. Repeat question 4 using matrix multiplication. Do you get the same three new locations?

Scaling

Matrix multiplication can also be used to scale objects in your game. Just like translation, if you scale each individual vertex, you end up scaling the whole object. Let's set up another matrix equation for scaling. Again, we'll start with 2D and then extend to 3D.

2D Scaling

$$\begin{bmatrix} x' \\ y' \\ 1 \end{bmatrix} = \begin{bmatrix} Sx & 0 & 0 \\ 0 & Sy & 0 \\ 0 & 0 & 1 \end{bmatrix} \begin{bmatrix} x \\ y \\ 1 \end{bmatrix}$$

where Sx = scale factor in the x direction and Sy = scale factor in the y direction.

As soon as you plug in the scale factors (Sx and Sy), the process is the same as translation: Plug in each vertex one at a time, and multiply the matrices to find its new location. If you want to perform a **uniform scale** to keep the proportions the same, just make sure that $Sx = Sy$. You don't have to perform a uniform scale, however. If you plug in two different values for Sx and Sy, you'll end up with a **differential scale**.

When choosing values for Sx and Sy, keep in mind that any number between 0 and 1 makes objects smaller, and any number greater than 1 scales objects larger. (Negative values flip the object into a different quadrant.) Let's look at a couple examples.

Example 6.5: 2D Uniform Scale

Set up a general matrix equation that will uniformly scale 2D objects 3 times larger, and then use it to scale the rectangle pictured in Figure 6.2.

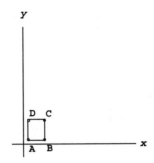

Figure 6.2   A rectangle to be uniformly scaled.

Solution

1. Set up the matrix equation. To uniformly scale objects 3 times larger, both scale factors must be equal to 3:

$$\begin{bmatrix} x' \\ y' \\ 1 \end{bmatrix} = \begin{bmatrix} 3 & 0 & 0 \\ 0 & 3 & 0 \\ 0 & 0 & 1 \end{bmatrix} \begin{bmatrix} x \\ y \\ 1 \end{bmatrix}$$

2. Now you have to plug in each old point and multiply the matrices to find the new location. First, plug in the old location of vertex A(10,10):

$$\begin{bmatrix} x' \\ y' \\ 1 \end{bmatrix} = \begin{bmatrix} 3 & 0 & 0 \\ 0 & 3 & 0 \\ 0 & 0 & 1 \end{bmatrix} \begin{bmatrix} 10 \\ 10 \\ 1 \end{bmatrix} = \begin{bmatrix} 3(10) + 0(10) + 0(1) \\ 0(10) + 3(10) + 0(1) \\ 0(10) + 0(10) + 1(1) \end{bmatrix} = \begin{bmatrix} 30 \\ 30 \\ 1 \end{bmatrix}$$

So A' is the point (30,30).

3. If you repeat step 2 with the old locations of B, C, and D, you get the new locations B'(150,30), C'(150,120), and D'(30,120). By scaling all four vertices, you have scaled the whole rectangle 3 times larger.

4. The old location and the new location are graphed in Figure 6.3.

Turning this into code isn't very difficult, but extends slightly as we try to make something more of it. Here is a function that will take a matrix and multiply the value by a scale passed to it:

```
Matrix3X1 scale2DByMultiplication(Matrix3X1 start, float dx, float dy)
    {
        Matrix3X3 temp;
        Matrix3X1 result;

        //Zero out the matrix.
        temp = createFixed3X3Matrix(0);

        //setup the 3x3 for multiplication;
        temp.index[0][0] = dx;
        temp.index[1][1] = dy;
        temp.index[2][2] = 1;

        result = multiplyMatrixNxM(temp,start);
        return result;
    }
```

Notice that this function will scale uniformly or nonuniformly based on the values passed through to dx and dy. If you want to make it scale uniformly, just ask for a single scale factor and assign them to be equal.

This is great for scaling up single points, but most objects that are scaled are of some geometric shape. Let's look at part of the driver function from the sample code that indicates how to scale a rectangle uniformly:

```
void scale2D()
    {
     Matrix3X1 start,temp;
     float dx,dy, height,width;
 cout<<"Please enter the coordinates and dimensions  of a
 ➥rectangle.\n";
        cout<<"X coordinates\n";
        cin>>start.index[0];
        cout<<"Now the Y coordinate.\n";
        cin>>start.index[1];
        cout<<"Enter the rectangle's height.\n";
        cin>>height;
        cout<<"Enter the rectangle's width.\n";
        cin>>width;
```

```
//make sure the last part of the matrix is a 1.
start.index[2] = 1;
cout<<endl;
cout<<"Now enter the amount to scale by.\n";
cin>>dx;
dy = dx;

temp = scale2DByMultiplication(start,dx,dy);
width = temp.index[0]+width;
height = temp.index[1]+height;

cout<<"The new position is
➥"<<temp.index[0]<<","<<temp.index[1]<<"\n";
cout<<"The right coord is
➥"<<width<<","<<temp.index[1]<<"\n";
cout<<"The bottom coord is
➥"<<height<<","<<temp.index[0]<<"\n";
}
```

This function will give the scaled position of all the points in the rectangle and is much more useful than just scaling a single point. We will look at a similar example when we focus on rotation a little later in this chapter.

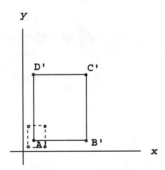

Figure 6.3   Old and new locations of a uniformly scaled rectangle.

Look at Figure 6.3 for a moment. Notice that the dimensions of the rectangle are indeed 3 times larger. However, the rectangle appears to have also moved away from the origin. Unfortunately, the scaling matrix is set up to scale objects with respect to the origin, which is why the rectangle moved away from the origin when it was scaled larger. If you had scaled it down, the rectangle would have moved closer to the origin. Unfortunately, if you want to keep the object in the same place and scale it (with respect to its own center), that is a combo. We'll examine that particular combo later in this chapter. In the meantime, let's look at an example of differential scaling with respect to the origin.

> **NOTE**
> One way to deal with this issue is to set up a local coordinate system with its own origin. For example, if I'm scaling a human figure who's standing on the ground, I can place the local origin on the soles of the figure's shoes and center it on the other two axes. Then a single scaling matrix would allow the figure to grow from the ground without moving laterally. Quite often, assets that look perfect in the preview applications get sent back to the artist after they start running in the game because their origins were misplaced.

Example 6.6: 2D Differential Scale

Suppose you have a rectangular-shaped object (see Figure 6.4) with vertices at A(20,0), B(50,0), C(50,100), and D(20,100), and a huge boulder falls on it. You want the object to look like it got squished, so set up a matrix equation that will scale objects 1.5 times in the x direction and 0.1 in the y direction, and then use it to scale the rectangle.

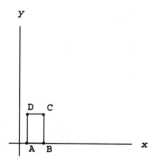

Figure 6.4   A rectangle to be differentially scaled.

Solution

1. Set up the matrix equation. In this case, the scale factor in the x direction is 1.5 and the scale factor in the y direction is 0.1:

$$\begin{bmatrix} x' \\ y' \\ 1 \end{bmatrix} = \begin{bmatrix} 1.5 & 0 & 0 \\ 0 & 0.1 & 0 \\ 0 & 0 & 1 \end{bmatrix} \begin{bmatrix} x \\ y \\ 1 \end{bmatrix}$$

2. Now you have to plug in each old point and multiply the matrices to find the new location. First, plug in the old location of vertex A(20,0):

$$\begin{bmatrix} x' \\ y' \\ 1 \end{bmatrix} = \begin{bmatrix} 1.5 & 0 & 0 \\ 0 & 0.1 & 0 \\ 0 & 0 & 1 \end{bmatrix} \begin{bmatrix} 20 \\ 0 \\ 1 \end{bmatrix} = \begin{bmatrix} 1.5(20) + 0(0) + 0(1) \\ 0(20) + 0.1(0) + 0(1) \\ 0(20) + 0(0) + 1(1) \end{bmatrix} = \begin{bmatrix} 30 \\ 0 \\ 1 \end{bmatrix}$$

So A' is the point (30,0).

3. If you repeat step 2 with the old locations of B, C, and D, you get the new locations B'(75,0), C'(75,10), and D'(30,10). By scaling all four vertices, you have scaled the whole rectangle.

4. The old location and the new location are graphed in Figure 6.5. Notice that the rectangle has become wider and flatter.

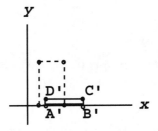

Figure 6.5   Old and new locations of a differentially scaled rectangle.

The scaling process works the exact same way in 3D. You just need to add an extra dimension to each matrix in the equation.

3D Scaling

$$\begin{bmatrix} x' \\ y' \\ z' \\ 1 \end{bmatrix} = \begin{bmatrix} Sx & 0 & 0 & 0 \\ 0 & Sy & 0 & 0 \\ 0 & 0 & Sz & 0 \\ 0 & 0 & 0 & 1 \end{bmatrix} \begin{bmatrix} x \\ y \\ z \\ 1 \end{bmatrix}$$

where Sx = scale factor in the x direction, Sy = scale factor in the y direction, and Sz = scale factor in the z direction.

Example 6.7: 3D Uniform Scale

Set up a general matrix equation that will uniformly scale 3D objects 5 times larger, and then use it to scale a triangle with vertices at A(50,0,–10), B(0,20,–100), and C(200,150,–50).

Solution

1. Set up the matrix equation. To uniformly scale objects 5 times larger, all three scale factors must be equal to 5:

$$\begin{bmatrix} x' \\ y' \\ z' \\ 1 \end{bmatrix} = \begin{bmatrix} 5 & 0 & 0 & 0 \\ 0 & 5 & 0 & 0 \\ 0 & 0 & 5 & 0 \\ 0 & 0 & 0 & 1 \end{bmatrix} \begin{bmatrix} x \\ y \\ z \\ 1 \end{bmatrix}$$

2. Plug in each old point, and multiply the matrices to find the new location. First, plug in the old location of vertex A(50,0,–10):

$$\begin{bmatrix} x' \\ y' \\ z' \\ 1 \end{bmatrix} = \begin{bmatrix} 5 & 0 & 0 & 0 \\ 0 & 5 & 0 & 0 \\ 0 & 0 & 5 & 0 \\ 0 & 0 & 0 & 1 \end{bmatrix} \begin{bmatrix} 50 \\ 0 \\ -10 \\ 1 \end{bmatrix} = \begin{bmatrix} 5(50) + 0(0) + 0(-10) + 0(1) \\ 0(50) + 5(0) + 0(-10) + 0(1) \\ 0(50) + 0(0) + 5(-10) + 0(1) \\ 0(50) + 0(0) + 0(-10) + 1(1) \end{bmatrix} = \begin{bmatrix} 250 \\ 0 \\ -50 \\ 1 \end{bmatrix}$$

So A' is the point (250,0,–50).

3. If you repeat step 2 with the old locations of B and C, you get the new locations B'(0,100,–500) and C'(1000,750,–250). By scaling all three vertices, you have scaled the whole triangle 5 times larger.

You can also perform differential scaling in 3D, so let's look at an example of that.

Example 6.8: 3D Differential Scale

Set up a general matrix equation that will scale 3D objects two times taller and half as deep (z direction), and then use it to scale a triangle with vertices at A(50,0,–10), B(0,20,–100), and C(200,150,–50).

Solution

1. Set up the matrix equation. To scale objects two times taller and half as deep, the scale factor in the x direction must be 1 (no change), the scale factor in the y direction must be 2, and the scale factor in the z direction must be 0.5:

$$\begin{bmatrix} x' \\ y' \\ z' \\ 1 \end{bmatrix} = \begin{bmatrix} 1 & 0 & 0 & 0 \\ 0 & 2 & 0 & 0 \\ 0 & 0 & 0.5 & 0 \\ 0 & 0 & 0 & 1 \end{bmatrix} \begin{bmatrix} x \\ y \\ z \\ 1 \end{bmatrix}$$

2. Now you have to plug in each old point and multiply the matrices to find the new location. First, plug in the old location of vertex A(50,0,–10):

$$\begin{bmatrix} x' \\ y' \\ z' \\ 1 \end{bmatrix} = \begin{bmatrix} 1 & 0 & 0 & 0 \\ 0 & 2 & 0 & 0 \\ 0 & 0 & 0.5 & 0 \\ 0 & 0 & 0 & 1 \end{bmatrix} \begin{bmatrix} 50 \\ 0 \\ -10 \\ 1 \end{bmatrix} = \begin{bmatrix} 1(50) + 0(0) + 0(-10) + 0(1) \\ 0(50) + 2(0) + 0(-10) + 0(1) \\ 0(50) + 0(0) + 0.5(-10) + 0(1) \\ 0(50) + 0(0) + 0(-10) + 1(1) \end{bmatrix} = \begin{bmatrix} 50 \\ 0 \\ -5 \\ 1 \end{bmatrix}$$

   So A' is the point (50,0,–5).

3. If you repeat step 2 with the old locations of B and C, you get the new locations B'(0,40,–50) and C'(200,300,–25). By scaling all three vertices, you have scaled the whole triangle.

Earlier, we saw a function that could process uniform and non-uniform 2D scaling. Here is a function that works the exact same way for 3D scaling:

```
Matrix4X1 scale3DByMultiply(Matrix4X1 start, float dx, float dy,
➥float dz)
    {
        Matrix4X4 temp;
        Matrix4X1 result;
```

```
        //Zero out the matrix to make sure nothing is left
        ➥uninitialized.
        temp = createFixed4X4Matrix(0);

        //setup the 3x3 for multiplication;
        temp.index[0][0] = dx;
        temp.index[1][1] = dy;
        temp.index[2][2] = dz;
        temp.index[3][3] = 1;

        result = multiplyMatrixNxM(temp,start);
        return result;
    }
```

This operation is performed the same way as the 2D scale function with the addition of a new variable in the form of dz. If you want this function to perform a uniform scale on a point or group of points, ask the user for one scale factor and assign the same value to dx, dy, and dz. The provided sample code for this chapter demonstrates this technique to rotate a set of vertices. Be sure to check it out!

Notice that the process for scaling objects is very similar to that of translating by matrix multiplication. This will make it easy to combine translation and scaling later in this chapter. In the meantime, practice scaling 2D and 3D objects with respect to the origin. This will make the combo of scaling with respect to any other point much easier when you get there.

Self-Assessment

1. Set up a general matrix equation that will uniformly scale 2D objects in half, and then use it to scale a triangle with vertices at A(–50,20), B(–10,20), and C(–30,40).

2. Set up a general matrix equation that will make objects tall and skinny by scaling $1/4$ in the x direction and 3 times in the y direction, and then use it to scale a triangle with vertices at A(–50,20), B(–10,20), and C(–30,40).

3. Set up a general matrix equation that will uniformly scale 3D objects 10 times larger, and then use it to scale a triangle with vertices at D(0,30,–100), E(–50,100,–20), and F(–20,0,–300).

4. Set up a general matrix equation that will scale objects twice as big in the x direction, no change in the y direction, and half as big in the z direction, and then use it to scale a triangle with vertices at D(0,30,–100), E(–50,100,–20), and F(–20,0,–300).

Rotation

There are actually two different approaches to rotating objects. One method uses quaternions, but the math is complex. The other method is very similar to that of scaling and translating, because it uses a similar matrix equation. This second method is called **Euler rotation** (pronounced "oiler rotation," not "yewler"). You'll set up a matrix equation first in 2D and then in 3D. As soon as the matrix equation is set up, all you have to do is plug in the vertices one at a time and multiply the matrices to find the new position.

2D Rotation

$$\begin{bmatrix} x' \\ y' \\ 1 \end{bmatrix} = \begin{bmatrix} \cos\theta & -\sin\theta & 0 \\ \sin\theta & \cos\theta & 0 \\ 0 & 0 & 1 \end{bmatrix} \begin{bmatrix} x \\ y \\ 1 \end{bmatrix}$$

where θ is the angle of rotation.

As soon as you know the angle of rotation, you can take the sine and cosine and turn them into decimal numbers so that you can multiply the matrices. You might need to revisit Chapter 3, "Trigonometry Snippets," for a discussion of angles. Remember that positive angles rotate counterclockwise, and negative angles rotate clockwise. Also, if you know the angle ahead of time and you're calculating the sine and cosine, you can leave the angle in degrees. However, if the computer program is fed the angle and it must take the sine and cosine, remember that the angle must be in radian measure.

Programming Transformations Using Matrices

When using the widely accepted `math.h` header, key functions such as sine and cosine have arguments that accept their parameters in radians. It's important to properly format the values passed to these functions before asking them to do any calculations. Here are a couple of quick macro functions that you can use when needed:

```
#define RadsToDegrees( radian ) ((radian) * (180.0f / M_PI))
```

As you probably recognize, this first method takes a radian argument and returns a degree conversion. More on the definition of `M_PI` in just a moment.

```
#define DegreesToRads( degrees ) ((degrees) * (M_PI/ 180.0f))
```

This function does the reverse and gives us radian arguments for our degree values.

The usage of `M_PI` comes from the `math.h` header. Make sure that you not only include the math header in your programs, but also set the directive to use the math header definitions for things like `PI`. The listed term `M_PI` comes from the math header and is used to represent pi throughout the chapter. If the math header defines are supported on your platform, you should be able to access them like this:

```
#define _USE_MATH_DEFINES
#include <math.h>
```

It's important to set the *USE_MATH_DEFINES* definition before you include the library so that it knows in advance to work with those parameters.

Example 6.9: 2D Rotation

Set up a general matrix equation that will rotate 2D objects 90°, and then use it to rotate the triangle pictured in Figure 6.6 with vertices at A(50,40), B(100,40), and C(75,200).

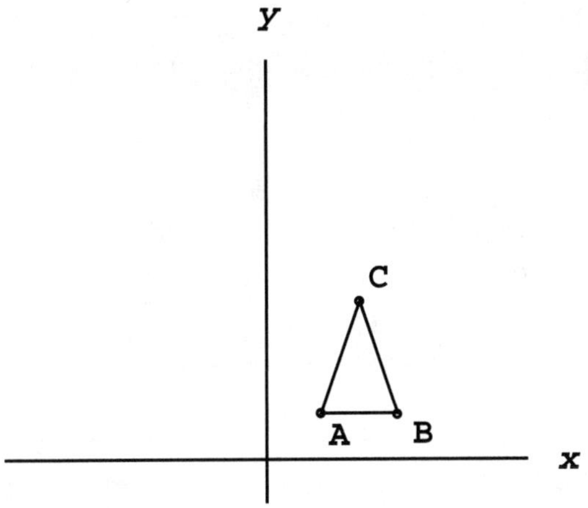

Figure 6.6   A 2D triangle to be rotated.

Solution

1. Set up the matrix equation. The angle of rotation is 90°:

$$\begin{bmatrix} x' \\ y' \\ 1 \end{bmatrix} = \begin{bmatrix} \cos 90° & -\sin 90° & 0 \\ \sin 90° & \cos 90° & 0 \\ 0 & 0 & 1 \end{bmatrix} \begin{bmatrix} x \\ y \\ 1 \end{bmatrix} = \begin{bmatrix} 0 & -1 & 0 \\ 1 & 0 & 0 \\ 0 & 0 & 1 \end{bmatrix} \begin{bmatrix} x \\ y \\ 1 \end{bmatrix}$$

2. Now you have to plug in each old point and multiply the matrices to find the new location. First, plug in the old location of vertex A(50,40):

$$\begin{bmatrix} x' \\ y' \\ 1 \end{bmatrix} = \begin{bmatrix} 0 & -1 & 0 \\ 1 & 0 & 0 \\ 0 & 0 & 1 \end{bmatrix} \begin{bmatrix} 50 \\ 40 \\ 1 \end{bmatrix} = \begin{bmatrix} 0(50) - 1(40) + 0(1) \\ 1(50) + 0(40) + 0(1) \\ 0(50) + 0(40) + 1(1) \end{bmatrix} = \begin{bmatrix} -40 \\ 50 \\ 1 \end{bmatrix}$$

So A' is the point (−40,50).

3. If you repeat step 2 with the old locations of B and C, you get the new locations B'(−40,100) and C'(−200,75). By rotating all three vertices, you have rotated the whole triangle. The original location and the new location are shown in Figure 6.7.

Rotating objects in 2D is an important thing to be able to process. The calculations are pretty straightforward. Let's take a look at a function that rotates a 2D point:

```
Matrix3X1 rotate2D(Matrix3X1 start, float theta)
    {
        Matrix3X3 temp;
        Matrix3X1 result;
        //Zero out the matrix.
        temp = createFixed3X3Matrix(0);
        //place the needed rotational values into the matrix.
        temp.index[0][0] = cos(DegreesToRads(theta));
        temp.index[1][1] = cos(DegreesToRads(theta));
        temp.index[2][2] = 1;
        temp.index[0][1] = -1*(sin(DegreesToRads(theta)));
        temp.index[1][0] = sin(DegreesToRads(theta));
        temp.index[2][2] = 1;
        result = multiplyMatrixNxM(temp,start);
        return result;
    }
```

You can see we are using the `DegreesToRads()` macro that was referenced at the beginning of the chapter. Stepping through, we initialize the values of the rotation matrix based on the amount of rotation specified by the user. Once the matrix is set up, we can then just multiply the current matrix by the rotation matrix and we will have the newly translated points.

Here is some sample code that will allow us to translate a whole rectangle around a center point:

```
void rotate2D()
    {
        Matrix3X1 start,temp;
        float height,width,theta;
        cout<<"Let's rotate a 2D!\n";
        cout<<"Please enter the coordinates and dimensions.\n";
        cout<<"X coordinates\n";
        cin>>start.index[0];
        cout<<"Now the Y coordinate.\n";
```

```
cin>>start.index[1];
cout<<"Enter the rectangle's height.\n";
cin>>height;
cout<<"Enter the rectangle's width.\n";
cin>>width;
//make sure the last part of the matrix is a 1.
start.index[2] = 1;
cout<<endl;
cout<<"Now enter the amount to rotate by in degrees.\n";
cin>>theta;
//Now that we have our info, lets rotate!
temp = rotate2D(start,theta);

//This gives the new locations calced from the temp matrix.
width = temp.index[0]+width;
height = temp.index[1]+height;

cout<<"The right coordinate of the rectangle
➥<<width<<","<<temp.index[1]<<"\n";
cout<<"The bottom coordiante of the rectangle
➥"<<height<<","<<temp.index[0]<<"\n";
}
```

The main reason that rotation is so important with respect to this square is that most 2D images are represented in a square format, even if the alpha channel blocks out some of the colors from the user. It is common to use the current position to handle the display of graphics. This rotation algorithm lets the user specify what facing he wants a particular graphic to have. Some games will directly tie the input from the user to the facing and process the updates using a similar rotation algorithm.

In Figure 6.7, notice that the triangle rotated and moved. You might have expected it to stay in the same place and rotate. Unfortunately, that is also a combo.

NOTE

Again, this issue can be resolved by setting up a local origin for the model (also called its pivot).

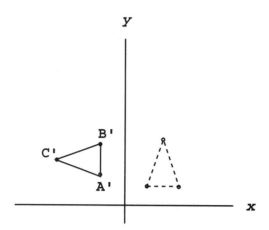

Figure 6.7 A 2D triangle before and after rotation.

By default, the rotation matrix rotates objects with respect to the origin, just like the scaling matrix does. The resulting effect is that the object appears to be orbiting about the origin. If you want the object to rotate about its own center or a particular vertex so that it appears to be tipping over, that is a combo, and we'll discuss that process in the next section.

In the meantime, let's take a look at 3D rotation. 2D has only one plane to rotate in, much like a flat screen. However, 3D has three different planes to rotate in—the *xy* plane, the *yz* plane, and the *xz* plane. These three planes are shown in Figure 6.8.

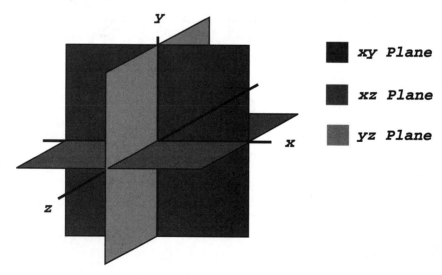

Figure 6.8 The three planes in 3D.

Notice that the *xy* plane is the same as the flat 2D plane you're used to working with for the computer screen. Because there are three separate planes to rotate within, there are three separate rotation matrices for 3D. Let's examine them one at a time.

3D Rotation About the Z-Axis (Roll)

$$\begin{bmatrix} x' \\ y' \\ z' \\ 1 \end{bmatrix} = \begin{bmatrix} \cos\theta & -\sin\theta & 0 & 0 \\ \sin\theta & \cos\theta & 0 & 0 \\ 0 & 0 & 1 & 0 \\ 0 & 0 & 0 & 1 \end{bmatrix} \begin{bmatrix} x \\ y \\ z \\ 1 \end{bmatrix}$$

where θ is the angle of rotation.

Remember that the z-axis comes in and out of the screen, so if you rotate around the z-axis it's the same as rotating inside the flat screen (*xy* plane). That's why this rotation matrix looks almost the same as the 2D rotation matrix; it just has an extra row and column of identity to make it a 4×4 matrix. Notice also that this particular rotation is labeled *roll*. This name comes from flight simulator terminology. If you stand up with your arms extended to the side and bend from side to side, it's the same motion as a plane rolling.

To rotate around the z-axis, use the following function:

```
Matrix4X1 rotate3DZ(Matrix4X1 start, float theta)
    {
        Matrix4X4 temp;
        Matrix4X1 result;

        //Zero out the matrix.
        temp = createFixed4X4Matrix(0);

        //put the needed rotation values into the matrix from
        ➥theta.
        temp.index[0][0] = cos(DegreesToRads(theta));
        temp.index[1][1] = cos(DegreesToRads(theta));
        temp.index[2][2] = 1;
        temp.index[3][3] = 1;
```

```
temp.index[0][1] = -1*(sin(DegreesToRads(theta)));
temp.index[1][0] = sin(DegreesToRads(theta));


result = multiplyMatrixNxM(temp,start);
return result;
}
```

Make sure that when you are setting up your own rotation algorithms that you watch the radian calculations. Also make sure you put the values in the proper positions.

3D Rotation About the X-Axis (Pitch)

$$\begin{bmatrix} x' \\ y' \\ z' \\ 1 \end{bmatrix} = \begin{bmatrix} 1 & 0 & 0 & 0 \\ 0 & \cos\theta & -\sin\theta & 0 \\ 0 & \sin\theta & \cos\theta & 0 \\ 0 & 0 & 0 & 1 \end{bmatrix} \begin{bmatrix} x \\ y \\ z \\ 1 \end{bmatrix}$$

where θ is the angle of rotation.

The x-axis runs left and right, so if you rotate around the x-axis, it's the same motion as standing up and bending over to take a bow.

In flight simulator terms, that's the same motion as pitching, so many programmers call rotation about the x-axis *pitch*. Notice the shift in the location of the sines and cosines. The first row and column typically represent *x* values, and in this case the first row and column have identity values. If you're rotating about the x-axis, the x-coordinates of the vertices shouldn't change, so that makes sense. This little trick might help you memorize the 3D rotation matrices. It works for rotating about the y- and z-axes as well.

Here's one way to rotate about the X-axis:

```
Matrix4X1 rotate3DX(Matrix4X1 start, float theta)
    {
        Matrix4X4 temp;
        Matrix4X1 result;
```

```
//Zero out the matrix.
temp = createFixed4X4Matrix(0);

//place needed rotation values into the matrix based on
➥theta.
temp.index[0][0] = 1;
temp.index[1][1] = cos(DegreesToRads(theta));
temp.index[2][2] = cos(DegreesToRads(theta));
temp.index[3][3] = 1;

temp.index[1][2] = -1*(sin(DegreesToRads(theta)));
temp.index[2][1] = sin(DegreesToRads(theta));


result = multiplyMatrixNxM(temp,start);
return result;
}
```

The main changes here are the locations of the sine and cosine values of theta. This example is used in the sample source code provided for this chapter.

3D Rotation About the Y-Axis (Yaw)

$$
\begin{bmatrix} x' \\ y' \\ z' \\ 1 \end{bmatrix} = \begin{bmatrix} \cos\theta & 0 & \sin\theta & 0 \\ 0 & 1 & 0 & 0 \\ -\sin\theta & 0 & \cos\theta & 0 \\ 0 & 0 & 0 & 1 \end{bmatrix} \begin{bmatrix} x \\ y \\ z \\ 1 \end{bmatrix}
$$

where θ is the angle of rotation.

Notice in this case that the second row and column (which represent y values) have identity values. Rotation about the y-axis in simulation terminology is the same as *yaw*. If you stand in place and spin around like a ballerina, that's the motion described as yaw. You can also visualize yaw by picturing someone spinning around a vertical pole. As soon as you have each matrix equation set up, all you have to do is plug in the original location of each vertex and multiply it to find the new location.

Unfortunately, these three types of rotation must be planned separately, but you'll see in the next section that they can eventually be combined.

Here's a function to rotate about the Y-axis:

```
Matrix4X1 rotate3DY(Matrix4X1 start, float theta)
    {
        Matrix4X4 temp;
        Matrix4X1 result;

        //Zero out the matrix.
        temp = createFixed4X4Matrix(0);

        //place the rotational values into the matrix based on
        ➥theta.
        temp.index[0][0] = cos(DegreesToRads(theta));
        temp.index[1][1] = 1;
        temp.index[2][2] = cos(DegreesToRads(theta));
        temp.index[3][3] = 1;

        temp.index[2][0] = -1*(sin(DegreesToRads(theta)));
        temp.index[0][2] = sin(DegreesToRads(theta));


        result = multiplyMatrixNxM(temp,start);
        return result;
    }
```

Remember to double-check the locations of the sine and cosine values.

NOTE

These three rotation matrices are also designed to rotate with respect to the origin, so they all have the same orbiting effect as the 2D rotation matrix. Again, if you want to rotate with respect to another point, that has to be set up as a combo.

Example 6.10: 3D Rotation About the Y-Axis

Set up a general matrix equation that will rotate 3D objects π^R about the y-axis, and then use it to rotate a triangle with vertices at A(100,0,–50), B(40,–30,0), and C(–20,100,50).

Solution

1. Set up the matrix equation. The angle of rotation is π^R or 180° (see Chapter 3 for the conversion):

$$\begin{bmatrix} x' \\ y' \\ z' \\ 1 \end{bmatrix} = \begin{bmatrix} \cos180° & 0 & \sin180° & 0 \\ 0 & 1 & 0 & 0 \\ -\sin180° & 0 & \cos180° & 0 \\ 0 & 0 & 0 & 1 \end{bmatrix} \begin{bmatrix} x \\ y \\ z \\ 1 \end{bmatrix} = \begin{bmatrix} -1 & 0 & 0 & 0 \\ 0 & 1 & 0 & 0 \\ 0 & 0 & -1 & 0 \\ 0 & 0 & 0 & 1 \end{bmatrix} \begin{bmatrix} x \\ y \\ z \\ 1 \end{bmatrix}$$

2. Now you have to plug in each old point and multiply the matrices to find the new location. First, plug in the old location of vertex A(100,0,–50):

$$\begin{bmatrix} x' \\ y' \\ z' \\ 1 \end{bmatrix} = \begin{bmatrix} -1 & 0 & 0 & 0 \\ 0 & 1 & 0 & 0 \\ 0 & 0 & -1 & 0 \\ 0 & 0 & 0 & 1 \end{bmatrix} \begin{bmatrix} 100 \\ 0 \\ -50 \\ 1 \end{bmatrix} = \begin{bmatrix} -1(100) + 0(0) + 0(-50) + 0(1) \\ 0(100) + 1(0) + 0(-50) + 0(1) \\ 0(100) + 0(0) - 1(-50) + 0(1) \\ 0(100) + 0(0) + 0(-50) + 1(1) \end{bmatrix} = \begin{bmatrix} -100 \\ 0 \\ 50 \\ 1 \end{bmatrix}$$

So A' is the point (–100,0,50).

3. If you repeat step 2 with the old locations of B and C, you get the new locations B'(–40,–30,0) and C'(20,100,–50). By rotating all three vertices, you have rotated the whole triangle.

If you can rotate about the y-axis, you can rotate about the other two axes as well. They all work the same way. Notice that the examples use multiples of 90°, so the sines and cosines are all 0s and 1s. However, be aware that for other angles, the sines and cosines have decimal numbers, so the new locations aren't always nice whole numbers. Also, remember that all rotation matrices are set up for rotation about the origin. The next section discusses how to rotate with respect to any other point.

The functions from last chapter that were used to create random matrices are a good way to test the matrix multiplications. You should also give the user a way to enter manual values as well. Check the sample source code for this chapter to see 3D rotation around each axis in action.

Self-Assessment

1. Set up a general matrix equation that will rotate 2D objects 30°, and then use it to rotate a triangle with vertices at A(–10,50), B(80,0), and C(–50,100).

2. Set up a general matrix equation that will make 3D objects stand in place and rotate 1 degree at a time (about the y-axis), and then use it to rotate a triangle with vertices at D(0,20,–50), E(–10,0,20), and F(30,20,0).

3. Set up a general matrix equation that will make 3D objects pitch 45°, and then use it to rotate a triangle with vertices at G(0,30,–100), H(–50,100,–20), and J(–20,0,–300).

4. Set up a general matrix equation that will rotate 3D objects $(\pi/2)^R$ about the z-axis, and then use it to rotate a triangle with vertices at L(0,30,–100), M(–50,100,–20), and N(–20,0,–300).

Concatenation

This whole chapter has been building up to this particular section. **Concatenation** is just a fancy name for combining transformation matrices into a single combo matrix. Earlier in this chapter I mentioned several common combinations: scaling with respect to an object's own center point, rotating with respect to the center point (or a vertex), and combining the 3D rotations. We'll use them as examples to demonstrate the concatenation process.

This process can be used for any combination of translation, scaling, and rotation, not just the examples mentioned earlier. Any time you plan to perform more than one transformation within the same frame, you can save *a lot* of processor time by combining them. It might take you more time up front when you're coding, but it will greatly enhance performance when the game is running.

Let's step through the process using the example of rotating an object about its own center point. Let's revisit the 2D triangle you rotated in Example 6.9. You rotated that triangle 90° with respect to the origin. This time, you'll rotate it 90° with respect to its own center point, which is (75,93). This particular combo is a three-step process (see Figure 6.9):

1. Translate so that the center is at the origin (left 75 and down 93).

2. Rotate 90°.

3. Translate so that the center is back in its original position (right 75 and up 93).

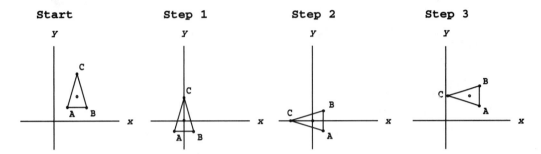

Figure 6.9 The three-step process.

By moving the center point to the origin, you almost trick the computer into rotating with respect to that point instead. You can use this same three-step process to scale with respect to any point other than the origin. As soon as you know the steps of your combo and the order in which you want to perform them, the next step is setting up a stack of transformation matrices so that they can be combined. Start with the old location on the far right. Then stack to the left (in order) the steps of your combo. In this case, the new location is equal to the following:

$$\begin{bmatrix} 1 & 0 & 75 \\ 0 & 1 & 93 \\ 0 & 0 & 1 \end{bmatrix} \begin{bmatrix} \cos 90° & -\sin 90° & 0 \\ \sin 90° & \cos 90° & 0 \\ 0 & 0 & 1 \end{bmatrix} \begin{bmatrix} 1 & 0 & -75 \\ 0 & 1 & -93 \\ 0 & 0 & 1 \end{bmatrix} \begin{bmatrix} x \\ y \\ 1 \end{bmatrix}$$

NOTE
This particular example has only three steps, but your combo can have as many steps as you like. As long as you want them all to happen in the same frame, go ahead and combine them.

Be very careful when setting up the stack. Remember from Chapter 5 that matrix multiplication is not commutative. This means that the order in which you multiply matrices is very important. If you accidentally flip two matrices in the stack, you end up at a completely different location than you expected, so always keep them in chronological order.

As soon as you have all the steps set up, the last step is to combine them into one matrix. The only way to do this is to multiply them all together. In this case, the new location matrix is equal to the following:

$$\begin{bmatrix} 1 & 0 & 75 \\ 0 & 1 & 93 \\ 0 & 0 & 1 \end{bmatrix} \begin{bmatrix} \cos 90° & -\sin 90° & 0 \\ \sin 90° & \cos 90° & 0 \\ 0 & 0 & 1 \end{bmatrix} \begin{bmatrix} 1 & 0 & -75 \\ 0 & 1 & -93 \\ 0 & 0 & 1 \end{bmatrix} \begin{bmatrix} x \\ y \\ 1 \end{bmatrix}$$

$$= \begin{bmatrix} 1 & 0 & 75 \\ 0 & 1 & 93 \\ 0 & 0 & 1 \end{bmatrix} \begin{bmatrix} 0 & -1 & 0 \\ 1 & 0 & 0 \\ 0 & 0 & 1 \end{bmatrix} \begin{bmatrix} 1 & 0 & -75 \\ 0 & 1 & -93 \\ 0 & 0 & 1 \end{bmatrix} \begin{bmatrix} x \\ y \\ 1 \end{bmatrix}$$

$$= \begin{bmatrix} 0 & -1 & 75 \\ 1 & 0 & 93 \\ 0 & 0 & 1 \end{bmatrix} \begin{bmatrix} 1 & 0 & -75 \\ 0 & 1 & -93 \\ 0 & 0 & 1 \end{bmatrix} \begin{bmatrix} x \\ y \\ 1 \end{bmatrix}$$

$$= \begin{bmatrix} 0 & -1 & 168 \\ 1 & 0 & 18 \\ 0 & 0 & 1 \end{bmatrix} \begin{bmatrix} x \\ y \\ 1 \end{bmatrix}$$

Just keep multiplying to the right until you get down to one matrix. This final matrix performs all three steps at once. In this particular case, all the player sees is the initial and final positions shown in Figure 6.9. The in-between steps are never seen, because they all happen within the same frame. Now, instead of placing all three matrices in the code, all you need is this combo matrix equation:

$$\begin{bmatrix} x' \\ y' \\ 1 \end{bmatrix} = \begin{bmatrix} 0 & -1 & 168 \\ 1 & 0 & 18 \\ 0 & 0 & 1 \end{bmatrix} \begin{bmatrix} x \\ y \\ 1 \end{bmatrix}$$

This might seem like a lot of work up front, and it is. However, it's better for you to do all that matrix multiplication once in the beginning than to have the computer repeat it for *every* vertex. A complex model has thousands of vertices, so this will have a significant effect.

At this point, the process is the same as all the others: Just plug in each vertex one at a time, and multiply the matrices to see where it moved to. By moving all the individual vertices, you end up moving the whole object. In this case, when you plug in the three original vertices A(50,40), B(100,40), and C(75,200), you get the new locations A'(128,68), B'(128,118), and C'(−32,93). Figure 6.10 shows both the original and final locations.

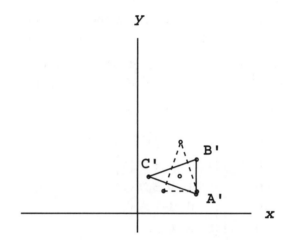

Figure 6.10   2D rotation with respect to the center point.

This same process also works in three dimensions. Let's look at an example of a 3D combo.

Example 6.11: 3D Scaling with Respect to the Center Point

Suppose you want a 3D model in your game to stay in the same place but scale down to half the size. Set up a general matrix equation that will scale any 3D object in half with respect to its own center point (x_c, y_c, z_c) using a single combo matrix.

Solution

1. Organize the three steps of the combo:

   ➤ Translate so that the center is at the origin.

   ➤ Uniformly scale in half.

   ➤ Translate so that the center is back in its original position.

2. Now you can set up a matrix equation with the individual transformation matrices stacked in order (right to left):

$$\begin{bmatrix} x' \\ y' \\ z' \\ 1 \end{bmatrix} = \begin{bmatrix} 1 & 0 & 0 & x_c \\ 0 & 1 & 0 & y_c \\ 0 & 0 & 1 & z_c \\ 0 & 0 & 0 & 1 \end{bmatrix} \begin{bmatrix} 0.5 & 0 & 0 & 0 \\ 0 & 0.5 & 0 & 0 \\ 0 & 0 & 0.5 & 0 \\ 0 & 0 & 0 & 1 \end{bmatrix} \begin{bmatrix} 1 & 0 & 0 & -x_c \\ 0 & 1 & 0 & -y_c \\ 0 & 0 & 1 & -z_c \\ 0 & 0 & 0 & 1 \end{bmatrix} \begin{bmatrix} x \\ y \\ z \\ 1 \end{bmatrix}$$

3. The last (but hardest) step is to multiply all the transformation matrices together. Remember that the order is important, so be sure to multiply left to right.

$$\begin{bmatrix} x' \\ y' \\ z' \\ 1 \end{bmatrix} = \begin{bmatrix} 1 & 0 & 0 & x_c \\ 0 & 1 & 0 & y_c \\ 0 & 0 & 1 & z_c \\ 0 & 0 & 0 & 1 \end{bmatrix} \begin{bmatrix} 0.5 & 0 & 0 & 0 \\ 0 & 0.5 & 0 & 0 \\ 0 & 0 & 0.5 & 0 \\ 0 & 0 & 0 & 1 \end{bmatrix} \begin{bmatrix} 1 & 0 & 0 & -x_c \\ 0 & 1 & 0 & -y_c \\ 0 & 0 & 1 & -z_c \\ 0 & 0 & 0 & 1 \end{bmatrix} \begin{bmatrix} x \\ y \\ z \\ 1 \end{bmatrix}$$

$$\begin{bmatrix} x' \\ y' \\ z' \\ 1 \end{bmatrix} = \begin{bmatrix} 0.5 & 0 & 0 & x_c \\ 0 & 0.5 & 0 & y_c \\ 0 & 0 & 0.5 & z_c \\ 0 & 0 & 0 & 1 \end{bmatrix} \begin{bmatrix} 1 & 0 & 0 & -x_c \\ 0 & 1 & 0 & -y_c \\ 0 & 0 & 1 & -z_c \\ 0 & 0 & 0 & 1 \end{bmatrix} \begin{bmatrix} x \\ y \\ z \\ 1 \end{bmatrix}$$

$$\begin{bmatrix} x' \\ y' \\ z' \\ 1 \end{bmatrix} = \begin{bmatrix} 0.5 & 0 & 0 & (0.5)x_c \\ 0 & 0.5 & 0 & (0.5)y_c \\ 0 & 0 & 0.5 & (0.5)z_c \\ 0 & 0 & 0 & 1 \end{bmatrix} \begin{bmatrix} x \\ y \\ z \\ 1 \end{bmatrix}$$

4. This last line is the final matrix equation that will scale any 3D object in half with respect to its own center point in just one step.

The preceding section talked about 3D rotation and showed that it must be broken into three separate parts: roll, pitch, and yaw. You might need to flip back to that section before tackling the next example, where you'll combine the three steps into one step.

Example 6.12: 3D Rotation Combined

Set up a general matrix equation that will make any 3D object roll 30°, pitch 180°, and yaw 90° using a single combo matrix. Then apply it to a triangle with vertices at A(200,0,–30), B(0,50,–150), and C(40,20,–100).

Solution

1. Organize the three steps of the combo:

   ➤ Rotate 30° about the z-axis.

   ➤ Rotate 180° about the x-axis.

   ➤ Rotate 90° about the y-axis.

2. Now you can set up a matrix equation with the individual transformation matrices stacked in order (right to left):

$$\begin{bmatrix} x' \\ y' \\ z' \\ 1 \end{bmatrix} = \begin{bmatrix} \cos 90° & 0 & \sin 90° & 0 \\ 0 & 1 & 0 & 0 \\ -\sin 90° & 0 & \cos 90° & 0 \\ 0 & 0 & 0 & 1 \end{bmatrix} \begin{bmatrix} 1 & 0 & 0 & 0 \\ 0 & \cos 180° & -\sin 180° & 0 \\ 0 & \sin 180° & \cos 180° & 0 \\ 0 & 0 & 0 & 1 \end{bmatrix} \begin{bmatrix} \cos 30° & -\sin 30° & 0 & 0 \\ \sin 30° & \cos 30° & 0 & 0 \\ 0 & 0 & 1 & 0 \\ 0 & 0 & 0 & 1 \end{bmatrix} \begin{bmatrix} x \\ y \\ z \\ 1 \end{bmatrix}$$

3. The last (but hardest) step is to multiply all the transformation matrices together. Order is important, so be sure to multiply left to right.

$$\begin{bmatrix} x' \\ y' \\ z' \\ 1 \end{bmatrix} = \begin{bmatrix} 0 & 0 & 1 & 0 \\ 0 & 1 & 0 & 0 \\ -1 & 0 & 0 & 0 \\ 0 & 0 & 0 & 1 \end{bmatrix} \begin{bmatrix} 1 & 0 & 0 & 0 \\ 0 & -1 & 0 & 0 \\ 0 & 0 & -1 & 0 \\ 0 & 0 & 0 & 1 \end{bmatrix} \begin{bmatrix} 0.8660 & -0.5 & 0 & 0 \\ 0.5 & 0.8660 & 0 & 0 \\ 0 & 0 & 1 & 0 \\ 0 & 0 & 0 & 1 \end{bmatrix} \begin{bmatrix} x \\ y \\ z \\ 1 \end{bmatrix}$$

$$\begin{bmatrix} x' \\ y' \\ z' \\ 1 \end{bmatrix} = \begin{bmatrix} 0 & 0 & -1 & 0 \\ 0 & -1 & 0 & 0 \\ -1 & 0 & 0 & 0 \\ 0 & 0 & 0 & 1 \end{bmatrix} \begin{bmatrix} 0.8660 & -0.5 & 0 & 0 \\ 0.5 & 0.8660 & 0 & 0 \\ 0 & 0 & 1 & 0 \\ 0 & 0 & 0 & 1 \end{bmatrix} \begin{bmatrix} x \\ y \\ z \\ 1 \end{bmatrix}$$

$$\begin{bmatrix} x' \\ y' \\ z' \\ 1 \end{bmatrix} = \begin{bmatrix} 0 & 0 & -1 & 0 \\ -0.5 & -0.8660 & 0 & 0 \\ -0.8660 & 0.5 & 0 & 0 \\ 0 & 0 & 0 & 1 \end{bmatrix} \begin{bmatrix} x \\ y \\ z \\ 1 \end{bmatrix}$$

4. Now that you have a matrix equation that performs all three rotations at once, all you have to do is plug in each vertex and multiply the matrices to find the new location, just like before. For example, if you plug in the old location of vertex A(200,0,–30), you get the following:

$$\begin{bmatrix} x' \\ y' \\ z' \\ 1 \end{bmatrix} = \begin{bmatrix} 0 & 0 & -1 & 0 \\ -0.5 & -0.8660 & 0 & 0 \\ -0.8660 & 0.5 & 0 & 0 \\ 0 & 0 & 0 & 1 \end{bmatrix} \begin{bmatrix} 200 \\ 0 \\ -30 \\ 1 \end{bmatrix} = \begin{bmatrix} 0(200) + 0(0) - 1(-30) + 0(1) \\ -0.5(200) - 0.8660(0) + 0(-30) + 0(1) \\ -0.8660(200) + 0.5(0) + 0(-30) + 0(1) \\ 0(200) + 0(0) + 0(-30) + 1(1) \end{bmatrix} = \begin{bmatrix} 30 \\ -100 \\ 173.2 \\ 1 \end{bmatrix}$$

So A' is the point (30,–100,173.2).

5. If you repeat step 4 with the old locations of B and C, you get the new locations B'(150,–43.3,25) and C'(100,–37.32,–24.64). By rotating all three vertices, you have rotated the whole triangle.

Programming combo matrices represent the last big step in transformations and require complete understanding of everything already presented in this chapter.

The first step is to actually create the combo matrix. Fortunately, we already have all the tools we need to build this matrix. Here is a function that will create a 3D combo matrix in preparation for the actual combo transformation:

```
Matrix4X4 createRotationCombo(float thetax,float thetay,float thetaz)
    {
        Matrix4X4 X,Y,Z,temp,result;

        X = createFixed4X4Matrix(0.0f);
        Y = createFixed4X4Matrix(0.0f);
        Z = createFixed4X4Matrix(0.0f);
        temp = createFixed4X4Matrix(0.0f);
        result = createFixed4X4Matrix(0.0f);

        //place the needed X rotational values into the matrix.
        X.index[0][0] = 1;
        X.index[1][1] = cos(DegreesToRads(thetax));
        X.index[2][2] = cos(DegreesToRads(thetax));
        X.index[3][3] = 1;

        X.index[2][1] = -1*(sin(DegreesToRads(thetax)));
        X.index[1][2] = sin(DegreesToRads(thetax));
```

```
//place the needed Y-Axis rotational values into the
➥matrix.
Y.index[0][0] = cos(DegreesToRads(thetay));
Y.index[1][1] = 1;
Y.index[2][2] = cos(DegreesToRads(thetay));
Y.index[3][3] = 1;

Y.index[2][0] = -1*(sin(DegreesToRads(thetay)));
Y.index[0][2] = 1;sin(DegreesToRads(thetay));

//place the needed Z-axis rotational values into the
➥matrix.
Z.index[0][0]  = cos(DegreesToRads(thetaz));
Z.index[1][1]  = cos(DegreesToRads(thetaz));
Z.index[2][2]  = 1;
Z.index[3][3]  = 1;

Z.index[0][1]  = -1*(sin(DegreesToRads(thetaz)));
Z.index[1][0]  = sin(DegreesToRads(thetaz));

//Create the single Combo Matrix.
temp = multiply4X4Matrices(Y,X);
result = multiply4X4Matrices(temp,Z);
return result;
    }
```

Most of this should look familiar. We took the guts out of each of the rotation functions we saw earlier in the chapter and set them up directly within this function. Once we have prepared the various matrices, we multiply them right to left. In this case, we are using temporary placeholders to bridge the limitation of our functions. You can process these in slightly faster ways without assigning the values to an intermediary matrix—just be careful and make sure that you are ordering them properly.

The final output of this function is just the finalized combo matrix; we will still need to process the translation. Now that the hard work is done, let's take a look at the transformation:

```
Matrix4X1 rotate3DWithCombo(Matrix4X4 combo, Matrix4X1 vertex)
    {
        Matrix4X1 temp;
        temp = multiplyMatrixNxM(combo,vertex);
        return temp;
    }
```

We continue through and multiply each vertex by the combo matrix. Remember that the rotation values for the different axis are contained within the single combo matrix. We need to make this rotation call against each vertex to discover the new orientation of the object. At this point, this process probably is starting to seem almost trivial.

By nature, programmers are always looking for math shortcuts. Unfortunately with combo matrices, the numbers become intertwined, so there's no shortcut here. The only way to find the correct values for each entry in the combo matrix is to stack them and multiply. There is some good news, though. When you go back to debug, an interesting pattern emerges. Let's look back at the example used to introduce this section: rotating 90° with respect to a triangle's own center point. The combo matrix equation you found is as follows:

$$\begin{bmatrix} x' \\ y' \\ 1 \end{bmatrix} = \begin{bmatrix} 0 & -1 & 168 \\ 1 & 0 & 18 \\ 0 & 0 & 1 \end{bmatrix} \begin{bmatrix} x \\ y \\ 1 \end{bmatrix}$$

If you look closely at this combo matrix, you can see that the rotation information is stored in the upper-left 2×2 section, and the overall translation information is stored in the last column.

Try setting up a few different combos; you should find the following pattern.

2D Combo Matrix

For every 2D combo matrix:

$$\begin{bmatrix} r_{00} & r_{01} & t_x \\ r_{10} & r_{11} & t_y \\ 0 & 0 & 1 \end{bmatrix}$$

entries with an r store scaling and rotation information, and entries with a t store overall translation information.

Notice that the bottom row of the combo is always $(0,0,1)$. This means that when you go back to debug, you might want to first check the bottom row, because that's an easy fix. If that's not the problem, look at the top two rows. If something is off with the translation, check the last column. If something is not right with scaling or rotation, check the first two columns. This process of elimination might save you some time when you go back to debug.

The same patterns also apply to 3D combo matrices.

3D Combo Matrix

For every 3D combo matrix:

$$
\begin{bmatrix}
r_{00} & r_{01} & r_{02} & t_x \\
r_{10} & r_{11} & r_{12} & t_y \\
r_{20} & r_{21} & r_{22} & t_z \\
0 & 0 & 0 & 1
\end{bmatrix}
$$

entries with an *r* store scaling and rotation information, and entries with a *t* store overall translation information.

Again, scaling and rotation information is stored in the upper-left 3×3 section. Examples 6.11 and 6.12 verify this. Again, the last column holds the overall translation information. You also might have noticed that the first row corresponds to *x*, the second row corresponds to *y*, the third row corresponds to *z*, and the bottom row is always the same: $(0,0,0,1)$. All these tricks should help you debug faster.

The last part of this section revisits the idea of the transpose, so you might need to flip back to Chapter 5 for a quick refresher. When you're ready, we'll look at 2D matrix equations. A typical combo matrix equation looks like this:

$$
\begin{bmatrix} x' \\ y' \\ 1 \end{bmatrix} =
\begin{bmatrix}
r_{00} & r_{01} & t_x \\
r_{10} & r_{11} & t_y \\
0 & 0 & 1
\end{bmatrix}
\begin{bmatrix} x \\ y \\ 1 \end{bmatrix}
$$

You might have noticed that this chapter uses single columns to represent the vertices. The good news is that OpenGL and most traditional mathematicians use the single-column format as well. The bad news is that DirectX uses single rows instead of single columns, so you have to make a few adjustments to convert from OpenGL format to DirectX.

The first step is to take the transpose of everything. That sends the single columns to single rows, and it adjusts the combo matrix to match. But you're not done yet. Remember that the order in which you multiply matrices is important. When you used single columns, you multiplied a 3×3 matrix by a 3×1. However, when you transposed everything, you ended up with a 3×3 times a 1×3, which is undefined. This leads to the second step, which is to reverse the order of multiplication. These two steps give you a matrix equation that is ready for DirectX:

$$\begin{bmatrix} x' & y' & 1 \end{bmatrix} = \begin{bmatrix} x & y & 1 \end{bmatrix} \begin{bmatrix} r_{00} & r_{10} & 0 \\ r_{01} & r_{11} & 0 \\ t_x & t_y & 1 \end{bmatrix}$$

Conversion Between the OpenGL and DirectX Formats

AB = B^{T}A^T for matrices A and B:

$$\underset{A}{\begin{bmatrix} r_{00} & r_{01} & t_x \\ r_{10} & r_{11} & t_y \\ 0 & 0 & 1 \end{bmatrix}} \underset{B}{\begin{bmatrix} x \\ y \\ 1 \end{bmatrix}} = \underset{B^T}{\begin{bmatrix} x & y & 1 \end{bmatrix}} \underset{A^T}{\begin{bmatrix} r_{00} & r_{10} & 0 \\ r_{01} & r_{11} & 0 \\ t_x & t_y & 1 \end{bmatrix}}$$

This same conversion process also works in 3D. Just remember to take the transpose of each matrix *and* reverse the order so that the matrix multiplication is defined.

> **NOTE**
> Even if you don't plan to use OpenGL, you might find it easier to set up the combos using single-column format and then switch to single rows at the last minute. Matrix multiplication is always easier going left to right.

This entire chapter built up to the point where you could finally construct combo matrices. You started by performing translation using matrix addition. Again, if all you want to do is translate, use matrix addition. However, if you know you need to set up a combo with scaling and/or rotation, you must use matrix multiplication. Remember to always start with the original vertex on the far right, stack to the left, and multiply to the right. In the end you can always switch to single-row format if you need to work with DirectX. I think you'll find that whether they use OpenGL or DirectX, transformation matrices are still at the heart of most 3D games.

Self-Assessment

1. Set up a combo matrix that will rotate a 2D object –90° with respect to its own center point, which is (10,50), all in one step.

2. Use the matrix in question 1 to rotate a triangle with vertices at A(–10,50), B(90,0), and C(–50,100).

3. Find a general matrix equation that will rotate any 2D object -90° with respect to its own center point, which is (x_c, y_c), all in one step.

4. Convert your answer to question 3 to a format that can be used by DirectX.

5. Set up a general matrix equation that will make any 3D object roll 45°, pitch 90°, and yaw –90° using a single combo matrix. Then apply it to a triangle with vertices at D(200,0,–30), E(0,50,–150), and F(40,20,–100).

6. Convert your matrix equation from question 3 to a format that can be used by DirectX.

Visualization Experience

On the CD-ROM, you will find a demo named Transformations. Here's a brief description from the programmers:

This program was designed to help you understand the principles of 2D transformations applied to an object. Matrices are used to rotate or translate a quad around the grid. Users can use this application to get a visual representation while learning the basics of matrix concatenation.

The user can add, select, move, and trace quads on the grid as well as undo and redo actions applied to a quad. During the experience, the user can view information about the current location of each quad.

—Michael Wigand and Michael Fawcett

This demo is also interactive. You can plug values into a transformation matrix and then see how the object moves as a result. You might want to try setting up a few examples by hand first and then run the demo to see if it has the effect you expected.

You can run the demo by double-clicking the Transformations.exe file. As soon as the demo is loaded, you should see a window with a red grid and a colored box in the middle. You can move this box around the screen using transformation matrices. The toolbar is labeled for you in Figure 6.11 so that you can follow the instructions listed next.

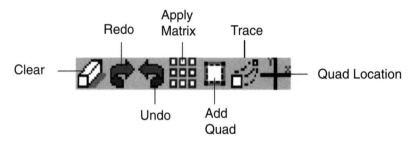

Figure 6.11   The toolbar for the Transformations demo.

To get started, click the Apply matrix button. A window pops up with a 3×3 matrix. Enter the following values:

$$\begin{bmatrix} 1 & 0 & 5 \\ 0 & 1 & 3 \\ 0 & 0 & 1 \end{bmatrix}$$

The box should move five units to the right and eight up.

Click the Trace button on the toolbar. This leaves an imprint of the current location. Click the Add a quad button on the toolbar. This adds a new box with the bottom-left vertex at the origin.

This time, try to move the box five units to the left and three up. After you have done so, leave the box selected (outlined in white), trace its location, and apply the following matrix to it:

$$\begin{bmatrix} 3 & 0 & 0 \\ 0 & 3 & 0 \\ 0 & 0 & 1 \end{bmatrix}$$

What happened this time? That's right—the object scaled 3 times larger with respect to the origin. This means that it moved away from the origin as it got larger. Click the Undo button to go back to the previous location. See if you can scale the box 3 times larger without moving away from the origin. Remember that this is a three-step combo:

$$\begin{bmatrix} 1 & 0 & -5 \\ 0 & 1 & 3 \\ 0 & 0 & 1 \end{bmatrix} \begin{bmatrix} 3 & 0 & 0 \\ 0 & 3 & 0 \\ 0 & 0 & 1 \end{bmatrix} \begin{bmatrix} 1 & 0 & 5 \\ 0 & 1 & -3 \\ 0 & 0 & 1 \end{bmatrix}$$

If you multiply these three matrices in the correct order, you should get the following combo matrix:

$$\begin{bmatrix} 3 & 0 & 10 \\ 0 & 3 & -6 \\ 0 & 0 & 1 \end{bmatrix}$$

This time you scaled 3 times larger with respect to the box's center instead of the origin. If your screen is starting to get too messy, you can click the Clear button at this point to wipe the slate clean. If not, just create a new quad for the next set of transforms.

This time, move the box nine units to the right and four units up using this matrix:

$$\begin{bmatrix} 1 & 0 & 9 \\ 0 & 1 & 4 \\ 0 & 0 & 1 \end{bmatrix}$$

Trace that location and then rotate 90° with this matrix:

$$\begin{bmatrix} \cos 90° & -\sin 90° & 0 \\ \sin 90° & \cos 90° & 0 \\ 0 & 0 & 1 \end{bmatrix} = \begin{bmatrix} 0 & -1 & 0 \\ 1 & 0 & 0 \\ 0 & 0 & 1 \end{bmatrix}$$

What happened? It looks like the box just translated up and to the left, but that's not entirely what happened. Look at the blue corner of the box. Press Undo and Redo a couple times. You might notice that the box did in fact rotate 90° in addition to translating. Otherwise, you can also view the coordinates of all four vertices by clicking the Quad position button on the toolbar. Write down the coordinates in the new position, press Undo, and view the coordinates of the old position. You can also verify that the box rotated that way. So what really happened is that the box rotated *with respect to* the origin.

Try to rotate the box with respect to the red corner instead. That way, it stays in the same place and looks like it's just tipping over. If you're not currently at the old location, click the Undo button to go back. Now you can view the quad position to find the coordinates of the red vertex. You should find that the red corner is currently at (9,4). Now you can set up a combo to rotate 90° with respect to the red vertex. You can either perform each of these steps individually or multiply them together for one combo matrix:

$$
\begin{bmatrix} 1 & 0 & 9 \\ 0 & 1 & 4 \\ 0 & 0 & 1 \end{bmatrix}
\begin{bmatrix} 0 & -1 & 0 \\ 1 & 0 & 0 \\ 0 & 0 & 1 \end{bmatrix}
\begin{bmatrix} 1 & 0 & -9 \\ 0 & 1 & -4 \\ 0 & 0 & 1 \end{bmatrix}
=
\begin{bmatrix} 0 & -1 & 13 \\ 1 & 0 & -5 \\ 0 & 0 & 1 \end{bmatrix}
$$

Did you get the outcome you expected? I suggest that you try a few combos of your own. Experiment with the demo a little bit. You might want to consider performing your own combos by hand first and then use the demo to check your work. You can write down the four original vertices and calculate where they should end up and then view the quad position to see if that's where the computer places them in the demo. Hopefully they come out to be the same!

Self-Assessment Solutions

Translation

1. D'(70,60)

2. E'(−10,180)

3. F'(140,−20)

4. G'(250,−330,−50), H'(140,−300,−40), J'(−350,−250,−100)

5. L'(−300,50), M'(−150,−60), N'(−130,20)

6. Yes. G'(250,−330,−50), H'(140,−300,−40), J'(−350,−250,−100)

Scaling

1. A'(–25,10), B'(–5,10), C'(–15,20)

2. A'(–12.5,60), B'(–2.5,60), C'(–7.5,120)

3. D'(0,300,–1000), E'(–500,1000,–200), F'(–200,0,–3000)

4. D'(0,30,–50), E'(–100,100,–10), F'(–40,0,–150)

Rotation

1. A'(–33.66,38.30), B'(69.28,40), C'(–93.3,61.6)

2. D'(–0.8725,20,–49.9925), E'(–9.6495,0,20.1715), F'(29.9955,20,–0.5235)

3. G'(0,91.91,–49.49), H'(–50,84.84,56.56), J'(–20,212.13,–212.13)

4. L'(–30,0,–100), M'(–100,–50,–20), N'(0,–20,–300)

Concatenation

1. $$\begin{bmatrix} 0 & 1 & -40 \\ -1 & 0 & 60 \\ 0 & 0 & 1 \end{bmatrix}$$

2. A'(10,70), B'(–40,30), C'(60,110)

3. $$\begin{bmatrix} x' \\ y' \\ 1 \end{bmatrix} = \begin{bmatrix} 0 & 1 & (-y_c + x_c) \\ -1 & 0 & (x_c + y_c) \\ 0 & 0 & 1 \end{bmatrix} \begin{bmatrix} x \\ y \\ 1 \end{bmatrix}$$

4.
$$\begin{bmatrix} x' & y' & 1 \end{bmatrix} = \begin{bmatrix} x & y & 1 \end{bmatrix} \begin{bmatrix} 0 & -1 & 0 \\ 1 & 0 & 0 \\ (-y_c + x_c) & (x_c + y_c) & 1 \end{bmatrix}$$

5. D'(–141.4,30,141.4), E'(–35.4,150,–35.4), F'(–42.4,100,14.1)

6.

$$[x' \quad y' \quad z' \quad 1] = [x \quad y \quad z \quad 1] \begin{bmatrix} -.707 & 0 & .707 & 0 \\ -.707 & 0 & -.707 & 0 \\ 0 & -1 & 0 & 0 \\ 0 & 0 & 0 & 1 \end{bmatrix}$$

Chapter 7

Unit Conversions

KEY TOPICS

- The Metric System
- Converting Units Between Systems
- Computer Conversions

As we prepare to transition into the physics chapters of this book, there's one last mathematical concept to master: unit conversions. In physics, we deal with physical quantities such as speed and displacement. The units in which they're measured often get overlooked to the detriment of many projects. You might remember that in the fall of 1999, the Mars Climate Orbiter was declared lost by NASA. The mission failed because one project group used English units and one used metric units when programming the maneuvering system. The Orbiter was eventually sent off target and got lost in space. Imagine what could happen in your game if the units aren't all consistent. If one team member programs in meters and another team member programs in miles, some interesting bugs will appear when the team members try to integrate their code. Unfortunately, a lot of time can be lost in debugging if nobody thinks to check the units, so this chapter is dedicated to the small but very important detail of units.

The Metric System

If you lived in almost any country other than the United States, you'd probably use metric units more than English units. This section is a quick review of how to work within the metric system, just in case it's been a while for you. I think after using it a bit you'll find that the metric system is much easier to work with because it's based on powers of 10.

When you're programming, the computer cannot distinguish between meters and centimeters. It understands only numbers, so it is up to you as the programmer to be consistent with the units of physical quantities in your program. We'll start with the metric system because it's much easier to work with. Your player will never know if you are working with miles or kilometers, yards or meters, so if you can do your measurements within the metric system, it will save you a lot of headaches. In addition, many licensed add-ins for game engines, such as the Havok physics engine, use metric units, so you might want to consider making it a habit to work with metrics.

Suppose you are tracking the motion of the main character in your game. You might estimate his displacement in meters while he's running, but it might be easier to estimate in centimeters when he's tiptoeing. If he runs for 10 meters and then tiptoes for 75 centimeters, it wouldn't make sense to add those two displacements together. You'd have to convert one of them to the same units as the other before you could add them. It doesn't matter which one you choose, as long as they're the same.

Converting within the metric system is simple because all the units represent powers of 10, so converting between them is as easy as sliding the decimal point. The following is a list in descending order of the metric prefixes. These prefixes would be followed by the word meter or gram.

> **NOTE**
> Remember that a meter is almost the same length as a yard—a little over 3 feet.
>
> Also, one gram is about the mass of a large thumbtack. A nickel has a mass of about 5 grams.

The Metric System						
kilo-	hecto-	deca-	meters, grams	deci-	centi-	milli-
1000	100	10	1	0.1	0.01	0.001

> **NOTE**
> These prefixes work the exact same way with grams if you're measuring mass.

Each time you slide to the right along that list, you multiply by 10 or slide the decimal point one slot to the right. For example, if you wanted to convert the 10 meters your character ran to centimeters, you'd slide right twice, so you have to slide the decimal point two places to the right, which would give you 1000 centimeters. Likewise, if you wanted to convert 75 centimeters to meters, that would be two prefixes to the left, so you'd slide the decimal point two places to the left, which yields 0.75 meters. This is the beauty of the metric system. Because it's a base-10 system, each time you slide to the left or right on the list, you multiply or divide the original value by the system's base, which is 10, just like our familiar decimal system.

Example 7.1: Converting Meters to Kilometers

Suppose the main character in your game runs 50 meters and then hops in his car and drives 25 kilometers. How far does he travel altogether in kilometers?

Solution

1. To add the two displacements, they must have the same units. In this case, you convert the 50 meters to kilometers. Looking at the list of prefixes, kilometers are three prefixes to the left of meters, so you must slide the decimal point three places to the left. This means that 50m = 0.05km.

2. Now you can add the two together, so the total displacement is 25.05km.

Example 7.2: Converting Kilometers to Meters

Suppose you find out that the rest of your team is programming in meters. How far does the main character in Example 7.1 travel altogether in meters?

Solution

1. You could start all over and convert the 25km to meters and then add again, or you could just convert the total, 25.05km, to meters.

2. Let's take the second approach. Meters are three prefixes to the right on the list, so you must slide the decimal point three places to the right, which gives you a total of 25,050 meters.

After stepping through two examples, you can see the beauty of the metric system. Converting within metrics is as simple as sliding the decimal point, because you're multiplying and dividing by powers of 10. The next section looks at the more complicated process of converting within the English system as well as converting between metrics and English units.

Self-Assessment

1. Convert 35 meters to centimeters.

2. Convert 35 meters to kilometers.

3. Convert 4567 millimeters to kilometers.

4. Convert a mass of 56 grams to kilograms.

5. Convert a mass of 3 kilograms to grams.

Converting Units Between Systems

Converting between different systems of units is a little more complicated than staying within metrics. That's why I suggest estimating distances in meters and estimating speeds in kilometers per hour. Unfortunately, if you grew up in the United States, it's a lot more natural to estimate quantities in English units, such as speeds in miles per hour.

In game programming, you'll mostly be dealing with length and time quantities, so we'll focus on those. There will be times when you'll need to convert within the English system, and there will be times when you'll need to convert between the English and metric systems. In either case, the process is the same.

When you are converting units, it is very important to keep your work organized. The premise behind this procedure is that when you multiply a number by 1, it stays the same. So if you start with the quantity you want to convert and multiply it by 1 several times, it will not change the quantity. Remember that any fraction whose numerator is equal to the denominator equals 1. The fraction $^3/3$ equals 1. The fraction (60 seconds/ 1 minute) equals 1. All you want to do is multiply the original quantity by a bunch of **conversion factors** (or ratios), all of which are fractions equal to 1, fractions whose numerator is equal to the denominator. An example of a conversion factor is (60min/1hr). We all know that 60 minutes equals 1 hour, so that fraction equals 1.

It is also a conversion factor, because it shows an equality between two different units. You can use that particular conversion factor to convert from hours to minutes. For example, to convert 3 hours to minutes, just multiply by (60min/1hr):

$$3hrs\left(\frac{60\,min}{1hr}\right) = 180\,min$$

Take a close look at the conversion factor (60min/1hr). If it were flipped, it would still be a conversion factor, but it would convert minutes to hours instead. Whenever you're not sure which way to flip, use the units as a guide. When you multiply, you want the old units to cancel out and the new units to stay. Always treat the original quantity as a number over 1 so that you know which way to flip the conversion factor for the units to line up and cancel the way you want. Table 7.1 lists all the conversion factors you should need.

Table 7.1 List of Conversion Factors

Length	Time
1m = 39.37in = 3.281ft	1s = 1000ms
1in = 2.54cm	1min = 60s
1km = 0.621mi	1hr = 3600s
1mi = 5,280ft = 1.609km	1 year = 365.242 days

When coding the solutions to these problems, it's a wise idea to make a few constants that can be referenced quickly in code. For example:

```
#define KM_TO_MILES 1.609
#define KM_TO_METERS 1000
#define DAYS_TO_WEEK 7
#define HOURS_TO_DAY 24
#define HOURS_TO_MIN 60
#define MIN_TO_SEC 60
```

These values are easy enough to determine from looking at Table 7.1 or other sources. Using a constant can make the actual calculation of the values in the game a little easier to read. We also gain the benefit of making wholesale changes throughout the application should one of these values need to be changed. On Earth that might be unlikely, but then again many games don't take place on Earth. A single day on Saturn is a little more than 10.5 Earth hours.

The best way to solidify this concept is to work through a few examples. Let's start with a simple time conversion.

Example 7.3: Time Conversion

How many seconds are in 2 weeks?

Solution

1. Start with the original quantity, 2 weeks.

2. Stack to the right a series of conversion factors that will convert weeks to seconds. Try to keep the fractions lined up so that you're less likely to make a mistake when you go back to multiply:

$$\frac{2wks}{1}\left(\frac{7days}{1wk}\right)\left(\frac{24hrs}{1day}\right)\left(\frac{60min}{1hr}\right)\left(\frac{60s}{1min}\right)$$

3. Make sure that the fractions are flipped in such a way that the units cancel the way you want.

4. Multiply all the fractions:

$$\frac{2wks}{1}\left(\frac{7days}{1wk}\right)\left(\frac{24hrs}{1day}\right)\left(\frac{60min}{1hr}\right)\left(\frac{60s}{1min}\right)=1,209,600s$$

As mentioned earlier, quite often you'll estimate quantities in English units but then program in metric units. Let's look at an example of that process.

Here's a quick function that will take a number of days and convert it to seconds. See if you can make your own derivatives of this function to approximate time conversion:

```
float convertDaysToSeconds(float days)
    {
        float seconds;
        seconds = days*HOURS_TO_DAY*HOURS_TO_MIN*MIN_TO_SEC;
        return seconds;
    }
```

Take note of how the constants are used here to make the code clean. This is a good technique for making code easy to read.

Example 7.4: Distance Conversion

Suppose you estimate that the character in your game has run 5 miles. Unfortunately, your team has decided to program in metric units. How many meters has he run?

Solution

1. Start with the original quantity, 5 miles.

2. Stack to the right a series of conversion factors that will convert miles to meters. Try to keep the fractions lined up so that you're less likely to make a mistake when you go back to multiply:

$$\frac{5mi}{1}\left(\frac{1.609km}{1mi}\right)\left(\frac{1000m}{1km}\right)$$

3. Make sure that the fractions are flipped in such a way that the units cancel the way you want.

4. Multiply all the fractions:

$$\frac{5mi}{1}\left(\frac{1.609km}{1mi}\right)\left(\frac{1000m}{1km}\right) = 8045m$$

Coding this out is also pretty straightforward:

```
float convertMilesToMeters(float miles)
    {
       float meters;
       meters = miles*KM_TO_MILES*KM_TO_METERS;
       return meters;
    }
```

> **NOTE**
> Most books use "mi" for miles and "m" for meters when labeling units. This book follows the same standard.

When dealing with quantities that have a fraction in the unit, this process becomes slightly more complicated. For example, speeds can be measured in miles per hour (mi/hr). Many errors are made when dealing with the hours on the bottom of the fraction. One way to avoid errors is to write a quantity such as 55mi/hr as 55mi/1hr instead. This might help you keep the conversion factors lined up the way you want. Example 7.5 demonstrates this process.

Example 7.5: Speed Conversion

Suppose you estimate that the car in your racing game is currently going 180mi/hr. Your team has decided to program in metric units. What is its speed in m/s?

Solution

1. Start with the original quantity, 180mi/hr. Write it as 180mi/1hr.

2. Stack to the right a series of conversion factors that will perform two separate conversions: miles to meters in the numerator and then hours to seconds in the denominator. Try to keep the fractions lined up so that you're less likely to make a mistake when you go back to multiply:

$$\frac{180mi}{1hr} \left(\frac{1.609km}{1mi}\right) \left(\frac{1000m}{1km}\right) \left(\frac{1hr}{60\,min}\right) \left(\frac{1\,min}{60s}\right)$$

3. Make sure that the fractions are flipped in such a way that the units cancel the way you want. Notice that by keeping the 1 hour on the bottom of the fraction, it is easier to determine which way to flip the last two conversion factors.

4. Multiply all the fractions:

$$\frac{180mi}{1hr} \left(\frac{1.609km}{1mi}\right) \left(\frac{1000m}{1km}\right) \left(\frac{1hr}{60\,min}\right) \left(\frac{1\,min}{60s}\right) = 80.45m/s$$

This conversion can also be coded out in a pretty straightforward manner:

```
float convertSpeed(float miles)
    {
        float meters;

        meters =
          (miles*KM_TO_MILES*KM_TO_METERS)/(HOURS_TO_MIN*MIN_TO_SEC);

        return meters;
    }
```

The last complication arises when you have a unit that is squared. For example, acceleration always has a unit of length divided by a unit of time squared, such as m/s^2. Remember that s^2 is s*s, not just seconds by itself. This means that when you convert, *both* seconds need to be converted. Let's look at an example to demonstrate this process.

Example 7.6: Acceleration Conversion

Suppose you estimate that the car in your racing game is currently accelerating at a rate of 20,000mi/hr^2. Unfortunately, your team has decided to program in metric units. What is the acceleration in m/s^2?

Solution

1. Start with the original quantity, 20,000mi/hr^2. Write it as 20,000mi/1hr^2 so that the time squared stays on the bottom of the fraction.

2. Stack to the right a series of conversion factors that will convert miles to meters and hours squared to seconds squared. Make sure you convert from hours to seconds *twice*, because the unit is hr^2, not just hours. Also, make sure the fractions are flipped in such a way that the units cancel the way you want. Try to keep them lined up so that you're less likely to make a mistake when you go back to multiply:

$$\frac{20,000mi}{1hr^2}\left(\frac{1.609km}{1mi}\right)\left(\frac{1000m}{1km}\right)\left(\frac{1hr}{60\,min}\right)\left(\frac{1\,min}{60s}\right)\left(\frac{1hr}{60\,min}\right)\left(\frac{1\,min}{60s}\right)$$

3. Multiply all the fractions:

$$\frac{20,000mi}{1hr^2}\left(\frac{1.609km}{1mi}\right)\left(\frac{1000m}{1km}\right)\left(\frac{1hr}{60\,min}\right)\left(\frac{1\,min}{60s}\right)\left(\frac{1hr}{60\,min}\right)\left(\frac{1\,min}{60s}\right)=2.48m/s^2$$

No matter what type of units you need to convert, the process is always the same: You multiply the original quantity by a series of fractions equal to 1 (conversion factors) that eventually bring you to the desired units. Be careful when doing this by hand. Try to keep the fractions lined up so that you don't accidentally divide when you meant to multiply. Also, keep in mind what units you're trying to reach. It's easy to start stacking conversion factors and forget where you were originally going with them. Most importantly, when you're working on a development team, always remember to establish a common set of units *before* you start programming anything. Conflicting units can lead to disastrous results—just ask NASA!

Let's take a look at how to code this conversion. Here is a function that will convert acceleration from MPH^2 to m/s^2:

```
float convertAccelMilesToMeters(float miles){
    float accelMeters;
    accelMeters = (miles*KM_TO_MILES*KM_TO_METERS) /
(HOURS_TO_MIN*MIN_TO_SEC*HOURS_TO_MIN*MIN_TO_SEC);
    return accelMeters;
    }
```

Note again the usage of defines in this formula. When the more commonly used conversions are known they are usually computed ahead. For example, instead of converting hours to minutes, then minutes to seconds, we could have just made the quicker jump from hours to seconds. The example is provided here to map with the previous explanation more than to identify the fastest way to handle the problem. Programming physics in a game that responds quickly is a big challenge that needs to reduce the processing as much as possible. Look for such opportunities in your own code.

Self-Assessment

1. How many minutes are in 3 days?

2. How many centimeters are in 10 inches?

3. Suppose you estimate that the car in your racing game has gone 12 miles. Unfortunately, your team has decided to program in metric units. How many meters has it traveled?

4. Suppose you estimate that the car in your racing game is currently going 225mi/hr. Your team has decided to program in metric units. What is the car's speed in km/hr?

5. After you convert the speed in question 4 to km/hr, you find out that the rest of your team is using meters and seconds. What is 225mi/hr in m/s?

6. What is 9.8m/s^2 in mi/hr^2?

Computer Conversions

Often, you hear people talk about 50-kilobyte files or 2-gig hard drives. These might sound like random numbers. It's important to understand how all these quantities are related. They all describe quantities of information that the computer can read or store. Remember that the computer actually reads binary code.

When you program code in a language such as C++, you need a compiler to translate your code into binary code. Then the computer flips a bunch of switches on (1) or off (0). Binary code is simply a series of 0s and 1s that state whether each individual switch is currently on or off. Each of these switches holds 1 bit of information: 0 or 1. Then these bits can be grouped into sets of eight, which is 1 byte of information. Each byte can be used to represent a number between 0 and 255. Here's where it gets tricky.

In "The Metric System" section, you saw how easy it was to work with a base-10 system. The decimal system is base 10. Each digit represents a power of 10. You might remember learning about the 1s digit, the 10s digit, the 100s digit, and so forth back in grade school. Now imagine that each digit represents a power of 2 rather than 10; that's how the binary system is set up. Table 7.2 compares decimal digits to binary digits.

Table 7.2   Digits in Decimal (Base 10) Versus Binary (Base 2)

Decimal (Base 10)							
10^7	10^6	10^5	10^4	10^3	10^2	10^1	10^0
10,000,000	1,000,000	100,000	10,000	1,000	100	10	1
Binary (Base 2)							
2^7	2^6	2^5	2^4	2^3	2^2	2^1	2^0
128	64	32	16	8	4	2	1

In the decimal system, a number like 702 is really 7 100s plus 0 10s plus 2 1s. In the binary system, each digit is worth a power of 2 rather than a power of 10. This means that the number 10011010 in binary is really one 128 plus no 64s plus no 32s plus one 16 plus one 8 plus no 4s plus one 2 plus no 1s, which is really $128 + 16 + 8 + 2 = 154$ as a decimal number. Table 7.3 illustrates the binary digits for the number 10011010.

Table 7.3 The Binary Number 10011010

2^7	2^6	2^5	2^4	2^3	2^2	2^1	2^0
128	64	32	16	8	4	2	1
1	0	0	1	1	0	1	0
128	0	0	16	8	0	2	0

Example 7.7: Converting Binary to Decimal

Convert the binary number 01001101 to decimal.

Solution

1. The easiest approach is to use a table like this to organize the binary digits:

2^7	2^6	2^5	2^4	2^3	2^2	2^1	2^0
128	64	32	16	8	4	2	1
0	1	0	0	1	1	0	1
0	64	0	0	8	4	0	1

2. Add the numbers in the bottom row:

   64 + 8 + 4 + 1 = 77

The binary number 01001101 is equal to 77 in decimal form.

If all eight digits are 0s, that's the equivalent of 0 in decimal. If all eight digits are 1s, that's the equivalent of 255 in decimal form. A unique binary number can represent each of the numbers between 0 and 255. The process of converting a number from decimal to binary can best be described with an example.

Example 7.8: Converting Decimal to Binary

Convert the decimal number 185 to binary.

Solution

1. Find the largest power of 2 that's less than 185. (The preceding table lists the first eight digits.) In this case, 128 is the largest power of 2 that is less than or equal to 185.

2. Subtract 128 from 185, which gives you 57.

3. Repeat the process using 57. The largest power of 2 that's less than or equal to 57 is 32.

4. Subtract 32 from 57, and you're left with 25.

5. Keep repeating the process until you reach 0.

6. The largest power of 2 that's less than or equal to 25 is 16.

7. Subtract 16 from 25, which leaves you with 9.

8. The largest power of 2 that's less than or equal to 9 is 8.

9. Subtract 8 from 9, and you get 1.

10. The largest power of 2 that's less than or equal to 1 is 1.

11. Subtract 1 from 1, and you get 0. Now you can stop.

12. The last step is to go through the list and, for every number you subtracted, give its corresponding digit a 1. For all the other powers of 2 that got skipped, give their digits a 0. You end up with the following:

2^7	2^6	2^5	2^4	2^3	2^2	2^1	2^0
128	64	32	16	8	4	2	1
1	0	1	1	1	0	0	1

This means that the binary number 10111001 is the same as decimal number 185.

Programming Binary and Decimal Conversions

The process of converting from binary to decimal and back again is a slightly different process in code than it is on paper. The algorithm works the same, but there are important things that have to be adjusted so that they work within the computer and still give the user the correct expected value from the conversion. First let's take a look at converting decimal to binary:

```
void decimaltoBinary()
    {
        int tobeconverted;
```

continues

continued

```
    int binaryplaceholder[32];

    cout<<"Please enter a binary number in ones and zeros\n";
    cin>>tobeconverted;


    for(int i =0;i<32;i++)
      {
        //take the number and process modulus to return a 1 or 0
        ➥binaryplaceholder[i] = tobeconverted%2;

        //then we divide the number by two and revisit the
        ➥number.
        tobeconverted = tobeconverted/2;
      }

  cout<<"Your decimal number converted to binary is: \n";

    //To make sure we are outputting in the proper order,
    //we print the array backwards.

    for(int j = 31; j>=0;j--)
      {
        cout<<binaryplaceholder[j];
      }
  }
```

First, the code takes a valid binary input. Then using the modulus operator, the number is determined to be currently even or odd (1 or 0) and the resulting value is stored in the `binaryplaceholderarray`, slowly constructing the converted number. Then we divide the number by two and continue the process. The last part of this function prints out the new binary number from left to right. In order to maintain the proper ordering of the binary number, it starts from the end and prints backwards. Pretty cool, eh?

Now let's look at the conversion process to turn a binary number into a decimal number. This process is similar, but requires us to use some additional tools:

```
void binarytoDecimal()
    {
        char tobeconverted[9];
        int finalvalue =0;
        int powerval = 0;

        cout<<"Please enter a binary value (8 bits max) MSB
        ➡first.\n";
        cin>>tobeconverted;

        //run from 0-7 = 8 bits total
        for(int j = 0; j<=7; j++)
          {
            //we have to reverse the power so the ordering is MSB
            ➡first,
            powerval = pow(2,(7-j));

            //test for a "1", otherwise it must be a zero.
            if(tobeconverted[j] == '1')
                finalvalue = finalvalue + powerval;

          }

        cout<<"The number from binary to decimal is
        ➡<<finalvalue<<"\n";
    }
```

This function first takes in an 8-bit binary value. 8 was chosen so the conversion could more easily be demonstrated. Feel free to increase the number of bits if you like; the algorithm is the same. Once the binary number is in the `char[]`, we move through one position at a time, calculating the current power of 2, then test to see if the value that is to be converted is a 1. If so, add the `final-value` to the `powerval`. The reason that we don't need to ask if its zero is because in a binary situation a number that is not one is always zero, or invalid. Since the Most Significant Bit (MSB) is the first one to come into the array, it has to have the highest possible power of the entire binary number. It is very easy to ignore this step and have the values in the reverse ordering giving incorrect values. These sort of conversions should always trap errors to keep from long debugging sessions. Make sure your code does.

From the unit of bits, you can build conversions to all the other binary units. Let's start with the smallest units and work our way up. I said earlier that a byte of information is equal to 8 bits. Most files such as text documents consist of thousands of bytes of information. It can be cumbersome to work with such large quantities, so often we convert them to kilobytes. One kilobyte equals 1,024 bytes. Some files, particularly those with many graphics, are much larger, so it might make sense to convert to an even larger unit, the megabyte. One megabyte equals 1,024 kilobytes. Let's take this thought one step further. Often, hard drives are described by the amount of information they can store. The most sensible unit for that is the gigabyte. One gigabyte equals 1,024 megabytes. All this information can be summarized as follows:

> 1 byte = 8 bits
>
> 1 kilobyte = 1,024 bytes
>
> 1 megabyte = 1,024 kilobytes
>
> 1 gigabyte = 1,024 megabytes

NOTE

These conversion factors might seem odd. Remember that you're working with binary now, which is base 2. That is why the conversion factors must be powers of 2.

The actual conversion process is the same as we discussed in the last section. You just have a new set of conversion factors this time. Let's look at an example.

Example 7.9: Computer Conversion

If your computer hard drive holds 20GB of information, how many bits is that?

Solution

1. Start with the original quantity, 20GB.

2. Stack to the right a series of conversion factors that will convert gigabytes to bits. Try to keep the fractions lined up so that you're less likely to make a mistake when you go back to multiply:

$$\frac{20GB}{1} \left(\frac{1024MB}{1GB}\right) \left(\frac{1024KB}{1MB}\right) \left(\frac{1024B}{1KB}\right) \left(\frac{8b}{1B}\right)$$

3. Make sure that the fractions are flipped in such a way that the units cancel the way you want.

4. Multiply all the fractions:

$$\frac{20GB}{1}\left(\frac{1024MB}{1GB}\right)\left(\frac{1024KB}{1MB}\right)\left(\frac{1024B}{1KB}\right)\left(\frac{8b}{1B}\right) = 1.718x10^{11}bits$$

One of the distinctive features of C++ is that it allows you to allocate memory as the application runs. If that's the case, you must be precise about the amount of space you need. If you're trying to get a rough estimate in your head, you can round the conversion factors to just 1,000, but if you're allocating memory or dealing with storage issues, it's imperative that you use 1,024 for all the conversion factors. If you're off by even a single byte, the program could crash. That is why these computer conversions are extremely important.

Self-Assessment

1. Convert the binary number 10101010 to decimal.

2. Convert the binary number 01101101 to decimal.

3. Convert the decimal number 176 to binary.

4. Convert the decimal number 205 to binary.

5. How many bits of information can be stored on a 100MB zip disk?

6. If you allocate 4KB of storage space, how many bits can it hold?

7. If you have a file that's 12,345,678 bits large, how many megabytes is that?

8. How many gigabytes are in 23,753,891,429 bytes?

Self-Assessment Solutions

The Metric System

1. 3,500cm

2. 0.035km

3. 0.004567km

4. 0.056kg

5. 3,000g

Converting Units Between Systems

1. 4,320 minutes

2. 25.4cm

3. 19,308m

4. 362.025km/hr

5. 100.5625m/s

6. 78,936mi/hr^2

Computer Conversions

1. 170

2. 109

3. 10110000

4. 11001101

5. 838,860,800 bits

6. 32,768 bits

7. 1.47MB

8. 22.12GB

Chapter 8

Motion in One Dimension

A video game is almost like a flipbook: As you loop through the program, all the objects move frame by frame. If you flip through fast enough, the motion appears to be smooth and realistic. But how does the computer know where to place objects in each frame? The laws of physics tell it exactly how the objects should move. Keep in mind that in the real world, so many factors influence motion that you can't possibly take all of them into account. Some factors must be sacrificed to achieve real-time physics, but the ones that are sacrificed are usually quite insignificant. This chapter introduces the world of game physics. It defines some basic physical quantities and addresses how to mathematically control the motion of objects in your game.

Speed and Velocity

Any time an object is moving, it has some speed. **Speed** measures how fast an object is moving. If an object has speed, it also has a **velocity**, which is simply the vector version of speed. You might want to flip back to Chapter 4, "Vector Operations," for a quick refresher on the difference between a vector and a scalar quantity. Velocity is speed with a direction. In one dimension, the direction is given by positive or negative. (Chapter 10, "Motion in Two and Three Dimensions," address how to deal with direction in 2D and 3D.) For now, just consider the motion of an object along a straight line, where positive velocity is forward and negative velocity is backward.

> **NOTE**
> The terms "speed" and "velocity" may be used interchangeably in dialogue. Whenever speed is used, the direction is ignored.

Let's first look at an object moving with a constant velocity. For example, suppose I set the cruise control on my car to 60mi/hr. If I maintain that constant speed for an hour, I should go 60 miles. If I keep the cruise control set, I should go 120 miles in 2 hours, 180 miles in 3 hours, and so forth. This leads to the following statement.

Displacement with Constant Velocity

displacement = velocity * time ($D = v * t$)

for any constant velocity v.

> **NOTE**
> If you chose to ignore direction because the road is not perfectly straight, the same formula applies to the scalar equivalents: distance = speed * time for any constant speed.

Example 8.1: Finding Displacement with Constant Velocity

Suppose you're programming a portion of a game in which the main character jumps into a vehicle with a constant velocity of 150px/s. How far has he moved after 1 second, 2 seconds, and 3 seconds?

Solution

1. Set up a formula to calculate displacement:

   $D = v * t = (150\text{px/s}) * t$

2. Plug in each time interval:

   After 1s: $D = (150\text{px/s}) * t = (150\text{px/s}) * (1\text{s}) = 150\text{px}$

   After 2s: $D = (150\text{px/s}) * t = (150\text{px/s}) * (2\text{s}) = 300\text{px}$

   After 3s: $D = (150\text{px/s}) * t = (150\text{px/s}) * (3\text{s}) = 450\text{px}$

Let's put this in programming terms. As I flip through my game frame by frame, I want to know how far my car moves between each frame. Remember that displacement is the change in position: new position, old position. If I plug that into the preceding formula, I get an equation that can go directly in the code:

```
//Passing through floats for velocity and time we return the
➥resulting displacement.
float calcDisplacement(float vel, float time)
    {
        return vel*time;
    }
```

Some game architectures try only to pass the relative change in an object's position over a network to reduce the overall size and amount of network data. This results in sending a net displacement of the object as opposed to the raw firing of the absolute position of an object in the game. Using this method, it is possible to calculate the displacement locally and then fire off a change to the server only if needed. Try to expand this example to work with multiple time periods and calculate an object's total displacement over a larger measure of time.

Displacement Between Frames

New_position = Old_position + Velocity * Time

where Time is one frame (usually 1/30th of a second).

NOTE

The framerate will most likely not stay constant at 30fps. Most developers calculate a "delta time" by subtracting the system clock's value at the last frame simulation from the value at this simulation and then use that as the time factor. This way, the simulations aren't thrown out of whack by the changes in framerate that naturally occur when new AIs are spawned or particle systems are introduced.

Example 8.2: Finding a New Position with Constant Velocity

Let's revisit Example 8.1. You really don't care how far the vehicle has moved after 1 whole second. What you really want to know is how far it moves between frames (assuming that the frame rate is 30fps). If the vehicle is at the 50-pixel mark in one frame, where should it be in the next frame?

Solution

1. Set up a formula to calculate the new position:

   New_position = Old_position + Velocity * Time = 50px + (150px/s) * Time

2. Because the frame rate is 30fps, the time interval of one frame is 1/30th of a second. Calculate the new position with a time of 1/30th of a second:

   New_position = 50px + (150px/s) * (1/30s) = 55px

Creating a function to handle this calculation works like this:

```
//Passing through floats for velocity and time we return the
➥resulting
//position at the time specified.

float calcPosition(float oldPosition, float vel, float time)
    {
        return oldPosition + (vel*time);
    }
```

All this works if you know the object is moving at a constant velocity. But how often do you drive around with the cruise control on? Certainly in some games, it's easy to set up sections in which a vehicle moves at a constant speed, but you probably wouldn't want to do this for a racing game. Next time you're in a car, watch the speedometer for a while; you'll probably notice that the speed constantly changes. Therefore, we need to discuss two different types of velocity: average and instantaneous. Let's look at average velocity first.

Suppose you take a road trip. You clock your miles using the odometer and find that you travel 200 miles in 4 hours. You might say that your average speed for the trip is 200 miles/4 hours, or 50mi/hr. However, you probably didn't maintain a constant speed of 50mi/hr (unless you had the cruise control on). Most likely you sped up at different times or even came to a stop for a red light, so your speed probably kept changing during the trip, but the *average speed* was 50mi/hr. The line over the *v* indicates that we're using the average velocity, as shown next.

Average Velocity

$$\bar{v} = \frac{\Delta x}{t} = \frac{x_f - x_i}{t}$$

for any displacement Δx and time interval t.

Example 8.3: Calculating Average Velocity

Suppose a police officer sets up a speed trap on a straight section of a busy road. He marks a 1/4-mile section on the road, as shown in Figure 8.1. Using a very accurate stopwatch, he times 8 seconds from the instant you cross the first line to the instant you cross the second line. If you're driving in a 60mph zone, will you get a ticket?

Figure 8.1 A speed trap.

Solution

1. Set up a formula to calculate the average velocity:

$$\bar{v} = \frac{\Delta x}{t} = \frac{x_f - x_i}{t} = \frac{0.25\,mi}{8s} = 0.03125\,mi/s$$

2. The average speed of 0.03125mi/s is probably meaningless to you, so convert that to mi/hr. (You might want to flip back to Chapter 7, "Unit Conversions," for a review of unit conversions.)

$$\left(\frac{0.03125\,mi}{1s}\right)\left(\frac{60s}{1\min}\right)\left(\frac{60\min}{1hr}\right) = 112.5\,mi/hr$$

You'd probably get a ticket!

Instantaneous velocity is somewhat different in concept. As you drive down the road, your speed (or velocity) keeps changing. At any moment you can look at your speedometer and see exactly how fast you're going at that instant. Of course, an instant later, it's probably something different, but whatever the speedometer shows is your instantaneous velocity at that moment in time. We'll look at how to calculate instantaneous velocity in the next section, so for now just focus on the concept. I could be driving on the interstate and average 60mi/hr for the whole trip, but the police officer that clocked me going 90mi/hr doesn't care about my average speed. All he cares about is how fast I was going the instant he clocked me. That's the difference between average velocity and instantaneous velocity.

If you're traveling at a constant velocity, the average velocity is the same as the instantaneous velocity at any point.

However, if your speed changes at all, the average will probably be different from the instantaneous at most times. Here's the good news for game programmers. Most games are approached on a frame-by-frame basis, and most programmers shoot for a frame rate of 30fps. This means that if you take an average velocity between two frames, the time interval is only 1/30th of a second, which is pretty darn close to an instant in time, so you can treat that as an instantaneous velocity.

Example 8.4: Average Velocity Between Frames

Suppose an object in your game is at the 50-pixel mark in one frame. In the next frame, it's positioned at the 52-pixel mark. What is its instantaneous velocity in that frame, assuming 30fps?

Solution

1. Set up a formula to calculate the average velocity between the two frames:

$$\bar{v} = \frac{\Delta x}{t} = \frac{x_f - x_i}{t} = \frac{2\,px}{(^1/_{30})s} = 60\,px/s$$

2. Because the time interval is so close to an instant in time (1/30th of a second), you can use it as a good approximation of the instantaneous velocity in that frame.

The code to handle this is also pretty straightforward. The start and end values specified here could be pixels or an absolute coordinate system. The solution works on the changes between the values over time so units don't matter as long as they are consistent. Apply any needed conversion in advance of calculating the average velocity.

```
float calcAvgVel(float start,float end, float time)
    {
        return (end - start)/ time;
    }
```

Velocity is one of the most important concepts in physics for game programming, because it controls how objects move. Remember that if all you care about is how fast an object is moving, just use the magnitude of the velocity vector, which is speed.

However, if you're trying to guide the motion of an object on the screen, always use velocity so that the computer knows in which direction the object is going. Also, as a programmer you should always be looking for simpler, faster ways to move things around. If you can use a constant velocity, the math is very simple. However, if you want more-realistic motion, you probably want the speed to constantly change. In this case, you must be careful and always use the instantaneous velocity rather than the average velocity over a longer time interval. We will revisit this concept in more detail in the next chapter.

Self-Assessment

1. You're on a straight highway, and you decide to set the cruise control at 65mi/hr. After 15 minutes, how far have you gone?

2. Suppose you're programming a moving platform for the player to jump on. The platform can move only left (–) and right (+). The platform is moving at a constant velocity of –5px/s. If it's currently at the 200-pixel mark, where should it be 3 seconds later (assuming that it hasn't reached the point where it turns around)?

3. Suppose your character runs 25 meters in 20 seconds. What's his average speed for that 20-second time interval?

4. Suppose the player in question 3 realizes he forgot something, so he turns the character around and runs back to where he started. What's his average velocity for the entire run?

5. Suppose an object in your game is at the 300-pixel mark in one frame. In the next frame, it's positioned at the 295-pixel mark. What is its instantaneous velocity in that frame, assuming 30fps?

Acceleration

In the preceding section, we discussed constant velocity as well as changing velocity. Any time an object's velocity changes, it experiences an *acceleration;* it speeds up or slows down. Acceleration simply measures the velocity's rate of change. The faster an object speeds up, the higher the acceleration. If the velocity is constant and doesn't change at all, the acceleration must be 0. Let's go back to the car example. The only way to avoid accelerating is to turn on the cruise control. Any time you step on the gas pedal, the car speeds up or accelerates. As soon as you release the gas pedal, the car starts to slow down or decelerate (negative acceleration). If you hit the brakes, you get an even larger deceleration. Let's use the car example to set up a numeric definition.

Take a look at Figure 8.2. At some initial time, t_i, the car has an instantaneous velocity, v_i. A few seconds later, t_f, the car has a new instantaneous velocity, v_f. The acceleration is the velocity's rate of change.

Figure 8.2 A car accelerating.

Acceleration

$$a = \frac{\Delta v}{\Delta t} = \frac{v_f - v_i}{t_f - t_i}$$

> **NOTE**
>
> Be careful with the units. Make sure the velocity units are consistent with the time units before you divide. For example, it doesn't make sense to divide mi/hr by seconds. Either convert everything to hours or convert everything to seconds.
>
> The units for acceleration should always be some unit of length divided by some unit of time squared.

Example 8.5: Calculating Acceleration

Suppose the car shown in Figure 8.2 starts out going 40mi/hr and 5 seconds later is going 50mi/hr. What is its acceleration in mi/hr²? What is it in m/s²?

Solution

1. Set up a formula to calculate the acceleration:

$$a = \frac{\Delta v}{\Delta t} = \frac{v_f - v_i}{t_f - t_i} = \frac{50 - 40 mi/hr}{5s} = \frac{10 mi/hr}{5s}$$

2. Wait! The units aren't consistent. You need to convert the 5 seconds to hours before you can divide. You might want to flip back to Chapter 7 for a review of the conversion process. After converting, you find that 5s = 0.00139hr, so now you can divide:

$$a = \frac{\Delta v}{\Delta t} = \frac{v_f - v_i}{t_f - t_i} = \frac{50 - 40 mi/hr}{5s} = \frac{10 mi/hr}{5s} = \frac{10 mi/hr}{0.00139hr} = 7200 mi/hr^2$$

3. You also need to find the acceleration in m/s², because metrics are easier to work with in the long run. So instead of converting the time, convert the change in velocity from mi/hr to m/s. After converting, you find that 10mi/hr = 4.47m/s, and you are ready to divide:

$$a = \frac{\Delta v}{\Delta t} = \frac{4.47 m/s}{5s} = 0.894 m/s^2$$

Let's take a closer look at the two answers we found in that example. First, you found an acceleration of 3600mi/hr². This means that if the car continues accelerating at the same rate, it will speed up 3600mi/hr every hour. Chances are the car won't be able to sustain that rate of acceleration for an entire hour, so this might be hard to visualize. This is one reason why metric units are nicer to work with. In this example, you found that 3600mi/hr² is the same acceleration as 0.894m/s². This means that at this rate the car will speed up almost 1m/s every second. Let's look at one more example.

Example 8.6: Calculating Deceleration

Suppose you're driving along, and you're forced to slam on the brakes. In 3 seconds you go from 50mi/hr to 10mi/hr. What is your deceleration in m/s²?

Solution

1. Set up a formula to calculate the acceleration:

$$a = \frac{\Delta v}{\Delta t} = \frac{v_f - v_i}{t_f - t_i} = \frac{10 - 50 mi/hr}{3s} = \frac{-40 mi/hr}{3s}$$

2. The units aren't consistent, so you need to convert the –40mi/hr to m/s. After converting, you find that –40mi/hr = –17.88m/s, and you are ready to divide:

$$a = \frac{\Delta v}{\Delta t} = \frac{-17.88 m/s}{3s} = -5.96 m/s^2$$

Notice this time you get a negative acceleration. This means that the object is slowing down rather than speeding up. Be careful. The negative number *does not* indicate that the object is moving backwards. In the car example, I said that pressing the gas pedal is the same as positive acceleration. Hitting the brakes is the same as negative acceleration. However, hitting the brakes does not mean you suddenly put the car in reverse. It just means you're slowing down. This is a very common misconception.

The code to define acceleration and deceleration is the same. The key comes in the interpretation as mentioned earlier. Here is a function that will calculate acceleration in units/seconds squared:

```
//This function will calculate the acceleration in seconds.
►float calcAccelerationSeconds( float startVel, float finalVel, float
►time)
    {

        return (finalVel-startVel)/time;
    }
```

This function can easily be modified to work with any unit of time that is needed for other components or calculations.

At this point, we have defined velocity and acceleration, so you're ready to use both quantities in some formulas in the next section. Keep in mind that we'll revisit these two quantities in the next chapter, where we'll examine them graphically and look even closer at the relationships between them. Then we'll extend these concepts to 2D and 3D in Chapter 10.

Self-Assessment

1. Suppose the car in Figure 8.2 starts out going 80mi/hr and 8 seconds later is going 100mi/hr. What is its acceleration in m/s²?

2. Suppose you're driving along and you're forced to slam on the brakes. In 5 seconds you go from 40mi/hr to a complete stop. What is your deceleration in m/s²?

3. A certain car can accelerate at a rate of 0.6m/s². How much time would it take this car to accelerate from 55mi/hr to 60mi/hr?

4. Another car is initially traveling 7m/s when it starts to accelerate at 0.8m/s². How fast will the car be going after 2 seconds?

Equations of Motion

Now that we've defined all the variables you'll be working with, you can move on to studying the equations that model one-dimensional motion. It is very important to note that these equations hold only when the acceleration is constant. Remember that the velocity section started by discussing constant velocity. It said that if the velocity does not change, the average velocity is the same as the instantaneous velocity at any time. The same applies to acceleration. Fortunately, most objects in nature move with a constant acceleration, like an object in free fall. If you have a scenario in which the acceleration changes, just break it into smaller time intervals of constant acceleration. This works perfectly in programming, because you address motion on a frame-by-frame basis, so within one frame you're sure to have a small-enough time interval for constant acceleration.

> **NOTE**
> To make the equations simpler, we'll use t to represent the entire time interval rather than $(t_f - t_i)$.

Let's start with the definition of acceleration:

$$a = \frac{\Delta v}{t} = \frac{v_f - v_i}{t}$$

If we do a little algebraic rearranging (multiply both sides by t and add v_i), we'll get the first equation of motion.

Equation 1

$$v_f = v_i + at$$

final velocity = initial velocity + acceleration * time

Remember that in this chapter you are working with constant acceleration. Because velocity is increasing or decreasing uniformly with time, you know that the average velocity over a time interval equals the average of the initial velocity, v_i, and the final velocity, v_f. This gives us the second equation.

Equation 2

$$\overline{v} = \frac{v_i + v_f}{2}$$

average velocity = (initial velocity + final velocity)/2

for constant acceleration only.

The first section of this chapter defined average velocity as displacement over time:

$$\overline{v} = \frac{\Delta x}{t}$$

Equation 2 also gives you a formula for average velocity as long as the acceleration is constant. If you set the two equal to each other, you get the following:

$$\frac{\Delta x}{t} = \frac{v_i + v_f}{2}$$

A little bit of algebra reveals equation 3:

$$\frac{\Delta x}{t} = \frac{v_i + v_f}{2}$$

$$\frac{\Delta x}{t} = \frac{1}{2}(v_i + v_f)$$

$$\Delta x = \frac{1}{2}(v_i + v_f)t$$

Equation 3

$\Delta x = 1/2(v_i + v_f)t$

displacement = $1/2$ (initial velocity + final velocity) * time

---

Now let's take equation 1 ($v_f = v_i + at$) and substitute it into equation 3 for v_f:

$$\Delta x = 1/2(v_i + v_i + at)t$$

$$\Delta x = 1/2(2v_i + at)t$$

$$\Delta x = (v_i + 1/2at)t$$

$$\Delta x = v_i t + 1/2at^2$$

Equation 4

$\Delta x = v_i t + 1/2at^2$

displacement = initial velocity * time + $1/2$ acceleration * time^2.

The final equation can be derived by another combination of equations 1 and 3. If you solve equation 1 for time ($t = (v_f - v_i)/a$) and then plug it into equation 3, you get the following:

$$\Delta x = \frac{1}{2}(v_i + v_f)\left(\frac{(v_f - v_i)}{a}\right)$$

$$\Delta x = \frac{(v_i + v_f)(v_f - v_i)}{2a}$$

$$\Delta x = \frac{v_f^2 - v_i^2}{2a}$$

$$2a\Delta x = v_f^2 - v_i^2$$

$$v_f^2 = v_i^2 + 2a\Delta x$$

Equation 5

$$v_f^2 = v_i^2 + 2a\Delta x$$

final velocity^2 = initial velocity^2 + 2*acceleration*displacement.

These five equations can help you solve any problem related to one-dimensional motion with constant acceleration. Remember that they are all derived from the definitions of velocity and acceleration. The best way to become familiar with them is to work through some examples.

A great way to approach 1D motion with constant acceleration is to follow these steps:

1. Make a list of what you know and what you want to solve for.

2. Check the units and make sure they're all consistent.

3. Use your list to choose an equation from the list in Table 8.1.

At this point, if you know the actual values, you can plug them into the equation and solve for the one you're looking for. If it's a programming situation and you're expecting values to be provided as the game progresses, simply use your rules of algebra to rearrange the equation you've chosen to solve for the variable you're looking for, as shown in Table 8.1.

Table 8.1 Five Equations of Motion

Equation 1	$v_f = v_i + at$
Equation 2	$\bar{v} = \dfrac{v_i + v_f}{2}$
Equation 3	$\Delta x = \frac{1}{2}(v_i + v_f)t$
Equation 4	$\Delta x = v_i t + \frac{1}{2}at^2$
Equation 5	$v_f^2 = v_i^2 + 2a\Delta x$

> **NOTE**
> The second equation might not be used very often, but it serves as a great reminder that average velocity is not the same as instantaneous velocity (unless $a = 0$).

Example 8.7: Race Car

Suppose you're driving along and you're forced to slam on the brakes. If you're going 50mi/hr when you apply the brakes, and you know the brakes can decelerate the car at a rate of –6.5m/s², how much time will it take to stop?

Solution

1. Make a list of everything you know and what you're looking for:

Given	Find
v_i = 50mi/hr	t = ?
v_f = 0mi/hr	
a = –6.5m/s²	

2. The units aren't consistent. You need to convert everything to either miles and hours or meters and seconds. Whenever you're given a choice, I encourage you to always go with metric units, so convert everything to meters and seconds.

Given	Find
v_i = 50mi/hr	
= 22.35m/s	t = ?
v_f = 0mi/hr	
= 0m/s	
a = –6.5m/s²	

3. Now you can use the list to choose an equation. One of the five equations will give a relationship between the four values listed. In this case, it's equation 1:

$$v_f = v_i + at$$

$$0\text{m/s} = 22.35\text{m/s} + (-6.5\text{m/s}^2)t$$

$$-22.35\text{m/s} = (-6.5\text{m/s}^2)t$$

$$t = 3.44\text{s}$$

Example 8.8: Race Car Revisited

Suppose you're in the same situation as in Example 8.7, and you realize the car you're about to hit is stopped about 10 meters away. Will you be able to stop in time?

Solution

1. In this case, you have the same list of given quantities. The only difference is that you're looking for displacement rather than time.

Given	Find
v_i = 50mi/hr	Δx = ?
v_f = 0mi/hr	
a = –6.5m/s^2	

2. Repeat the same unit conversions as last time.

Given	Find
v_i = 50mi/hr	
= 22.35m/s	Δx = ?
v_f = 0mi/hr	
= 0m/s	
a = –6.5m/s^2	

3. Now you can use the list to choose an equation. This time, equation 5 relates the values on your list:

$$v_f^2 = v_i^2 + 2a\Delta x$$

$$(0m/s)^2 = (22.35m/s)^2 + 2(-6.5m/s^2)\Delta x$$

$$0 = 499.5235m^2/s^2 + (-13m/s^2)\Delta x$$

$$-499.5235m^2/s^2 = (-13m/s^2)\Delta x$$

$$\Delta x = 38.425m$$

Therefore, the answer is no you will not be able to stop in time.

Notice that the last two examples started out with the same information but ended quite differently. Always be clear about what you're looking for, because that determines which equation you use. Also, be careful with the units. Remember that they must be consistent before you can plug values into the equations. You can even carry the units through the calculations and use them as a double check. If the units make sense for the quantity you're looking for, chances are you did the algebra correctly. In the last example, you were looking for displacement and you ended up with meters for the units, which makes sense. Let's look at a slightly more complicated example.

Example 8.9: Using More Than One Equation

Suppose you're driving along a straight highway. You look at the speedometer, and it reads 45mi/hr just before you hit the gas. If you know the car accelerates at a rate of 2m/s², how long will it take to go 0.25 miles?

Solution

1. Start with a list.

Given	Find
v_i = 45mi/hr	t = ?
Δx = 0.25mi	
a = 2m/s²	

2. Check the units. They don't match, so convert everything to metrics.

Given	Find
v_i = 45mi/hr	
= 20.11m/s	t = ?
Δx = 0.25mi	
= 402.25m	
a = 2m/s²	

3. Now you can use the list to choose an equation. Normally it would make sense to use equation 4:

$$\Delta x = v_i t + 1/2 a t^2$$

$$402.25\text{m} = (20.11\text{m/s})t + 1/2(2\text{m/s}^2)t^2$$

But how do you solve for time? You could pull out the old quadratic formula, but that's expensive (it has a square root). One way to get around this problem is to bypass equation 4 by using two others. Notice that v_f does not appear in the list. Even though you don't care what it is, you can still use v_f in a different equation to find time. Let's do that.

4. Use equation 5 to find v_f:

$$v_f^2 = v_i^2 + 2a\Delta x$$

$$v_f^2 = (20.11\text{m/s})^2 + 2(2\text{m/s}^2)(402.25\text{m})$$

$$v_f^2 = 404.41\text{m}^2/\text{s}^2 + 1609\text{m}^2/\text{s}^2$$

$$v_f^2 = 2013.41\text{m}^2/\text{s}^2$$

$$v_f = 44.87\text{m/s}$$

5. Now you can use v_f in equation 1 to calculate time:

$$v_f = v_i + at$$

$$44.87\text{m/s} = 20.11\text{m/s} + (2\text{m/s}^2)t$$

$$24.76\text{m/s} = (2\text{m/s}^2)t$$

$$t = 12.38\text{s}$$

There is usually more than one way to solve every problem, so allow yourself to be a little creative. Any time you want to avoid using a particular equation, you can simply bypass it by using two others.

So far, we've only talked about horizontal one-dimensional motion. These same equations can be used for vertical one-dimensional motion as well. Just replace Δx in all the equations with Δy. One additional detail applies to vertical motion—gravity. On Earth, all objects fall to the ground with the same acceleration due to gravity (if you ignore air resistance). That gravitational constant is $g = 9.8m/s^2 = 32.1ft/s^2$. In the five equations of motion, you can now substitute $-g$ or $-9.8m/s^2$ for a any time the motion is vertical. The negative sign in front indicates that the direction is downward. Let's look at an example.

Example 8.10: Vertical Motion

Suppose your game has a monster that drops rocks from a raised platform. How long would it take for a rock to fall 50m to the ground?

Solution

1. Start with a list.

Given	Find
$v_i = 0m/s$	$t = ?$
$\Delta x = -50m$	
$a = -9.8m/s^2$	

The initial velocity is 0 because the rocks are being dropped, not thrown. Also notice that the displacement is negative because the rock falls down. Finally, you already know the acceleration because the motion is vertical.

2. Check the units. Everything is in meters and seconds, so there's no need for conversions.

3. Now you can solve for time using equation 4:

$$\Delta x = v_i t + \frac{1}{2}at^2$$

$$-50m = (0m/s)t + \frac{1}{2}(-9.8m/s^2)t^2$$

$$-50m = 0 + (-4.9m/s^2)t^2$$

$$t^2 = 10.20s^2$$

$$t = 3.19s$$

As you can see, vertical 1D motion works the same way as horizontal 1D motion. This section opened with five equations that can be used to describe one-dimensional motion. The next chapter closely looks at both velocity and acceleration. The following chapter expands these concepts into two and three dimensions.

Self-Assessment

1. A speedboat increases its speed from 20m/s to 30m/s over a distance of 200m. What is its rate of acceleration?

2. How much time would it take the boat in question 1 to go the 200m?

3. A race car reaches the finish line going 40m/s. The driver applies the brakes, and the car comes to rest 5 seconds later. What is its rate of deceleration?

4. How far does the car in question 3 travel before finally coming to a stop?

5. A ball is thrown upward at a speed of 25m/s. How much time does it take to reach its maximum height?

6. What is the maximum height the ball in question 5 reaches?

Visualization Experience

On the CD-ROM, you will find a demo named 1D Racer. Here's a brief description from the programmer, Kaveh Kahrizi:

1D Racer demonstrates the motion of an object with constant acceleration moving through space. First you choose the formula you want, and then you choose the unknown variable. After you have entered valid values for the three known parameters, the race begins. The formulas are clearly marked in the Game class's header (Game.h) by the large comment block. The workspace was created in Visual Studio 6.0, although the files can easily be added to any existing workspace without your having to change the project settings, as long as the compiler is configured to know where DirectX include and library files are located. The program's executable requires that DirectX 8.1 runtime or higher be installed on the machine. To compile the code yourself, you must have the DirectX 8.1 SDK (Software Developer's Kit) or higher. Both of these can be downloaded for free from Microsoft's website at www.Microsoft.com.

Go ahead and run the demo by double-clicking 1DRacer.exe. The first thing you'll see is four of the five equations listed on the screen. Choose the first one ($v_f = v_i + at$). Next the application asks you which variable you want to solve for; choose a. Then you can enter the three variables you know. Enter the following values:

$v_i = 0$

$v_f = 50$

$t = 10$

Press Enter to begin the race. The application tracks time, displacement, and current velocity as the race progresses. You can pause the car at any point by pressing the P key. Try repeating this process, and pause halfway through ($t = 5$) to see how fast the car is going compared to its speed at the very end. To repeat the race, press the Backspace key.

When you're done, press Backspace, and try using a different equation. You can repeat the examples to see the actual motion. Let's go back to Example 8.8. After the units were converted, you had the following list:

Given	Find
$v_i = 50$mi/hr	
$= 22.35$m/s	$\Delta x = ?$
$v_f = 0$mi/hr	
$= 0$m/s	
$a = -6.5$m/s^2	

Start a new race using the last equation ($v_f^2 = v_i^2 + 2a\Delta x$). You want to solve for Δx. Then enter the metric values from the table, and run the race. Did you get a displacement close to $\Delta x = 38.425$m?

You might want to use this demo to check your answers to the self-assessment questions. Also try making up your own questions, and see what you get. You might want to try pausing the car at different times to track the motion as the race progresses.

Next, you can view the source code by double-clicking 1DRacer_code.txt. If you scroll down far enough, you'll see the sections where the actual equations were coded. Notice that each equation had to be rewritten four times—once for each variable the user could ask for. You might want to consider attempting a text-based application that performs similar operations.

Self-Assessment Solutions

Speed and Velocity

1. 16.25 miles

2. 185-pixel mark

3. 1.25m/s

4. 0m/s

5. −150px/s

Acceleration

1. $1.12m/s^2$

2. $−17.88m/s^2$

3. 3.7 seconds

4. 8.6m/s

Equations of Motion

1. $1.25m/s^2$

2. 8 seconds

3. $−8m/s^2$

4. 100m

5. 2.55 seconds

6. 31.9m

Chapter 9

Derivative Approach to Motion in One Dimension

The preceding chapter defined the quantities of velocity and acceleration and took a numerical approach to working with the new quantities. As promised, this chapter takes a more in-depth look at both velocity and acceleration. We'll start with a graphical approach to help you visualize the motion, and then we'll use that graph to define the concepts of the limit and the derivative. This chapter briefly introduces the huge world of Newtonian Calculus; you might be inspired to pursue this subject even further. You'll find a list of suggested readings in Appendix B, "Suggested Reading," to continue your study.

Visualizing Velocity and Derivative

Let's start by revisiting the concept of velocity. Remember that **velocity** is a vector, so it has direction, and in one dimension that direction is either positive or negative. I also said that average velocity is defined as displacement divided by time. To help visualize the motion of an object, you can start by graphing position versus time on a traditional Cartesian coordinate system. Let's step through the process with a vertical 1D situation like throwing something into the air.

Suppose your game character throws a tomato into the air. You can track the tomato's height as time increases, which gives you the values shown in Table 9.1.

Table 9.1 A Tomato's Height at Various Times

t (in sec)	y (in ft)
0	6
1	90
2	142
3	162
4	150
5	106
6	30

You can then graph these points to see how the tomato moves over time, as shown in Figure 9.1.

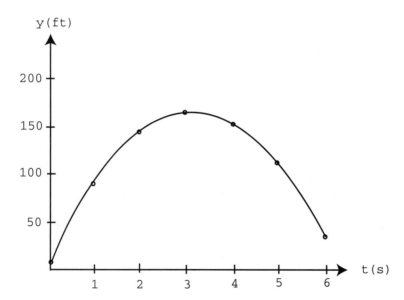

Figure 9.1 A graph of the values shown in Table 9.1.

As you can see in the graph, as time increases, the tomato goes up and then falls back down. You can also say that the height (y) is a function of time (t). That is, the height changes as time increases from 0 to 6 seconds. Mathematically, this can be written as $y = f(t)$ and can be read as "y is a function of time." This notation is used throughout the rest of this chapter.

Let's use the graph shown in Figure 9.1 to reexamine the concept of average velocity. Suppose you wanted to know the average velocity of the tomato over the first 4 seconds. If you approached this numerically, you'd have to calculate the displacement and then divide it by the 4-second time interval. Using the new notation, it would look like this:

$$\bar{v} = \frac{f(4) - f(0)}{4 - 0} = \frac{150 - 6}{4} = \frac{144}{4} = 36\,\text{ft/s}$$

Average Velocity

$$\bar{v} = \frac{f(b) - f(a)}{b - a}$$

= the slope between two points on position *v*. Time graph for any time interval $a \le t \le b$.

You can also use the graph to visualize this. Remember the good old slope formula? Slope = rise over run. In this case, the rise is the displacement, and the run is the time interval, so the average velocity is simply the slope of the line between those two points on the graph. This is illustrated in Figure 9.2.

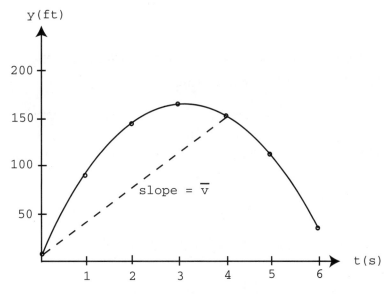

Figure 9.2   The average velocity over the first 4 seconds.

Try plugging the coordinates of those two points into the slope formula, and you'll find that you repeated the same process we did earlier. So the slope of the line between any two points on a position-versus-time graph gives you the average velocity over that time interval.

Example 9.1: Finding Average Velocity

Using the data just discussed, find the average velocity of the tomato for the time interval $3 \leq t \leq 5$ seconds.

Solution

1. Looking at the data, you need to know the height of the tomato at $t = 3$s and $t = 5$s:

   $f(3) = 162$

   $f(5) = 106$

2. Calculate the average velocity, or the slope between those two points:

   $$\bar{v} = \frac{f(5) - f(3)}{5 - 3} = \frac{106 - 162}{2} = \frac{-56}{2} = -28 \text{ft/s}$$

> **NOTE**
> If you look at that portion of the graph, you can see that the tomato is falling between 3 and 5 seconds, which is why the average velocity is negative.

At this point, you can calculate the average velocity over any time interval. Let's look at what happens when you take smaller and smaller time intervals. Suppose you want a better understanding of what's happening to the tomato at exactly $t = 1$s. You can calculate the average velocity between 1 and 4 seconds:

$$\bar{v} = \frac{f(4) - f(1)}{4 - 1} = \frac{150 - 90}{3} = \frac{60}{3} = 20 \text{ft/s}$$

You can calculate the average velocity between 1 and 3 seconds:

$$\bar{v} = \frac{f(3) - f(1)}{3 - 1} = \frac{162 - 90}{2} = \frac{72}{2} = 36 \text{ft/s}$$

You can calculate the average velocity between 1 and 2 seconds:

$$\bar{v} = \frac{f(2) - f(1)}{2 - 1} = \frac{142 - 90}{1} = \frac{52}{1} = 52\,\text{ft/s}$$

These smaller and smaller time intervals are illustrated in Figure 9.3.

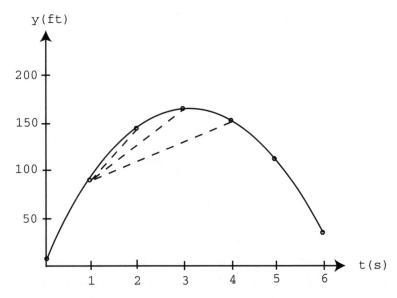

Figure 9.3   Smaller time intervals close to t = 1.

You can continue to take smaller and smaller time intervals until the line segment approaches a point or an instant in time. This leads to the concept of instantaneous velocity. Look at the dashed lines in Figure 9.3. As the time intervals get smaller and smaller, the dashed lines approach the bold line shown in Figure 9.4. This bold line represents the slope at the point where $t = 1\text{s}$. That slope is the instantaneous velocity at exactly 1 second.

NOTE
The bold line shown in Figure 9.4 is called the tangent line.

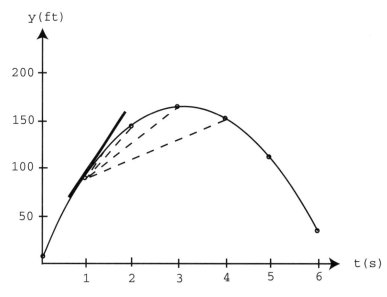

Figure 9.4 Instantaneous velocity at t = 1.

The average velocity is the slope of a line segment over a time interval on a position-versus-time graph, and the instantaneous velocity is the slope at a point on the graph. This leads to the concept of the limit. As you take smaller and smaller time intervals, you'll find that the average velocity approaches some number. That is the instantaneous velocity.

Instantaneous Velocity

$$v = \lim_{h \to 0} \frac{f(a+h) - f(a)}{h}$$

at *t* = *a* for any function *f*(*t*) that gives position as a function of time.

The limit notation might look intimidating, but all it means is keep recalculating the average velocity over smaller and smaller time intervals as close to 0 as you can get.

Example 9.2: Finding Instantaneous Velocity

Suppose you're coding a game like *Half Life* and the player can throw a grenade into the air, and its height is a function of time, just like the tomato. If its height is $y = f(t) = t^2 + 5$, find the instantaneous velocity at *t* = 3s.

Solution

1. To find the instantaneous velocity at exactly $t = 3$s, you need to take the average velocity over smaller and smaller time intervals. In other words, take the limit of $f(t)$ as the change in time approaches 0:

$$\lim_{h \to 0} \frac{f(3+h) - f(3)}{h}$$

2. Calculate both heights using the formula $y = f(t) = t^2 + 5$:

$$\lim_{h \to 0} \frac{f(3+h) - f(3)}{h}$$

$$= \lim_{h \to 0} \frac{(3+h)^2 + 5 - (3^2 + 5)}{h}$$

$$= \lim_{h \to 0} \frac{9 + 6h + h^2 + 5 - (9 + 5)}{h}$$

$$= \lim_{h \to 0} \frac{6h + h^2}{h}$$

$$= \lim_{h \to 0} \frac{6 + h}{1}$$

Here's where the limit notation comes into play. If h keeps getting closer and closer to 0, the instantaneous velocity gets closer and closer to 6.

Believe it or not, you just computed a derivative! A **derivative** is the rate of change of a quantity as the time interval shrinks to an instant. In this case, you calculated **instantaneous velocity**, which is the rate of change of height as the time interval approaches 0. The notation for the derivative is the ' (pronounced "prime"). For example, the derivative of $f(t)$ is written $f'(t)$.

Instantaneous Velocity

$v = f'(t)$

for any position equation that's a function of time, $f(t)$.

Example 9.3: Finding the Derivative

Suppose a racecar in *Need For Speed Under Ground* is traveling across the screen, and its position is a function of time defined as $y = f(t) = 15t + 10$. Find the derivative, or the instantaneous velocity at $t = 2s$.

Solution

1. To find the instantaneous velocity at exactly $t = 2s$, you need to find the derivative, or the average velocity as the time interval approaches 0. Use the limit notation:

$$f'(2) = \lim_{h \to 0} \frac{f(2+h) - f(2)}{h}$$

2. Calculate both positions using the formula $y = f(t) = 15t + 10$:

$$\lim_{h \to 0} \frac{f(2+h) - f(2)}{h}$$

$$= \lim_{h \to 0} \frac{(15(2+h)+10) - (15(2)+10)}{h}$$

$$= \lim_{h \to 0} \frac{30 + 15h + 10 - (30+10)}{h}$$

$$= \lim_{h \to 0} \frac{40 + 15h - 40}{h}$$

$$= \lim_{h \to 0} \frac{15h}{h}$$

$$= \lim_{h \to 0} \frac{15}{1}$$

3. At this point, it doesn't matter what h is. The derivative is simply 15.

In this section, you computed two derivatives. You used simple polynomial functions (powers of t) to model the motion of the objects discussed here. However, you could use any function to describe an object's position as time increases. The process is the same; take the limit as the time interval approaches 0, and see what the function approaches. This is only a brief introduction, however. Volumes have been written about tricks and tips for taking the derivative of various functions. If you want to investigate this further, several suggested readings are listed in Appendix B.

Self-Assessment

1. Looking back at the tomato described in Example 9.1, find its average velocity for the following time intervals:

   $3 \le t \le 6$

   $3 \le t \le 5$

   $3 \le t \le 4$

2. Looking back at the grenade described in Example 9.2, find its instantaneous velocity at $t = 1$s.

3. Suppose an object is thrown into the air, and its height is a function of time. If its height is $y = f(t) = 3t^2 + 1$, find its instantaneous velocity at $t = 5$s.

4. Suppose a vehicle is traveling across the screen, and its position is a function of time defined as $y = f(t) = 5t + 2$. Find the derivative, or the instantaneous velocity, at $t = 3$s.

Visualizing Acceleration and Second Derivative

The preceding section took a closer look at instantaneous velocity, and you ended up computing derivatives. This section goes one step further by delving deeper into the realm of acceleration, which leads to the concept of a second derivative. Let's start by taking a graphical approach again.

Rather than graph an object's position versus time, let's graph an object's speed or velocity versus time. Suppose a race car driver starts at a dead stop and floors the gas pedal. At regular intervals, his instantaneous velocity is recorded. These values are shown in Table 9.2.

Table 9.2 A Race Car's Velocity at Various Times

t (in sec)	v (in m/s)
0	0
1	3
2	12
3	27
4	48
5	75
6	108

You can graph these points to see how the race car speeds up over time, as shown in Figure 9.5.

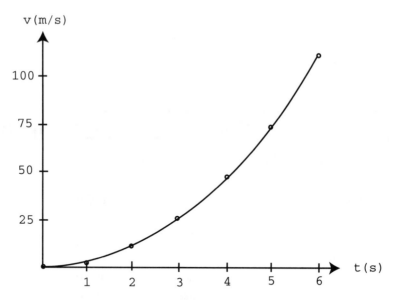

Figure 9.5 A graph of the values shown in Table 9.2.

As you can see in the graph, as time increases, the race car continues to speed up. We can also say that the velocity (v) is a function of time (t). That is, the velocity changes as the time increases from 0 to 6 seconds. Mathematically, this can be written as v = f(t) and read as "Velocity is a function of time." Notice the parallel between the preceding section and this one. So far, they're almost identical.

Just as you did last time, use the graph shown in Figure 9.5 to reexamine the concept of acceleration. Suppose you wanted to know the average acceleration of the race car over the full 6 seconds. If you approached this numerically, as you did in the preceding chapter, you'd have to calculate the change in velocity and then divide it by the 6-second time interval. Using the new notation, it would look like this:

$$\bar{a} = \frac{f(6) - f(0)}{6 - 0} = \frac{108 - 0}{6} = 18\,\text{m/s}^2$$

Average Acceleration

$$\bar{a} = \frac{f(b) - f(a)}{b - a}$$

= the slope between two points on velocity v. Time graph for any time interval $a \le t \le b$.

You can also use the graph to visualize this. Remember the good old slope formula? Slope = rise over run. In this case, the rise is the change in velocity, and the run is the time interval, so the average acceleration is simply the slope of the line between those two points on the graph, as shown in Figure 9.6.

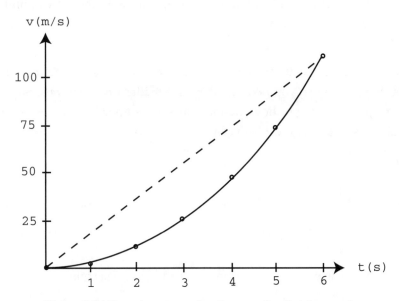

Figure 9.6 The average acceleration over the first 6 seconds.

Try plugging the coordinates of those two points into the slope formula. You'll find that you repeat the same process you did earlier. The slope of the line between any two points on a velocity-versus-time graph gives you the average acceleration over that time interval, just like the slope of the position-versus-time graph gives you the average velocity.

Example 9.4: Finding Average Acceleration

Using the data from Table 9.2, find the average acceleration of the race car for the time interval $2 \leq t \leq 4$ seconds.

Solution:

1. Looking at the data, you need to know the instantaneous velocity of the race car at $t = 2$s and $t = 4$s:

$f(2) = 12$

$f(4) = 48$

2. Calculate the average acceleration, or the slope between those two points:

$$\bar{v} = \frac{f(4) - f(2)}{4 - 2} = \frac{48 - 12}{2} = \frac{36}{2} = 18 \text{m/s}^2$$

At this point, you can calculate the average acceleration over any time interval. Let's look at what happens when you take smaller and smaller time intervals. Suppose you want a better understanding of how the race car speeds up at exactly $t = 1$s. You can calculate the average acceleration between 1 and 4 seconds:

$$\bar{a} = \frac{f(4) - f(1)}{4 - 1} = \frac{48 - 3}{3} = \frac{45}{3} = 15 \text{m/s}^2$$

You can calculate the average acceleration between 1 and 3 seconds:

$$\bar{a} = \frac{f(3) - f(1)}{3 - 1} = \frac{27 - 3}{2} = \frac{24}{2} = 12 \text{m/s}^2$$

You can calculate the average acceleration between 1 and 2 seconds:

$$\bar{a} = \frac{f(2) - f(1)}{2 - 1} = \frac{12 - 3}{1} = \frac{9}{1} = 9 \text{m/s}^2$$

These smaller and smaller time intervals are illustrated in Figure 9.7.

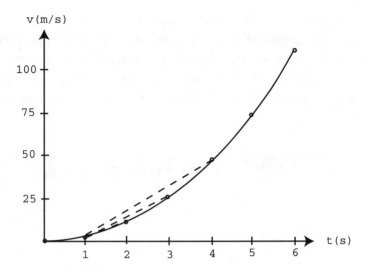

Figure 9.7 Smaller time intervals close to t = 1.

You can continue to take smaller and smaller time intervals until the line segment approaches a point or an instant in time. This leads to the concept of instantaneous acceleration. Look at the dashed lines in Figure 9.7. As the time intervals get smaller and smaller, the dashed lines approach the bold line shown in Figure 9.8. This bold line represents the slope at the point where t = 1s. That slope is the instantaneous acceleration at exactly 1 second.

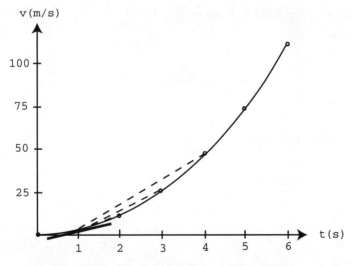

Figure 9.8 The instantaneous velocity at t = 1.

The average acceleration is the slope of a line segment over a time interval on a velocity-versus-time graph. The instantaneous acceleration is the slope at a point on the graph. This follows the same exact pattern as velocity did with the position-versus-time graph. Again, the smaller time intervals lead to the concept of the limit. As you take smaller and smaller time intervals, you'll find that the average acceleration approaches some number. That is the instantaneous acceleration.

Instantaneous Acceleration

$$a = \lim_{h \to 0} \frac{f(t+h) - f(t)}{h}$$

for any function $f(t)$ that gives velocity as a function of time.

Example 9.5: Finding Instantaneous Acceleration

Suppose another grenade is thrown into the air in a game like *Half Life*, and its instantaneous velocity is a function of time. If its velocity is $v = f(t) = -9.8t + 25$, find the instantaneous acceleration at $t = 3$s.

Solution

1. To find the instantaneous acceleration at exactly $t = 3$s, you need to take the average acceleration over smaller and smaller time intervals. In other words, take the limit of $f(t)$ as the change in time approaches 0:

    $$\lim_{h \to 0} \frac{f(3+h) - f(3)}{h}$$

2. Calculate both heights using the formula $y = f(t) = -9.8t + 25$:

    $$\lim_{h \to 0} \frac{f(3+h) - f(3)}{h}$$

    $$= \lim_{h \to 0} \frac{-9.8(3+h) + 25 - (-9.8(3) + 25)}{h}$$

    $$= \lim_{h \to 0} \frac{-29.4 - 9.8h + 25 + 29.4 - 25}{h}$$

    $$= \lim_{h \to 0} \frac{-9.8h}{h}$$

    $$= \lim_{h \to 0} \frac{-9.8}{1}$$

Here's where the limit notation comes into play. If h keeps getting closer and closer to 0, the instantaneous velocity gets closer and closer to –9.8.

Just like before, you just computed a derivative. Acceleration is actually the derivative of velocity with respect to time. If $v(t)$ gives instantaneous velocity as a function of time, acceleration is $v'(t)$.

Instantaneous Acceleration

$a = v'(t)$

for any velocity equation that's a function of time, $v(t)$.

Here's where we take a big step. If acceleration is the derivative of a velocity function, and velocity is the derivative of a position function, acceleration is the second derivative of position; it's the derivative of the derivative. The second derivative is written as $f''(t)$.

Instantaneous Acceleration

$a = v'(t) = y''(t)$

for any velocity equation that's a function of time, $v(t)$

and any position equation that's a function of time, $y(t)$.

Although this notation might look intimidating, it's just a repeat of the preceding section. If you're looking for the acceleration at a point and you know an equation for the instantaneous velocity, simply take the derivative. However, if all you have is an equation for the position with respect to time, simply repeat the derivative process (take two limits).

Example 9.6: Finding the Second Derivative

Let's revisit the grenade one more time. Suppose all you have is an equation for the height as a function of time: $y = f(t) = 10t - 4.9t^2$. Find the instantaneous acceleration at $t = 2s$.

Solution

1. To find the instantaneous acceleration at exactly $t = 2$s, you need to take the derivative twice. In other words, take the limit of $f(t)$ as the change in time approaches 0, and then do it again. Take the first derivative, and wait until the end to plug in $t = 2$s:

$$f'(t) = \lim_{h \to 0} \frac{f(t+h) - f(t)}{h}$$

$$f'(t) = \lim_{h \to 0} \frac{10(t+h) - 4.9(t+h)^2 - (10t - 4.9t^2)}{h}$$

$$f'(t) = \lim_{h \to 0} \frac{10t + 10h - 4.9(t^2 + 2th + h^2) - 10t + 4.9t^2}{h}$$

$$f'(t) = \lim_{h \to 0} \frac{10h - 4.9(t^2 + 2th + h^2) + 4.9t^2}{h}$$

$$f'(t) = \lim_{h \to 0} \frac{10h - 4.9t^2 - 9.8th - 4.9h^2 + 4.9t^2}{h}$$

$$f'(t) = \lim_{h \to 0} \frac{10h - 9.8th - 4.9h^2}{h}$$

$$f'(t) = \lim_{h \to 0} \frac{10 - 9.8t - 4.9h}{1}$$

As h approaches 0, $f'(t)$ becomes $10 - 9.8t$.

2. Take the derivative again to get acceleration:

$$f''(t) = \lim_{h \to 0} \frac{f'(t+h) - f'(t)}{h}$$

$$f''(t) = \lim_{h \to 0} \frac{10 - 9.8(t+h) - (10 - 9.8t)}{h}$$

$$f''(t) = \lim_{h \to 0} \frac{10 - 9.8t - 9.8h - 10 + 9.8t}{h}$$

$$f''(t) = \lim_{h \to 0} \frac{-9.8h}{h}$$

$$f''(t) = \lim_{h \to 0} \frac{-9.8}{1}$$

As you can see, $a = f''(t) = -9.8$. So in this case, at $t = 2$s (or at any time during this motion), the acceleration is -9.8.

This chapter not only explored a graphical approach to the concepts of velocity and acceleration, but it also looked at using derivatives to express velocity and acceleration. You even found an interesting link between position, velocity, and acceleration: The derivative of position is velocity, and the derivative of velocity is acceleration. If you can model an object's position as a function of time, you can use the derivative to get two simple equations for velocity and acceleration to put into your code. This chapter used polynomial functions (powers of t) to model the position because they are easy to work with. Again, if you want to model an object's position with a different equation (other than polynomial), Appendix B lists texts that provide you with tricks for finding the derivative of other equations. I encourage you to investigate this further.

Self-Assessment

1. Using the data from Table 9.2, find the average acceleration of the race car for the time interval $1 \leq t \leq 5$ seconds.

2. The velocity of the grenade in Example 9.5 is a function of time: $v = f(t) = -9.8t + 25$. Find its instantaneous acceleration at $t = 1$s.

3. Suppose an object's velocity is a function of time: $v(t) = 30t + 5t^2$. Find its acceleration at $t = 3$s.

4. Suppose an object's position is a function of time: $y(t) = 8t + 3t^2$. Find its acceleration at $t = 2$s.

Self-Assessment Solutions

Visualizing Velocity and Derivative

1. For $3 \leq t \leq 6$, average velocity = -44ft/s

   For $3 \leq t \leq 5$, average velocity = -28ft/s

   For $3 \leq t \leq 4$, average velocity = -12ft/s

2. $v = 2$ft/s

3. $v = 30$ft/s

4. $v = 5$ft/s

Visualizing Acceleration and Second Derivative

1. 18m/s^2

2. -9.8

3. 60

4. 6

Chapter 10

Motion in Two and Three Dimensions

Now that we've discussed 1D motion extensively, I'm sure you're wondering how these equations extend to two and three dimensions. It all comes back to vectors. If you're a little rusty on dealing with vectors, you might want to revisit Chapter 4, "Vector Operations," for a quick review. As soon as you feel confident performing vector operations, you'll be amazed at how simple the transition from 1D to 2D and 3D really is!

Using Vectors

The biggest difference between one-dimensional and two- or three-dimensional motion involves the direction. Remember that displacement, velocity, and acceleration are all vector quantities and that in one dimension we satisfied the direction requirement with either a positive or negative sign.

However, to completely describe motion in two or three dimensions, we must incorporate vectors. This means that all the vector operations discussed in Chapter 4 can be applied to displacement, velocity, and acceleration. Believe it or not, this section has no new information. It simply combines the concepts of motion discussed in Chapter 8, "Motion in One Dimension," with the vector operations discussed in Chapter 4.

Let's start by revisiting the idea of displacement. In one dimension, there are only two possible directions—positive or negative. Displacement in 1D is the same as motion up and down a number line. For example, in Figure 10.1 the first object moves from the 50-pixel mark to the 450-pixel mark, so the total displacement is positive 400 pixels. Below that, the second object moves from the 450-pixel mark to the 50-pixel mark, so its displacement is –400 pixels.

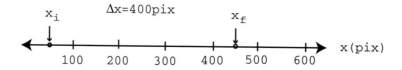

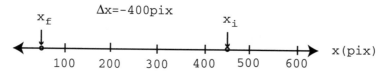

Figure 10.1 Displacement in 1D.

In two dimensions, we're no longer restricted to two directions. Now there are 360° worth of directions. This means that positive or negative is no longer descriptive enough. We need to incorporate vectors. In 2D displacement is still final position minus initial position, but now we need to use vectors to describe those positions. So rather than subtract two numbers on a number line, now we must subtract two vectors. Remember that vectors must be in component form before you can subtract them. Look at the two positions in Figure 10.2—P and P'.

You can use 2D vectors anchored at the origin to describe those positions. Because you need to subtract them, you must express the two vectors in component form (distance in the x direction and distance in the y direction). Figure 10.3 shows the two vectors in component form.

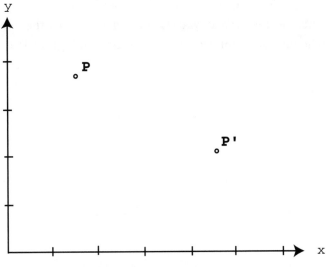

Figure 10.2 Initial and final positions in 2D.

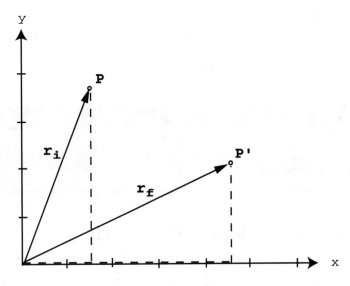

Figure 10.3 Positions in 2D as vectors.

NOTE

When you venture into 2D, you can no longer use x for position, because each position has both x and y components. To avoid confusion, we will use r to represent position and Δr for displacement in 2D.

Now we can talk about displacement. Remember that displacement is simply final position minus initial position, so all you have to do is subtract the two position vectors $(r_f - r_i)$. The displacement vector (Δr) is shown in Figure 10.4.

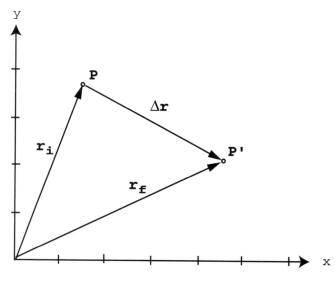

Figure 10.4 Displacement in 2D.

2D Displacement

$\Delta r = r_f - r_i$

for position vectors r_i (initial) and r_f (final).

Example 10.1: Finding Displacement in 2D

Suppose an object in your game moves from point P(50,400) to point P'(550,100). What is its displacement?

Solution

1. Express the initial and final positions as vectors: P = [50 400] and P' = [550 100].

2. Displacement is change in position, so

$$P' - P = [550\ 100] - [50\ 400] = [500\ -300]$$

3. The overall displacement is 500 pixels to the right and 300 pixels down, which written as a vector is [500 −300].

When you use vectors for position and displacement, it's very simple to extend the process to 3D: You simply add a z component to all the vectors. Then all you have to do is subtract two 3D vectors.

Example 10.2: Finding Displacement in 3D

Suppose an object in your game moves from point P(150,0,250) to point P'(400,250,−300). What is its displacement?

Solution

1. Express the initial and final positions as vectors: P = [150 0 250] and P' = [400 250 −300].

2. Displacement is change in position, so

    P' − P = [400 250 −300] − [150 0 250] = [250 250 −550]

3. The overall displacement is 250 pixels to the right, 250 pixels up, and 550 pixels back, which written as a vector is [250 250 −550].

If we take a look at Chapter 4 where we defined our 3Dvector class, solving this problem in our code would be extremely easy. We'd simply need to define our initial and final positions as vectors, then use the subtraction operator (which we defined) to return our solution:

```
#include "3Dvector.h"

int main()
{
    // Define our 2 vectors
    3Dvector initial(150, 0, 250);
    3Dvector final(400, 250, -300);
    // Calculate our solution
    3Dvector displacement = final - initial;

    return 0;
}
```

Let's look back at the definition of velocity in one dimension. Velocity is the rate of change of position. In two dimensions velocity is still displacement divided by time. The only difference is that now displacement is a 2D or 3D vector instead of a positive or negative number. This means that to calculate average velocity, you need to divide the vector displacement by the scalar time.

If the vector is in polar coordinates, simply divide the magnitude by time and keep the direction the same. If it's in Cartesian coordinates, divide each component by time. In either case, the definition is the same.

Average Velocity in 2D and 3D

$$\bar{v} = \frac{\Delta r}{t} = \frac{r_f - r_i}{t}$$

for any displacement vector Δr and time interval t.

Example 10.3: Calculating Average Velocity in 3D

Suppose a character in your game moves from point P(150,0,250) to point P'(400,250,–300) in 5 seconds. What is its average velocity over the 5-second time interval?

Solution

1. In Example 10.2, you found the displacement between points P and P'. The displacement vector was [250 250 –550].

2. The average velocity is displacement divided by time. Because you have displacement in Cartesian coordinates, all you have to do is divide each component by the 5 seconds:

$$\bar{v} = \frac{\Delta r}{t} = \frac{\begin{bmatrix} 250 & 250 & -550 \end{bmatrix}}{5} = \begin{bmatrix} 50 & 50 & -110 \end{bmatrix}$$

Calculating average velocity is extremely important for interpolation and keyframing animations. When creating and loading 3D animations in a game, we use keyframing to save memory by storing only the initial and final frames of the animations, then calculating all of the in-between positions in the code. Once again, using our 3Dvector class defined in Chapter 4, a function to calculate average velocity would look like this:

```
3Dvector averageVelocity(const 3Dvector &Pi, const 3Dvector &Pf,
                float intervals)
{
    // Calculate the displacement between our start and finish
    3Dvector temp(Pf.x - Pi.x, Pf.y - Pi.y, Pf.z - Pi.z);
    // Divide our displacement by our number of intervals
    temp = temp * (1 / intervals);
    // Return our answer
    return temp;
}
```

As you might have guessed, the definition of acceleration, or the first equation of motion, also holds for 2D and 3D. Again, the only difference is that all the mathematical operations are performed on vectors instead of just scalar numbers. In fact, all the equations of motion work in 2D and 3D. The ones that are used most often in programming are the first, third, and fourth equations.

Equations of Motion in 2D and 3D

$$v_f = v_i + at$$

$$\Delta x = \tfrac{1}{2}(v_f + v_i)t$$

$$\Delta x = v_i t + \tfrac{1}{2}at^2$$

for vectors a, v_f, v_i, and Δx and scalar t.

NOTE

These three equations are called **parametric equations** because they are functions of time. You'll find that they are used the most in game programming.

Here are the previous three equations as they would appear in code:

```
// purpose: calculate final velocity, given initial velocity,
➥acceleration,
//            and time
// input:   vi- initial velocity
//          a-  acceleration
//          t-  time
// output:  our final velocity
float eqOne_vf(float vi, float, a, float t)
{
    return vi + a * t;
}


// purpose: calculate change in distance, given final velocity,
➥initial
//          velocity, and time
// input:   vf- final velocity
//          vi- initial velocity
//          t-  time
// output:  our change in distance
float eqTwo_x(float vf, float vi, float t)
{
    return .5f * (vf - vi) / t;
}


// purpose: calculate change in distance, given initial velocity,
//          acceleration, and time
// input:   vi- initial velocity
//          t-  time
//          a-  acceleration
// output:  our change in distance
float eqThree_x(float vi, float t, float a)
{
    return vi * t + .5f * a * t * t;
}
```

Any of these equations can be changed to solve for one of the other variables present in the equation—for instance, the third equation can be algebraically altered to solve for acceleration, and would appear as follows:

```
// purpose: calculate acceleration, given initial velocity,
//           change in distance, and time
// input:   vi- initial velocity
//           t-  change in distance
//           a-  acceleration
// output:  our acceleration
float eqThree_a(float vi, float x, float a)
{
    return (x - vi * t) * 2 / (t * t);
}
```

These equations work the same way in two and three dimensions as they do in one dimension. Just remember that any time you add or subtract vector quantities, they must be in component form. Also, any time you must multiply a vector by time, simply multiply each component by the scalar quantity time.

Example 10.4: Using Equations of Motion in 2D

Suppose a vehicle in your game has a current velocity of 10m/s at 53° when it gets accelerated at a rate of 5m/s² @ 30°. How fast will it be going after 3 seconds?

Solution

1. Make a list of what you know and what you're looking for:

Given	Find
v_i = 10m/s @ 53°	v_f = ?
t = 3s	
a = 5m/s² @ 30°	

2. Because you've estimated the initial velocity and the acceleration in polar coordinates, you must convert them to Cartesian coordinates. Remember that the x-component is equal to the magnitude times the angle's cosine and that the y-component is equal to the magnitude times the angle's sine.

Given	Find
$v_i = 10\text{m/s} @ 53°$	
$= [6\ 8]$	$v_f = ?$
$t = 3\text{s}$	
$a = 5\text{m/s}^2 @ 30°$	
$= [4.3\ 2.5]$	

3. You need to choose an equation based on the list. In this case, the first equation ($v_f = v_i + at$) will work, because it is the only one that relates the four quantities in the list.

4. All that's left is to plug in and solve for v_f:

$$v_f = v_i + at = [6\ 8] + [4.3\ 2.5]3 = [6\ 8] + [12.9\ 7.5] = [18.9\ 15.5]$$

So v_f is the vector $[18.9\ 15.5]$.

Example 10.5: Using Equations of Motion in 3D

Suppose you're coding a racing game like *Need for Speed Under Ground* and the car is at rest on the starting line. If the acceleration is given by the vector $[3\ 0\ -2]$, how far will the care have gone 5 seconds after the start of the race?

Solution

1. Make a list of what you know and what you're looking for:

Given	Find
$v_i = [0\ 0\ 0]$	$\Delta x = ?$
$t = 5\text{s}$	
$a = [3\ 0\ -2]$	

2. Choose an equation based on the list. In this case, the fourth equation ($\Delta x = v_i t + \frac{1}{2}at^2$) will work, because it relates the three quantities you know with the one quantity you're looking for.

3. All that's left is to plug in and solve for Δx:

$\Delta x = v_i t + \frac{1}{2}at^2 = [0\ 0\ 0]5 + \frac{1}{2}[3\ 0\ -2](5)^2$

$=[0\ 0\ 0] + 12.5[3\ 0\ -2]$

$=[37.5\ 0\ -25]$

So the displacement vector is $[37.5\ 0\ -25]$.

As you can see, everything that was discussed in Chapter 8 also works in two and three dimensions. The only complication is the way in which vector quantities such as displacement, velocity, and acceleration are handled. The formulas still work; you just have to use vector operations instead of the scalar operations you're used to. The beauty of vector quantities is that they can always be broken into components, which simplifies the mathematical operations.

Self-Assessment

1. Give a vector in both forms that can be used to describe the 2D position of (40,75).

2. Find the displacement between the following two points on the screen: (250,300) and (75,100).

3. Find the displacement between the two 3D points (20,30,40) and (50,0,–50).

4. Find the average velocity of an object that goes from the point (150,200) to (25,0) in 10 seconds.

5. Find the average velocity of an object that goes from the point (50,400,–50) to (250,100,–100) in 10 seconds.

6. Find the acceleration of an object that goes from 30m/s @ 30° to 25m/s @ 45° in 5 seconds.

7. Find the displacement of the object described in question 6.

8. Suppose an object in your game starts at rest, and its acceleration is given by the vector [4 1 2]. How far will it have gone after 5 seconds?

9. How fast will the object described in question 8 be going at the end of the 5 seconds?

Projectiles

One of the easiest types of motion to spot in a game is projectile motion. Any object that has been thrown, kicked, or shot and that is flying through the air is considered a **projectile**. Think about the last time you threw a baseball or kicked a soccer ball. What type of path did the ball follow? That's right—it followed a parabolic path! You might want to flip back to Chapter 2, "Geometry Snippets," for a quick review of the parabola. Check out the parabola that opens downward. Doesn't it look like the trajectory of a missile that's just been shot at an angle? Any first-person or third-person shooter will have tons of projectiles, so how do we model them mathematically?

The easiest way to approach a 2D projectile is to break all the vector quantities into components, as you did in the preceding section, and then separate the horizontal components from the vertical ones. The components are completely independent of each other, so mathematically you can treat them separately. If you don't believe me, try this simple experiment. Get two identical balls or pencils, and find a table with a nice smooth surface. Roll one ball off the edge of the table, and watch it fall to the floor in a parabolic path. Now repeat the process, but this time drop the other ball from the same height as the table at the exact same time that the first ball reaches the edge of the table. Do they both hit the floor at the same time? They should. This tells you that the horizontal motion of the first ball does not affect its vertical motion. Both balls fall vertically in the same way. Figure 10.5 shows what happens from the side view.

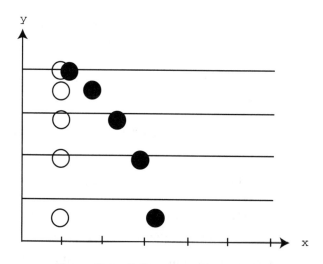

Figure 10.5 Ball experiment side view.

If you watch the experiment from the front view, where you have no depth perception, the motion of both balls appears identical, as shown in Figure 10.6.

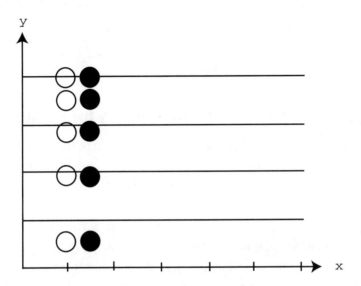

Figure 10.6 Ball experiment front view.

Now that we have established that vertical motion is completely independent of horizontal motion, let's address them separately. The best part of separating them is that we're back to 1D motion, which means just dealing with positive and negative numbers. Let's look at vertical motion first.

If we look at just the vertical components of the displacement, velocity, and acceleration vectors, we're really back to vertical 1D motion, which was discussed in Chapter 8. Looking at the displacement, the object goes up to a maximum height and then falls back down. The velocity starts out positive, decreases to 0 at the maximum height, and then speeds up in the negative direction as it falls down. This, of course, is caused by negative acceleration due to gravity (-9.8m/s^2). Because we're back to 1D motion with constant acceleration, we can use the five equations of motion discussed in Chapter 8.

Vertical Components of a Projectile

$a_y = -9.8\text{m/s}^2$

$v_{fy} = v_{iy} + at$

$\Delta y = v_{iy}t + \frac{1}{2}a_yt^2$

Example 10.6: Vertical Components of a Projectile

Suppose you're coding a game like *Spyro the Dragon* where the player climbs onto a cannon, and it launches cannon balls at a speed of 20m/s at a 30° angle. How much time will it take a cannon ball to come back down to the ground?

Solution

1. The cannon ball's initial velocity is not straight up in the air. It's at an angle, so you need to find the vertical component. Remember that the vertical component is equal to the overall magnitude times the angle's sine:

   $v_{iy} = 20\text{m/s}(\sin 30°) = 10\text{m/s}$

2. You're back to 1D vertical motion. Find the time it takes to get to the maximum height, and then double it for the total time up and down. List what you know and what you're trying to find:

Given	Find
$v_i = 10\text{m/s}$	$t = ?$
$v_f = 0\text{m/s}$	
$a = -9.8\text{m/s}^2$	

3. Choose an equation based on the list. In this case, the first equation ($v_f = v_i + at$) will work:

   $v_f = v_i + at$

   $0\text{m/s} = 10\text{m/s} + (-9.8\text{m/s}^2)t$

   $-10\text{m/s} = (-9.8\text{m/s}^2)t$

   $t = 1.02\text{s}$

4. Remember that this is only the time up to the maximum height. The total time up and back down is twice that, so $t = 2.04$s.

Now let's turn our attention to the horizontal components of the projectile's vector quantities. The horizontal components are even easier to work with, because as soon as a projectile is airborne, it does not speed up or slow down in the horizontal direction (if we ignore air resistance). This means that the horizontal component of the acceleration is always 0. In other words, the horizontal velocity does not change; it stays constant. And that constant velocity is equal to the horizontal displacement divided by time. Again, we're back to 1D motion with constant velocity, so we can use the five equations of motion just like we did in Chapter 8. What's even nicer about the projectile is that the horizontal acceleration is 0, and if you plug that into the equations of motion, they all reduce to one equation: $v_x = \Delta x/t$. That's the only equation you need to worry about for the horizontal components.

Horizontal Components of a Projectile

$a_x = 0$m/s^2

$v_x = \Delta x/t$

Example 10.7: Horizontal Components of a Projectile

Once again, you're coding a game like *Spyro the Dragon* where he's climbed onto a cannon, and it launches water balloons at a speed of 20m/s at a 30° angle. If the edge of the screen is 30 meters away from the launch, how much time will it take the cannon ball to fly out of view?

Solution

1. The cannon ball's initial velocity is at an angle, so you need to find the horizontal component. Remember that the horizontal component is equal to the magnitude times the angle's cosine:

$v_{iy} = 20$m/s$(\cos 30°) = 17.32$m/s

2. Now you're back to 1D horizontal motion. Make a list of what you know and what you're looking for:

Given	Find
v = 17.32m/s	t = ?
Δx = 30m/s	
a = 0m/s^2	

3. Because this is a projectile, the acceleration is 0, which means that the velocity stays constant. You need to worry about only one equation, so use it to find the time:

$v = \Delta x / t$

17.32m/s = 30m/t

t = 30m/(17.32m/s)

t = 1.73s

The cannon ball will go off the edge of the screen 1.73 seconds after it has been launched.

Now let's put the two pieces together. Earlier I said that all the projectile's vector quantities can be broken into components and then separated. You've been working with one more quantity that's not a vector. Time is a scalar quantity, so it has no direction. This means that time is the one element that can bridge the horizontal and vertical parts of projectile motion. For example, the water balloon you looked at in the last two examples had both horizontal and vertical components to its motion. You found in Example 10.6 that it took 2.04 seconds for the water balloon to go up and back down to the ground. That's the same amount of time it takes the water balloon to travel horizontally before it hits the ground. You can use the same 2.04 seconds to calculate how far away the balloon will hit the ground. That takes you to the horizontal information, so make a list:

Given	Find
$v = 17.32$m/s	$\Delta x = ?$
$t = 2.04$s	
$a = 0$m/s^2	

Because the acceleration is 0, you can use the equation $v = \Delta x/t$ to find the horizontal displacement:

$v = \Delta x/t$

17.32m/s $= \Delta x/2.04$s

$\Delta x = 35.33$m

The trick here is that it takes 2.04 seconds to go up and back down, so it also takes 2.04 seconds to travel 35.33 meters horizontally before hitting the ground.

Let's look at a few examples where this comes in handy. In these examples, you'll see that I place the horizontal and vertical components on opposite sides of the page. You also might want to consider sketching the motion to help organize all the numbers.

Example 10.8: Falling from a Known Height

Suppose you're making a 2D game like Joust with platforms at various heights. One platform is 8 meters above the ground. If the player (on his ostrich) runs off the ledge at 10m/s without jumping, how far away from the edge will he land on the ground?

Solution

1. Start by sketching the motion. This is done in Figure 10.7.

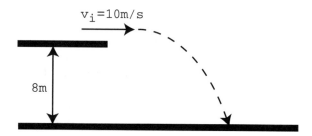

Figure 10.7 The player runs off the ledge.

2. Break all the vectors into components, and separate the horizontal from the vertical in two lists:

Horizontal		Vertical	
Given	**Find**	**Given**	**Find**
$v_x = 10\text{m/s}$	$\Delta x = ?$	$v_{iy} = 0\text{m/s}$	
$a_x = 0\text{m/s}^2$		$a_y = -9.8\text{m/s}^2$	
		$\Delta y = -8\text{m}$	

Because the player does not jump, his initial velocity is completely horizontal, so all 10m/s goes to the horizontal component, and the vertical initial velocity is 0m/s. Also notice that Δy is negative because the player is falling.

3. You're looking for horizontal displacement, so start with the horizontal list. Because the acceleration is 0, you have only one equation to worry about—$v_x = \Delta x/t$. Unfortunately, you can't use it until you know the time. The good news is that time is neither horizontal nor vertical, so it is the same value in both lists. This means that if you can find out how long it takes the player to fall, you can use the same time to calculate the horizontal displacement.

4. Go to the vertical list and see if you can find the time. You're right back to vertical 1D motion, and you have a list, so choose the appropriate equation:

$$\Delta y = v_{iy}t + {}^{1}/2a_yt^2$$

$$-8m = (0m/s)t + {}^{1}/2(-9.8m/s^2)t^2$$

$$-8m = {}^{1}/2(-9.8m/s^2)t^2$$

$$t^2 = 1.633s^2$$

$$t = 1.28s$$

5. Now revisit the lists. You've found the time it takes to fall to the ground. You can also use that for the horizontal time:

Horizontal		Vertical	
Given	**Find**	**Given**	**Find**
$v_x = 10m/s$	$\Delta x = ?$	$v_{iy} = 0m/s$	$t = 1.28s$
$a_x = 0m/s^2$		$a_y = -9.8m/s^2$	
$t = 1.28s$		$\Delta y = -8m$	

6. Now you have enough information on the horizontal side to calculate Δx:

$$v_x = \Delta x/t$$

$$10m/s = \Delta x/1.28s$$

$$\Delta x = 12.8m$$

The player lands 12.8 meters from the edge of the platform.

In this example, the player's initial velocity is completely horizontal. Let's look at the same situation but with an initial velocity at an angle.

Generally in a game, we don't calculate where a player is going to land or strike another object unless it is vital to some form of prediction code we're implementing. In the scenario previously described, once the player leaves the platform, in every frame we would apply gravity to his motion while also adjusting his position accordingly until we detected a collision with either the ground or another platform. Let's take a look at how this works. The player's position and his current direction of movement could be stored in arrays of two floats. Let's assume a screen coordinate of (200, 200) for the player and a velocity at 10 pixels/second:

```
float player_pos[2] = { 200, 200 };
float player_motion[2] = { 10, 0 };
```

In every frame, we would call a function to update the player's position, as follows:

```
// purpose: to update the player's position
// input:   none
// output:  the updated position
void updatePlayerPos()
{
    for(int i = 0; i < 2; ++i)
        player_pos[i] += player_motion[i];
}
```

We would also need to call a function to update the player's motion. In the game of *Joust*, horizontal motion would be affected by things like player input and collisions with objects, but in this instance, we're concerned more with the vertical motion, which is affected by gravity until it is affected by a collision. So in every frame, we would need to check to see if there was something underneath the player, and if not, we would need to allow gravity to affect his motion:

```
// purpose: to update the player's motion if there is nothing
➥under him
// input:   accel - the amount of constant vertical acceleration
➥per second
//          fps - our frames per second, in other words our time
➥interval
// output:  update player_motion[1] (vertical velocity)
void updatePlayerVertMotion(float accel, float fps)
{
    if(/*check to see if there is nothing underneath the player*/)
    {
```

```
            player_motion[1] = player_motion[1] + accel * fps;
    }
}
```

This same code could be used to solve the following problem as well, the only difference being that the player would begin the scenario with a negative initial velocity in the Y direction. You may be confused by this statement, because generally in this book a negative y-component for velocity represents downward motion, but keep in mind that in a game the Y axis decrements in the upward direction, so negative velocity in the vertical would indicate upwards travel.

Example 10.9: Jumping from a Known Height

Suppose you're making the same Joust-like game with platforms at various heights. One platform is 8 meters above the ground. If the player (on his ostrich) stands at the ledge and jumps off with an initial speed of 10m/s at a 30° angle, how far from the edge will he land on the ground?

Solution

1. Start by sketching the motion. This is done in Figure 10.8.

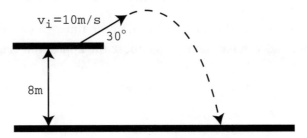

Figure 10.8   The player jumps off the ledge.

2. Break all the vectors into components, and separate the horizontal from the vertical in two lists:

Horizontal		Vertical	
Given	**Find**	**Given**	**Find**
$v_x = 10\cos30°$			
$= 8.66$m/s	$\Delta x = ?$	$v_{iy} = 10\sin30°$	
$= 5$m/s			
$a_x = 0$m/s^2		$a_y = -9.8$m/s^2	
		$\Delta y = -8$m	

Notice that Δy is still –8m even though the player jumps up first. Remember that Δy is displacement, not the actual distance.

3. You're looking for horizontal displacement, so start with the horizontal list. Because the acceleration is 0, you have only one equation to worry about—$v_x = \Delta x/t$. Unfortunately, you can't use it until you know the time. The good news is that time is neither horizontal nor vertical, so it is the same value in both lists. This means that if you can find out how long it takes the player to jump and fall, you can use the same time to calculate the horizontal displacement.

4. Go to the vertical list, and see if you can find the time. You're right back to vertical 1D motion, and you have a list, so choose the appropriate equation:

$$\Delta y = v_{iy}t + 1/2a_yt^2$$

$$-8m = (5\text{m/s})t + 1/2(-9.8\text{m/s}^2)t^2$$

5. You can use the quadratic formula here, or you can bypass this by finding v_{fy} and then use a different equation for time. Because the quadratic formula has a square root (which is an expensive operation) and it's difficult to remember, use the second option:

$$v_{fy}^2 = v_{iy}^2 + 2a\,\Delta y$$

$$v_{fy}^2 = (5\text{m/s})^2 + 2(-9.8\text{m/s}^2)(-8\text{m})$$

$$v_{fy}^2 = 181.8$$

$$v_{fy} = -13.48\text{m/s}$$

(Remember that you want the negative root because the player is falling when he hits the ground.)

6. Use v_{fy} in a different equation to find the time:

$v_{fy} = v_{iy} + a_y t$

$-13.48\text{m/s} = 5\text{m/s} + (-9.8\text{m/s}^2)t$

$t = 1.89\text{s}$

7. Now revisit the lists. You've found the time it takes to jump and fall to the ground. You can also use that for the horizontal time:

Horizontal		Vertical	
Given	**Find**	**Given**	**Find**
$v_x = 10\cos30°$			
$= 8.66\text{m/s}$	$\Delta x = ?$	$v_{iy} = 10\sin30°$	
$= 5\text{m/s}$		$v_{fy} = -13.48\text{m/s}$	
$a_x = 0\text{m/s}^2$		$a_y = -9.8\text{m/s}^2$	$t = 1.89\text{s}$
$t = 1.89\text{s}$		$\Delta y = -8\text{m}$	

8. Now you have enough information on the horizontal side to calculate Δx:

$v_x = \Delta x / t$

$8.66\text{m/s} = \Delta x / 1.89\text{s}$

$\Delta x = 16.33\text{m}$

This time, the player lands 16.33 meters from the edge of the platform.

In Examples 10.8 and 10.9, you were ultimately looking for the horizontal displacement. That won't always be the case. Let's look at one more example where you try to find the vertical displacement.

Example 10.10: Shooting Paintballs

Suppose the character in your game is shooting paintballs at the side of a building 20 meters from where he's lying on the ground. If the pellets leave the gun with an initial speed of 25m/s, and the character is aiming at a 40° angle, how high above the ground will the splattered paint appear on the wall?

Solution

1. Start by sketching the motion. This is done in Figure 10.9.

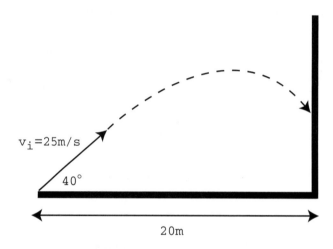

Figure 10.9 Shooting paintballs.

2. Break all vectors into components, and separate the horizontal from the vertical in two lists:

Horizontal		Vertical	
Given	**Find**	**Given**	**Find**
$v_x = 25\cos40°$			
$= 19.15$m/s		$v_{iy} = 25\sin40°$	
$= 16.07$m/s	$\Delta y = ?$		
$a_x = 0$m/s^2		$a_y = -9.8$m/s^2	
$\Delta x = 20$m			

3. You're looking for vertical displacement, so start with the vertical list. Unfortunately, you don't have enough information to use any of the equations of motion yet. However, because time has no direction, it is the same value in both lists. This means that if you can find out how long it takes the paintball to travel 20m toward the building, you can use the same time to calculate the vertical displacement.

4. Go to the horizontal list and see if you can find the time. Because $a = 0$, there's only one equation:

$$v_x = \Delta x/t$$

$$19.15\text{m/s} = 20\text{m}/t$$

$$t = 20\text{m}/(19.15\text{m/s})$$

$$t = 1.04\text{s}$$

5. Now revisit the lists. You've found the time it takes to hit the wall. You can also use that for the vertical time:

Horizontal		Vertical	
Given	**Find**	**Given**	**Find**
$v_x = 25\cos40°$			
$= 19.15\text{m/s}$	$t = 1.04\text{s}$	$v_{iy} = 25\sin40°$	
$= 16.07\text{m/s}$			$\Delta y = ?$
$a_x = 0\text{m/s}^2$		$a_y = -9.8\text{m/s}^2$	
$\Delta x = 20\text{m}$		$t = 1.04\text{s}$	

6. Now you have enough information on the vertical side to calculate Δy:

$$\Delta y = v_{iy}t + 1/2a_yt^2$$

$$\Delta y = (16.07\text{m/s})(1.04\text{s}) + 1/2(-9.8\text{m/s}^2)(1.04\text{s})^2$$

$$\Delta y = 11.48\text{m}$$

So the paintball will go splat on the wall at a height of 11.48 meters.

> **NOTE**
> All these examples began with all metric units. Be careful if you estimate initial values in different units. Always convert all values to the same units before plugging anything into an equation.

All the examples we've looked at have been flat on a 2D screen. You might be wondering how this translates to 3D. Well, it works the same way. A parabola is a 2D shape, so ultimately any projectile moves in a flat 2D plane—it just might not be the xy plane. The math still works. Just think of the components as horizontal and vertical, not necessarily parallel to the x- and y-axes. In the end, any horizontal component you find might need to be rotated in the xz plane, but the vertical components will always stay the same.

Self-Assessment

1. A grenade is thrown from the top of a cliff at an angle of 25° with an initial speed of 15m/s. After 3 seconds in flight, how far will it have fallen below the ledge?

2. Tom, the cat, is chasing Jerr,y the mouse, across the kitchen table, which is 1.5m high. At the last second, Jerry steps out of the way and lets Tom slide off the edge of the table going 5m/s. How far from the edge of the table will Tom land?

3. An enemy in your game stands on the edge of a rooftop 10m above the ground and throws a boulder with an initial velocity of 15m/s @ 37°. How far from the building would the player have to be standing to get hit by the boulder?

4. Your game character has set up a slingshot on the ground that fires eggs with an initial speed of 15m/s at a 37° angle. If a building is positioned 16 meters away from the slingshot, how high on the wall will the egg go splat?

5. If a quarterback throws a football downfield with an initial velocity of 20m/s at 35°, how far away should a receiver position himself to catch the ball?

Visualization Experience

On the CD-ROM, you will find a demo named *Cannon Physics*. Here's a brief description from the programmers, Michael Fawcett and Mike Wigand:

> *The* Cannonball *program is meant to look and feel a little like a* Tank Wars *or* Scorched Earth *clone, because we felt that many people would be familiar with the simple interface, and it lent itself to simple projectile physics nicely. The framework is kept to a minimum so that you can concentrate on the physics code rather than getting lost in files of collision code, Win32 code, image loaders, and so on.*

Run the demo by double-clicking Cannon Physics.exe. You see a black background with two small cannons at the bottom of the screen and a bunch of information at the top of the screen. Basically, two cannons shoot back and forth at each other. Above each cannon, certain variables are tracked. In the middle are the instructions so that you don't need to memorize the hot keys.

Start by experimenting with player 1 (on the left). Use the right arrow to change the angle to 60°, use the up arrow to change the force to 50N, and leave the mass at 1kg. Press the spacebar to launch the cannonball. You see the numbers above start to change, and the projectile path is a white dotted line. When the cannonball finally comes to rest, a Settings window pops up. You'll change those settings later, so just click OK for now. On the top-left side of the screen you see that the initial velocity is 10m/s. Chapter 12, "Energy," addresses how to calculate that value, so for now just let the program calculate it for you. This tells you that the initial velocity when the cannonball is shot is 10m/s @ 60°.

Now it's player 2's turn to shoot back. Use the left arrow to change the angle to 120°, use the up arrow to change the force to 50N, and leave the mass at 1kg. These are essentially the same settings that player 1 had, but this time you're shooting toward the left. This means that the initial velocity is 10m/s @ 120°. Calculate what the maximum height of the cannonball should be on paper before you press the spacebar. Your calculations should look similar to this:

Horizontal		Vertical	
Given	Find	Given	Find
$v_x = 10\cos 120°$			
$= 10\text{m/s}$		$v_{iy} = 10\sin 120°$	
≈ 8.660	$\Delta y = ?$		
$a_x = 0\text{m/s}^2$		$a_y = -9.8\text{m/s}^2$	
		$v_{fy} = 0\text{m/s}$	

On the vertical side, you can use equation 5 to calculate the height:

$$v_{fy}{}^2 = v_{iy}{}^2 + 2a\,\Delta y$$

$$(0\text{m/s})^2 = (8.660)^2 + 2(-9.8\text{m/s}^2)\,\Delta y$$

$$\Delta y = 3.8263$$

Be careful; it's tempting to stop here. Keep in mind that you just calculated Δy, which is the change in y. Did the cannonball leave from the ground? No, it was shot from the top of the cannon. If you look at the top of the screen, you see that the initial height (labeled Launch Pos_y) is 2.87m above the ground, so you need to add that to the change in y. Therefore, the maximum height should be 6.69m.

Press the spacebar and see what happens. The maximum height is reported at the top of the screen. Is it the same height you calculated? It should be. You might want to retry this process with a different angle and/or a different force for extra practice.

Notice that the Settings window appears at the completion of the launch. This time, put up a wall. In the Settings window, check the box next to Wall, and input the following three values for the wall:

Left: 5 m

Width: 1 m

Height: 20 m

Before launching player 1 again, calculate by hand how high the cannonball will be when it hits the wall. If you use the same settings as before (60°, 50N, 1kg), the magnitude of the initial velocity should still be 10m/s. If the wall is at the 5m mark (3m away from the cannon), how high (Δy) will the cannonball be after traveling 3m horizontally (Δx)? Again, don't forget to add the cannon's height.

After you calculate the answer, get ready to press the spacebar. Also get ready to press the P key quickly so that you can pause the motion and read the current height. Press the spacebar, and then try to pause the cannonball just as it hits the wall. What is its current height? Were you close?

When the Settings window appears, you can either leave the wall there or uncheck the box next to the wall to remove it. Now it's player 2's turn. Leave the cannon at 120° and the mass at 1kg, but use the up arrow to change the force to 200N. When you press the spacebar, the cannonball launches, and you can see at the top of the screen that this time the initial velocity is 20m/s.

The Settings window appears again. Create a new wall with the following dimensions:

Left: 25 m

Width: 1 m

Height: 15 m

Now it's player 1's turn. Let's keep the angle at 60° and the mass at 1kg. Use the up arrow to increase the force to 200N. Just like last time, the initial velocity should have a magnitude of 20m/s. With these settings, will the cannonball make it over the wall 23 meters away? Try to calculate the answer on paper first. Then press the spacebar to see if you are correct. The cannonball should clear!

What about the other side? Leave the wall exactly where it is. Make sure player 2 has an angle of 120°, a force of 200N, and a mass of 1kg. This should give you an initial velocity of 20m/s. If the wall is 23 meters away from the cannon, will the cannonball clear the wall again? Try calculating an answer on paper first. Then press the spacebar to see if you are correct. The cannonball should clear again!

Here's a final challenge. With a force of 250N and a mass of 1kg, what angle allows you to hit the other cannon, which is approximately 46 meters away? See if you can figure it out on paper, and then use the program to see if you're correct!

Self-Assessment Solutions

Using Vectors

1. [40 75] = 85 @ 62°

2. [−175 −200]

3. [30 −30 −90]

4. [−12.5 −20]

5. [20 −30 −5]

6. [−1.66 0.54]

7. [109.15 81.70]

8. [50 12.5 25]

9. [100 25 50]

Projectiles

1. 25.08 meters below the ledge

2. 2.77 meters away from the table

3. 31.44 meters away from the building

4. 3.26 meters high on the wall

5. 19.18 meters down the field

Chapter 11

Newton's Laws

So far, we've discussed how to describe motion: how far an object has moved, how fast it's going, and even how quickly it's speeding up or slowing down. At any point in that discussion, did you ever wonder what *causes* that motion? This chapter takes a step back in the process and examines what sets the object in motion before describing how it moves.

Forces

When you're getting ready to start the physics simulation portion of the code, the first step is to brainstorm all the forces that are acting on the object you want to move. The sum (or total) of all those forces determines how the object moves. Some of the forces are obvious: an enemy punches or kicks the player, the player pushes a large object out of the way, a ball is thrown, or a missile is launched. However, some less-obvious forces often get overlooked: gravity, friction, wind resistance (if it's significant), or the normal force. Let's stop and take a closer look at how each of these forces works, starting with gravity.

Earlier, we discussed acceleration due to gravity, which is represented in most formulas as the constant g.

Whenever we looked at the vertical components of the motion, we used $-g$ or -9.8m/s^2 for the acceleration. Now you can use that gravitational constant to calculate the force due to gravity, also known as *weight*. Weight is actually a force, which means it's a vector, and its direction is always down toward the center of the earth. The magnitude of weight is actually the object's mass times the acceleration due to gravity.

Weight

w = *m*g

where *m* = mass and g = acceleration due to gravity

(−9.8m/s^2 on Earth).

While most games won't need to differentiate between mass and weight, in extremely detailed games (or any simulation) such a distinction is needed. An example of some instances where this would be true is rag-doll physics or any form of driving simulation where the amount that the tires skid on turns needs to be calculated. The following function calculates weight. Notice that the return is not simply a number, but an array of three numbers. Why? Because weight is a vector which acts upon the object, not simply a scalar value.

```
// purpose: to calculate the weight of an object based on its mass
// input:   mass - the mass of the object
//          grav - the amount of constant acceleration due to
            ➥gravity
// output:  an array of 3 floats representing the vector of weight
float *calcWeight3D(float mass, float grav)
{
    // This will hold the weight of the object until it is returned
    // The value in [1] will be the only number changed, since
        ➥gravity
    // is only applied along the Y axis
    float weight[3] = { 0, };

    // Calculate the weight, it is assumed that grav is a
        ➥negative number
    weight[1] = mass * grav;
```

```
    // Return our answer
    return weight;
}
```

Let's look a little closer at mass and weight. The biggest difference between the two is that mass is a scalar quantity, and weight is a vector quantity. Even though we tend to use these two terms interchangeably in everyday language, in physics they are two very different quantities. The units are often a dead giveaway as to which quantity you are working with. Mass often is measured in either grams or kilograms, whereas weight is measured in pounds or newtons.

You might not be familiar with newtons, so let's define this new unit. If mass is measured in kilograms, when you multiply it by the acceleration due to gravity ($g = -9.8m/s^2$) to calculate the object's weight on Earth, you end up with the unit of $kg*m/s^2$. This unit is quite awkward to say, so it has been named the Newton (written N) after Sir Isaac Newton. Unfortunately, you might be accustomed to approximating weights in pounds, so you might need to convert a weight from pounds to newtons. The conversion factor is $1N = 0.2248lbs$.

Newtons

$1N = 1kg*m/s^2$

$1N = 0.2248lbs$

Example 11.1: Calculating Weight

If an object in your game has a mass of 50kg, what is its weight in pounds?

Solution

1. Find the weight in newtons:

$$w = mg = 50kg(-9.8m/s^2) = -490kg*m/s^2 = -490N$$

2. Convert from newtons to pounds:

$$-490N\left(\frac{0.2248\,lbs}{1N}\right) = 110.152\,lbs$$

More often in game programming, you'll find that you estimate an object's weight in pounds out of habit, and then you can convert it to newtons or use it to find the mass.

Example 11.2: Calculating Mass

Suppose you estimate a character's weight (on Earth) to be 200lbs. What is its mass?

Solution

1. Convert from pounds to newtons:

$$-200\,lbs\left(\frac{1N}{0.2248\,lbs}\right) \approx -890N$$

2. Use the weight in newtons to calculate the mass in kilograms:

$$w = mg$$

$$-890N = m(-9.8m/s^2)$$

$$m = -890N/-9.8m/s^2 = 90.78kg$$

Have you ever wondered why, if gravity (or your weight) is always pulling you down, you don't perpetually fall? Something is stopping you from falling all the way to the Earth's core. That's right—the ground. The ground actually exerts a force on you as well; it's called the *normal force*. The normal force is the force of the surface your object is sitting on that counteracts gravity and keeps it from falling any farther. If the surface is suddenly removed, the object falls until it hits another surface with a normal force that counteracts gravity. It's called the normal force because the term "normal" indicates perpendicular, and this force is always perpendicular to the surface the object is on. Chapter 4, "Vector Operations," discussed how to find the surface normal by taking the cross-product of the two vectors that define the surface.

Therefore, if you are simply standing on the ground, gravity is pulling you down, but the ground is exerting a force straight up (perpendicular to the ground) to keep you from falling through.

Example 11.3: Normal Force on a Flat Surface

Suppose you estimate a vehicle's weight (on Earth) to be 1,000lbs. What must the normal force of the road be to keep the car from sinking?

Solution

1. Convert the weight from pounds to newtons:

$$-1000\,lbs\left(\frac{1N}{0.2248\,lbs}\right) \approx -4448.4N$$

The normal force needs to cancel out the weight of the car so that it doesn't float up in the air or sink through the road. Therefore, the normal force must be 4448.4N.

> **NOTE**
> Weight is always a negative value, because the direction is down toward the center of the Earth. That is why the normal force must always have a positive value.

Example 11.4: Normal Force on an Inclined Plane

Suppose a ball that weighs 0.25lbs is rolling down a ramp, which is positioned at a 30° incline. What is the normal force of the ramp?

Solution

1. Convert the weight from pounds to newtons:

$$-0.25\,lbs\left(\frac{1N}{0.2248\,lbs}\right) \approx -1.112N$$

2. Remember that the normal force must be perpendicular to the surface of the ramp, so it's not simply the opposite of the weight this time. You want the opposite of the component of the weight that is perpendicular to the ramp, as shown in Figure 11.1.

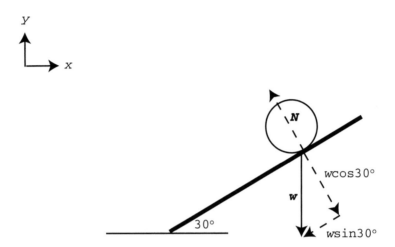

Figure 11.1 Normal force on an inclined plane.

3. Notice that the component of the weight that's perpendicular to the ramp's surface is $w\cos30° = -1.112N(\cos30°) = -0.963N$. Therefore, the normal force must be 0.963N.

> **NOTE**
> This normal force accounts for the ball's slower acceleration downward compared to freefall if there were no surface.

Another type of force that often gets ignored is the force due to friction. In gaming it might be a good idea to ignore friction, but that's entirely up to the programmer. If the force of friction is relatively insignificant, and the player won't even notice it, why waste precious processing power on it? However, if you are attempting to code a perfectly realistic simulator, it might be extremely important to spend the extra clock cycles calculating friction. It all depends on how you want to balance speed against realism.

There are actually two types of friction: static and kinetic. **Static friction** is the force that keeps an object from moving initially, and **kinetic friction** is the force that slows down an object after it gets moving.

Always calculate static friction first. If all the other forces added up are less than the static friction, the object will not move. As soon as the other forces become greater than the static friction, the object starts to move, and kinetic friction takes over. Both types of friction are completely dependent on the two surfaces coming into contact with each other. The smoother the surfaces, the less friction there is. This means that a metal object on ice has significantly less friction than rubber tires on dry pavement. When you're ready to calculate friction, you need a table of coefficients to use as a guide. Table 11.1 lists some common surfaces to give you an idea of what some coefficients are. Just remember that the smoother the surfaces, the lower the coefficient.

NOTE

The Greek letter μ (mu) is the standard symbol for the coefficient of friction.

Table 11.1 Coefficient of Friction

Surface Friction (μ_K)	Static Friction (μ_S)	Kinetic
Steel on steel (dry)	0.6	0.4
Steel on steel (greasy)	0.1	0.05
Teflon on steel	0.041	0.04
Brake lining on cast iron	0.4	0.3
Rubber on concrete (dry)	1.0	0.9
Rubber on concrete (wet)	0.30	0.25
Metal on ice	0.022	0.02
Steel on steel	0.74	0.57
Aluminum on steel	0.61	0.47
Copper on steel	0.53	0.36

continues

Table 11.1 Coefficient of Friction *continued*

Surface Friction (μ_K)	Static Friction (μ_S)	Kinetic
Nickel on nickel	1.1	0.53
Glass on glass	0.94	0.40
Copper on glass	0.68	0.53
Oak on oak (parallel to grain)	0.62	0.48
Oak on oak (perpendicular to grain)	0.54	0.32

Now you can use these coefficients to calculate both types of friction.

Static friction:

$$F_S = -\mu_S N$$

where N is the normal force.

Note that the static frictional force is always the opposite direction of the normal force of the surface.

Kinetic friction:

$$F_K = -\mu_K N$$

where N is the normal force.

Example 11.5: Calculating Friction

Suppose you're coding a racing game, and the car weighs approximately 1,500lbs. What values might you use for the static and kinetic friction of the rubber tires on a dry road?

Solution

1. Convert the weight from pounds to newtons:

$$-1500\,lbs\left(\frac{1N}{0.2248\,lbs}\right) \approx -6672.6N$$

2. Find the normal force. If the road is flat, the normal force must be N = 6672.6N.

3. To find the static friction, look up the coefficient of static friction between rubber and dry concrete in Table 11.1. In this case $\mu_S = 1.0$, so the static friction is

$$F_S = -\mu_S N = -1.0(6672.6N) = -6672.6N$$

4. To find the kinetic friction, look up the coefficient of kinetic friction between rubber and dry concrete in Table 11.1. In this case $\mu_K = 0.9$, so the kinetic friction is

$$F_K = -\mu_K N = -0.9(6672.6N) = -6005.3N$$

So now it's time to combine everything we've learned about normals and friction into some functions which may have an applicable use in a game. Suppose we are presented with the problem of an object—for instance a box, which is sitting at rest on an incline that is slowly increasing in angle. For a realistic simulation, at some point the box must begin to slide down the ramp, so how can we figure this out? First and foremost, we must be able to calculate the normal force applied to the object from the ramp, and secondly, the opposing perpendicular force which is trying to pull the box down the ramp. Using the normal force and the coefficient of friction between the two surfaces, we can then determine the amount of force needed for the object to begin moving. Once the force perpendicular to the normal exceeds that force, the box will begin to slide. Finally, note that weight has been simplified to a scalar quantity here, for ease of use.

```
// purpose: to determine whether an object on an incline will
➥slide
// input:    angle - the current angle of the incline
//           weight - the weight of the object
//           fric_coeff - the coefficient of static friction
             ➥between surfaces
// output:   true if the object should slide, else false
bool checkForMotion(float angle, float weight, float fric_coeff)
{
    // Calculate the normal force being exerted by the ramp
    float normal = weight * cosf(angle * PI / 180);
    // Calculate the force perpendicular to the normal
    float perpForce = weight * sinf(angle * PI / 180);
    // Calculate the amount of static friction keeping the object
    ➥at rest
```

```
    float stat_friction = fric_coeff * normal;
    // Return true if the object should slide, else false
    return perpForce > stat_friction;
}
```

Let's take this problem one step further and calculate just how fast the box should be accelerating. If we subtract the amount of the kinetic friction (the force which is trying the stop the object) from the amount of force which is perpendicular to the normal (the force which is trying to move the object), we will end up with the amount of force which is actually being applied to the object. Knowing that F = ma and subsequently that a = F / m, we can easily figure out the acceleration and return it. Note that this function call should only be allowed if the checkForMotion() function call returns true, as otherwise it would return a negative acceleration and the box would actually slide up the ramp.

```
// purpose: to determine whether an object on an incline will
➥slide
// input:    angle - the current angle of the incline
//           weight - the weight of the object
//           fric_coeff - the coefficient of kinetic friction
             ➥between surfaces
//           mass - the mass of the object
// output:   the acceleration of the object
float calcAccel(float angle, float weight, float fric_coeff, float
➥mass)
{
    // Calculate the normal force being exerted by the ramp
    float normal = weight * cosf(angle * PI / 180);
    // Calculate the force perpendicular to the normal
    float perpForce = weight * sinf(angle * PI / 180);
    // Calculate the amount of static friction keeping the object
    ➥at rest
    float kin_friction = fric_coeff * normal;
    // Calculate the sum of forces acting upon the object
    float total_force = perpForce - kin_friction;
    // return the acceleration of the object
    return total_force / mass;
}
```

After you've brainstormed all the significant forces acting on an object, the next step is to add them all up to find the net or total force, which is often written as ΣF.

NOTE
If you've never seen the sigma (Σ) notation, it's often used to indicate the sum or total.

In one dimension, finding ΣF is very easy, because the direction of the forces is given by a positive or negative value. So when you are ready to add them up, you're simply adding positive and negative numbers. For example, consider the vertical forces acting on you as you sit in your chair and read this book. The force due to gravity is a negative value (your weight), and the normal force of the chair is a positive value (the opposite of your weight), so when you add them up, in this case you get a net force of 0. This is illustrated in Figure 11.2.

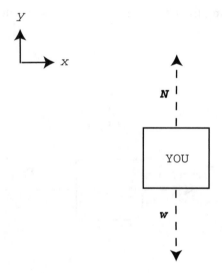

Figure 11.2   Net force in 1D.

Now let's extend that scenario to 2D. Suppose your chair has wheels on it, and someone sneaks up from behind and starts to push you across the floor. Now you have both horizontal and vertical forces to contend with. Here's where all your work with vectors in Chapter 4 comes in handy. All you're really doing is adding 2D vectors in component form. Just remember to always keep the horizontal components of the forces separate from the vertical.

The best way to organize all the forces and their components is to use a *free-body diagram*. This is a standard diagram that uses arrows to represent the forces on an object in a very specific way. Standards can be extremely useful if you adhere to the same rules as everyone else. In this case, you can quickly get a feel for the total force just by glancing at the diagram *if* it adheres to the standards. The free-body diagram has two basic rules:

➤ Use arrows of relative lengths to represent forces.

➤ Draw all arrows originating from the center of the object and pointing in the appropriate direction.

Let's use a free-body diagram to organize all the forces acting on you as you're pushed in the chair. We've discussed four different forces so far: weight, normal, friction, and the force of your friend pushing the chair. These four forces are pictured in Figure 11.3.

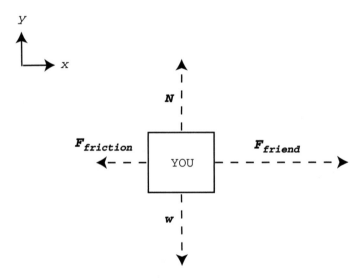

Figure 11.3 A sample free-body diagram.

Just glancing at the diagram allows you to see that the net force is in the general direction that your friend is pushing. Now that you have a general feel for the net force, you can attach numeric values to each of the forces and add them up. Remember that when you add vector quantities such as forces in 2D, they can be added only in component form.

Example 11.6: Calculating Net Force in 2D

Suppose you're coding an ice world level of your game, and the main character is pulling a sled piled with treasure across the ice. The sled's rope is at a 60° incline, and the player pulls with an overall force of 100N. If the loaded sled weighs approximately 80lbs, what is the net force?

Solution

1. Draw a free-body diagram to organize all the forces. This has been done in Figure 11.4.

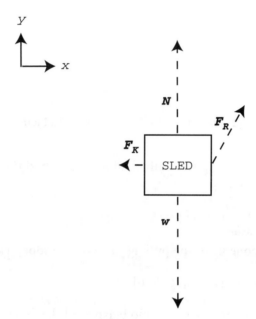

Figure 11.4   A free-body diagram for net force.

2. Use the diagram to break all the forces into components. This has been done in Figure 11.5.

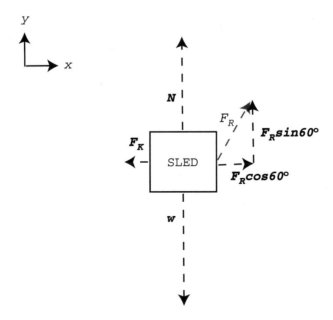

Figure 11.5 All forces in component form.

3. Calculate the values of all the individual forces. To find the weight, convert it from pounds to newtons:

$$w = -80\,lbs \left(\frac{1N}{0.2248\,lbs}\right) \approx -355.9N = [0\ -355.9]$$

To find the components of the pulling force on the rope, use sine and cosine:

$$F_R = [100\cos60°\ 100\sin60°] = [50\ 86.6]$$

To find the normal force, you need to balance all the downward forces, taking into account the slight upward force of the rope:

$$N = -(-355.9N + 86.6N) = 355.9N - 86.6N = 269.3N = [0\ 269.3]$$

To find the kinetic friction, use the formula $F_K = -\mu_K N$ with the appropriate value for μ_K from Table 11.1. Just remember that the direction is always in the direction opposite the motion.

$$F_K = -\mu_K N = -0.02(269.3N) = -5.4N = [-5.4\ 0]$$

4. Now all that's left is to add these vector quantities. Remember to always add in component form!

$$w + F_R + N + F_K = [0 \; -355.9] + [50 \; 86.6] + [0 \; 269.3] + [-5.4 \; 0]$$

$$=[44.6 \; 0]$$

Therefore, the net force is [44.6 0].

The free-body diagram is a very useful tool for organizing all the forces acting on the object. After you work with them for a while, it becomes easier to glance at them and quickly get an instinctive feel for what the net force is. It's also a nice tool for organizing any forces that might come in at a strange angle and need to be broken into components. Unfortunately, when you move into 3D, it's pretty difficult to sketch a clear diagram. In that case, simply keep all the forces' components organized in vectors, and in the end, add the vectors for the net force. The next section examines how the net force changes an object's motion after you've calculated it.

Self-Assessment

1. If a monster in your game has a mass of 80kg, what is its weight in pounds?

2. Suppose you estimate a weapon's weight (on Earth) to be 10lbs. What is its mass?

3. Suppose you estimate an object's weight (on Earth) to be 25lbs. What must the normal force of the table it's sitting on be to keep the object from falling through?

4. Suppose a 50kg cart is sitting on a loading ramp with a 20° incline. What's the ramp's normal force?

5. Suppose the cart described in question 4 has rubber wheels. What's the static and kinetic friction between the wheels and the concrete ramp after a good rainstorm?

6. What is the net force for the object in the free-body diagram shown in Figure 11.6?

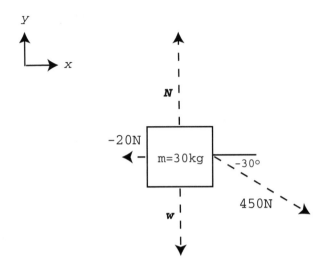

Figure 11.6 Another free-body diagram.

7. Draw a free-body diagram for the following scenario: You spot a buddy sitting in a chair with wheels, and you decide to get him back for pushing your chair earlier. He weighs 150lbs, and the chair is another 10lbs. You push him with a force of 1200N at a –60° angle. The coefficient of kinetic friction between the wheels and the floor is 0.3.

8. Find the net force on your buddy in the chair described in question 7.

Using Newton's Laws to Determine How Forces Affect an Object's Motion

Now that we have discussed how to find the net force, Newton's laws will tell us how that net force affects an object's motion. Sir Isaac Newton is credited with, among other things, inventing calculus as well as discovering three laws that govern all motion on Earth (except for on the molecular level) in the late 17th century. These three laws tell us how forces affect an object's motion. We'll address them one at a time.

Newton's First Law specifies what happens when the net or total force on an object is 0. If all the individual forces cancel each other out, there should be no change in the motion. A perfect example of this law is you sitting in your chair right now. Your weight is pulling you down, but the normal force of the chair cancels that out, so there's nothing left to force you to move.

Newton's First Law

If $F_{net} = 0$, there's no change in motion.

In other words, if an object is at rest, it stays at rest until a net external force changes it. Likewise, if an object is moving, it continues at the same speed in the same direction until a net force changes it. At this point, you might be thinking, "But if I roll a ball across the floor, it slows down and eventually comes to rest." That's true. But the net force is not 0. Don't forget about friction; that is the net external force responsible for slowing down the ball.

Example 11.7: Newton's First Law on Air Hockey

Suppose you're coding an air hockey game. An ideal table should have no friction. A player hits the puck and gives it an initial velocity of [10 5]. As the puck approaches the wall 3 seconds later, what is its current velocity just before it hits the wall?

Solution

If the game takes place on a good air hockey table with no friction, there's no net external force. Therefore, the puck will still be moving with a constant velocity of [10 5].

> **NOTE**
> In Example 11.7, the puck changes its motion only when it hits the wall or the other player's paddle.

Newton's First Law tells us what happens when the net force is 0. At this point, are you wondering what happens when the net force is something other than 0? You already know that a net external force changes an object's motion, but by how much? That's precisely what Newton's Second Law tells us.

Newton's Second Law

$F_{net} = ma$

where m = mass and a = acceleration.

> **NOTE**
> Note that when the net force is 0, the acceleration must be 0, which is exactly what Newton's First Law says.

This law tells us several things. First, it shows that the more force you place on an object, the faster it speeds up. It also tells us that if two objects receive the same amount of force, the smaller object speeds up faster than the larger object. Most importantly, Newton's Second Law lets you numerically calculate an object's acceleration based on its mass and the net force.

Example 11.8: Newton's Second Law

In Example 11.6, you found that the net force on the sled was [44.6 0]. What's the resulting acceleration?

Solution

1. Remember that the loaded sled weighs –355.9N. Use that to calculate the mass:

   $w = mg$

   $-355.9N = m(-9.8m/s^2)$

   $m = 36.3kg$

2. Use the net force and mass to calculate the acceleration:

   $F_{net} = ma$

   $$\begin{bmatrix} 44.6 \\ 0 \end{bmatrix} = 36.3 \begin{bmatrix} a_x \\ a_y \end{bmatrix}$$

   $$a = \begin{bmatrix} 1.2 \\ 0 \end{bmatrix}$$

After you calculate the acceleration, you're right back to the five equations of motion from Chapter 10, "Motion in Two and Three Dimensions." The most important thing to remember about Newton's Second Law is that the net force can change at any time. An object accelerates only when the net force is applied. When the force stops, the acceleration stops, and the velocity becomes constant (Newton's First Law). Fortunately, in game programming everything is recalculated on a frame-by-frame basis, so as soon as the net force stops, the next frame is based on 0 acceleration. So overall, the process starts with the forces, which determine acceleration, which determines velocity and displacement. Ultimately, you need to track where an object should be located as time is incremented.

Example 11.9: Newton's Second Law with the Five Equations of Motion

Suppose you're coding a game with a top-down view, and the player needs to roll a large boulder into a stand in order to unlock a door. The boulder is sitting still, and it weighs 50lbs. If the player pushes with a constant force of 400N @ 30°, and the coefficient of kinetic friction is 0.25, how far will the boulder move after 1, 2, and 3 seconds?

Solution

1. Start with a free-body diagram to organize all the forces. This is done in Figure 11.7.

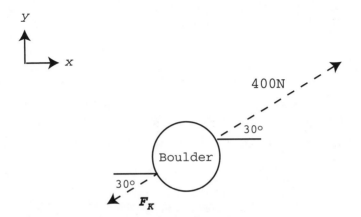

Figure 11.7   A free-body diagram for a boulder.

2. Numerically calculate F_K:

w = −50lbs = −222.42N

N = 222.42N

$F_K = -\mu_K N = -0.25(222.42N) = -55.605N$ (opposite of F_P)

3. Calculate the net force. Remember that all forces must be added in component form, so break both forces into components:

F_P = 400N @ 30° = [346.41 200]

F_K = 55.605N @ 210° = [−48.16 −27.80]

$F_{net} = F_P + F_K$ = [298.25 172.20]

4. To use Newton's Second Law, you need to know the boulder's mass:

w = mg

−222.42N = m(−9.8m/s²)

m = 22.7kg

5. Use the net force and mass to calculate the acceleration:

F_{net} = ma

$$\begin{bmatrix} 298.25 \\ 172.20 \end{bmatrix} = 22.7 \begin{bmatrix} a_x \\ a_y \end{bmatrix}$$

$$a = \begin{bmatrix} 13.14 \\ 7.59 \end{bmatrix}$$

6. Now that you know the acceleration, you can use the five equations of motion just like before. If the boulder starts from rest, v_i = [0 0]. If you know the acceleration, initial velocity, and time, you can use the 4th equation of motion to find displacement:

$$\Delta r = v_i t + \tfrac{1}{2}at^2$$

$$\begin{bmatrix} r_x \\ r_y \end{bmatrix} = \begin{bmatrix} 0 \\ 0 \end{bmatrix} t + 0.5 \begin{bmatrix} 13.14 \\ 7.59 \end{bmatrix} t^2$$

$$\begin{bmatrix} r_x \\ r_y \end{bmatrix} = 0.5 \begin{bmatrix} 13.14 \\ 7.59 \end{bmatrix} t^2$$

7. Use that equation to solve for displacement for each of the three times:

At $t = 1s$:

$$\begin{bmatrix} r_x \\ r_y \end{bmatrix} = 0.5 \begin{bmatrix} 13.14 \\ 7.59 \end{bmatrix} (1)^2 = \begin{bmatrix} 6.57 \\ 3.80 \end{bmatrix}$$

At $t = 2s$:

$$\begin{bmatrix} r_x \\ r_y \end{bmatrix} = 0.5 \begin{bmatrix} 13.14 \\ 7.59 \end{bmatrix} (2)^2 = \begin{bmatrix} 26.28 \\ 15.18 \end{bmatrix}$$

At $t = 3s$:

$$\begin{bmatrix} r_x \\ r_y \end{bmatrix} = 0.5 \begin{bmatrix} 13.14 \\ 7.59 \end{bmatrix} (3)^2 = \begin{bmatrix} 59.13 \\ 34.16 \end{bmatrix}$$

Even though Newton's Third Law does not appear often in code, this discussion would be incomplete without it, so let's quickly mention it. You might have heard the saying "For every action there's an equal and opposite reaction." Newton's Third Law basically says that for every force there's an equal and opposite force. For example, if I punch my opponent in a fighting game, I am putting a force on that person. At the same time, that person's body is exerting a force back on my fist, which is why my fist slows down (and why it hurts!)

Newton's Third Law

For every force there is an equal and opposite force, or, when two objects come into contact, they exert equal and opposite forces upon each other.

This chapter actually took a step backwards in the overall framework of a physics simulation. Before you can track the motion of an object, you must examine what causes the motion, and that means forces. After you have brainstormed all the forces acting on the object being modeled, you can add them up to find the net force. If the net force is 0, the object continues to move with a constant velocity. If the net force is nonzero, you can use the mass to numerically calculate the acceleration, which then determines how fast and how far the object moves.

Self-Assessment

1. If you lay this book on a table, and nothing touches it, where should it be 2 minutes later?

2. If you're in the space station, where there's no friction, and you toss a pen to your partner with an initial velocity of 5m/s @ 45°, what's its velocity when it reaches your partner?

3. What is the acceleration for the object in the free-body diagram shown in Figure 11.8?

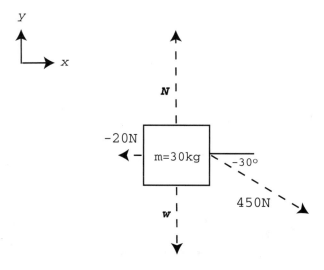

Figure 11.8   The free-body diagram for question 3.

4. If the forces listed in question 3 are applied for 5 seconds, and the object starts from rest, how far will the object move?

5. Suppose you're coding a game with a top-down view, and the player needs to push a cart full of treasure back to home base. The cart is sitting still, and it weighs 35lbs. If the player pushes with a constant force of 200N @ –60°, and the coefficient of kinetic friction is 0.05, what's the cart's acceleration?

6. If the player in question 5 pushes the cart with a constant force for 3 seconds, what's the cart's displacement?

Self-Assessment Solutions

Forces

1. –176.24lbs

2. 4.54kg

3. 111.2N

4. 460.45N

5. $F_S = -\mu_S N = -0.3(460.45) = -138.13N$ and $F_K = -\mu_K N = -0.25(460.45) = -115.11N$

6. $F_{net} = [369.7\ 0]$

7. The answer is shown in Figure 11.9.

8. $F_{net} = [88.05\ 0]$

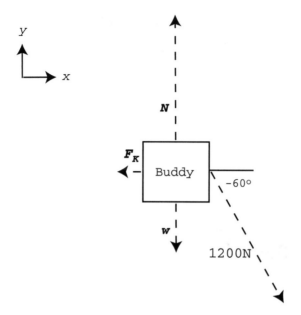

Figure 11.9 The free-body diagram for question 7.

Using Newton's Laws to Determine How Forces Affect an Object's Motion

1. In the same place

2. 5m/s @ 45°

3. a = [12.32 0]

4. 154m

5. a = [6.05 –10.48]

6. Δr = [27.22 –47.15]

Chapter 12

Energy

KEY TOPICS

- Work and Kinetic Energy
- Potential Energy and the Conservation Law

Have you ever gotten on a roller coaster and noticed that after the car was carried up the first hill, there were no more motors to speed you up? In addition, did you notice that there were no brakes to slow you down until the very end of the ride? And yet the speed kept changing the whole time. That is the power of mechanical energy.

This chapter examines energy as an alternative approach to modeling motion. Depending on the type of game, this might or might not be more efficient, but it's always good to have options.

> **NOTE**
> The morph ball in *Metroid Prime* uses this to outstanding effect.

Work and Kinetic Energy

Before we can delve into the energy-based model, we must define a couple new quantities. Two of them are work and kinetic energy. We all use the term work in our everyday language, so I'm sure you have a sense of what it means. Be careful, though: In physics, work has a very precise definition. **Work** is equal to force times displacement.

Work

$W = F\Delta x$

where

Δx = displacement

and

F = force in the direction of displacement.

If work is defined as force times displacement, this means that the object must move for work to be done. This might contradict your current perception of work. For example, if you push against a brick wall until you work up a sweat, you might think you've worked really hard. However, a physicist will tell you that you've done no work at all, because the brick wall hasn't moved.

Another important aspect of this definition is that the force must be in the same direction as the displacement. It can be a negative force, but it must be in the same direction as the displacement. You might have noticed that force and displacement are both vector quantities, so the only way you can multiply them together is if their directions are the same.

For example, suppose your game character must pull a wagon filled with treasure, as shown in Figure 12.1. He'll probably pull the handle at an angle, but the wagon will roll horizontally across the ground. What that means in terms of work is that you need to use the horizontal component of the force, not the total force, to calculate the work.

Before looking at examples, it's important to discuss a few quick facts about vectors. Chapter 4, "Vector Operations," detailed several operations that may need to be calculated in order to process some vector operations. This chapter will require several of those methods including the dot product, normalization, and scalar multiplication. Standing with the emphasis on readability over robustness, the code in this chapter is centered around a vector definition that looks like this:

2D vector

```
    typedef struct
    {
      float x;
      float y;
    } vector2D;
```

3D vector

```
    typedef struct
    {
      float x;
      float y;
      float z;
    } vector3D;
```

These vectors are used from here on out for the sake of simplicity and so that the mathematics can be emphasized. If you prefer an earlier or different implementation, feel free to substitute it in the examples. The vector library that is provided with the sample source code contains all the details needed for operations that are not explicitly defined within this chapter.

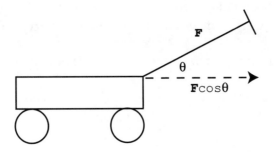

Figure 12.1   Pulling a wagon at an angle.

One last detail concerning work is the issue of units. If you haven't discovered this already, metric units are always the easiest to work with in physics simulation. If you choose to keep everything metric for consistency, the force is measured in Newtons, and the displacement is measured in meters, which means that the work is measured in Newton-meters (N*m). This unit has been renamed the **joule** (J), so 1J = 1N*m. If you insist on using British units, work is measured in foot-pounds (ft*lbs).

Joule (J)
1J = 1N*m

Example 12.1: Calculating Work

Suppose the player in your game must push a secret stone wall at least 2 meters to gain access to a bonus level. If the player's character can push with a horizontal force of 1500N and a kinetic frictional force of 50N is working against him, how much work total will it take to move the wall out of the way?

Solution

Let's start with the definition of work, $W = F\Delta x$. The net force in this case is 1500N − 50N = 1450N, and the displacement is 2m.

$W = F\Delta x$

$= 1450N(2m)$

$= 2900N*m$

$= 2900J$

Programming the calculation for work is fairly straightforward. Here is a function that returns the amount of work done given a force, a friction force, and a displacement:

```
float calculateWork(float force, float friction, float displacement)
    {
        //calculate the difference of the forces.
        float netForce = force-friction;

    //multiply by displacement
        float temp = displacement*netForce;
        return temp;
    }
```

This function will return a float value of the work in Joules. Always make sure to double check your units when setting up calculations. Refer to Chapter 6, "Transformations," for more information on unit calculations.

> **NOTE**
> Both units N*m and J are equally acceptable, so use whichever one you like better.

Example 12.2: Calculating Work with Angled Force

Let's go back to the wagon example. If your character pulls the wagon with a force of 1600N@60° and the kinetic friction is 25N, how much work will it take to pull the wagon 5m?

Solution

1. Notice that the force of the character pulling the wagon is at an angle, and the displacement is horizontal. This means that you can use only the horizontal component of that force:

$$F_{Cx} = F_C(\cos\theta)$$

$$= 1600N(\cos 60°)$$

$$= 1600N(0.5)$$

$$= 800N$$

2. Now you can find the net force:

$$F_{net} = F_{Cx} - F_f$$

$$= 800N - 25N$$

$$= 775N$$

3. Finally, all you need is the definition of work:

$$W = F_{net}\,\Delta x$$

$$= 775N(5m)$$

$$= 3875N*m$$

$$= 3875J$$

Angled forces may frequently be calculated depending on how a game models physics.

Here is a function that will return the amount of work done considering an angled force:

```
float calculateAngledWork(vector2D vect, float friction,float
➥displacement)
    {
        float temp;
        //don't forget to convert to rads....
        temp = cos(DegreesToRads(vect.y));

        //calculate the horizontal force;
        float horizForce = vect.x*temp;

        float work = calculateWork(horizForce,friction,
        ➥displacement);
        return work;
    }
```

Here we see the first usage of our 2Dvector type. Using the quick conversion macros from Chapter 6, we get the cosine of the angled force, and then continue on to calculate the horizontal force. The final amount of work is determined when we reuse the work function that was listed in Example 12.1.

Example 12.3: Calculating Work with Force and Displacement at Different Angles

Suppose you're coding a top-down game where the object being moved is free to move in both the x and y directions. A net force of 2000N@60° is applied to the object, but due to constraints, the object moves 3m@30°. How much work is done to move the object?

Solution

1. The challenge here is that the two vectors are at different angles. First, break both vector quantities into components so that you can work with them more easily:

   F = 2000N@60° = [2000(cos60°) 2000(sin60°)] = [1000 1732]

   Δr = 3m@30° = [3(cos30°) 3(sin30°)] = [2.6 1.5]

2. Now you need to find the component of the force that is in the same direction as the displacement. You can use the dot product for this. Remember that the dot product of the force and the normalized displacement vector produce the length of the projection. That projection times the normalized displacement reveals the component of the force in the direction of the motion:

$$\hat{\Delta r} = [2.6/3 \ 1.5/3] = [0.866 \ 0.5]$$

$$|F_r| = F \bullet \hat{\Delta r} = [1000 \ 1732] \bullet [0.866 \ 0.5] = 1732$$

$$F_r = |F_r| * \hat{\Delta r} = 1732[0.866 \ 0.5] = [1500 \ 866] = 1732N@30°$$

3. Now that both the force and displacement are in the same direction (30), you can multiply their magnitudes together. All you need is the definition of work:

$$W = F_r \ \Delta r$$

$$= 1732N(3m)$$

$$= 5196N*m$$

$$= 5196J$$

Programming code to illustrate this example begins to work with some of the more complex calculations that were defined in Chapter 4. This code follows along with the explanation provided in the previous example:

```
float calculateAngledWorkFromVector(vector2D initial, vector2D
➥change)
    {
        vector2D force, displacement,displacementNormal, temp;
        float projectionLength, work;

        //change vectors from Polar to Cartesian.
        force = polarToCartesian(initial);
        displacement = polarToCartesian(change);

        //Normalize the displacementNormal
        displacementNormal = normalizeVector(displacement);
```

```
//the length of the project is the dot product of the
➥force against the displacement normal.
projectionLength = dotProduct(force,displacementNormal);

//Let's see what that length is.
cout<<"Projection Length "<< projectionLength<<"\n";

//multiply projection times normalized displacement
➥Vector
temp =
➥scalarMultiply(projectionLength,displacementNormal);

//Get back to Polar coordinates to calculate work. Don't
➥forget about radians.
temp = cartesianToPolar(temp);

//Finally, our work is calculated.
work = temp.x * change.x;
return work;


}
```

This function does take some work. The first step is to convert from polar coordinates to Cartesian so that we can process our force and displacement vector components properly.

The next step is to determine the displacement Normal. This is done through the use of the `normalizeVector()` function. We then use the `dotProduct()` function to determine the projection length. Now that the projection length is known, we multiply it by the `displacementNormal` and get the final vector that we can use to calculate work.

This function admittedly takes a bit of reading to understand fully. You can take a look at the sample documentation and see this function in action. Here are quick reminders of the calculation of vector normals and the dot product:

```
vector3D normalizeVector(vector3D vect)
    {
        float mag,square;
```

```
    vector3D temp;
    square = squareVector(vect);
    mag = sqrt(square);

    temp.x = vect.x/mag;
    temp.y = vect.y/mag;
    temp.z = vect.y/mag;
    return temp;
}
```

Remember that the normal calculates the magnitude of the vector and then divides each element in the vector by that amount resulting in the normal of the original vector.

```
float dotProduct(vector3D a, vector3D b)
    {
        vector3D temp;
        float scalar;
        temp.x = a.x*b.x;
        temp.y = a.y*b.y;
        temp.z = a.z*b.z;
        scalar = sumVector(temp);
        return scalar;
    }
```

The dot product multiplies the two vectors resulting in a vector that is summed. Remember that the dot product returns a scalar value. If you have forgotten either of these functions, refresh your memory with a quick trip back to Chapter 4.

NOTE

Remember that work is a scalar quantity, so as soon as the force and displacement are in the same direction, you can ignore it and simply multiply the magnitudes.

The second quantity we need to define is kinetic energy. **Kinetic energy** is the amount of energy an object has because it is moving. Therefore, the faster it's moving, the more kinetic energy it has. In that respect, it's very similar to momentum, which is mass times velocity.

The definition of kinetic energy is one-half of the mass times the speed squared, $^1/_2mv^2$.

Kinetic Energy

$KE = {}^1/_2mv^2$

where m = mass and v = speed.

Notice that the definition is based on speed rather than velocity. (Remember that speed is the scalar version of velocity, so it's the velocity minus its direction.)

Because kinetic energy is also a scalar quantity, the direction doesn't matter. Just as speed changes on an instantaneous basis, so does kinetic energy. Any time the speed changes, the kinetic energy changes also, so quite often you'll find that we designate initial and final kinetic energy over a period of time, just as we did with velocity in earlier chapters.

Also, this is another place where metric units are much easier to work with. If the speed is measured in m/s and the mass is measured in kg, the kinetic energy can also be measured in joules:

$kg(m/s)^2 = kg(m^2/s^2) = (kg*m/s)*m = N*m = J$

Example 12.4: Calculating Kinetic Energy

Suppose you have a device that can clock the speed of a baseball as it crosses the plate, and it registers 90mi/hr for a particular pitch. If the baseball has a mass of 145g, how much kinetic energy does it have at that instant?

Solution

1. The first thing you need to do is convert all the units. The speed must be measured in m/s, and the mass must be in kg:

$$\left(\frac{90\,mi}{1\,hr}\right)\left(\frac{1609\,m}{1\,mi}\right)\left(\frac{1\,hr}{60\,min}\right)\left(\frac{1\,min}{60\,s}\right) = 40.225\,m/s$$

$145g = 0.145kg$

2. Now you can plug these values into the definition of kinetic energy:

$$KE = \frac{1}{2}mv^2 = \frac{1}{2}(0.145\text{kg})(40.225\text{m/s})^2 = 117.3\text{J}$$

Programming this calculation is fairly straightforward. Here is a function that will calculate kinetic energy given a mass in kilograms and a speed in meters per second:

```
float calculateKineticEnergy(float mass, float speed)
    {
        float KE;
        KE = (mass/2)*(pow(speed,2));
        return KE;
    }
```

Now that we've defined both work and kinetic energy, we're ready to use a new theorem that describes a direct relationship between the two. Not surprisingly, it's called the **work-energy theorem**. This theorem states that the net or total work done on an object is equal to the change in its kinetic energy.

Work-Energy Theorem

$$W = \Delta KE = KE_f - KE_i$$

or

$$F\Delta x = \frac{1}{2}mv_f^2 - \frac{1}{2}mv_i^2$$

where the force and displacement are in the same direction, and v is speed.

This theorem basically says that if work is done on an object (a force moves it a certain distance), the object either speeds up or slows down. Conceptually, this sounds exactly like Newton's Second Law (and it is), but this version can be used to track the object's final speed after any given displacement. Let's use an example to show how this might be the easier version to work with in a gaming example.

Example 12.5: Work-Energy Theorem

Suppose you're programming a baseball game, and the shortstop needs to throw the ball to the first baseman. It takes some work for him to get the ball moving. If he can produce a force of 400N for a distance of 0.75m (from behind his head to the point where he lets go of the ball), and the baseball has a mass of 145g, what speed should the ball have when he lets go?

Solution

This is a great opportunity to use the work-energy theorem:

$$W = \Delta KE = KE_f - KE_i$$

$$F\Delta x = \tfrac{1}{2}mv_f^2 - \tfrac{1}{2}mv_i^2$$

$$400N(0.75m) = \tfrac{1}{2}(0.145kg)(v_f)^2 - 0$$

$$300J = 0.0725kg(v_f)^2$$

$$4137.93m^2/s^2 = v_f^2$$

$$64.33m/s = v_f$$

The basis for the work energy theorem provides the foundation for all the conservation theorems presented later. Each of them needs to be organized for fairly specific purposes inside a game. This function will tell us the final speed using the work energy theorem:

```
float calculateWorkEnergy(float force, float mass,
                       float displacement, float velocityInitial)
    {
       float work,vFinal;
       work = calculateWork(force,displacement);
       vFinal = work/((mass/2) - calculateKE(mass,
       ⮕velocityInitial));
       velocityFinal = sqrt(Final);
       return vFinal;
    }
```

This function does quite a bit of calculation to determine the final speed of the object. First, it calculates the work done by the force and displacement. Then the value for work is plugged directly into the function to determine the final velocity. The right side terms come straight out of the work energy theorem. Once those have resolved, the square root is taken and returned as the final speed of the object. Very cool.

In game programming, finding the final speed is more helpful than finding the acceleration, so you might find this theorem quite useful. Remember that there is always more than one way to approach a physics model. You could have just as easily used Newton's Second Law and the five equations of motion, but that would probably require more steps. As a game programmer, always look for the most optimized formula for your particular scenario. In some cases, the work-energy theorem might hit the spot.

Self-Assessment

1. A tugboat exerts a constant force of 5500N to pull a ship through the harbor. If the tugboat pulls the ship 5km, how much work is done?

2. If the main character in your game has to push a cart 5 meters down the road, and he pushes with a force of 30N at a –60° angle, how much work is being done?

3. If the cart described in question 2 starts from rest and has a mass of 50kg, how fast will it be going at the end of the 5 meters?

4. What is the kinetic energy of a 3000-kg car moving at 55mi/hr?

5. A 2-g bullet leaves the barrel of a gun going 300m/s. What is its kinetic energy?

6. If the length of the barrel of the gun described in question 5 is 50cm, find the average force exerted on the bullet to move it the length of the barrel.

Potential Energy and the Conservation Law

Now that we've defined work and kinetic energy, there's one more type of energy to define before we can tackle another formula for modeling motion. That energy is called **gravitational potential energy (GPE)**. Basically, GPE is the energy stored in an object due to its height off the ground. If you picked up this book and held it in the air, it would have gravitational potential energy. How do you know that energy is stored in the book? Just let go. Did the book move? Sure—it fell to the ground because of gravity. This tells you that potential energy was stored in the book until it was released.

How do you measure the amount of energy stored in that book? Well, it's based on the object's mass and, most importantly, its height above the ground. In fact, it's simply the product of the object's weight in Newtons and its height.

Gravitational Potential Energy

$GPE = mgy$

where m = mass, g = acceleration due to gravity, and y = height.

> **NOTE**
> There are other types of potential energy, but they are relatively insignificant in terms of motion in a video game, so it's safe to ignore them. From this point forward we'll just use PE to represent gravitational potential energy, because it's the only type we're concerned with.

Looking closer at the definition of gravitational potential energy, you might be curious about the units. If we stay consistent with previous chapters, metric units are the most convenient. If you measure the mass in kilograms, the acceleration due to gravity in m/s^2, and the height in meters, the potential energy is measured in joules (J), just like kinetic energy. Also, it is important to note that potential energy is a scalar quantity as well; it's simply an amount of energy with no direction. This means that you can ignore the direction of g and just use a positive $9.8 m/s^2$.

Example 12.6: Gravitational Potential Energy

Suppose this book weighs 1.5 pounds, and you raise it 2 meters off the ground. What is its gravitational potential energy?

Solution

1. Notice that the definition is based on mass, not weight. So let's first use the weight to calculate the mass:

$$1.5\,lbs\left(\frac{1N}{0.2248\,lbs}\right) = 6.6726N$$

$$w = mg$$

$$-6.6726N = m(-9.8m/s^2)$$

$$m = 0.6809kg$$

2. Now you go to the definition:

$$PE = mgy = 0.6809kg(9.8m/s^2)(2m) = 13.35J$$

The calculation for potential energy is also fairly straightforward. Before using any calculations involving gravity, you should be sure to define how gravity will be used in your game. For most games this should suffice (assuming metric units):

```
#define GRAVITY 9.81
```

With this definition in hand, let's look at how to calculate potential energy. This function will give us the value of potential energy in Joules:

```
float calculatePotentialEnergy(float mass,float height)
    {
        float PE;
        PE = mass*GRAVITY*height;
        return PE;
    }
```

Now that we've defined kinetic and potential energy, you can use them to model certain types of motion. Have you ever wondered how a roller coaster works? Think about the last time you rode one.

After being towed up the first hill, do you recall any additional motors or brakes until you reached the very end? If it was a traditional roller coaster, there weren't any. The entire ride was governed by a conservation law known as the **law of conservation of mechanical energy**. This particular law says that energy cannot be created or destroyed. It can only switch forms. The two forms of energy we've discussed so far are kinetic and potential.

Conservation of Mechanical Energy (Simplified)

$KE_i + PE_i = KE_f + PE_f$

or

$\frac{1}{2}mv_i^2 + mgy_i = \frac{1}{2}mv_f^2 + mgy_f$

Remember from the definitions that the faster an object moves, the more kinetic energy it has, and the higher it is off the ground, the more potential energy it has. What's fascinating is that the total amount of energy always remains the same; it just shifts between the different forms. Picture the roller coaster at the top of the first hill. It's really high, so it has a lot of potential energy. However, it's moving pretty slowly, so it has only a little bit of kinetic energy. Then it starts down the first big drop, and as it loses height, the coaster picks up speed. The potential energy is converting to kinetic. By the time the coaster gets down to the bottom of the hill, almost all the potential energy has switched to kinetic, and now the coaster is at its maximum speed. Then, as it goes up the next hill, the kinetic switches back to potential. It's a constant trade-off so that the total amount stays the same. This is illustrated in Figure 12.2.

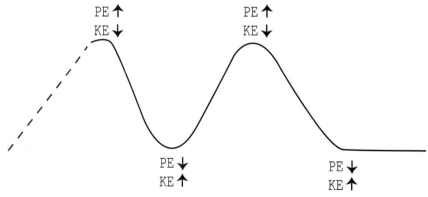

Figure 12.2 A traditional roller coaster.

Example 12.7: Conservation of Mechanical Energy

Suppose you're programming an *Indiana Jones* game and you get to the part where he jumps into the mining cart and rides the track up and down a series of hills. If the cart is at a height of 100m when Indy jumps in, and together he and the cart weigh 300 pounds, how fast should they be going when they reach the bottom of the first hill (ground level)?

Solution

1. Notice that both definitions require mass instead of weight, so first convert the weight to mass:

$$300lbs\left(\frac{1N}{0.2248lbs}\right) = 1334.52N$$

$$w = mg$$

$$-1334.52N = m(-9.8m/s^2)$$

$$m = 136.18kg$$

2. Now you can plug everything you know into the conservation law and solve for v_f:

$$\frac{1}{2}mv_i^2 + mgy_i = \frac{1}{2}mv_f^2 + mgy_f$$

$$\frac{1}{2}(136.18kg)(0)^2 + (136.18kg)(9.8m/s^2)(100m) = \frac{1}{2}(136.18kg)(v_f)^2 + (136.18kg)(9.8m/s^2)(0m)$$

$$0 + (136.18kg)(9.8m/s^2)(100m) = \frac{1}{2}(136.18kg)(v_f)^2 + 0$$

$$(136.18kg)(9.8m/s^2)(100m) = \frac{1}{2}(136.18kg)(v_f)^2$$

$$133451.96J = 68.09kg(v_f)^2$$

$$1960m^2/s^2 = v_f^2$$

$$v_f = 44.27m/s$$

> **NOTE**
>
> When you're working with this conservation law, remember that it holds true for any two points on the roller coaster, not just the top and bottom of the hill.
>
> Also note that there is an *m* in each term of the conservation law. If you divide both sides of the equation by *m,* it cancels out, so the mass really is irrelevant.

Also note that this law is not limited to roller coasters. It holds true for any type of motion as long as no outside forces interfere. A roller coaster is a good example because it's an isolated scenario with no major outside forces. I say no "major" outside forces because you can take into account a few small forces such as friction and air resistance if you want to add a little more realism to the motion. In real life, some energy is lost to heat and sound because of friction and air resistance, but calculating the precise amount can be quite expensive in terms of processing power. However, there is a simple way to work this into your model. As time goes on, energy is lost. Adding an extra term that represents heat and sound energy to the left side of the conservation law forces a reduction in kinetic and potential energy, which produces a more realistic result. As time progresses, the vehicle never goes quite as high or quite as fast as it did in the beginning because of the slight loss of energy.

Conservation of Mechanical Energy (Modified)

$KE_i + PE_i = KE_f + PE_f + E_0$

or

$\frac{1}{2}mv_i^2 + mgy_i = \frac{1}{2}mv_f^2 + mgy_f + E_0$

where E_0 represents other energy (heat/sound).

When you use this modified form, just make sure your extra term for heat and sound energy is relatively small compared to the other two forms of energy. This is a simple (and fast) cheat for modeling more realistic motion.

Example 12.8: Modified Conservation of Mechanical Energy

Suppose you go back to the *Indiana Jones* game, and you get to the part where he jumps in the mining cart and rides the track up and down a series of hills. This time you want to make it a little more realistic. If the cart is at a height of 100m when Indy jumps in, and together he and the cart weigh 300 pounds, *and* about 2000J of energy is lost to heat and sound, how fast should they be going when they reach the bottom of the first hill (ground level)?

Solution

1. Notice that both definitions require mass instead of weight, so first convert the weight to mass:

$$300lbs\left(\frac{1N}{0.2248lbs}\right) = 1334.52N$$

$$w = mg$$

$$-1334.52N = m(-9.8m/s^2)$$

$$m = 136.18kg$$

2. Now you can plug everything you know into the modified conservation law and solve for v_f:

$$^1/_2mv_i^2 + mgy_i = {}^1/_2mv_f^2 + mgy_f + E_o$$

$$^1/_2(136.18kg)(0)^2 + (136.18kg)(9.8m/s^2)(100m) = {}^1/_2(136.18kg)(v_f)^2 + (136.18kg)(9.8m/s^2)(0m) + 2000J$$

$$0 + (136.18kg)(9.8m/s^2)(100m) = {}^1/_2(136.18kg)(v_f)^2 + 0 + 2000J$$

$$(136.18kg)(9.8m/s^2)(100m) = {}^1/_2(136.18kg)(v_f)^2 + 2000J$$

$$133451.96J = 68.09kg(v_f)^2 + 2000J$$

$$131451.96J = 68.09kg(v_f)^2$$

$$1930.56m^2/s^2 = v_f^2$$

$$v_f = 43.94m/s$$

Notice that with the modified version of the conservation law, the final speed is slightly lower because some energy is lost. If this doesn't seem noticeable, you might want to bump up the amount of lost energy. If the vehicle were a sled going down an icy hill, you might even choose to use a smaller value for the energy loss. After you experiment a little, you'll get a feel for how large or small to make E_o.

> **NOTE**
> This (E_o) is one variable you might be wise to expose to your designers to allow them to tune it for feel.

At this point, you have several choices for modeling an object's motion. You can always go back to Newton's Second Law and the five equations of motion. However, in some cases you might find this energy approach to be more efficient, because there might be fewer calculations. It all depends on the situation you are modeling, so it's great to have options.

Self-Assessment

1. If a 50-kg boulder is teetering on the edge of a cliff 300 meters high, what is its gravitational potential energy?

2. If the boulder described in question 1 falls, how fast is it going when it hits the ground?

3. A couple of troublemakers set up a slingshot on the ground to launch water balloons. If the slingshot gives the balloons an initial speed of 20m/s, find the maximum height the balloons should reach.

4. Find the speed of the water balloons described in question 3 when they get halfway up to the maximum height.

Self-Assessment Solutions

Work and Kinetic Energy

1. 27,500,000J

2. 75J

3. 1.732m/s

4. 906,408 J

5. 90J

6. 180N

Potential Energy and the Conservation Law

1. 147,000J

2. 76.68m/s

3. 20.4m

4. 14.14m/s

Chapter 13

Momentum and Collisions

So far, we've talked about how individual objects move around in a simulated world. The next step is to look at how these objects interact. What happens when two billiard balls collide or when one player jumps up and kicks another? So far, we've only discussed how to model the motion of an isolated object. By now, you might be wondering how to model these types of interactions between objects.

First, we'll examine collisions where one object is stationary, and then we'll look more closely at the effects that two moving objects have on each other when they come into contact.

Collision with a Stationary Object

The simplest type of collision to model is one in which a moving object collides with a fixed stationary object, such as a billiard ball hitting the bumper. The bumper doesn't move, so you only need to model the resulting motion of one object, the ball. This type of scenario can be modeled using **vector reflection**, which refers to the motion of the moving object—in this case, the ball. An interesting symmetry exists: The angle that the ball comes in at must equal the angle at which it leaves. In other words, the **angle of incidence** (incoming) must equal the **angle of reflection** (outgoing), as shown in Figure 13.1.

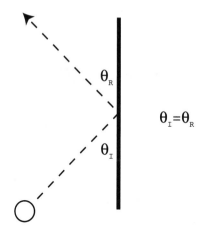

Figure 13.1   Vector reflection.

This process is very simple to program if the wall is perfectly horizontal or perfectly vertical. Likewise, if the stationary object is in an **axis-aligned bounding box**, which means that the sides of the box are perfectly horizontal and vertical, the vector reflection is simple to model. We'll tackle the non-axis-aligned case next. For now, let's go back to the billiard ball about to hit the bumper. Hopefully, after working through Chapter 10, "Motion in Two and Three Dimensions," you're tracking the ball's velocity with a vector in component form: ball velocity = $[v_x \ v_y]$. If the bumper is vertical, all you have to do is reverse the horizontal component of the velocity when the ball hits, as shown in Figure 13.2.

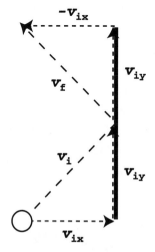

Figure 13.2   Vector reflection with a vertical wall.

Similarly, if the wall is horizontal, all you have to do is reverse the direction of the vertical component of the ball's velocity when it hits.

Axis-Aligned Vector Reflection

If the stationary boundary is vertical, $v_f = [-v_{ix}\ v_{iy}]$ and

if the stationary boundary is horizontal, $v_f = [v_{ix}\ -v_{iy}]$

for incoming velocity $v_i = [v_{ix}\ v_{iy}]$.

Example 13.1: Axis-Aligned and Non-Axis-Aligned Vector Reflection

Suppose you're coding a simple *Pong* game, and you want to model the collision of the ball with the paddle. If the ball is approaching the paddle with an incoming velocity of [40 75] when it hits, what should its resulting velocity be?

Solution

In *Pong*, the ball goes back and forth across the screen, so when it hits the paddle, it collides with the vertical edge. That means you must reverse the horizontal component of the velocity and leave the vertical component the same. Therefore, the final velocity vector must be [–40 75].

Now that we've discussed axis-aligned vector reflection, let's tackle non-axis-aligned. What if the stationary object is oriented in such a way that its edges are no longer parallel to the x- and y-axes? The angle of incidence must still equal the angle of reflection, but now it's more complicated than just reversing one component. Let's start with two dimensions and then extend the process to 3D.

Typically when you approach this scenario, you know the moving object's incoming velocity vector (v_i), you know the boundary line of the stationary object it is about to bounce off of (B), and you're looking for the new resulting velocity vector (v_f). This is shown in Figure 13.3.

To implement this form of reflection in code, we can use this function:

```
vector2D axisAlignedCollision(vector2D vect, char b)
    {
       vector2D temp = vect;

       if(b == 'v')
             temp.x = temp.x*= -1;
        else if(b =='h')
             temp.y = temp.y*= -1;

       return temp;
    }
```

This particular function requires that we know if the user is making a horizontal or vertical reflection. Normally, you don't ask the player to give this information. The key here would be to nest the guts of this reflection inside a collision algorithm. Remember that collision detection is only half the process. As the game designer and developer, you have to determine what the outcome is going to be.

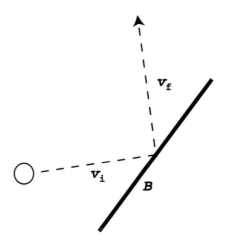

Figure 13.3   Non-axis-aligned vector reflection.

The first thing you need to find is the normal (N) to the line of the stationary object. Chapter 1, "Points and Lines," discussed perpendicular lines. It said that slopes are negative reciprocals of each other. So if the slope of the boundary line (B) is $\Delta y/\Delta x$, the slope of the normal (N) must be $-\Delta x/\Delta y$. In vector form, that's the same as saying B = $[\Delta x\ \Delta y]$; therefore, N = $[\Delta y\ -\Delta x]$. Then you need to normalize N so that it has a length of 1. Chapter 4, "Vector Operations," discussed normalizing. It said that to normalize a vector, you must divide it by its own magnitude. In Figure 13.4, normalized N is written as N'.

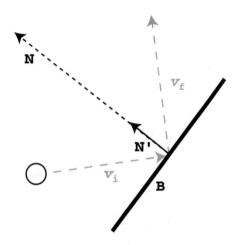

Figure 13.4 The normal to the boundary line.

The next step is to find the projection (P) of $-v_i$ onto the normal (N').

> **NOTE**
> Note that you need to reverse v_i before taking the dot product because it's facing the wrong way with respect to P.

Back in Chapter 4, you found that the dot product gives you the magnitude of the projection, so the magnitude of P = $-v_i \bullet$ N'.

To get P to point in the same direction as the normal, you must multiply the magnitude of P by the normal, so the vector P = $(-v_i \bullet$ N') * N', as shown in Figure 13.5.

Now to find v_f, all you need is a bit of geometry. Figure 13.6 adds a new vector, V. Look at how vectors v_i and P are lined up tip-to-tail (see Chapter 4). This means that V = v_i + P.

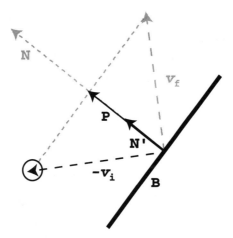

Figure 13.5 Projection added.

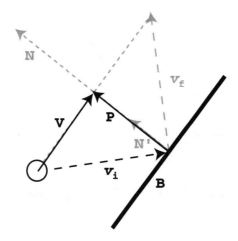

Figure 13.6 A new vector v added.

Look at Figure 13.6; you see that $P + V = v_f$. Now just substitute the previous line for V:

If $V = v_i + P$ and

$P + V = v_f$ then

$v_f = P + (v_i + P)$

This brings you to the final line you are looking for:

$v_f = 2 * P + v_i$

Non-Axis-Aligned Vector Reflection

$v_f = 2 * P + v_i$

where v_i = the incoming velocity and P = the projection of $-v_i$ onto the normal of the boundary line.

Example 13.2: Non-Axis-Aligned 2D Vector Reflection

Suppose you're coding a modified *Pong* game that has additional objects on the screen, and you want to model the collision of the ball with one of these obstacles. Suppose you have already determined that a collision is about to happen in the next frame. The obstacle's closest boundary goes from the point (50,25) to the point (200,250). If the ball is approaching the obstacle with an incoming velocity of [50 10] when it hits, what should its resulting velocity be?

Solution

1. Find a vector to describe the boundary line:

    B = [Δx Δy]

    = [200 250] – [50 25]

    = [150 225]

2. Find the normal (or perpendicular) vector:

    N = [Δy $-\Delta x$]

    = [225 –150]

3. Normalize N:

    $\|N\| = \sqrt{225^2 + (-150)^2} = \sqrt{50625 + 22500} = \sqrt{73125} \approx 270.416$

    N = [225 –150]

$$N' = \hat{N} = \left[\frac{225}{270.416} \quad \frac{-150}{270.416}\right] \approx [0.832 \quad -0.555]$$

4. Find P by calculating the length of the projection and multiplying that by N':

$$P = (-v_i \bullet N') * N'$$

$$= ([-50 \ -10] \bullet [0.832 \ -0.555]) * N'$$

$$= (-36.05) * N'$$

$$= (-36.05) * [0.832 \ -0.555]$$

$$\approx [-30 \ 20]$$

5. The final step is to calculate the final velocity:

$$v_f = 2 * P + v_i$$

$$= 2 * [-30 \ 20] + [50 \ 10]$$

$$= [-60 \ 40] + [50 \ 10]$$

$$= [-10 \ 50]$$

Let's look at how we can turn this big calculation into a function that will properly calculate non-axis aligned reflections for a 2D object:

```
vector2D nonAxisAlignedCollision(vector2D a, vector2D b)
    {
        vector2D temp,temp2,temp3,length,reflection;
        float projection;

        temp = normalizeVector(a);

        //reverse the vector.
        temp2 = scalarMultiply(-1,b);

        //find the project length using the dot product.
        projection = dotProduct(temp2,temp);
```

```
        length = scalarMultiply(projection,temp);

        //the reflection is going to be twice the length.
        reflection = scalarMultiply(2,length);

        //sum them all together making sure the reflection is
     ➥ inverted.
        temp3 = sumVectors(scalarMultiply(-1,reflection),temp2);

        //tada!!
        return temp3;
    }
```

This function follows right along with the solution to the previous example. First, we normalize the vector that describes the boundary. Then we determine the projection length by reversing the colliding object's vector and calculating the dot product. Multiply the projection with the boundary normal. We then determine the length component of the reflection by multiplying the projection by the boundary normal. The reflection is determined to be twice the size of the length. Sum all the vectors with the reversed object vector, and we have a non-axis aligned reflection.

You might be wondering how to extend this to 3D. If you know the incoming velocity and the 3D plane about to be hit, you can calculate the final velocity using the same vector operations. The only slight difference is that in 3D the object bounces off a plane rather than a 2D line. Two vectors define the plane, so the normal vector can be found using the cross-product of those two vectors, as discussed in Chapter 4. Let's look at a 3D example.

Example 13.3: Non-Axis-Aligned 3D Vector Reflection

Now suppose you're coding a modified 3D *Pong* game that has additional objects on the screen, and you want to model the collision of the ball with one of these obstacles. Suppose you have already determined that a collision is about to happen in the next frame. The obstacle's closest boundary is a plane defined by the vectors [200 250 –300] and [50 200 –25]. If the ball is approaching the obstacle with an incoming velocity of [100 –50 –50] when it hits, what should its resulting velocity be?

Solution

1. Find the surface normal, as you did in Chapter 4:

   N = [200 250 –300] * [50 200 –25]

   = [(250 * –25) – (–300 * 200) (–300 * 50) – (200 * –25) (200 * 200) – (250 * 50)]

   = [(–6250 + 60000) (–15000 + 5000) (40000 – 12500)]

   = [53750 –10000 27500]

   $$\|N\| = \sqrt{53750^2 + (-10000)^2 + 27500^2} = \sqrt{3745312500} \approx 61{,}199$$

   $$N' = \hat{N} = \left[\frac{53750}{61199} \quad \frac{-10000}{61199} \quad \frac{27500}{61199}\right] \approx [0.8783 \quad -0.1634 \quad 0.4494]$$

2. Find P by calculating the length of the projection and multiplying that by N':

   P = $(-v_i \bullet N') * N'$

   = ([–100 50 50] $\bullet$ [0.8783 –0.1634 0.4494]) * N'

   = (–73.53) * N'

   = (–73.53) * [0.8783 –0.1634 0.4494]

   $\approx$ [–64.5814 12.0148 –33.0444]

3. The last step is to calculate the final velocity:

   v_f = 2 * P + v_i

   = 2*[–64.5814 12.0148 –33.0444] + [100 –50 –50]

   = [–129.1628 24.0296 –66.0888] + [100 –50 –50]

   = [–29.1628 –25.9704 –116.0888]

This calculation is almost identical to the non-axis aligned 2D reflection. The major changes are the implementation of the 3D vector:

```
vector3D nonAxisAlignColl(vector3D a, vector3D b,vector3D
➥ velocity)
```

```
{
    vector3D temp,normal, velocityTemp,velocityFinal,length,
➡  reflection;

        velocityTemp = scalarMultiply(-1,velocity);

        float projection;
        temp = crossProduct(a,b);

        //get the surface normal
        normal = normalizeVector(temp);

        //calculate the projection.
        projection = dotProduct(velocityTemp,normal);

        //Take the length of the projection against the normal.
        length = scalarMultiply(projection,normal);

        //Lets obtain the final vector.
        reflection = scalarMultiply(2,length);
        velocityFinal = sumVectors(reflection,velocity);
        return velocityFinal;
    }
```

If you need to refer back to the function definition for the dotProduct, normalizeVector, or scalarMultiply methods, take a look at the last chapter or check out the source code for this chapter.

Now that we've discussed the motion of a moving object bouncing off a fixed object, we can move on to two moving objects. The rest of this chapter examines how two objects interact when one object is still when it gets hit and when both objects are moving when they collide.

Self-Assessment

1. Suppose you're coding a 2D pool game with a top-down view. If the sides of the table are parallel to the x- and y-axes, and one of the balls has an incoming velocity of [–30 50] when it hits the bumper at the top of the screen, what should its resulting velocity be?

2. Suppose you're coding a 2D pool game where the camera can rotate around the table. If the bumper that the cue ball is about to hit goes from (40,150) to (240,300), and the ball is approaching it with an incoming velocity of [80 20], what should the ball's resulting velocity be?

3. Suppose you're coding a full 3D pool game where the camera can be oriented any way the player wants. If the bumper is now the plane defined by vectors [30 100 −50] and [200 −50 −25], and the cue ball has an incoming velocity of [20 −10 −50] when it hits, what should its resulting velocity be?

Momentum and Impulse Defined

The fist step in the process of modeling collisions between two moving objects is to define a new quantity—momentum. **Momentum** (p) is defined as mass times velocity. This means that the more massive an object is, the more momentum it has. That's why it's extremely difficult to bring a tractor-trailer to an abrupt stop. Likewise, a large velocity also results in a lot of momentum, so even if you're driving a little sports car, it's still difficult to stop at 100mph.

Momentum

$p = mv$

where m = mass and v = velocity.

NOTE
Because momentum is based on velocity, which constantly changes, it makes sense to talk about instantaneous momentum at specific points in time or change in momentum over a time interval.

Let's quickly address the issue of units again. If you stay consistent with metric units, mass is measured in kilograms, and velocity is measured in meters per second, so the unit for momentum is kg*m/s. Be careful. This is often confused with Newtons, but remember that $1N = 1kg*m/s^2$, not kg*m/s.

Also, if you look closely at the definition, you'll see that momentum is equal to a scalar (mass) times a vector (velocity). This means that momentum is also a vector quantity, and its direction is always the same as the velocity. In one dimension that direction can be only positive or negative. In two dimensions, the angle of the velocity in polar coordinates is the same as the direction of the momentum. In 2D or 3D, you'll most likely leave these vector quantities in component form for programming. The great thing about vectors is that each of these components can be treated separately, which brings you right back to one dimension.

Example 13.4: Calculating Momentum in 1D

If a truck weighs approximately 5500lbs, and it is traveling at 60mph down a straight road, what is its momentum?

Solution

1. Notice that the truck's weight is approximated in pounds, but the definition requires mass in kilograms, so you need to do a conversion:

$$5500\,lbs\left(\frac{1N}{0.2248\,lbs}\right) = 24{,}466.19N$$

$$w = mg$$

$$24{,}466.19N = m(9.8\text{m/s}^2)$$

$$m = 2496.55\text{kg}$$

2. Also, the velocity needs to be converted to meters per second:

$$\left(\frac{60\,mi}{1\,hr}\right)\left(\frac{1609m}{1\,mi}\right)\left(\frac{1\,hr}{3600s}\right) = 26.82m/s$$

3. Now you can plug these two values into the definition:

$$p = mv$$

$$p = 2496.55\text{kg}(26.82\text{m/s})$$

$$p = 66{,}957.47\text{kg*m/s}$$

The momentum function looks like this:

```
float momentum(float velocity, float mass)
    {
       float momentum;
       momentum = mass*velocity;
       return momentum;
    }
```

This example is one-dimensional, so the positive momentum indicates that the direction is forward, just like the velocity. Let's look at a 3D situation next.

Example 13.5: Calculating Momentum in 3D

If a spaceship has an approximate mass of 4500kg, and its current velocity vector is

$$\begin{bmatrix} 30 \\ 50 \\ -20 \end{bmatrix}$$

what is its momentum at that instant?

Solution

This time the velocity is expressed as a 3D vector, so calculate momentum as a 3D vector:

$$p = mv$$

$$\begin{bmatrix} p_x \\ p_y \\ p_z \end{bmatrix} = m \begin{bmatrix} 30 \\ 50 \\ -20 \end{bmatrix} = 4500 \begin{bmatrix} 30 \\ 50 \\ -20 \end{bmatrix} = \begin{bmatrix} 135{,}000 \\ 225{,}000 \\ -90{,}000 \end{bmatrix}$$

3D momentum is also straightforward in code. Here is a function the calculates the solution using a scalar multiplication:

```
vector3D momentum3D(vector3D velocity, float mass)
    {
          vector3D temp;
          temp = scalarMultiply(mass,velocity);
          return temp;
    }
```

Now that you've defined momentum, there's only one more quantity to define—impulse. To do so, revisit Newton's Second Law from Chapter 11, "Newton's Laws":

$$F = ma$$

Substitute the definition of acceleration:

$$F = m(v_f - v_i)/t$$

$$F = (mv_f - mv_i)/t$$

Do you recognize the top of that fraction? That's right—it's actually the change in momentum:

$$F = (\Delta p)/t$$

Believe it or not, this was actually the original form of Newton's Second Law. Initially, he stated that force equals the rate of change of momentum. Eventually, most texts adopted the $F = ma$ version.

The last step is to multiply both sides by time:

$$Ft = (\Delta p)$$

The left side of this equation is actually the impulse.

Impulse

Impulse $= Ft$

where $F =$ net force and $t =$ a very small time.

Typically, an impulse is a force delivered in a very small amount of time, such as an instant. For example, if a golfer tees up and hits the ball with his club, he delivers an impulse to the ball. The club is in contact with the golf ball for a fraction of a second, but it sends the ball flying. This brings us back to the equation you just derived:

$$Ft = (\Delta p)$$

This tells you that an impulse changes an object's momentum. In other words, a force delivered quickly results in a change of momentum. This means that if the mass does not change, the object either speeds up or slows down. This formula has a special name—the **impulse-momentum theorem**.

Impulse-Momentum Theorem

Impulse = $Ft = (\Delta p)$

where F = net force, t = a very small amount of time, and p = momentum.

Conceptually, the impulse-momentum theorem is the same as Newton's Second Law. Both formulas support the idea that a net force applied to an object results in a change in velocity. However, you might find that the impulse-momentum theorem is more optimized for programming. Let's revisit the golfer getting ready to tee up. Chapter 11 discussed assigning a force for the club hitting the ball. Then you can calculate the resulting acceleration and use the five equations of motion to calculate the resulting velocity. A faster approach might be to assign a value to the impulse based on user input. Then, if you know the mass of the golf ball and its initial velocity (in this case, 0), you can calculate the final velocity as a result of hitting the golf ball with the club. Just like before, this final velocity then becomes the initial velocity of the projectile motion. The impulse-momentum theorem performs the same process, just with fewer steps.

The trick is to remember that this all happens very quickly. The golf club is in contact with the ball for only a fraction of a second. So the ball's motion has two separate segments—the collision with the club, which is an extremely small time interval, and the projectile motion.

Example 13.6: Impulse-Momentum Theorem

Suppose you're coding a golf game, and the ball has a mass of 45g (0.045kg). The player determines the club's impulse using a sliding scale. If the player selects enough force to deliver an impulse of

$$\begin{bmatrix} 3 \\ 2 \\ -4 \end{bmatrix}$$

(measured in kg*m/s), what is the ball's resulting velocity?

Solution

Go straight to the impulse-momentum theorem and plug in what you know:

$$\text{impulse} = \Delta p = mv_f - mv_i$$

$$\begin{bmatrix} 3 \\ 2 \\ -4 \end{bmatrix} = 0.045 \begin{bmatrix} v_x \\ v_y \\ v_z \end{bmatrix} - 0.045 \begin{bmatrix} 0 \\ 0 \\ 0 \end{bmatrix}$$

(The initial velocity is 0 because the ball is sitting on the tee.)

$$\begin{bmatrix} 3 \\ 2 \\ -4 \end{bmatrix} = 0.045 \begin{bmatrix} v_x \\ v_y \\ v_z \end{bmatrix}$$

$$\begin{bmatrix} v_x \\ v_y \\ v_z \end{bmatrix} = \frac{1}{0.045} \begin{bmatrix} 3 \\ 2 \\ -4 \end{bmatrix}$$

$$\begin{bmatrix} v_x \\ v_y \\ v_z \end{bmatrix} = \begin{bmatrix} 66.67 \\ 44.44 \\ -88.89 \end{bmatrix}$$

Here is what the impulse momentum theorem looks like in code:

```
vector3D impulse3D (vector3D final, vector3D initial, float mass)
    {
        vector3D impulse,momentumFinal, momentumInitial;
        momentumFinal = momentum3D(final,mass);
        momentumInitial = momentum3D(initial,mass);
        impulse = subtractVectors(momentumFinal,momentumInitial);
        return impulse;
    }
```

> **NOTE**
> Remember that the final velocity you calculate here becomes the initial velocity for the projectile motion.

We've just scratched the surface of modeling collisions by examining the effects on one object in a collision. The impulse momentum theorem shows you how an object's motion changes as a result of being hit by something else. The next section takes this idea one step further and looks at how both objects should move as a result of colliding with each other. Just remember that momentum is at the root of all collisions.

Self-Assessment

1. If a boulder weighs approximately 100lbs, and it rolls horizontally across the screen toward your player going 15m/s, what is its momentum at that instant?

2. In a 3D game, your vehicle has a current velocity vector of

$$\begin{bmatrix} 50 \\ 25 \\ -10 \end{bmatrix}$$

    and a mass of 2000kg. What is its current momentum?

3. In a fighting game, one player is standing still when the other player kicks him. If he weighs approximately 250lbs, and he gets hit with an impulse of 5000kg*ms/s, how fast should he go flying as a result of the kick?

4. Suppose the player described in question 3 is not standing still when he gets kicked. Instead, he's running toward his attacker with an initial speed of 5m/s. What's his final velocity?

5. Suppose you're coding a 3D fighting game. The player who gets hit still weighs approximately 250lbs. This time he's hit with an impulse of

$$\begin{bmatrix} 2500 \\ 6000 \\ -1000 \end{bmatrix}$$

    What's his resulting velocity in 3D?

Modeling Collisions

The last section took a one-sided approach by looking at the effects of a collision on just one object using the impulse-momentum theorem. Now let's look at the effects on both objects involved in the collision. If two objects collide, and both can move, they both apply an impulse to each other due to the collision. Let's look at the impulse-momentum theorem one more time:

$$Ft = (\Delta p)$$

Let's divide both sides by time:

$F = (\Delta p)/t$

Newton's Third Law states that for every action there's an equal and opposite reaction. In this case, one object places a force on another object, and at the same time, the second object places an equal and opposite force on the first object:

$F_1 = -F_2$

Now let's substitute the impulse-momentum theorem on both sides:

$(\Delta p_1)/t = -(\Delta p_2)/t$, or
$\Delta p_1 = -\Delta p_2$

Now let's insert the definition of momentum on both sides:

$m_1 v_{1f} - m_1 v_{1i} = -(m_2 v_{2f} - m_2 v_{2i})$
$m_1 v_{1f} - m_1 v_{1i} = -m_2 v_{2f} + m_2 v_{2i}$
$m_1 v_{1i} + m_2 v_{2i} = m_1 v_{1f} + m_2 v_{2f}$

This last line has a special name: **conservation of momentum theorem**. This theorem states that the total amount of momentum stays the same when two objects collide. It simply transfers from one object to the other.

Conservation of Momentum Theorem

$m_1 v_{1i} + m_2 v_{2i} = m_1 v_{1f} + m_2 v_{2f}$

where the 1 subscript represents object 1 and the 2 subscript represents object 2.

This theorem applies to any isolated collision between two objects. If an outside force interferes with the collision, the theorem no longer holds up. However, due to the speed at which a collision occurs, very rarely does another force interfere.

> **NOTE**
> Remember that momentum is a vector quantity, so this theorem works the same way whether the collision occurs in 1D, 2D, or 3D.

Example 13.7: Conservation of Momentum Theorem

Suppose you're coding a 3D pool game, and you're focused on the cue ball hitting another ball at rest. If the cue ball has a mass of 0.5kg and an initial velocity of [50 10 −30], and it completely stops when it hits the other ball with a mass of 0.45kg, what should the final velocity of the second ball be as a result of the collision?

Solution

Go straight to the conservation of momentum theorem, and fill in everything you know:

$$m_1 v_{1i} + m_2 v_{2i} = m_1 v_{1f} + m_2 v_{2f}$$

$$0.5kg \begin{bmatrix} 50 \\ 10 \\ -30 \end{bmatrix} + 0.45kg \begin{bmatrix} 0 \\ 0 \\ 0 \end{bmatrix} = 0.5kg \begin{bmatrix} 0 \\ 0 \\ 0 \end{bmatrix} + 0.45kg \begin{bmatrix} v_{2fx} \\ v_{2fy} \\ v_{2fz} \end{bmatrix}$$

$$0.5kg \begin{bmatrix} 50 \\ 10 \\ -30 \end{bmatrix} = 0.45kg \begin{bmatrix} v_{2fx} \\ v_{2fy} \\ v_{2fz} \end{bmatrix}$$

$$\begin{bmatrix} 25 \\ 5 \\ -15 \end{bmatrix} = 0.45kg \begin{bmatrix} v_{2fx} \\ v_{2fy} \\ v_{2fz} \end{bmatrix}$$

$$\begin{bmatrix} 55.56 \\ 11.11 \\ -33.33 \end{bmatrix} = \begin{bmatrix} v_{2fx} \\ v_{2fy} \\ v_{2fz} \end{bmatrix}$$

You can see that all the cue ball's momentum is transferred to the second ball when they collide.

Let's see this converted into a programming function:

```
vector3D conserveMomentum(vector3D object1Start,vector3D
➥ object1Stop, vector3D object2Start, float mass1, float mass2)
    {
        vector3D temp,temp2,sum,result;

        //First calculate the left hand side of the equation.
        temp  =  scalarMultiply(mass1,object1Start);
        temp2 =  scalarMultiply(mass2,object2Start);
        sum   =  sumVectors(temp,temp2);

        //Divide the left hand side by the second object's
        ➥ mass to
    //get the vector;
        result = scalarDivide(mass2,sum);
        return result;
    }
```

Using this function, we can find out the final vector of the second object after the collision. This function is used in the provided sample code and is capable of taking different start and stop vectors for the objects.

This is a simple example. However, it's quite possible that both objects will move together as a result of the collision. Let's look at such an example.

Example 13.8: Perfectly Inelastic Collision

Suppose you're coding a 2D football game with a top-down view. The player with the ball weighs 180lbs and is running down the field toward the end zone with a velocity of [0 30]. One of his opponents, who weighs 220lbs, is on the other side of the field when he starts running at [25 5] to make the tackle. After he makes the tackle, what is the players' final velocity as they go flying across the field together as a result of the tackle?

Solution

1. The players' weights are approximated in pounds, but the theorem requires mass in kilograms. Convert the two weights to mass, as you did in Chapter 11:

$$180\,lbs\left(\frac{1N}{0.2248\,lbs}\right) = 800.71N$$

$$m_1 = \frac{w}{g} = \frac{800.71N}{9.8m/s^2} = 81.71kg$$

$$220\,lbs\left(\frac{1N}{0.2248\,lbs}\right) = 978.65N$$

$$m_2 = \frac{w}{g} = \frac{978.65N}{9.8m/s^2} = 99.86kg$$

2. Now that you have both masses, plug everything you know into the conservation of momentum theorem:

$$m_1 v_{1i} + m_2 v_{2i} = m_1 v_{1f} + m_2 v_{2f}$$

$$81.71kg\begin{bmatrix}0\\30\end{bmatrix} + 99.86kg\begin{bmatrix}25\\5\end{bmatrix} = 81.71kg\begin{bmatrix}v_{1fx}\\v_{1fy}\end{bmatrix} + 99.86kg\begin{bmatrix}v_{2fx}\\v_{2fy}\end{bmatrix}$$

$$\begin{bmatrix}0\\2451.3\end{bmatrix} + \begin{bmatrix}2496.5\\499.3\end{bmatrix} = 81.71kg\begin{bmatrix}v_{1fx}\\v_{1fy}\end{bmatrix} + 99.86kg\begin{bmatrix}v_{2fx}\\v_{2fy}\end{bmatrix}$$

$$\begin{bmatrix}2496.5\\2950.6\end{bmatrix} = 81.71kg\begin{bmatrix}v_{1fx}\\v_{1fy}\end{bmatrix} + 99.86kg\begin{bmatrix}v_{2fx}\\v_{2fy}\end{bmatrix}$$

3. The trick to this example is that the two players go down together, which means that they both have the same final velocity. In other words, $v_{1fx} = v_{2fx}$ and $v_{1fy} = v_{2fy}$, so just call them v_{fx} and v_{fy}:

$$\begin{bmatrix}2496.5\\2950.6\end{bmatrix} = 81.71kg\begin{bmatrix}v_{fx}\\v_{fy}\end{bmatrix} + 99.86kg\begin{bmatrix}v_{fx}\\v_{fy}\end{bmatrix}$$

$$\begin{bmatrix}2496.5\\2950.6\end{bmatrix} = 181.57kg\begin{bmatrix}v_{fx}\\v_{fy}\end{bmatrix}$$

$$\begin{bmatrix}13.75\\16.25\end{bmatrix} = \begin{bmatrix}v_{fx}\\v_{fy}\end{bmatrix}$$

The only reason you can calculate the final velocities is because they are the same. There's one more case to consider—when both objects are moving as a result of the collision but they have different final velocities. If you have two unknown variables, v_{1f} and v_{2f}, you need a second equation to calculate both. This takes you back to Chapter 1, where you looked at linear combination and substitution. If you think of v_{1f} as x and v_{2f} as y, it's actually the same process. Use linear combination or substitution to find one final velocity, and then plug it in to find the other final velocity. To help you find that second equation, we need to discuss different types of collisions.

Every collision falls somewhere along a spectrum where one extreme is the **elastic collision** and the other extreme is the **perfectly inelastic collision**. An elastic collision is one in which no kinetic energy is lost when the two objects hit. The result is a collision where the objects appear to just bounce off each other like billiard balls. Example 13.8 showed a perfectly inelastic collision, where two objects stuck together and had the same final velocity. In real life, most collisions fall somewhere in between: Some energy is lost, but the two objects have different final velocities. You control how much energy is lost by defining a variable called the **coefficient of restitution** (ε). For an elastic collision, $\varepsilon = 1$, and for a perfectly inelastic collision, $\varepsilon = 0$. For most realistic collisions, ε falls somewhere between 0 and 1.

Linear Collision

$$(v_{1f} - v_{2f}) = -\varepsilon(v_{1i} - v_{2i})$$

where ε = the coefficient of restitution ($0 < \varepsilon < 1$).

Let's look at this formula more closely. If you plug in 0 for ε, the whole right side disappears, and essentially v_{1f} must equal v_{2f}. This is exactly what you saw happen in Example 13.8, so it makes sense. If you plug in 1 for ε, notice how the equation quickly simplifies to just $(v_{1f} - v_{2f}) = -(v_{1i} - v_{2i})$. This is why most programmers often opt to just make all collisions elastic. However, you as the programmer get to choose the value of ε if you want to make the collision more realistic. The closer ε is to 0, the more energy that is lost in the collision. The closer it is to 1, the more it resembles an elastic collision such as billiard balls.

Example 13.9: Elastic Collision

Suppose you're coding a 2D pool game with a top-down view, and you're focused on the elastic collision of two identical billiard balls. If one ball has an initial velocity of [30 20] and the other has an initial velocity of [−40 10] when they hit on center, what must their final velocities be?

Solution

1. In this case, you don't know either final velocity, so you need to use both equations. First, fill in all you know for the conservation of momentum theorem:

$$m_1v_{1i} + m_2v_{2i} = m_1v_{1f} + m_2v_{2f}$$

$$m_1\begin{bmatrix} 30 \\ 20 \end{bmatrix} + m_2\begin{bmatrix} -40 \\ 10 \end{bmatrix} = m_1v_{1f} + m_2v_{2f}$$

Because the balls are identical ($m_1 = m_2$), the mass cancels out of every term:

$$\begin{bmatrix} 30 \\ 20 \end{bmatrix} + \begin{bmatrix} -40 \\ 10 \end{bmatrix} = v_{1f} + v_{2f}$$

$$\begin{bmatrix} -10 \\ 30 \end{bmatrix} = v_{1f} + v_{2f}$$

2. Set up the second equation. Because it's an elastic collision, $\varepsilon = 1$.

$$(v_{1f} - v_{2f}) = -\varepsilon(v_{1i} - v_{2i})$$

$$(v_{1f} - v_{2f}) = -1(v_{1i} - v_{2i})$$

$$(v_{1f} - v_{2f}) = -v_{1i} + v_{2i}$$

$$(v_{1f} - v_{2f}) = \begin{bmatrix} -30 \\ -20 \end{bmatrix} + \begin{bmatrix} -40 \\ 10 \end{bmatrix}$$

$$(v_{1f} - v_{2f}) = \begin{bmatrix} -70 \\ -10 \end{bmatrix}$$

3. Here's where you can use linear combination or substitution. Either method will work. For this example, use linear combination:

$$v_{1f} - v_{2f} = \begin{bmatrix} -10 \\ 30 \end{bmatrix}$$

$$v_{1f} - v_{2f} = \begin{bmatrix} -70 \\ -10 \end{bmatrix}$$

Subtract the bottom equation from the top:

$$0 + 2v_{2f} = \begin{bmatrix} 60 \\ 40 \end{bmatrix}$$

$$v_{2f} = \begin{bmatrix} 30 \\ 20 \end{bmatrix}$$

Substitute the top equation to find v_{1f}:

$$v_{1f} + \begin{bmatrix} 30 \\ 20 \end{bmatrix} = \begin{bmatrix} -10 \\ 30 \end{bmatrix}$$

$$v_{1f} = \begin{bmatrix} -40 \\ 10 \end{bmatrix}$$

Note that the two balls transfer momentum because it is elastic. Imagine what might happen if you made $\varepsilon = 0.9$ instead of 1. Right—the two final velocities would be a little slower.

Here is a look at elastic collision in code. This function will process the final velocity of two objects with the same mass given the current vectors of each. In this particular example, we have defined restitution at 1 like this:

```
#define RESTITUTION 1
void elasticCollision(vector2D object1, vector2D object2, float
➡ mass)
    {
    vector2D object1Temp,object2Temp, sum, sum2,
    object1Velocity,object2Velocity,temp;

        //First calculate the left hand side of the equation.
        object1Temp  =  scalarMultiply(mass,object1);
        object2Temp =  scalarMultiply(mass,object2);
        sum     =  sumVectors(object1Temp,object2Temp);

        //setup right side of equation; multiply through by
        //restitution value.

        //This is only for illustration purposes in this example.
```

```
objectlTemp = scalarMultiply(RESTITUTION,objectlTemp);
object2Temp = scalarMultiply(RESTITUTION,object2Temp);

//for example purposes, since the equation switched to
// the right side.

objectlTemp = scalarMultiply(-1,objectlTemp);
sum2 = sumVectors(objectlTemp,object2Temp);

//Now we have the two vectors we will need to complete the
//solution and calculate the vectors.
temp = subtractVectors(sum,sum2);
object2Velocity = scalarDivide(2,temp);

objectlVelocity = subtractVectors(sum,object2Velocity);

//print the resulting velocities
cout<<"The first object's resulting velocity vector is ";
printVector(objectlVelocity);
cout<<"The second object's resulting velocity vector is \n";
printVector(object2Velocity);

}
```

Here, we immediately multiply both vectors by the coefficient of restitution. As you can see, we then follow through completing the equation to solve for the final velocity. This function will give us our answer but is fairly limited to solving one kind of problem.

At this point, you have a solid foundation to start experimenting with different types of collisions. The next section shows you how one programmer took this foundation and ran with it to make a remarkably realistic pool simulation.

Self-Assessment

1.   Suppose you're coding a 3D pool game, and you're focused on the cue ball hitting another ball at rest. The cue ball has a mass of 0.5kg and an initial velocity of [–40 50 –20]. It completely stops when it hits the other ball with a mass of 0.45kg. What is the second ball's final velocity as a result of the collision?

2. Suppose you're coding a car crash in a 3D racing game. A car with a mass of 1500kg has a velocity of [30 −20 −40] when it hits another car of mass 1800kg going [−50 40 −20]. If the two cars become entangled in the crash, what's their final velocity?

3. Suppose you're coding a car crash in a 3D racing game, but this time the cars don't get stuck together. A car with a mass of 1500kg has a velocity of [30 −20 −40] when it hits another car of mass 1800kg going [−50 40 −20]. Using e = 0.5, what should their final velocities be?

Visualization Experience

On the CD-ROM, you will find a demo named Basement Billiards. Here's a brief description from the programmer:

Basement Billiards is a practical demonstration of 2D collision between circles. Although the program is written in OpenGL and encompasses 3D space, the world has been rotated so that the negative z-axis faces down (as opposed to the traditional arrangement, in which the negative y-axis defines the down direction). This lets all calculations be done in the XY plane. Conservation of momentum is also demonstrated through perfectly elastic collisions, such as those between balls, and inelastic collisions, such as those between a ball and the rails. The entirety of the game code has been placed in the function `DrawGLScene`, *which resides in* `OGL_Wrapper.cpp`. *This was done for ease of comprehension. Each section of code that ordinarily would have been allocated to a separate function is clearly marked by a large comment block. All game collision calculations are done in the section "Shooting Code," and some basic ray-to-circle collision techniques appear in the section "Prediction Code." Because this is a demo, no game mechanics are implemented, such as players taking turns or reracking the balls after they have all been pocketed.*

You can move the camera with the arrow keys and zoom in and out with the A and Z keys, respectively. The C key toggles the camera's focus from the center of the table to the cue ball's current position. Clicking the cue ball begins the game's aiming phase, at which point the left and right arrows aim and the up and down arrows decrease and increase the shot's power. Holding down the Shift key allows for more precise aiming.

Clicking the large cue ball in the upper-left corner adjusts the English placed on the shot. Right-clicking at any time cancels the aiming phase without shooting, and clicking fires the shot. Rinse and repeat as desired. Pressing Esc quits the game, and pressing F1 toggles between windowed and full-screen (full-screen is recommended).

—Kaveh Kahrizi

Go ahead and run the demo by double-clicking Pool.exe. You'll see a pool table ready for you to break. Go ahead and play the game, paying close attention to the different types of collisions (balls colliding with each other, balls colliding against the bumper). The code for this game can be quite intimidating for a new programmer. Listing 13.1 shows the section that handles the collisions. See if you can figure out which formulas are at the root of this code.

Listing 13.1 Basement Billiards

```
/////////////////////////////////////////////////////////////////
// Ball-to-ball collision
/////////////////////////////////////////////////////////////////
        for(int j = i + 1; j < 16; ++j)
        {
            if(!ball[j].pocketed)
            {
                if(ball[i].collision(ball[j]) && !invalid
                ➥_collision[i][j])
                {
                    // Allow top or bottom english to affect the
                    // cue ball
                    if(!i)
                    {
                        apply_english = true;
                    }

                    invalid_collision[i][j] = invalid_collision[j][i]
                    ➥ =1;

                    GLT_VECTOR3 intersect = { 0, };
                    // Calculate the unit length vector defined by the
```

```
// centers of the two balls
// This is a special case where the cue ball is
// colliding with the ball which was predicted
// before the shot was taken. In this
// we apply pixel-perfect collision
if(i == 0 && j == predicted_ball)
{
    intersect[0] = ball[j].x - col.x;
    intersect[1] = ball[j].y - col.y;
    predicted_ball = 0;
    ball[0].x = col.x;
    ball[0].y = col.y;
}
// Otherwise, proceed as normal
else
{
    intersect[0] = ball[j].x - ball[i].x;
    intersect[1] = ball[j].y - ball[i].y;
}


gltNormalize(intersect);


// Small optimization; no need to calculate vectors
// and whatnot if the ball isn't moving
bool b1_moving = false;
bool b2_moving = false;

if(ball[i].vec[0] || ball[i].vec[1])
    b1_moving = true;
if(ball[j].vec[0] || ball[j].vec[1])
    b2_moving = true;


// Unify the forward vectors of the two balls in
// question
if(b1_moving)
    gltNormalize(ball[i].vec);
if(b2_moving)
    gltNormalize(ball[j].vec);
```

continues

Listing 13.1 Continued

```
                   if(ball[i].vec[0] > .95f && fabs(ball[i].vec[1]) <
                ➧ .05f)
                      bool what_the_heck = true;
                   // Calculate the angle between the balls and the
                   // vector of collision
                   float angle1 = 0, angle2 = 0;
                   if(b1_moving)
                       angle1 = acosf(gltDotProduct(ball[i].vec,
                   ➧ intersect));
                   if(b2_moving)
                       angle2 = acosf(fabs(gltDotProduct(ball[j].vec,
                   ➧ intersect)));

                   // This occurs only in the event that this
                   // collision is invalid and is a result of
                   // a previous collision's not being completely
                   // resolved from the last frame. This collision
                   // will be ignored.
//                              if(angle1 > (90 * GLT_PI_DIV_180) &&
                                ➧ angle1 < 270 * GLT_PI_DIV_180)
//                              continue;

                   if(i == 0)
                       started = true;
                   // These variables hold the components of the
                   // respective ball's vector.
                   // comp1 will hold the component transferred to
                   // the owning ball, and comp2 will hold the
                   // component transferred to the colliding ball.
                   float b1_comp1 = 0, b1_comp2 = 0, b2_comp1 = 0, b2
                ➧ _comp2 =0;

                   // Calculate the components of ball1 (defined by
                   // [i])
                   if(b1_moving)
                   {
                       b1_comp1 = sinf(angle1) * ball[i].velocity;
```

```
      b1_comp2 = cosf(angle1) * ball[i].velocity;
}
// Calculate the components of ball2 (defined by
// [j])
if(b2_moving)
{
    b2_comp1 = sinf(angle2) * ball[j].velocity;
    b2_comp2 = cosf(angle2) * ball[j].velocity;
}

// Calculate the vector that is perpendicular to
// the vector of collision
GLT_VECTOR3 norm_intersect = { 0, };
gltCrossProduct(world_up, intersect, norm
➥_intersect);

// These are the resultant component vectors of
➥the
// ball's travel vector
GLT_VECTOR3 b1_vcomp1 = {0, };
GLT_VECTOR3 b1_vcomp2 = {0, };
GLT_VECTOR3 b2_vcomp1 = {0, };
GLT_VECTOR3 b2_vcomp2 = {0, };

// Calculate the resultant vector of ball1 ([i])
if(gltGetAngleDeg(ball[i].vec, norm_intersect) <
➥ 90)
{
    b1_vcomp1[0] = norm_intersect[0] * b1_comp1;
    b1_vcomp1[1] = norm_intersect[1] * b1_comp1;
}
else
{
    b1_vcomp1[0] = -norm_intersect[0] * b1_comp1;
    b1_vcomp1[1] = -norm_intersect[1] * b1_comp1;
}
b1_vcomp2[0] = -intersect[0] * b2_comp2;
b1_vcomp2[1] = -intersect[1] * b2_comp2;
```

continues

Listing 13.1 Continued

```
        ball[i].vec[0] = b1_vcomp1[0] + b1_vcomp2[0];
        ball[i].vec[1] = b1_vcomp1[1] + b1_vcomp2[1];

        ball[i].velocity = sqrtf(ball[i].vec[0] *
➥ball[i].vec[0] + ball[i].vec[1] * ball[i].vec[1]);

        // Calculate the resultant vector of ball2 ([j])
        if(gltGetAngleDeg(ball[j].vec, norm_intersect) <
➥ 90)
        {
            b2_vcomp1[0] = norm_intersect[0] * b2_comp1;
            b2_vcomp1[1] = norm_intersect[1] * b2_comp1;
        }
        else
        {
            b2_vcomp1[0] = -norm_intersect[0] * b2_comp1;
            b2_vcomp1[1] = -norm_intersect[1] * b2_comp1;
        }
        b2_vcomp2[0] = intersect[0] * b1_comp2;
        b2_vcomp2[1] = intersect[1] * b1_comp2;

        // Finally we sum up each ball's respective
        // vector and assign it to the ball
        ball[j].vec[0] = b2_vcomp1[0] + b2_vcomp2[0];
        ball[j].vec[1] = b2_vcomp1[1] + b2_vcomp2[1];
        ball[j].velocity = sqrtf(ball[j].vec[0] *
➥ball[j].vec[0] + ball[j].vec[1] * ball[j].vec[1]);

        // Update the vector perpendicular to our forward
        // vector for purposes of spinning the balls
        ball[i].nvec[0] = -ball[i].vec[1];
        ball[i].nvec[1] = ball[i].vec[0];
        ball[j].nvec[0] = -ball[j].vec[1];
        ball[j].nvec[1] = ball[j].vec[0];
        gltNormalize(ball[i].nvec);
        gltNormalize(ball[j].nvec);
```

```
//                    soundPlayer.playSample(collision);
            }
            // Small buffer to correct some minor collision
            // glitches
            else
            {
                invalid_collision[i][j] = invalid_collision[j][i]
                ➥ = 0;
            }
        }
    }
  }
}
```

Self-Assessment Solutions

Collision with a Stationary Object

1. [−30 −50]

2. [41.6 71.2]

3. [38.634 24.478 30.132]

Momentum and Impulse Defined

1. 680.88kg*m/s

2. $\begin{bmatrix} 100,000 \\ 50,000 \\ -20,000 \end{bmatrix}$

3. 44m/s

4. 39m/s

5. $\begin{bmatrix} 22.03 \\ 52.87 \\ -8.81 \end{bmatrix}$

Modeling Collisions

1. [−44.44 55.56 −22.22]

2. [−13.636 12.727 29.091]

3. v_{1f} = [−35.455 29.091 −23.636], v_{2f} = [4.545 −0.909 −33.636]

Chapter 14

Rotational Motion

The preceding chapter discussed linear (head-on) collisions. By now, you might be wondering about all the other collisions in which two objects hit off-center. Think about the last time you played pool. Even when you wanted the cue ball to hit dead center, how often did that really happen? Most times the balls hit off-center, which not only causes them to move off in different directions but also forces them to spin. As you investigate further, you'll find that there are two parts to the collision response. The linear part causes a translation in which the object moves in a different direction. The other part causes rotation as a result of being hit off-center. You already know how to handle the linear part, so this chapter on rotational motion is the last piece of the puzzle.

Circular Motion

Believe it or not, you already understand all the underlying concepts of circular motion. Previous chapters defined quantities such as displacement, velocity, and acceleration. Now all you have to do is apply these same concepts to rotational motion. Let's start by looking at the motion of a CD-ROM when your computer is reading it. Figure 14.1 shows a top-down view of the spinning CD.

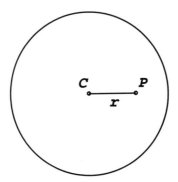

Figure 14.1 Point P on a CD-ROM.

The center point (C) represents the axis of rotation. A point on the CD (P) therefore rotates about the center, which means that it travels along a circular path with a fixed radius (r). After some time has passed (Δt), point P has moved a certain distance (s) along the circular path. This distance is called the **arc length**, and it is illustrated in Figure 14.2.

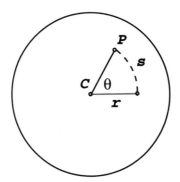

Figure 14.2 Point P has moved.

Also in Figure 14.2, you see that the angle of rotation (θ) for this time interval is labeled. This angle must always be measured in radians. Chapter 3, "Trigonometry Snippets," discussed the conversion between degrees and radians. This angle of rotation (θ) represents the **angular displacement**, and it's defined as the arc length divided by the radius.

Angular Displacement

$\theta = s/r$

where s = arc length and r = radius.

> **NOTE**
>
> Notice that if the arc length (s) is equal to the radius (r), $\theta = 1$ radian. This is precisely how the radian was originally defined.

Here is an example of a function that can calculate the angular displacement given the arc length and radius:

```
float angDisplacement(float arc, float radius)
    {
       float theta;
       theta = arc/radius;
       return theta;
    }
```

Now that angular displacement has been defined, we can look at **average angular velocity** (ω). As you might have guessed, angular velocity is the rate of change of the angular displacement. In other words, angular velocity is the angular displacement divided by time, just like linear velocity.

Average Angular Velocity

$$\overline{\omega} = \frac{\Delta\theta}{\Delta t} = \frac{\theta_f - \theta_i}{t_f - t_i}$$

where θ = angular displacement and t = time.

> **NOTE**
>
> The symbol for angular displacement (ω) is the Greek letter omega.

If you look closely at the definition of angular velocity, you can probably guess the appropriate units. If angular displacement is measured in radians and time is measured in seconds, angular velocity must be measured in radians/second (rad/s).

Example 14.1: Average Angular Velocity of a CD-ROM

A certain manufacturer of CD-ROM drives advertises a speed of 9500rpm (revolutions per minute). What is the angular velocity in rad/s?

Solution

1. Calculate the angular displacement. If one revolution equals 2π radians, then

$$9500\,rev\left(\frac{2\pi^R}{1\,rev}\right) = 19000\,\pi^R$$

2. Convert the time to seconds. 1 minute equals 60 seconds.

3. Plug those two values into the definition:

$$\omega = \frac{\Delta\theta}{\Delta t} = \frac{19000\,\pi^R}{60\,s} \approx 316.67^R/s$$

Here is one way to turn this into a function.

```
float avgAngularVelocity(float arcStart, float arcEnd, float time,
➥float radius)
    {
    float initialDisplacement, endDisplacement,omega;

        //calculate the angular displacement.
        initialDisplacement = arcStart/radius;
        endDisplacement = arcEnd/radius;

        //apply the formula.
        omega = (endDisplacement - initialDisplacement) / time;
        return omega;
    }
```

This particular version will take the beginning and ending points of the arc, the total radius, and the overall time interval to calculate against. This function determines the angular displacement internally, and then applies the formula to determine the average angular velocity.

While this is a useful method, in general it is best to try to find the smallest possible chunk of work that can be done, then write a function to process it. A function like the previous one is useful, but only in the situation where the arc lengths and radius are known. Bear this in mind when designing your own functions.

At this point, we can make a distinction between linear velocity and angular velocity. Looking at the CD-ROM described in Example 14.1, you can see that any point on the CD-ROM moves with the same *angular velocity* because the CD is a solid (rigid body) object. However, if you look at *linear velocity,* points on the outside of the CD have to move faster than points close to the center in order to keep up.

So far, we've discussed only average angular velocity. Chapter 8, "Motion in One Dimension," discussed the difference between average linear velocity and instantaneous linear velocity. The same concept applies here as well. The **instantaneous angular velocity** is simply the average angular velocity over an extremely small time interval, as close to an instant as you can get.

Now let's redefine acceleration in terms of circular motion. Chapter 8 also said that linear acceleration is the rate of change of linear velocity. In other words, linear acceleration is equal to the change in linear velocity divided by time. The same definition carries over to circular motion: **Average angular acceleration ($\bar{\alpha}$)** is equal to the rate of change of angular velocity.

Average Angular Acceleration

$$\bar{\alpha} = \frac{\Delta \omega}{\Delta t} = \frac{\omega_f - \omega_i}{t_f - t_i}$$

where ω = angular displacement and t = time.

NOTE
The symbol for angular acceleration (α) is the Greek letter alpha.

If you look closely at the definition, you can see that the units for angular acceleration are rad/s^2, which is very similar to the m/s^2 that you're used to seeing for linear acceleration. Also similar to linear acceleration, the **instantaneous angular acceleration** is the average angular acceleration over a tiny time interval, as close to an instant as you can get.

Example 14.2: Average Angular Acceleration of a Wheel

Suppose you're coding a racing game like *Need for Speed Under Ground*, and the car's wheels have an angular velocity of 5rad/s when the player pushes the acceleration button. If 2 seconds later the angular velocity is 15rad/s, what was the wheel's average angular acceleration?

Solution

Let's go straight to the definition:

$$\bar{\alpha} = \frac{\Delta\omega}{\Delta t} = \frac{\omega_f - \omega_i}{t_f - t_i} = \frac{15 rad/s - 5 rad/s}{2s} = \frac{10 rad/s}{2s} = 5 rad/s^2$$

Just as you saw with the CD-ROM, notice that the angular acceleration is the same for every point on the wheel even though the linear acceleration is different depending on how far the point is from the axis of rotation.

To calculate alpha in code, we can use a function that takes the angular displacement and divides by time:

```
float avgAngAcceleration(float angVelBegin, float angVelEnd, float
➥time)
    {
       float alpha;
       alpha = (angVelEnd - angVelBegin)/time;
       return alpha;
    }
```

Note here that again, the change in time has been pre-computed and put through as a final value instead of performing the subtraction of start and end times. This function could also calculate the instantaneous angular acceleration if it were passed a sufficiently small time interval. If you need to modify this function to take degree measurements, don't forget to convert!

Now that we've redefined displacement, velocity, and acceleration for circular motion, you can see that basically the same concepts carry over from linear motion. As you might have guessed, the five equations of motion (discussed in Chapter 8) also carry over from linear motion. The only difference is that the variables change slightly.

Displacement goes from Δx to $\Delta\theta$, velocity changes from v to Ω, and acceleration changes from a to α. The revised equations are listed in Table 14.1.

Table 14.1 The Five Equations of Motion Revisited

Equation 1	$\omega_f = \omega_i + \alpha t$
Equation 2	$\overline{\omega} = \dfrac{\omega_i + \omega_f}{2}$
Equation 3	$\Delta\theta = \frac{1}{2}(\omega_i + \omega_f)t$
Equation 4	$\Delta\theta = \omega_i t + \frac{1}{2}\alpha t^2$
Equation 5	$\omega_f^2 = \omega_i^2 + 2\alpha\Delta\theta$

The process is the same as before. The only difference is that you plug in angular variables instead of linear variables.

Example 14.3: *Wheel of Fortune*

Suppose you're coding a *Wheel of Fortune* game. If the player gives the wheel an initial angular velocity of 8rad/s, and the pegs decelerate it at a rate of -2rad/s^2, what will its angular displacement be after 3 seconds?

Solution

1. Make a list of everything you know and what you're looking for, just like you did for linear motion:

Given	Find
$\omega_i = 8$rad/s	$\Delta\theta = ?$
$t = 3$s	
$\alpha = -2$rad/s^2	

2. Based on this list, you can choose an equation. In this case, equation 4 will work.

3. Plug in the known values, and solve for $\Delta\theta$:

$$\Delta\theta = \omega_i t + \frac{1}{2}\alpha t^2$$

$$\Delta\theta = (8\text{rad/s})(3\text{s}) + \frac{1}{2}(-2\text{rad/s}^2)(3\text{s})^2$$

$$\Delta\theta = 24\text{rad} - 3\text{rad}$$

$$\Delta\theta = 21\text{rad}$$

Until now, we've focused on the similarities between linear motion and circular motion. The only difference that has been mentioned is the idea that angular velocity and acceleration are the same for all points on a fixed object where linear velocity and acceleration differ based on how far the point is from the center or axis of rotation. Let's take that one step further and look for a relationship between the linear and angular values, starting with linear and angular velocity.

At the beginning of this chapter, we said that angular displacement is equal to the arc length divided by the radius:

$$\Delta\theta = \frac{\Delta s}{r}$$

To get angular velocity, we must divide by time, so let's divide both sides of that equation by time:

$$\omega = \frac{\Delta\theta}{\Delta t} = \frac{1}{r}\left(\frac{\Delta s}{\Delta t}\right)$$

Here's where we take a big jump. Remember that to calculate instantaneous angular velocity, we must use a very small time interval. If we use smaller and smaller time intervals, you'll see that the arc length approaches a straight line. As soon as it becomes that tiny straight line, the linear velocity equals ($\Delta s/\Delta t$). The equation then becomes

$$\omega = \frac{v}{r}$$

If you look back at the CD-ROM shown in Figure 14.2 and picture smaller and smaller time intervals, θ becomes smaller, and s approaches a straight line that is tangent to the circular path. That is why the linear velocity at this point is called the **tangential velocity**, v_t. This is shown in Figure 14.3.

Tangential Velocity

$v_t = \omega r$

where ω = instantaneous angular velocity and r = radius.

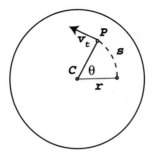

Figure 14.3   Tangential velocity at point P.

Tangential velocity is also pretty easy to turn into a function for programming purposes. Here is an example:

```
float tangVelocity(float omega, float radius)
    {
       float velT;
       velT = omega*radius;
       return velT;
    }
```

This function returns the finalized tangential velocity given omega and time.

One way you can visualize this idea of tangential velocity is to find a ball with a string attached to it, or even a yo-yo. Take the end of the string and swing the ball so that it ends up circling your hand, which is fixed at some location. What do you suppose would happen if the ball came loose from the string? At the instant it detached, the ball would follow a straight-line path tangent to the circular path at the point where it was released, as shown in Figure 14.4.

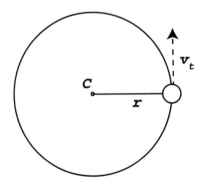

Figure 14.4 A ball on a string.

Example 14.4: Throwing a Baseball

Suppose you're coding a baseball game like *All Star Base*. If the player throwing the ball has a forearm that measures 0.5m, and the ball has an instantaneous angular acceleration of 100rad/s when he releases it, what is the ball's initial linear velocity at the beginning of the projectile motion?

Solution

If $v_t = \omega r$, the tangential velocity must be 100rad/s * 0.5m, which is 50m/s in the direction that is tangent to the curve at the instant the player releases the ball.

You can also derive a relationship between linear and angular acceleration. Let's start with the equation that relates the velocities:

$$v_t = \omega r$$

To get acceleration, divide both sides by time:

$$\frac{v_t}{\Delta t} = \frac{\omega}{\Delta t}(r)$$

$$a_t = \alpha r$$

Tangential Acceleration
$a_t = \alpha r$
where α = instantaneous angular acceleration and r = radius.

Example 14.5: *Wheel of Fortune* Revisited

Suppose you're back to coding that *Wheel of Fortune* game. The player gives the wheel an initial angular velocity of 8rad/s, and it takes 10 seconds to come to rest. If the wheel has a 3-meter radius, and one of the pegs on the wheel's exterior comes loose the second the player sets the wheel in motion, what is the wheel's tangential acceleration?

Solution

1. The first thing you need to find is the angular acceleration. Make a list of what you know:

Given	Find
ω_i = 8rad/s	α = ?
t = 10s	
ω_f = 0rad/s	

2. Now you can choose an equation. In this case, use equation 1:

$\omega_f = \omega_i + \alpha t$

0rad/s = 8rad/s + α(10s)

α = −0.8rad/s²

3. Now that you know the angular acceleration, you can find the tangential acceleration:

$a_t = \alpha r$

a_t = −0.8rad/s²(3m)

a_t = −2.4m/s²

As you can see, the basic definitions of displacement, velocity, and acceleration carry over from linear motion to angular motion. Linear motion is based on translation, whereas angular motion is based on rotation. Remember that for rigid bodies the angular velocity and acceleration are consistent for all points on the object, but linear velocity and acceleration vary depending on the distance from the center. The next section uses these definitions to investigate what causes rotational motion.

Self-Assessment

1. If a merry-go-round completes 10 revolutions in 30 seconds, what is its average angular velocity in rad/s?

2. If a merry-go-round has an initial angular velocity of 5rad/s when a parent gives it a good push to speed it up to 15rad/s in 3 seconds, what is the angular acceleration due to the push?

3. As soon as the merry-go-round hits its top angular velocity of 15rad/s, it starts to slow down at a rate of −3rad/s². At that rate, how long will it take to come to a complete stop?

4. As soon as the merry-go-round hits its top angular velocity of 15rad/s, it starts to slow down at a rate of −3rad/s². What is its total angular displacement when it finally comes to rest?

5. One of the children on the merry-go-round is not holding on tight enough. If the radius of the merry-go-round is 2.5m, and the child falls off the edge at the maximum angular velocity of 15rad/s, what is his new linear (tangential) velocity?

Rotational Dynamics

The preceding section described the angular equivalent of Chapter 8. Now we can talk about angular displacement, velocity, and acceleration. The last thing we need to look at is what causes rotational motion. In Chapter 11, "Newton's Laws," you looked at what causes linear motion. Basically, Newton's Second Law says that adding up all the forces acting on an object determines how the object accelerates as a result of the net force being applied. We assumed that all these forces were acting on the object's center of mass, so the result was a simple translation. But what if the force is applied to one of the vertices? That would cause the object to rotate about the center of mass rather than just translating the entire object.

Suppose an object gets hit by a tangential force on one of the vertices rather than head-on. According to Newton's Second Law:

$F_t = ma_t$

Now multiply each side by the radius from that vertex to the center of mass:

$$F_t(r) = ma_t(r)$$

In the preceding section, we found that

$$a_t = r\alpha$$

so that means

$$F_t(r) = m(r\alpha)(r) = mr^2\alpha$$

The left side of that equation is the **torque** (τ), which rotates an object about its axis of rotation through the center of mass.

Torque

$\tau = mr^2\alpha$

where m = mass, r = radius, and α = angular acceleration.

NOTE
As long as you stay consistent with metric units for everything else, the units for torque are N*m.

By now, you should hopefully start spotting similarities between linear motion and rotational motion. A minute ago, we mentioned Newton's Second Law, $F = ma$. If torque is the angular equivalent of force, there should be an angular version of Newton's Second Law, right? You just learned that $\tau = mr^2\alpha$. Mass has an angular equivalent— **inertia** (I)—which equals mr^2. This means that torque must be equal to the inertia times the angular acceleration. Sounds a lot like Newton's Second Law, doesn't it?

Newton's Second Law Revisited

$\tau = I\alpha$

where I = inertia (mr^2) and α = angular acceleration.

Just as net force causes linear acceleration, torque causes angular acceleration. Also as before, as soon as you know the angular acceleration, you can use the equations of motion to calculate the resulting velocity or displacement.

Example 14.6: Car Crash

Suppose you're coding a game like *Grand Theft Auto*, and one car hits another on the corner of the rear bumper with 5000N*m of torque. If the car that gets hit has a mass of 1200kg, and the distance from the bumper to the center of mass is 3m, what's the resulting angular acceleration?

Solution

Let's go straight to the equation derived earlier:

$$\tau = mr^2\alpha$$

$$5000N\text{*}m = 1200kg(3m)^2(\alpha)$$

$$\alpha = 0.463rad/s^2$$

Just as you did with linear acceleration, as soon as you know the angular acceleration, you can use it in the five equations of motion to calculate the resulting angular velocity and displacement. Remember that in game programming it all goes back to how the object moves as time is incremented frame by frame.

Two more quantities can be translated from linear motion into rotational motion—momentum and kinetic energy. Think about how you used these quantities to model linear motion. In both cases, you ended up calculating a final speed or velocity so that you could track displacement as time incremented. The same concepts can be applied to rotational dynamics. Let's look at kinetic energy first.

If inertia is related to mass, and angular velocity is related to speed, you might be able to guess the definition of rotational kinetic energy.

> **Rotational Kinetic Energy**
>
> $KE_R = \frac{1}{2}I\omega^2$
>
> where I = inertia (mr^2) and ω = angular velocity.

NOTE

From this point forward, linear (or translational) kinetic energy will be labeled as KE_T and rotational kinetic energy will be labeled as KE_R.

As discussed in Chapter 12, "Energy," conservation of energy still holds. You just have one additional type of energy to add to each side of the equation—rotational kinetic energy.

Example 14.7: Rolling Ball

Suppose you're coding a game like *Crash Bandicoot* where the player moves around in a hamster ball for one level. The ball with a mass of 0.5kg starts from rest and rolls down a hill from an initial height of 10m. If the inertia of a sphere equals $(2/5)mr^2$, what is the ball's linear speed when it reaches the bottom of the hill?

Solution

Let's revisit conservation of energy with the additional kinetic energy:

$$PE_i + KE_{Ti} + KE_{Ri} = PE_f + KE_{Tf} + KE_{Rf}$$

$$mgy_i + \tfrac{1}{2}mv_i^2 + \tfrac{1}{2}I\omega_i^2 = mgy_f + \tfrac{1}{2}mv_f^2 + \tfrac{1}{2}I\omega_f^2$$

$$mgy_i + \tfrac{1}{2}m(0)^2 + \tfrac{1}{2}I(0)^2 = mg(0) + \tfrac{1}{2}mv_f^2 + \tfrac{1}{2}I\omega_f^2$$

$$mgy_i = \tfrac{1}{2}mv_f^2 + \tfrac{1}{2}I\omega_f^2$$

$$0.5\text{kg}(9.8\text{m/s}^2)(10\text{m}) = \tfrac{1}{2}(0.5\text{kg})v_f^2 + \tfrac{1}{2}((2/5)(0.5\text{kg})r^2)\omega_f^2$$

$$49\text{J} = 0.25\text{kg}(v_f^2) + 0.1\text{kg}(r^2)\omega_f^2$$

Remember that $v = r\omega$, so $v^2 = r^2\omega^2$:

$$49J = 0.25kg(v_f^2) + 0.1kg(v_f^2)$$

$$49J = 0.35kg(v_f^2)$$

$$49J = 0.35kg(v_f^2)$$

$$140 \text{ m}^2/\text{s}^2 = v_f^2$$

$$v_f \approx 11.832 \text{ m/s}$$

Tackling this mathematical model is a bit more complicated, but let's give it a try. Here is a function that will calculate the linear speed of the ball given the height, mass, and inertia as provided in the previous example:

```
#define GRAVITY 9.81
void LinearSpeed()
    {
    //lots of floats.
    float mass,initialHeight,inertia,energy =0.0f;
float halfMass,halfInertiaMass linearSpeed,temp = 0.0f;

    cout<<"Let's calculate the linear speed of a rolling
    ➥object!\n";
    cout<<"First, we need some information...\n";
    cout<<"Please specify a mass for the ball in kg\n";
    cin>>mass;

    cout<<"Next, give us an initial height for the ball in
    ➥meters\n";
    cin>>initialHeight;

    cout<<"Lastly, give us an inertia for the ball\n";
    cin>>inertia;
    cout<<"\n";

    //first figure out what is known for sure.
    energy = mass*initialHeight*GRAVITY;
```

```
//this term is used to hold the math equivalent of
➥1/2(m)vf^2
halfMass = mass/2;

//this term hold on to the formula equivalent of
//1/2(inertia)*(mass) r^2 * ωf^2

halfInertiaMass = inertia*mass/2;

//make a holding place.
temp = energy/(halfMass+halfInertiaMass);

//take the square root to find the speed in m/s
linearSpeed = sqrt(temp);

cout<<"The final linear speed is "<<linearSpeed<< "
meters/second\n";

}
```

There's lots of stuff happening in here, so let's look it over. The first thing to do is figure out the initial Potential Energy. Then the term `halfMass` is assigned to hold the mass/2. This value skips to the chase in code dividing the mass by two. Then we assign the result of half the inertia*mass and assign it to `halfInertiaMass`. Energy is then divided by the sum of those two terms. The linear speed of the ball at the bottom of the hill is the square root of the temp value. The square root function is from the `math.h`. It is CPU-intensive and should be used as sparingly as possible.

The trick with modeling math code for a game is to understand the function well enough to be able to distill out the most basic components, and then build code that will compute the values as quickly as possible. Getting the speed for complete calculations is usually the difficult part.

The other quantity that you can extend to rotational motion is momentum. If you follow the same parallel, angular momentum must be the product of inertia and angular velocity.

Angular Momentum

$L = I\omega$

where I = inertia (mr^2) and ω = angular velocity.

Remember how in Chapter 13, "Momentum and Collisions," we rearranged Newton's Second Law from $F = ma$ to the impulse-momentum theorem? We ended up saying that an impulse applied to an object results in a change in momentum. We can apply this same concept to rotation. Any angular (off-center) impulse results in a change in angular momentum.

As you can see, rotational motion is a natural extension of all the concepts we've discussed in terms of linear motion. The formulas stay the same, and the quantities are modified only slightly to fit a rotating object. If you understood all the chapters that discussed linear motion in depth, you should be able to start drawing your own parallels to rotation. At this point you have a strong-enough foundation to start experimenting with commercial physics engines such as Havok and MathEngine. In fact, a number of commercial game engines that incorporate physics subsystems make their development tools freely available to the mod community. For example, Unreal Tournament 2003 ships with an editor that incorporates MathEngine's Karma physics library. Although they generally don't expose the underlying mathematics directly, it's certainly a good opportunity to explore the ways in which physics can support gameplay. Or, with enough programming experience, you can start coding your own simulations from scratch. Please don't close this book and think you have arrived. I hope you put this book down only to venture out and discover all the other texts that will now make sense to you. This is just the beginning!

Self-Assessment

1. Suppose a parent gives the merry-go-round another good push. This push delivers an angular acceleration of 6rad/s². If the radius is still 2.5m, and the total mass with the kids is 500kg, how much torque does the parent deliver?

2. Suppose you're coding a crazy taxi type of game. The taxi hits a parked 1000kg car on the edge of the bumper with 3000N*m or torque. If the distance from the point of collision and the car's center of mass is 2m, what was the resulting angular acceleration?

Self-Assessment Solutions

Circular Motion

1. $(2/3)\pi$rad/s

2. 5rad/s^2

3. 5s

4. 37.5rad

5. 37.5m/s

Rotational Dynamics

1. 18,750N*m

2. 0.75rad/s^2

Chapter A

List of Formulas

Symbols

Symbol	Name	Description
α	Alpha	Often used to represent an angle
Δ	Delta	Means "change in"
ε	Epsilon	Coefficient of restitution
$f'(t)$		The derivative of function f with respect to t
μ	Mu	Coefficient of friction
ω	Omega	Used here to represent angular velocity
π	Pi	Constant ≈ 3.14
θ	Theta	Often used to represent an angle

Chapter 1, "Points and Lines"

Equation of a Line

The graph of an equation of the form $Ax + By = C$, where A and B are not both 0, is a straight line.

Slope

$$slope = m = \frac{\Delta y}{\Delta x} = \frac{y_2 - y_1}{x_2 - x_1}.$$

For any line in standard form, $Ax + By = C$, the slope $m = -A/B$.

Parallel Lines

If two lines are parallel, their slopes must be equal.

Perpendicular Lines

If two lines are perpendicular, $m_1 m_2 = -1$, or $m_1 = -\dfrac{1}{m_2}$ or $m_2 = -\dfrac{1}{m_1}$.

Equation of a Line

Slope-intercept form: $y = mx + b$

Point-slope form: $(y - y_1) = m(x - x_1)$

where (x_1, y_1) is a point on the line.

System of Linear Equations

A system of two linear equations in the same plane has

➤ Exactly *one* solution if the two graphs have different slopes.

➤ An *infinite* set of solutions if both graphs have the same slope and y-intercept.

➤ *No* solution if the graphs have the same slope but different y-intercepts.

Chapter 2, "Geometry Snippets"

Pythagorean Theorem

In a right triangle, the square of the length c of the hypotenuse is equal to the sum of the squares of the lengths a and b of the other two sides: $c^2 = a^2 + b^2$.

Distance Formula in 2D

$$P_1P_2 = \sqrt{(x_2 - x_1)^2 + (y_2 - y_1)^2}$$

where $P_1(x_1,y_1)$ and $P_2(x_2,y_2)$ are points on the line.

Distance Formula in 3D

$$P_1P_2 = \sqrt{(x_2 - x_1)^2 + (y_2 - y_1)^2 + (z_2 - z_1)^2}$$

where $P_1(x_1,y_1,z_1)$ and $P_2(x_2,y_2,z_2)$ are points on the line.

Midpoint Formula in 2D

$$M\left(\frac{x_1 + x_2}{2}, \frac{y_1 + y_2}{2}\right)$$

is the midpoint between $P_1(x_1,y_1)$ and $P_2(x_2,y_2)$.

Midpoint Formula in 3D

$$M\left(\frac{x_1 + x_2}{2}, \frac{y_1 + y_2}{2}, \frac{z_1 + z_2}{2}\right)$$

is the midpoint between $P_1(x_1,y_1,z_1)$ and $P_2(x_2,y_2,z_2)$.

Parabola with a Vertical Axis

$y = a(x - h)^2 + k$, with vertex (h,k) and axis of symmetry $x = h$.

Parabola with a Horizontal Axis

$x = a(y - k)^2 + h$, with vertex (h,k) and axis of symmetry $y = k$.

Equation of a Circle

$(x - h)^2 + (y - k)^2 = r^2$

where the center is (h,k) and the radius is r.

Equation of a Circle Centered at the Origin

$x^2 + y^2 = r^2$

where the center is (0,0) and the radius is r.

Equation of a Sphere

$(x - h)^2 + (y - k)^2 + (z - l)^2 = r^2$

where the center is (h,k,l) and the radius is r.

Equation of a Sphere Centered at the Origin

$x^2 + y^2 + z^2 = r^2$

where the center is (0,0,0) and the radius is r.

Circle-Circle Collision Detection

Given two circles $(x - h_1)^2 + (y - k_1)^2 = r_1^2$ and $(x - h_2)^2 + (y - k_2)^2 = r_2^2$, if $\sqrt{(h_2 - h_1)^2 + (k_2 - k_1)^2} \le (r_1 + r_2)$, a collision occurs.

Optimized Circle-Circle Collision Detection

Given two circles $(x - h_1)^2 + (y - k_1)^2 = r_1^2$ and $(x - h_2)^2 + (y - k_2)^2 = r_2^2$, if $(h_2 - h_1)^2 + (k_2 - k_1)^2 \le (r_1 + r_2)^2$, a collision occurs.

Optimized Sphere-Sphere Collision Detection

Given two spheres $(x - h_1)^2 + (y - k_1)^2 + (z - l_1)^2 = r_1^2$ and $(x - h_2)^2 + (y - k_2)^2 + (z - l_2)^2 = r_2^2$, if $(h_2 - h_1)^2 + (k_2 - k_1)^2 + (l_2 - i_1)^2 \le (r_1 + r_2)^2$, a collision occurs.

Chapter 3, "Trigonometry Snippets"

Degrees to Radians

Angle in degrees $*$ $\left(\dfrac{\pi^R}{180°}\right)$ = angle in radians.

Radians to Degrees

Angle in radians $*$ $\left(\dfrac{180°}{\pi^R}\right)$ = angle in degrees.

Trigonometric Functions

$$\sin \alpha \ = \ \frac{opp}{hyp} = \frac{b}{c}$$

$$\cos \alpha \ = \ \frac{adj}{hyp} = \frac{a}{c}$$

$$\tan \alpha \ = \ \frac{opp}{adj} = \frac{b}{a}$$

where opp = the side opposite α, adj = the side adjacent to α, and hyp = the hypotenuse.

Other Trigonometric Functions

$$\csc \alpha \ = \ \frac{1}{\sin\alpha} = \frac{hyp}{opp}$$

$$\sec \alpha \ = \ \frac{1}{\cos\alpha} = \frac{hyp}{adj}$$

$$\cot \alpha \ = \ \frac{1}{\tan\alpha} = \frac{adj}{opp}$$

where opp = the side opposite α, adj = the side adjacent to α, and hyp = the hypotenuse.

Period of the Sine Wave

For $y = \sin(Bx)$, the period $= \dfrac{360°}{|B|}$.

Amplitude of the Sine Wave

For $y = A\sin(x)$, the amplitude $= |A|$.

Unit Circle Identity

$\cos^2\alpha + \sin^2\alpha = 1$

Tangent and Cotangent

$\tan \alpha = \dfrac{\sin\alpha}{\cos\alpha}$

$\cot \alpha = \dfrac{\cos\alpha}{\sin\alpha}$

Negative Angles

$\sin(-\alpha) = -\sin\alpha$

$\cos(-\alpha) = \cos\alpha$

$\tan(-\alpha) = -\tan\alpha$

Sum and Difference Identities for Sine

$\sin(\alpha_1 + \alpha_2) = \sin\alpha_1\cos\alpha_2 + \cos\alpha_1\sin\alpha_2$

$\sin(\alpha_1 - \alpha_2) = \sin\alpha_1\cos\alpha_2 - \cos\alpha_1\sin\alpha_2$

Sum and Difference Identities for Cosine

$\cos(\alpha_1 + \alpha_2) = \cos\alpha_1\cos\alpha_2 - \sin\alpha_1\sin\alpha_2$

$\cos(\alpha_1 - \alpha_2) = \cos\alpha_1\cos\alpha_2 + \sin\alpha_1\sin\alpha_2$

Chapter 4, "Vector Operations"

Vector Versus Scalar

Scalar = magnitude only.

Vector = magnitude + direction.

Displacement

Displacement = final position − initial position.

$$\Delta x = x_f - x_i$$

Polar Coordinates

Vector A = $\|A\|$ @ θ

where $\|A\|$ is the magnitude of A and θ is the direction.

Cartesian Coordinates (Components)

Vector B = $b_1\hat{i} + b_2\hat{j}$

where $\hat{i}$ is one unit in the x direction and $\hat{j}$ is one unit in the y direction.

Converting from Polar to Cartesian Coordinates

For vector A = $\|A\|$ @ θ,

$$A = a_1\hat{i} + a_2\hat{j}$$

where $a_1 = \|A\| \cos\theta$ and $a_2 = \|A\| \sin\theta$.

Converting from Cartesian to Polar Coordinates

For vector $B = b_1\hat{i} + b_2\hat{j}$,

$\|B\| = \sqrt{(b_1)^2 + (b_2)^2}$ and $\theta = \tan^{-1}\left(\dfrac{b_2}{b_1}\right)$.

Cartesian Coordinates (Components) in 3D

Vector $B = b_1\hat{i} + b_2\hat{j} + b_3\hat{k}$

where $\hat{i}$ is one unit in the x direction, $\hat{j}$ is one unit in the y direction, and $\hat{k}$ is one unit in the z direction.

Commutative Law of Vector Addition

$A + B = B + A$

for any vectors A and B.

Adding 2D Vectors Numerically

$A + B = (a_1 + b_1)\hat{i} + (a_2 + b_2)\hat{j}$

for vectors $A = a_1\hat{i} + a_2\hat{j}$ and $B = b_1\hat{i} + b_2\hat{j}$.

Adding 3D Vectors Numerically

$A + B = (a_1 + b_1)\hat{i} + (a_2 + b_2)\hat{j} + (a_3 + b_3)\hat{k}$

for vectors $A = a_1\hat{i} + a_2\hat{j} + a_3\hat{k}$ and $B = b_1\hat{i} + b_2\hat{j} + b_3\hat{k}$.

Subtracting Vectors Numerically

$A - B = (a_1 - b_1)\hat{i} + (a_2 - b_2)\hat{j}$

for vectors $A = a_1\hat{i} + a_2\hat{j}$ and $B = b_1\hat{i} + b_2\hat{j}$.

Subtracting 3D Vectors Numerically

$A - B = (a_1 - b_1)\hat{i} + (a_2 - b_2)\hat{j} + (a_3 - b_3)\hat{k}$

for vectors $A = a_1\hat{i} + a_2\hat{j} + a_3\hat{k}$ and $B = b_1\hat{i} + b_2\hat{j} + b_3\hat{k}$.

Scalar Multiplication in Polar Coordinates

$cA = c\|A\|$ @ θ

for any scalar c and vector $A = \|A\|$ @ θ.

Scalar Multiplication in Cartesian Coordinates

$cA = ca_1\hat{i} + ca_2\hat{j}$

for any scalar c and vector $A = a_1\hat{i} + a_2\hat{j}$.

Normalizing a 2D Vector

$$\hat{A} = \frac{1}{\|A\|}A = \begin{bmatrix} \dfrac{a_1}{\|A\|} & \dfrac{a_2}{\|A\|} \end{bmatrix}$$

for any vector $A = [a_1 \ a_2]$.

Normalizing a 3D Vector

$$\hat{A} = \frac{1}{\|A\|}A = \begin{bmatrix} \dfrac{a_1}{\|A\|} & \dfrac{a_2}{\|A\|} & \dfrac{a_3}{\|A\|} \end{bmatrix}$$

for any vector $A = [a_1 \ a_2 \ a_3]$.

Dot Product in 2D

$A \bullet B = a_1b_1 + a_2b_2$

for any 2D vectors $A = [a_1 \ a_2]$ and $B = [b_1 \ b_2]$.

Dot Product in 3D

$A \bullet B = a_1b_1 + a_2b_2 + a_3b_3$

for any 3D vectors $A = [a_1\ a_2\ a_3]$ and $B = [b_1\ b_2\ b_3]$.

Perpendicular Check

If $A \bullet B = 0$, $A \perp B$.

Positive or Negative Dot Product

If $A \bullet B < 0$ (negative), $\theta > 90°$

If $A \bullet B > 0$ (positive), $\theta < 90°$

where θ is the angle between vectors A and B.

Angle Between Two Vectors

$A \bullet B = \|A\|\|B\| \cos\theta$

where θ is the angle between vectors A and B.

Cross-Product

$A \times B = [(a_2b_3 - a_3b_2)\ (a_3b_1 - a_1b_3)\ (a_1b_2 - a_2b_1)]$

for any two vectors $A = [a_1\ a_2\ a_3]$ and $B = [b_1\ b_2\ b_3]$.

Perpendicular Vectors

$A \times B$ is perpendicular to both vectors A and B.

Cross-Product Is Not Commutative

$A \times B \neq B \times A$

In fact, $A \times B = -(B \times A)$ for any two 3D vectors A and B.

Surface Normal

Surface normal = $(A\hat{x}B) = \dfrac{AxB}{\|AxB\|}$

for any two 3D vectors A and B.

Angle Between Two Vectors

$\|AxB\| = \|A\|\|B\|\sin\theta$

for any two 3D vectors A and B.

Chapter 5, "Matrix Operations"

Equal Matrices

Two matrices are equal if

➤ Both matrices have equal dimensions.

➤ *All* corresponding entries are equal.

Adding Matrices

For two matrices of the same size, add the corresponding entries.

Subtracting Matrices

For two matrices of the same size, subtract the corresponding entries.

Scalar Multiplication

$$cA = \begin{bmatrix} ca_{00} & ca_{01} & \cdot & \cdot & \cdot \\ ca_{10} & \cdot & & & \\ \cdot & & \cdot & & \\ \cdot & & & \cdot & \\ \cdot & & & & ca_{nn} \end{bmatrix}$$

for any scalar value c and any size matrix A.

Multiplying Two 2×2 Matrices

$$AB = \begin{bmatrix} (a_{00}b_{00} + a_{01}b_{10}) & (a_{00}b_{01} + a_{01}b_{11}) \\ (a_{10}b_{00} + a_{11}b_{10}) & (a_{10}b_{01} + a_{11}b_{11}) \end{bmatrix}$$

for any matrix $A = \begin{bmatrix} a_{00} & a_{01} \\ a_{10} & a_{11} \end{bmatrix}$ and $B = \begin{bmatrix} b_{00} & b_{01} \\ b_{10} & b_{11} \end{bmatrix}$.

Is the Product Defined?

For matrix multiplication AB, the number of columns in A must equal the number of rows in B.

Size of the Product

If AB is defined, the size of matrix AB is the number of rows in A by the number of columns in B.

Matrix Multiplication Is Not Commutative

$AB \neq BA$

for any size matrices A and B.

Transpose for a 3×3 Matrix

If $A = \begin{bmatrix} a_{00} & a_{01} & a_{02} \\ a_{10} & a_{11} & a_{12} \\ a_{20} & a_{21} & a_{22} \end{bmatrix}$, $A^T = \begin{bmatrix} a_{00} & a_{10} & a_{20} \\ a_{01} & a_{11} & a_{21} \\ a_{02} & a_{12} & a_{22} \end{bmatrix}$.

Transpose

For any size matrix A, each entry a_{mn} moves to a_{nm} in A^T.

Chapter 6, "Transformations"

2D Translation by Addition

$$\begin{bmatrix} x' \\ y' \end{bmatrix} = \begin{bmatrix} x \\ y \end{bmatrix} + \begin{bmatrix} dx \\ dy \end{bmatrix}$$

where dx = change in x and dy = change in y.

3D Translation by Addition

$$\begin{bmatrix} x' \\ y' \\ z' \end{bmatrix} = \begin{bmatrix} x \\ y \\ z \end{bmatrix} + \begin{bmatrix} dx \\ dy \\ dz \end{bmatrix}$$

where dx = change in x, dy = change in y, and dz = change in z.

2D Translation by Multiplication

$$\begin{bmatrix} x' \\ y' \\ 1 \end{bmatrix} = \begin{bmatrix} 1 & 0 & dx \\ 0 & 1 & dy \\ 0 & 0 & 1 \end{bmatrix} \begin{bmatrix} x \\ y \\ 1 \end{bmatrix}$$

where dx = change in x and dy = change in y.

3D Translation by Multiplication

$$\begin{bmatrix} x' \\ y' \\ z' \\ 1 \end{bmatrix} = \begin{bmatrix} 1 & 0 & 0 & dx \\ 0 & 1 & 0 & dy \\ 0 & 0 & 1 & dz \\ 0 & 0 & 0 & 1 \end{bmatrix} \begin{bmatrix} x \\ y \\ z \\ 1 \end{bmatrix}$$

where dx = change in x, dy = change in y, and dz = change in z.

2D Scaling

$$\begin{bmatrix} x' \\ y' \\ 1 \end{bmatrix} = \begin{bmatrix} Sx & 0 & 0 \\ 0 & Sy & 0 \\ 0 & 0 & 1 \end{bmatrix} \begin{bmatrix} x \\ y \\ 1 \end{bmatrix}$$

where Sx = scale factor in the x direction and Sy = scale factor in the y direction.

3D Scaling

$$\begin{bmatrix} x' \\ y' \\ z' \\ 1 \end{bmatrix} = \begin{bmatrix} Sx & 0 & 0 & 0 \\ 0 & Sy & 0 & 0 \\ 0 & 0 & Sz & 0 \\ 0 & 0 & 0 & 1 \end{bmatrix} \begin{bmatrix} x \\ y \\ z \\ 1 \end{bmatrix}$$

where Sx = scale factor in the x direction, Sy = scale factor in the y direction, and Sz = scale factor in the z direction.

2D Rotation

$$\begin{bmatrix} x' \\ y' \\ 1 \end{bmatrix} = \begin{bmatrix} \cos\theta & -\sin\theta & 0 \\ \sin\theta & \cos\theta & 0 \\ 0 & 0 & 1 \end{bmatrix} \begin{bmatrix} x \\ y \\ 1 \end{bmatrix}$$

where θ is the angle of rotation.

3D Rotation About the z-Axis (Roll)

$$\begin{bmatrix} x' \\ y' \\ z' \\ 1 \end{bmatrix} = \begin{bmatrix} \cos\theta & -\sin\theta & 0 & 0 \\ \sin\theta & \cos\theta & 0 & 0 \\ 0 & 0 & 1 & 0 \\ 0 & 0 & 0 & 1 \end{bmatrix} \begin{bmatrix} x \\ y \\ z \\ 1 \end{bmatrix}$$

where θ is the angle of rotation.

3D Rotation About the x-Axis (Pitch)

$$\begin{bmatrix} x' \\ y' \\ z' \\ 1 \end{bmatrix} = \begin{bmatrix} 1 & 0 & 0 & 0 \\ 0 & \cos\theta & -\sin\theta & 0 \\ 0 & \sin\theta & \cos\theta & 0 \\ 0 & 0 & 0 & 1 \end{bmatrix} \begin{bmatrix} x \\ y \\ z \\ 1 \end{bmatrix}$$

where θ is the angle of rotation.

3D Rotation About the y-Axis (Yaw)

$$\begin{bmatrix} x' \\ y' \\ z' \\ 1 \end{bmatrix} = \begin{bmatrix} \cos\theta & 0 & \sin\theta & 0 \\ 0 & 1 & 0 & 0 \\ -\sin\theta & 0 & \cos\theta & 0 \\ 0 & 0 & 0 & 1 \end{bmatrix} \begin{bmatrix} x \\ y \\ z \\ 1 \end{bmatrix}$$

where θ is the angle of rotation.

2D Combo Matrix

For every 2D combo matrix

$$\begin{bmatrix} r_{00} & r_{01} & t_x \\ r_{10} & r_{11} & t_y \\ 0 & 0 & 1 \end{bmatrix}$$

entries with an r store scaling and rotation information, and entries with a t store overall translation information.

3D Combo Matrix

For every 3D combo matrix

$$\begin{bmatrix} r_{00} & r_{01} & r_{02} & t_x \\ r_{10} & r_{11} & r_{12} & t_y \\ r_{20} & r_{21} & r_{22} & t_z \\ 0 & 0 & 0 & 1 \end{bmatrix}$$

entries with an r store scaling and rotation information, and entries with a t store overall translation information.

Conversion Between OpenGL and DirectX Formats

$AB = B^T A^T$ for matrices A and B:

$$
\underset{A}{\begin{bmatrix} r_{00} & r_{01} & t_x \\ r_{10} & r_{11} & t_y \\ 0 & 0 & 1 \end{bmatrix}} \underset{B}{\begin{bmatrix} x \\ y \\ 1 \end{bmatrix}} = \underset{B^T}{\begin{bmatrix} x & y & 1 \end{bmatrix}} \underset{A^T}{\begin{bmatrix} r_{00} & r_{10} & 0 \\ r_{01} & r_{11} & 0 \\ t_x & t_y & 1 \end{bmatrix}}
$$

Chapter 7, "Unit Conversions"

Metric System

kilo-   hecto-   deca-   **meters**   deci-   centi-   milli-

grams

List of Conversion Factors

Length	Time
1m = 39.37in. = 3.281ft.	1s = 1000ms.
1in = 2.54cm.	1min. = 60s
1km = 0.621mi.	1hr. = 3600s
1mi = 5280ft. = 1.609km.	1 year = 365.242 days

Computer Conversions

1 byte = 8 bits

1 kilobyte = 1024 bytes

1 megabyte = 1024 kilobytes

1 gigabyte = 1024 megabytes

Chapter 8, "Motion in One Dimension"

Displacement with Constant Velocity

displacement = velocity * time ($D = v * t$)

for any constant velocity v.

Displacement Between Frames

new_position = old_position + velocity * time

where time is one frame (usually $1/30$ of a second).

Average Velocity

$$\bar{v} = \frac{\Delta x}{t} = \frac{x_f - x_i}{t}$$

for any displacement Δx and time interval t.

Acceleration

$$a = \frac{\Delta v}{\Delta t} = \frac{v_f - v_i}{t_f - t_i}$$

Equation 1

$$v_f = v_i + at$$

Equation 2

$$\bar{v} = \frac{v_i + v_f}{2}$$

for constant acceleration only.

Equation 3

$$\Delta x = 1/2(v_i + v_f)t$$

Equation 4

$\Delta x = v_i t + \frac{1}{2}at^2$

Equation 5

$v_f^2 = v_i^2 + 2a\Delta x$

Chapter 9, "Derivative Approach to Motion in One Dimension"

Average Velocity

$$\bar{v} = \frac{f(b) - f(a)}{b - a}$$

equals the slope between two points on position v. Time graph for any time interval $a \leq t \leq b$.

Instantaneous Velocity

$$v = \lim_{h \to 0} \frac{f(a+h) - f(a)}{h}$$

at $t = a$ for any function $f(t)$ that gives position as a function of time.

Instantaneous Velocity

$v = f'(t)$

for any position equation that's a function of time, $f(t)$.

Average Acceleration

$$\bar{a} = \frac{f(b) - f(a)}{b - a}$$

equals the slope between two points on velocity v. Time graph for any time interval $a \leq t \leq b$.

Instantaneous Acceleration

$$a = \frac{\lim_{h \to 0} \frac{f(t+h) - f(t)}{h}}{}$$

for any function $f(t)$ that gives velocity as a function of time.

Instantaneous Acceleration

$a = v'(t)$

for any velocity equation that's a function of time, $v(t)$.

Instantaneous Acceleration

$a = v'(t) = y''(t)$

for any velocity equation that's a function of time, $v(t)$, and any position equation that's a function of time, $y(t)$.

Chapter 10, "Motion in Two and Three Dimensions"

2D Displacement

$\Delta r = r_f - r_i$

for position vectors r_i (initial) and r_f (final).

Average Velocity in 2D and 3D

$$\bar{v} = \frac{\Delta r}{t} = \frac{r_f - r_i}{t}$$

for any displacement vector Δr and time interval t.

Equations of Motion in 2D and 3D

$v_f = v_i + at$

$\Delta x = \frac{1}{2}(v_f + v_i)t$

$\Delta x = v_i t + \frac{1}{2}at^2$

for vectors a, v_f, v_i, and Δx and scalar t.

Vertical Components of a Projectile

$a_y = -9.8 \text{m/s}^2$

$v_{fy} = v_{iy} + at$

$\Delta y = v_{iy}t + \frac{1}{2}a_y t^2$

Horizontal Components of a Projectile

$a_x = 0 \text{m/s}^2$

$v_x = \Delta x/t$

Chapter 11, "Newton's Laws"

Weight

w = mg

where m = mass and g = acceleration due to gravity (-9.8m/s^2 on Earth).

Newtons

$1\text{N} = 1\text{kg}*\text{m/s}^2$

$1\text{N} = 0.2248\text{lbs}$

Static Friction

$F_S = -\mu_S N$

where N is the normal force.

Kinetic Friction

$F_K = -\mu_K N$

where N is the normal force.

Free-Body Diagram

1. Use arrows of relative lengths to represent forces.

2. Draw all arrows originating from the center of the object and pointing in the appropriate direction.

Newton's First Law

If $F_{net} = 0$, no change in motion occurs.

Newton's Second Law

$F_{net} = ma$

where m is mass and a is acceleration.

Newton's Third Law

For every force there is an equal and opposite force, or, when two objects come into contact, they exert equal and opposite forces upon each other.

Chapter 12, "Energy"

Work

$W = F\Delta x$

where Δx = displacement and F = force in the direction of displacement.

Kinetic Energy

$KE = 1/2mv^2$

where m = mass and v = speed.

Work-Energy Theorem

$W = \Delta KE = KE_f - KE_i$

or

$F\Delta x = 1/2mv_f^2 - 1/2mv_i^2$

where the force and displacement are in the same direction and v is speed.

Gravitational Potential Energy

$GPE = mgy$

where m = mass, g = acceleration due to gravity, and y = height.

Conservation of Mechanical Energy (Simplified)

$KE_i + PE_i = KE_f + PE_f$

or

$1/2mv_i^2 + mgy_i + 1/2mv_f^2 + mgy_f$

Conservation of Mechanical Energy (Modified)

$$KE_i + PE_i = KE_f + PE_f + E_o$$

or

$$1/2mv_i^2 + mgy_i + 1/2mv_f^2 + mgy_f + E_o$$

where E_o represents other energy (heat/sound).

Chapter 13, "Momentum and Collisions"

Axis-Aligned Vector Reflection

If the stationary boundary is vertical, $v_f = [-v_{ix} \ v_{iy}]$ and if the stationary boundary is horizontal, $v_f = [v_{ix} \ -v_{iy}]$ for incoming velocity $v_i = [v_{ix} \ v_{iy}]$.

Non-Axis-Aligned Vector Reflection

$$v_f = 2 * P + v_i$$

where v_i = the incoming velocity and P = the projection of $-v_i$ onto the normal of the boundary line.

Momentum

$$p = mv$$

where m = mass and v = velocity.

Impulse

Impulse = Ft

where F = net force and t = a very small amount of time.

Impulse-Momentum Theorem

Impulse = $Ft = (\Delta p)$

where F = net force, t = a very small amount of time, and p = momentum.

Conservation of Momentum Theorem

$m_1 v_{1i} + m_2 v_{2i} = m_1 v_{1f} + m_2 v_{2f}$

where the 1 subscript represents object 1 and the 2 subscript represents object 2.

Linear Collision

$(v_{1f} - v_{2f}) = -\varepsilon(v_{1i} - v_{2i})$

where ε = coefficient of restitution ($0 < \varepsilon < 1$).

Chapter 14, "Rotational Motion"

Angular Displacement

$\theta = s/r$

where s = arc length and r = radius.

Average Angular Velocity

$$\overline{\omega} = \frac{\Delta\theta}{\Delta t} = \frac{\theta_f - \theta_i}{t_f - t_i}$$

where ω = angular displacement and t = time.

Average Angular Acceleration

$$\overline{\alpha} = \frac{\Delta\omega}{\Delta t} = \frac{\omega_f - \omega_i}{t_f - t_i}$$

where ω = angular displacement and t = time.

Tangential Velocity

$v_t = \omega r$

where ω = instantaneous angular velocity and r = radius.

Tangential Acceleration

$a_t = \alpha r$

where α = instantaneous angular acceleration and r = radius.

Appendix B

Suggested Reading

Math

Dolciani, Mary P. et al. *Algebra 2 and Trigonometry*. Boston: Houghton Mifflin, 1992.

Finney, Ross L. et al. *Calculus: Graphical, Numerical, Algebraic*. Reading: Addison-Wesley, 1995.

Lecky-Thompson, Guy. *Infinite Game Universe: Mathematical Techniques*. Rockland: Charles River Media, 2001.

Leduc, Steven A. *Linear Algebra*. Lincoln: Cliffs Notes, 1996.

Stewart, James. *Calculus*. Pacific Grove: Brooks/Cole, 2002.

Strang, Gilbert. *Introduction to Linear Algebra*. Wellesley: Wellesly-Cambridge Press, 1993.

Thompson, Silvanus P. and Martin Gardner. *Calculus Made Easy*. New York: St. Martin's Press, 1998 (original copyright 1910).

Physics

Bourg, David M. *Physics for Game Developers*. Cambridge: O'Reilly, 2002.

Gonick, Larry and Art Huffman. *The Cartoon Guide to Physics*. New York: HarperPerennial, 1990.

Huetinck, Linda. *Physics*. Lincoln: Cliffs Notes, 2001.

Serway, Raymond A. and Jerry S. Faughn. *College Physics*. Philadelphia: Saunders College Publishing, 2003.

3D Game Engineering

DeLoura, Mark, ed. *Game Programming Gems*. Rockland: Charles River Media, 2000.

DeLoura, Mark, ed. *Game Programming Gems 2*. Rockland: Charles River Media, 2001.

Dunn, Fletcher and Ian Parberry. *3D Math Primer for Graphics & Game Development*. Wordware, 2002.

Eberly, David H. *3D Game Engine Design*. San Francisco: Morgan Kaufmann Publishers, 2001.

Foley, J.D. and A. Van Dam. *Fundamentals of Interactive Computer Graphics*. Reading: Addison-Wesley, 1982.

LaMothe, Andre. *Tricks of the Windows Game Programming Gurus*. Indianapolis: Sams, 1999.

Lengyel, Eric. *Mathematics for 3D Game Programming & Computer Graphics*. Rockland: Charles River Media, 2001.

Watt, Alan and Fabio Policarpo. *3D Games: Real-time Rendering and Software Technology*. Reading: Addison-Wesley, 2001.

General Programming

Eckel, Bruce. *Thinking in C++, Volume I: Introduction to Standard C++*, Second Edition. Upper Saddle River: Prentice Hall, 2000.

Meyers, Scott. *Effective C++: 50 Specific Ways to Improve Your Programs and Designs*. Reading: Addison-Wesley, 2001.

Prata, Stephen. *C++ Primer Plus,* Third Edition. Indianapolis: Sams, 1998.

Appendix C

What's on the CD-ROM

The accompanying CD-ROM is packed with all sorts of exercise files and products to help you work with this book. The following sections contain detailed descriptions of the CD's contents.

For more information about the use of this CD, please review the ReadMe.txt file in the root directory. This file includes important disclaimer information, as well as information about installation, system requirements, troubleshooting, and technical support.

Technical Support Issues

If you have any difficulties with this CD, you can access our website at
`http://www.newriders.com`.

Loading the CD Files

To load the files from the CD, insert the disc into your CD-ROM drive. If autoplay is enabled on your machine, the CD-ROM setup program starts automatically the first time you insert the disc. You may copy the files to your hard drive, or use them right off the disc.

> **NOTE**
> This CD-ROM uses long and mixed-case filenames, requiring the use of a protected mode CD-ROM driver.

Exercise Files

This CD contains all the files you'll need to complete the exercises in *Beginnning Math and Physics for Game Programmers*. These files can be found in the root directory's Book Files folder.

Third-Party Programs

This CD also contains several third-party programs and demos from leading industry companies. These programs have been carefully selected to help you strengthen your professional skills.

Please note that some of the programs included on this CD-ROM are shareware-"try-before-you-buy"-software. Please support these independent vendors by purchasing or registering any shareware software that you use for more than 30 days. Check with the documentation provided with the software on where and how to register the product.

➤ **Circles** demonstrates the movement and collision of two circles with the bounds of the screen and each other (Chapter 2, "Geometry Snippets").

➤ **Matrix Vortex** teaches familiarity with the various matrix and vector operations in a visually stimulating setting (Chapter 4, "Vector Operations").

➤ **Transformations** helps explain the principles of 2D transformations applied to an object (Chapter 6, "Transformations").

➤ The **1D Racer** demonstrates the motion of an object with constant acceleration moving through space (Chapter 8, "Motion in One Dimension").

➤ **Cannon Physics** is a demonstration in simple projectile physics (Chapter 10, "Motion in Two and Three Dimension").

➤ **Basement Billiards** is a practical demonstration of 2D collision between circles (Chapter 13, "Momentum and Collisions").

Read This Before Opening the Software

By opening the CD package, you agree to be bound by the following agreement:

You may not copy or redistribute the entire CD-ROM as a whole. Copying and redistribution of individual software programs on the CD-ROM is governed by terms set by individual copyright holders.

The installer, code, images, actions, and brushes from the author(s) are copyrighted by the publisher and the authors.

This software is sold as-is, without warranty of any kind, either expressed or implied, including but not limited to the implied warranties of merchantability and fitness for a particular purpose. Neither the publisher nor its dealers or distributors assumes any liability for any alleged or actual damages arising from the use of this program. (Some states do not allow for the exclusion of implied warranties, so the exclusion may not apply to you.)

Glossary

acceleration   The rate of change of velocity; it measures how quickly an object speeds up or slows down.

affine   As in "affine transformation," indicates that the essential shape of the object being moved is preserved.

amplitude   Measures the range of output values for the sine or cosine function.

angle of incidence   The incoming angle of a moving object when it collides with a fixed object.

angle of reflection   The outgoing angle of a moving object when it collides with a fixed object.

angular displacement (θ)   A vector quantity that measures rotation. It is equal to the arc length divided by the radius of a rotating object.

Angular Momentum   ($L = I\omega$) where I=inertia (mr^2) and ω=angular velocity.

arc length (s)   A certain distance along a circular path.

array   A gridlike system for organizing any type of information (such as numbers, variables, text, and even arrays).

average angular acceleration (α)   The rate of change of angular velocity (change in angular velocity divided by time).

average angular velocity ($\bar{\omega}$)   The rate of change of angular displacement (change in angular displacement divided by time).

axis-aligned bounding box   A box with sides that are perfectly horizontal and vertical, meaning parallel to the x- and y-axes.

axis of symmetry   A horizontal or vertical line that goes through the vertex of a parabola and splits it right down the middle so that each side is a reflection of the other.

Cartesian coordinates   x, y, and z values that describe displacement parallel to the three axes.

Cartesian coordinate system   A gridlike system that uses a horizontal x-axis and a vertical y-axis to pinpoint a 2D location or an x-, y-, and z-axis to pinpoint a 3D location.

circle   The set of all 2D points at a given distance, called the radius, from a given fixed point, the center.

class   The basic type used in object oriented design.

coefficient of restitution (ε)   A measure of how much energy is lost during a collision. For an elastic collision, $\varepsilon = 1$, and for a perfectly inelastic collision, $\varepsilon = 0$.

complete solution   All the points that satisfy a given equation.

concatenation   The process of combining transformation matrices into a single combo matrix.

conservation of momentum theorem   States that the total amount of momentum stays the same when two objects collide. It simply transfers from one object to the other.

corresponding entries   Entries in any matrix that are in the same row and column location.

differential scale   A scaling process with two different scale factor values for Sx and Sy.

displacement   The vector version of distance—distance plus direction.

elastic collision   A collision in which no kinetic energy is lost when the two objects hit.

entry   Each individual number in a matrix.

Euler rotation   Pronounced "oiler." A process that uses three variables, commonly called roll, pitch, and yaw, to rotate objects. Distinguished from Quaternions, an alternative method of rotation.

formula   An equation.

free-body diagram   A standard diagram that uses arrows to represent the forces on an object in a very specific way. All the arrows originate at the object's center, and all have relative lengths.

function   A rule that takes in information (input) and returns new information (output).

fundamental period $360°$ or $2\pi^R$ measures how often the sine and cosine functions repeat.

gravitational potential energy (GPE)   The energy stored in an object due to its height off the ground.

impulse-momentum theorem   States that a force delivered quickly results in a change of momentum. This means that if the mass does not change, the object either speeds up or slows down.

individual solution   A single point that makes an equation true.

Inertia (I)   measures an object's resistance to motion. It's the angular equivalent to mass and is equal to mr^2.

instantaneous angular acceleration   The average angular acceleration over an extremely small time interval, as close to an instant as you can get.

instantaneous angular velocity   The average angular velocity over an extremely small time interval, as close to an instant as you can get.

instantaneous velocity   The average velocity over an extremely small time interval, as close to an instant as you can get.

interpolation   The process of predetermining intermediate values between two

key framing   Identifying important points of transition in an animation.

kinetic energy   The amount of energy an object has because it is moving.

kinetic friction   The force that slows down an object after it gets moving.

law of conservation of mechanical energy   States that energy cannot be created or destroyed; it can only switch forms.

linear combination   A process that uses the rules of equality to solve for two unknown variables when two equations are given.

matrix   An array that is limited to storing numbers.

midpoint   The point that is exactly halfway between two other points.

momentum (p)   An object's mass times velocity.

Newton's Second Law Revisited   ($\tau = I\alpha$) where I=inertia (mr^2) and α=angular acceleration.

normal force   The force of the surface an object is sitting on that counteracts gravity and keeps it from falling any farther.

normalization   A process that scales the magnitude of a vector down to 1.

orthogonal   A synonym for perpendicular.

parabola   A fancy name for a symmetric bump, or arc.

parallel lines   Two lines that never cross because they have equal slopes.

perfectly inelastic collision   A collision in which two objects stick together and have the same final velocity.

period   The measurement of how often a trigonometric function repeats.

perpendicular lines   Two lines that intersect at right angles.

polar coordinates   A length plus an angle in standard position.

projectile   Any object that has been thrown, kicked, or shot and is flying through the air.

Pythagorean theorem   States that, for any right triangle, the length of the hypotenuse squared is equal to the sum of the squares of the other two sides ($a^2 + b^2 = c^2$).

quadrant   One segment of the Cartesian system of coordinates.

radius   The distance from any point on a circle or sphere to its center.

Rotational Kinetic Energy   ($KE_R = {}^1\!/_2 I\omega^2$) where I=inertia (mr^2) and ω=angular velocity.

scalar   A number, sometimes called a magnitude, without any direction.

slope   The measure of steepness (rise over run).

solution set   The set of all the points that satisfy two equations.

speed   The measure of how fast an object is moving.

sphere   The set of all 3D points at a given distance, called the radius, from a given fixed point, the center. It's what you get when a circle revolves about its center point.

static friction   The force that keeps an object from initially moving.

structure   a user-created programming construct that is used as a new data

substitution   A method for solving a system of two linear equations.

surface normal   A vector that is perpendicular to the surface and that has a length of 1.

system of linear equations   Two equations put together.

tangential velocity (v_t)   The linear velocity of a spinning object if it were to break free from rotation.

transformation   A way to move objects around in a 2D or 3D coordinate system. It encompasses movement such as forward-and-backward or up-and-down motion, scaling objects larger or smaller, and rotating objects.

translation   The process of moving objects left, right, up and down, or in and out.

transpose   A matrix operation that swaps rows with columns.

uniform scale   A scale with equal scale factors that keeps the proportions of the object being scaled the same.

unit circle   A circle centered at the origin with a radius of 1.

vector   A quantity that has both magnitude and direction.

vector reflection   The motion of a moving object when it bounces off a fixed object.

velocity   The vector version of speed—speed plus direction.

vertex   A point. For a parabola, the vertex is the very tip of the bump, the extreme maximum or minimum.

weight   The force due to gravity.

work   The scalar measurement of force times displacement.

work-energy theorem   States that the net or total work done on an object is equal to the change in its kinetic energy.

y-intercept   The point where a line crosses the y-axis.

Index

Symbols

1D momentum calculations (Example 13.4), 373-374

2D
average velocity, 290, 433
combo matrices, debugging, 218, 429
differential scale (Example 6.6), 194-195
displacement, 288-289, 433
distance between points, 417
dot product, 132, 423
equations of motion, 291-294, 434
locations, graphing (Example 1.1), 3
midpoint formula, 417
non-axis-aligned vector reflection
   (Example 13.2), 367-369
points. *See* screen points
rotation, 200-204, 428
scaling, 428
translation by addition, 181-182, 427
translation by multiplication, 185-186, 427
uniform scale (Example 6.5), 190-194
vector normalization, 130, 423

3D
average velocity, 290, 433
Cartesian coordinates in, 120
combo matrices, debugging, 219, 429
differential scale (Example 6.8), 197-198
displacement (Example 10.2), 289
distance between points, 417
dot product, 133, 424
equations of motion, 291-295, 434
lines, determining equation for (Example 1.10),
   21-22
locations, graphing (Example 1.2), 6
midpoint formula, 417
momentum calculations (Example 13.5), 374

non-axis-aligned vector reflection
   (Example 13.3), 369-371
numerical vector addition, 126
numerical vector subtraction, 127
points
   distance between (Example 2.3), 47
   midpoint between (Example 2.5), 49
rotation, 204-208, 428
   about the y-axis (Example 6.10), 209
   Example 6.12, 215-218
scaling, 428
   with respect to center point (Example 6.11),
   213-214
translation by addition, 182-183, 427
translation by multiplication, 187-188, 427
uniform scale (Example 6.7), 196
vector class, 139-141
vector normalization, 131, 423

A

acceleration, 252, 431
angular acceleration (Example 14.6), 408
average acceleration, 278-279, 432
   Example 9.4, 278
   graphing, 275-278
average angular acceleration, 399-400, 438
calculating (Example 8.5), 253
deceleration, calculating (Example 8.6), 254
equations of motion, 255-259, 291-293, 431-434
   in 2D (Example 10.4), 293-294
   in 3D (Example 10.5), 294-295
   CD-ROM demos, 264, 266
   multiple equations Example (8.9), 261-262
   race car examples (8.7 and 8.8), 259-260
   self-assessment, 264

W

waves. *See* graphing, sine and cosine

weeks, converting to seconds (Example 7.3), 232

weight, 316-318, 434. *See also* gravity

Wheel of Fortune examples
  equations of motion, 401-402
  tangential acceleration, 405

Wigand, Mike (Cannon Physics CD-ROM demo), 311

work, 339-341, 436
  calculating (Example 12.1), 342
    with angled force (Example 12.2), 343-344
    with force and displacement at different angles (Example 12.3), 344-347
  self-assessment, 351
  units of measurement, 341

work-energy theorem, 349-351, 436

X-Z

x-axis
  3D rotation about (pitch), 206-207, 429
  in Cartesian coordinate system, 3-5

x-intercept in slope-intercept linear equations, 18

y-axis
  3D rotation about (yaw), 207-209, 429
  in Cartesian coordinate system, 3-5

y-intercept in slope-intercept linear equations, 18

y-up, right-handed coordinate system, 4-5

yaw (3D rotation about the y-axis), 207-209, 429

z-axis
  3D rotation about (roll), 205-206, 428
  in Cartesian coordinate system, 4-5

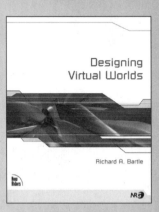
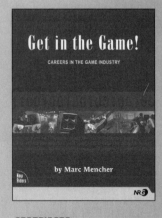